Denise Valdés

VOICING CHICANA FEMINISMS

QUALITATIVE STUDIES IN PSYCHOLOGY

This series showcases the power and possibility of qualitative work in psychology. Books feature detailed and vivid accounts of qualitative psychology research using a variety of methods, including participant observation and fieldwork, discursive and textual analyses, and critical cultural history. They probe vital issues of theory, implementation, interpretation, representation, and ethics that qualitative workers confront. The series mission is to enlarge and refine the repertoire of qualitative approaches to psychology.

GENERAL EDITORS
Michelle Fine and Jeanne Marecek

VOICING CHICANA FEMINISMS

Young Women Speak Out
on Sexuality and Identity

AÍDA HURTADO

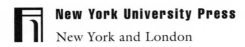

New York University Press

New York and London

NEW YORK UNIVERSITY PRESS
New York and London
www.nyupress.org

Library of Congress Cataloging-in-Publication Data
Hurtado, Aída.
Voicing Chicana feminisms : young women speak out
on sexuality and identity / Aída Hurtado.
p. cm. — (Qualitative studies in psychology)
Includes bibliographical references and index.
ISBN 0-8147-3573-8 (alk. paper) —
ISBN 0-8147-3574-6 (pbk : alk. paper)
1. Mexican American women—Social conditions.   2. Mexican
American women—Sexual behavior.   3. Mexican American
women—Interviews.   4. Young women—United States—
Social conditions.   5. Young women—United States—
Sexual behavior.   6. Young women—United States—Interviews.
7. Mexican Americans—Ethnic identity.   8. Mexican Americans—
Statistics.   9. Sex role—United States.   10. Feminisim—
United States.   I. Title.   II. Series.
E184.M5 H87 2003
305.48'86872073—dc21   2002011269

New York University Press books are printed on acid-free paper,
and their binding materials are chosen for strength and durability.

Manufactured in the United States of America

10 9 8 7 6 5 4 3

Reclamation

A history was denied me
My grandmother's tongue ripped out of my mouth
I was too young to know how to grieve the loss
  properly

the wound healed
  in the shape of my Americanness

"Work hard and you'll succeed," I heard
  And so I did

My 22nd year the truth was revealed to me
  "White man is on top"
"And you? Sorry honey, you're somewhere near
  the bottom"

Anger
Anger turned my insides into a seething crimson

The death of my ignorance shook me hard and
  choked me out of my complacency
I have fallen many times since the first breaths of
truth were inhaled
        But I always come back to standing
  And now
A language has been found
The language of the colonizer twisted
and shape-shifted
to resist
to empower

Their words, now mine, woven into a
*   tempestuous cloth that's wrapped protectively*
*   around my shoulders*
Their words, now mine, used to reclaim my
*   history*
*   to reclaim what was taken from me*

And to make the promise
*   to speak the words*
That this is only the beginning

Jessica Roa, a student in my Chicana Feminisms course at the University of California, Santa Cruz, wrote this poem. Jessica, together with Maya Madrigal, Ana Inez Hyatt, and Natalie Rodríguez, painted the images on the cover for their class presentation, where Jessica recited her poem.

To the young women in this book who gave of their time and
of themselves so that we could better understand our collective existence.
And to the pioneers and emergent pioneers who helped me
understand the field of Chicana feminisms:

Norma Alarcón, Gloria Anzaldúa, Judy Baca, Maxine Baca Zinn, Maylei Blackwell, Yolanda Broyles-González, Norma E. Cantú, Ana Castillo, Lorna Dee Cervantes, Angie Chabram-Dernersesian, Sandra Cisneros, Marta Cotera, Gloria Cuádraz, Yvette G. Flores-Ortiz, Rosa Linda Fregoso, Alma García, Alicia Gaspar de Alba, Deena González, Jennifer González, Elena Gutiérrez, Michelle Habell-Pallán, Clara Lomas, Yolanda M. López, Josie Mendez-Negrete, Amalia Mesa-Bains, Pat Mora, Cherríe Moraga, Anna NietoGomez, Sandra Pacheco, Mary Pardo, Emma Pérez, Beatríz Pesquera, Alvina Quintana, Mary Romero, Vicki Ruiz, Sonia Saldívar-Hull, Elba R. Sánchez, Rosaura Sánchez, Chela Sandoval, Denise Segura, Carla Trujillo, Yvonne Yarbro-Bejarano, Patricia Zavella.

Contents

■　■　■　■

Tables

∎　　∎　　∎　　∎

Preface

Los Angeles, Aug. 10—In the latest in a string of seemingly inexplicable shootings, a balding, white, middle-aged man walked into a Jewish community center in the middle-class neighborhood of Granada Hills this morning and shot five people, including three young boys at a day camp, then fled.   —Sterngold 1999

AS I WAS IN THE MIDST of writing this book, Buford O'Neal Furrow Jr. wounded five people, including three children, at a Jewish community center, and then continued his rampage ten miles down the road, where he shot to death a letter carrier named Joe Ileto (May 1999, 26A). Furrow admitted that the shootings were racially motivated. He told FBI agents that he wanted the shootings "to be a wake-up call to America to kill Jews" (Witt, Kaplan, and Bailey 1999, 1A). Furthermore, according to newspaper reports, Furrow chose to kill Joe Ileto because he was "a good target of opportunity, a non-white, federal employee" (May 1999, 26A). At different points during his life, Furrow had been associated with white supremacist groups and was an "official" in the Aryan Nations Church (Van Derbeken et al. 1999, 1A). A year earlier, I had found on the Web a review of my book *The Color of Privilege* by a hate group. The shooting at the Granada Hills Jewish Community Center brought back memories of what it felt like to draw the attention of such individuals.

So, as I wrote this book, I worried. I worried about many things, but primarily I worried about my respondents. We, as people of Color, exist in a social milieu of racial hatred that is overwhelming and life threatening. To be sure, Furrow represents the most extreme version of it, but there are more insidious "nonconscious ideologies," to quote the social psychologists Sandra Bem and Daryl Bem (1997), that are also detrimental to our existence. In many ways, Furrow's actions, however misguided and offensive to our sense of common humanity, are easier to deal with because they are honest. He acted upon his beliefs and owned both his ideology and his actions. I do not like either and I fear both, but as a person of Color, I know where I stand in Furrow's universe.

But the Furrows of the world are not whom I fear most. I am much more afraid of those individuals who are not as clearheaded, as honest, and perhaps not as outwardly insane as Furrow. I fear those who will take my respondents' lives and distort them to fit their own biased conceptions of who women of Color are. The women I interviewed gave me a great gift— their honesty. They spoke candidly about their pains, sorrows, triumphs, defeats, secrets, humiliations, joys, happiness, *sueños* (dreams), *inspiración* (inspiration), *dolor* (pain), and accomplishments. Their intelligence, commitment, trust, love, strength, humor, and willingness to be vulnerable overwhelmed me. I did not expect all of this. Maybe because I, too, in spite of my best efforts to fight against it, had succumbed to the view that "we couldn't be that good," that we must have some "hidden injuries of class" (Sennett and Cobb 1993), suffer from "stigma vulnerability" (Steele 1997), and experience "acculturation stress" (Allen, Amason, and Holmes 1998) as we moved from predominantly working-class Chicano environments and families to predominantly white institutions. The social science literature, often repackaged in the popular media, had partly convinced me that our individual "possible selves" (Oyserman and Markus 1990) suffer from a commitment to the "collective" (Triandis 1995) and we are forever in psychological "limbo" (Ogbu 1987), unable to fully integrate our "multiple worlds" (Cooper and Denner 1998).

I did not worry about my credibility when I wrote about my respondents' strengths rather than their weaknesses; but I worried that many readers would remember only the confessions of abortions, incest, rape, bisexuality, homosexuality, poverty, a family's alcoholism, moments of despair, and loneliness. I worried that the overall triumphs of these young lives would be lost in the need to fit new and contradictory information into our existing paradigms rather than change them. We live in times when redemption is dead. My fear was that my respondents' candidness would be used against them.

This anxiety only subsided as I listened again to the voices of the young women who spoke to me. They were teaching me a very profound lesson—you cannot hide because of the fear of being misunderstood. You cannot put a sugarcoating around your life in efforts to fend off those who are invested in hate and distortion. Loving, courageous honesty is the only hope we, as people of Color, have for recuperating our humanity. We are not angels, but neither are we the pathological, biologically inferior, subhuman individuals many believe us to be (Herrnstein and Murray 1994). We produce great intellects as well as those who make foolish choices or who, because of tragic circumstances, end up in prison. Many of my respondents' families produced all three. As I went back to my respondents' interviews and tried to piece together the fabric of their lives, I finally learned the biggest feminist lesson of all—we must tell the truth whether others believe us or not, and whether it is used against us or not. After this realization, I finally put my fears aside and with a joyful heart embraced the courage and truth these young women gave me.

Overview of the Book

I begin in chapter 1 by delineating the research context. I review the main theoretical concepts proposed by Chicana feminisms as central to understanding the gender subordination of Chicanas. I also provide an overview of my respondents' background characteristics to situate the sample as well as a general description of how I conducted this study. The rest of the book is divided into three parts. After each part, I review the implications of the data for feminist theorizing.

Part 1, "The Development of Self: Existing within a Family," is composed of chapters 2 and 3. Chicana feminisms argue that to understand the enforcement of patriarchy within Chicano communities we must comprehend the internal dynamics of families. It is within the socialization practices of families that gender beliefs are first inculcated and practiced. Many beliefs about gender revolve around the biological maturation of girls as they transition from childhood, to adolescence, to early adulthood. Chapter 2, "Growing Up Female," chronicles my respondents' transformation as they started menstruation, began dating, and became sexually active. Besides the physical changes entailed in growing up female, respondents also learned the social aspects of "becoming family," the topic of chapter 3.

The biological aspects of development happen naturally, but respondents had to learn how to be family. My respondents had many definitions of what constituted "family." Many were raised by two parents; others grew up in single-headed households; several were raised by grandparents; and still others were socialized primarily by older siblings. Families were also not static. Family members often emigrated from Mexico at different points in time, struggling to integrate once they were reunited. Many respondents and their families kept contact with relatives in Mexico. Parents also divorced, remarried, and had children with other partners; in one instance, both parents abandoned my respondent and her siblings. In the midst of all these evolutions, combinations, and changes, my respondents learned to become family.

In Part 2, "Multiple Group Identities: Existing in the World," I move from the internal dynamics of the family life of my respondents to their existence in the public sphere. Chicana feminisms place great importance on how social identities, largely determined by significant group memberships, affect the functioning of Chicanas outside their communities. The socialization received in their families and communities is largely at odds with their experiences outside these spheres. My respondents experienced their ethnic and racial difference as they joined the workforce, entered college, practiced their religion away from home, and (in some cases) married and/or had children. That is, my respondents experienced a disjuncture between their upbringing and the social worlds they were entering. Their racial, ethnic, and, many times, class differences led to an examination of their social existence. Chicana feminisms propose that Chicanas acquire a "*mestiza* consciousness" (Anzaldúa 1987) through the scrutiny of their disjunctures. My respondents had to understand that the negative judgments of their stigmatized group memberships were socially constructed and therefore could be refuted and not accepted as absolute fact. At the same time, they had to become comfortable in predominantly white institutions and in social contexts that did not necessarily reflect the values and norms they had grown up with. In chapter 4, "Believers," I explore these disjunctures in the realm of religion. Chapter 5, "Workers," contains my respondents' reflections on their class identities, and chapter 6, "Lovers," probes how they view themselves within romantic relationships.

Part 3, "Living and Speaking Feminisms," directly addresses my respondents' views on gender issues. Chicana feminisms maintain that the historical exclusion of working-class women from the academy has led to a lack of recognition of Chicanas' feminisms as expressed in their everyday interactions. Chapter 7, "Negotiating the Color Line," focuses on my respondents' experiences with being racialized in and outside their families. Chapter 8, "Chicanas Speak Feminisms," offers my respondents' answers to questions about their own and their family members' feminisms. In this chapter they articulate their multiple definitions of feminism and how it is expressed in their own lives. Chapter 9, "Political Understandings," further explores my respondents' views on issues that have been defined as part of a feminist agenda, such as the right to abortion, commitment to social change, and political engagement with their communities of origin.

In chapter 10, "Conclusions and Ruminations," I integrate and further theorize the feminisms expressed by my respondents. Their feminisms resonate with many of the writings by Chicana feminists and illustrate how young Chicanas live and speak their feminisms.

Acknowledgments

AS ALWAYS, my deepest appreciation goes to my family, whose unfailing support is the only reason I write. In particular I thank my husband, Craig Haney, who gives me sustenance, love, nurturing, and morning coffee every day and has for our eighteen years together. Above all, he always tells me that writing is my mission in life.

Essential to the completion of this book were my friends all around the country who helped me conduct this study on a shoestring budget. My gratitude goes to those who put me in touch with potential respondents, housed me, fed me, picked me up at airports, and read various versions of this book. My gratitude also goes to others, who were strangers but became friends in the research process, as I made connections through the circuitous Chicana/o-Feminist-Loca/o networks around the country. A special thanks that cannot be captured in words goes to my research assistants, who are my intellectual *hijas* and who worked endless hours transcribing tapes, coding data, checking and double checking quotes, chasing down references, and hearing me talk interminably about my respondents. Their insights, support, good cheer, and brilliance made this book partly theirs and infinitely better.

In the appendix I acknowledge all of my respondents who gave generously of their time, often driving long distances to tell me their life stories. The appendix lists the names of those respondents who chose to disclose their names as well as the list of pseudonyms respondents chose when they wanted to preserve their anonymity. Next to each respondent are the chapters where they are mentioned. Although not all of the respondents were quoted, all of the interviews were used to write this book. When a respondent is quoted for the first time, the respondent's age and academic degrees are listed in a note. In addition, each chapter also contains information on the respondent that is pertinent to the chapter. For example, the notes for chapter 6 contain information on the respondents' marital status and whether they have children. This "mini-biography" is both to acknowledge the respondents' educational successes and to give the reader additional information to provide a context for the respondent's quote.

I would like to use the remaining space to name all the people who made this project possible. I consider them my invisible research team, who gave of their time, their resources, and themselves.

Olga Aguilar, Tomás Almaguer, Gina Amaro, Gabriela Arredondo, Judith Arroyo, Jennifer Ayala, Jan Beals, Norma E. Cantú, Martin Chemers, Lakeya Reneé Cherry, Francie Córdova, Eleanor Fernández, Michelle Fine, Sarah Firestein, Shane Timberlake Fisher, Lilia Flores, Hector Garza, Irasema Garza, Juanita Garza, Alicia González, Erin Haney, Francisco Hernández, Eva Hernández Fatigoni, Arcelia Hurtado, María Hurtado, Norma Klahn, Sylvia Hurtado, Chanel Hurtado-Treviño, Laura Joyce, Tami Kasamatsu, Leslie Kuo, Clara Lomas, Salina López, Beatriz López-Flores, Raquel Márquez, Diana Martinez, Esperanza Martínez, Paola Martínez, Gabriel Melendez, Jimmy Mendiola, Maritza Mendoza, Bernadette Miera, Douglas Monroy, Erin Morimoto, Olga Nájera-Ramírez, Victor Nelson-Cisneros, Elvia Niebla, Renae Mari Olivas, Reena Panchal, Carmen Pérez, Laura Rendón, Maria Celina Reyes, Jessica Roa, Rudy Rocha, Mary Romero, Rolando Romero, Rodolfo Rosales, José Sahagún, Janelle Melissa Silva, Christina Santana, Leticia Sedano, Martha Serrano, Mariela Shaiken, Abby Stewart, Andrew K. Sandoval-Strausz, Adriana Torres, Jamie Torres, Armando Trujillo, Rhoda Unger, Patricia Valencia, Annie Valva, Gloria S. Vaquera, Richard Vasquez, Jessica Gabriela Vázquez, William Vega, Tara Yasso, Patricia Zavella.

The following units at the University of California, Santa Cruz, provided partial funding for this study: the Social Science Division, Dean Martin Chemers; Student Affairs Division, Vice-Chancellor Francisco Hernández; the Chicano/Latino Research Center, Director Patricia Zavella.

1

■　■　■　■　■　■　■　■　■

The Research Context

IT IS CUSTOMARY in academic books to write a chapter describing previous research to situate the current work within the framework of existing scholarship. This is a useful convention but one that holds little interest for the general reader. Every audience I have spoken to, whether union workers in Detroit or high school principals in Albuquerque, has been interested in existing research but not in the conventional framework. They prefer facts, which are combined with a range of arguments and analyses. I follow their preference in the hope that it will make this book more accessible to a wider range of audiences than is usual for an academic book. Therefore, instead of a chapter for the review of the literature and a chapter for the methods used to gather the data, I combine both into an overview of the book to better prepare the reader to understand what follows.

Introduction

We have come a long way since the anthropologist William Madsen wrote in the 1960s the following description of Mexican American women in relation to their husbands:

> The wife is expected to give comfort and pleasure to her husband. She must acknowledge his authority and superiority and think of his needs before her

own. She is supposed to accept abuse without complaint and avoid resentment of his pastimes and extramarital affairs. Her in-laws may criticize her and her husband may beat her for demanding that he spend too much time at home. . . . She sets the tone of the home atmosphere, ideally by radiating love and understanding. In her role as wife and mother, she is frequently compared with the Virgin of Guadalupe. This holy model for female behavior possesses all the most prized values of womanhood: purity, sanctity, tolerance, love, and sympathy. By extension but rarely by direct comparison, the husband and father is seen as a human image of God. He is aloof, absolute, and forceful in administering justice. (1964, 48)

In spite of vigorous and challenging scholarship by Chicana feminists, many of these inaccurate descriptions first proposed by Madsen still persist.

I first encountered William Madsen's work as an undergraduate student at Pan American University in South Texas, the area where he conducted his fieldwork. In fact, he was speaking about my family, my community, and me. It was the incongruence between my lived everyday experience and what I saw in scholarly work about us that prompted my academic career. I was not unusual; many feminist scholars were spurred by the same motivation. It was not only white male scholars like William Madsen producing this type of scholarship, but also white women (Heller 1966) and some Mexican scholars as well (Paz 1961; Díaz Guerrero 1975). Therefore, when Chicana feminists wrote in protest to these dominant views, they were in fact writing against multiple constituencies, some of whom were members of their own community.

In the last ten years there has been a revolution in the publishing of feminist theory by Chicanas. Their writing is provocative, incendiary, and a true call to action not only to dismantle the masculinist and racist scholarship on ethnic minorities but also to mount a challenge to the stronghold white feminists have had on the production of feminist theory. Although many scholars have used Chicana feminist theoretical writings to interpret and theorize the results of their empirical studies (Zavella forthcoming; Ruiz 1998; Pardo 1998; Bernal 1998a, 1998b; E. Gutiérrez 1999), most Chicana feminist theorizing has relied on literary texts or autobiographical writings. Only a few studies have asked Chicanas directly their views on feminist issues (most notably Segura 2001; Pesquera and Segura 1993.) The challenge remains, especially for psychologists, to transform Chicana feminist theory into viable empirical projects. This book focuses on the results of a qualitative study conducted with a cohort of Chicanas between the ages of twenty and thirty who have participated in higher education. The purpose was to verify whether the basic tenets of Chicana feminisms are validated in the life experiences of these young women.

Theoretical Background

Contemporary Chicana feminisms are truly children of the U.S. progressive political movements of the 1960s. Chicanas' activism on behalf of women's issues has a long, mostly undocumented, history prior to this historical moment. Contemporary writing by Chicana feminists largely began in the late 1960s and was contemporaneous with the Chicano movement, the free speech movement, the Black Power movement, the Asian American movement, the civil rights movement, the women's liberation movement, and other progressive movements of that time. Many Chicana feminists simultaneously participated in more than one of these movements (Martínez 1989), challenging stigmatization on the basis of sexuality, race and ethnicity, class, and gender. Chicana scholarship benefited from developments made by other groups in deciphering their oppression as well as their liberation. From the beginning, many Chicana feminists have not been concerned with reaching consensus or avoiding disruption (A. García 1989) as they voice their condition as women, lesbians, members of ethnic and racial groups, and predominantly members of the working class (Sandoval 1991). They confronted their internal diversity earlier than many other groups, including the white women's movement. In other words, they readily ascribed to many feminisms and, in fact, expected there to be more than one. Their disruptive voices have been raised within the context of overwhelming solidarity and political coalition vis-à-vis various progressive movements like Third World feminism, the white women's movement, the Chicano movement, socialist and Marxist movements, and revolutionary movements primarily in Latin America (Sandoval 2000).

A Word about Ethnic Labels

I use *people of Color* to refer to Chicanos, Asians, Native Americans, and Blacks, all of whom are U.S. minorities. Therefore, I capitalize *Color* because it refers to specific ethnic groups. I also capitalize *Black*, following the argument that it refers not merely to skin pigmentation but also to a

> heritage, an experience, a cultural and personal identity, the meaning of which becomes specifically stigmatic and/or glorious and/or ordinary under specific social conditions. It is socially created as, and at least in the American context no less specifically meaningful or definitive than, any linguistic, tribal, or religious ethnicity, all of which are conventionally recognized by capitalization. (MacKinnon 1982, 516)

On the other hand, *white* is left in lowercase letters because it refers not to one ethnic group or to specified ethnic groups but to many.

People of Mexican origin as well as from other Latin American origins residing in the United States have many labels available to them to identify their ethnicity. Some labels, like Mexican, Nicaraguan, and Salvadorian, refer to the specific country of origin and are most commonly, although by no means exclusively, used by recent immigrants. Other labels refer to U.S. geographical origins and highlight regional identities and cultural practices, for example, Tejano (Texan), Manito (from New Mexico), and Californiano (Californian). There are also labels that refer to different views on cultural assimilation and are inherently political, for example, Chicano for Mexican descendants and Boricua for Puerto Ricans. Both terms highlight ethnic cultural pride and the hybridity of cultural and language practices in these U.S. communities. Other labels, like Latino and Hispanic, demonstrate the necessity of expressing cultural and political solidarity among different national groups. However, it is worth mentioning that Latino is often viewed as a more politically progressive pan-ethnic label than is the term Hispanic, which many feel had its origins in the U.S. government rather than being an organic label emerging from the different U.S. Latino communities. Hispanic is also viewed by many as emphasizing the European ancestry of Latin Americans and ignoring indigenous roots. Nonetheless, Hispanic has great currency on the East Coast and more recently in Texas, whereas Latino is much more acceptable on the West Coast and is claimed by many in direct opposition to the use of Hispanic. Also, following Spanish language conventions, gender is indicated in many of these labels by the ending vowel—labels ending in *a* indicate female, whereas labels ending in *o* indicate male. For example, Latin*o* refers to male and Latin*a* refers to female. As is common in English, the generic is usually male, so in references to the group the male pronoun is preferred—Latin*os*. In an effort to avoid the sexism in the language, many writers use Latin*os/as* or vice versa, Latin*as/os*. Some authors choose to use the female Latin*a* as generic in effort to raise gender consciousness. Still others switch randomly between the use of male and female to equalize language use. Most individuals in the United States with origins in Latin America use multiple labels depending on the social context and their own particular historical and immigration experiences.

In this book I use the term Chicana to refer to women of Mexican origin. I use Latinas as a more inclusive term that includes Mexican-origin as well as other women of Latin American descent. I use Latinos/as as the pan-ethnic term to label the group as a whole. When these labels end in *o*, they refer to males in the different groups outlined above. Later in this chapter I also elaborate the theoretical underpinnings of using the label Chicana to refer to all my respondents when they themselves may or may not use this label.

Chicana Feminisms: Claiming *un Sitio y una Lengua* (a Space and a Language)

In 1991 Emma Pérez wrote about Chicana feminist production and the intellectual production of other women of Color.

> [O]ur works emerge from *un sitio y una lengua* [a space and language] that rejects colonial ideology and the by-products of colonialism and capitalist patriarchy—sexism, racism, homophobia, etc. The space and language is rooted in both the words and silence of Third-World-Identified-Third-World-Women who create a place apart from white men and women and from men of color. . . . Chicanas seize sociosexual power [to create] our own *sitio y lengua*. [I move] from deconstructing male centralist theory about women to reconstructing and affirming a Chicana space and language in an antagonistic society. (161–62)

Pérez's phrases *un sitio* (a space) and *una lengua* (a language) capture the essence of the Chicana feminist project. Both parts of the phrase—space and language—have multiple layers of meaning. Claiming a *lengua* meant claiming a language, a tongue, and a discourse. Claiming a *sitio* involved a historical place, a geographical location, and a philosophical space.

Lenguas (Discourses)

Claiming a Language

> Lacan imparted to us the "symbolic law of the father" entrenched in language. Language, he argues, is ensconced with symbols that dictate patriarchal power. But in his discussion he, like Freud, dismisses women, and exalts the phallus, again because women do not have "one."
>
> —Pérez 1991, 164

Chicanas reclaim their native language, Spanish. Reclaiming Spanish is a public acknowledgment of the linguistic limbo many experience as they are socialized in Spanish at home and then confront language repression when they enter school (Hurtado and Rodríguez 1989). Learning the "colonizer's language" was a traumatic event for many Chicana feminist writers and one that deeply influenced their thinking about the meaning of having their own *lengua*. As Emma Pérez related,

> Like many tejanas/os [Texans] who attended Anglo schools through grade school, I too was punished for speaking my parent's [*sic*] tongue on playgrounds and classrooms. Spanish set my brother and me apart. Anglo teachers peered at us when we spoke Spanish, the way white women peer at me now when they try to interfere in a circle of Chicanas speaking together in Spanglish, reaffirming our *mestizaje* [hybridity/mixed-race heritage]. As a child in Anglo schools, I realized quickly that I had to learn English, to pronounce it accurately, precisely. I was ridiculed for my accent, I was pushed into dark closets, disciplined for calling a student *gringo*. I practiced at night, staring up at the ceiling in my bedroom, reciting the alphabet. In English. Forgetting *la lengua de mi gente* [the language of my people]. Not knowing that the loss of language is loss of memory. (1991, 174)

The loss of their native *lengua* and the shame around those who retained it propelled Chicana feminists' understandings of the political nature of all discourse. Sonia Saldívar-Hull (2000) refused to translate, italicize, or otherwise mark the shift between English and Spanish in the first few chapters of her book. She wanted non-Spanish readers to experience the disjuncture felt by many monolingual Spanish speakers, especially children, as they enter mainstream circles not understanding English:

> In a consciously political act, what Gloria Anzaldúa calls "linguistic terrorism," I will not italicize Spanish words or phrases unless they are italicized in direct quotations. I invite readers not fluent in Spanish to experience a sense of life on the border as we switch from English to Spanish. Sometimes we translate, at other times we assume the nonnative speaker will understand from the context. Many Chicanas/os speak only English. Reading Chicana texts puts several demands on the reader, including the expectation that the reader will be knowledgeable in multiple Chicana and Chicano linguistic, cultural, and historical contexts. While most contemporary Chicana writers and critics have been formally educated in the United States and are fluent in English and Spanish, many of the writers code-switch between the two languages in a conscious act of identity politics. . . . My political practice as a transfrontera border feminista informs my linguistic acts of "identitarian collectivities." Once I have given the non-Spanish-literate reader a sense of "alien" disorientation in the text, I move toward more inclusionary tactics and offer translations in [later chapters]. (2000, 173)

Having access to multiple discourses in two languages—from formal English, to Spanglish, to Caló—provides insight into the fact that intellectual "merit" is defined politically. Many Chicana feminists who came from working-class backgrounds experienced the derogation of their parents by schools and other institutions because their parents did not speak English.

> When I entered the first grade, I cried each day after school. I lay my head on my mother's lap, a woman who was denied the right to read and write the language of the colonizer in a land that belonged to her ancestors. She brushed my hair back, comforting me. I couldn't articulate what I say so easily now. I couldn't say that the woman who comforted me, the woman who held power, beauty, and strength in my eyes, that Anglos dismissed her because she couldn't fill out their damn forms. I couldn't say that the school

was infested with white students, so alien to me. And that day the white teacher shoved me against a wall because I didn't recite the "Pledge of Allegiance." I didn't know it. But I knew "El Rancho Grande." (Pérez 1991, 177–78)

The use of Spanish by Chicana feminists in intellectual production became a political assertion of the value of their heritage and the means to create a feminist discourse directly tied to a Chicana experience.

Claiming a Tongue

> *A Gift of Tongues*
> *this tongue of mine*
> *sets fires*
> *licking hot*
> *all in its path*
> *scorches the old*
> *announces the new*
>
> *this tongue of mine*
> *breaks through walls*
> *setting free*
> *imagery of feelings*
> *odors of dreams*
> *tasting the bitter*
> *the rancid*
> *quenching the thirst*
>   —Sánchez 1992

Another translation for *lengua* is tongue, which captures the sexuality implicit in the word. Claiming sexuality has been central to the Chicana feminist project. Chicana feminists have written explicitly about sexual pleasure to counteract the silence and repression around sex in Chicano communities. Central to this has been the recognition that although Chicanas experience sexual restrictions in their communities and although virginity is highly valued (Hurtado 1996a, 59), within these spaces of restriction they also seek pleasure. As Patricia Zavella concludes from analyzing her interviews with Mexicana/Chicana respondents on their sexual practices,

> Catholic-based repressive ideology should be seen as only a cultural template. Women's cultural poetics (the social meaning of sexuality) entails struggling with the contradictions of repressive discourses and social practices of control that are often violent towards women and their desires. Women contest or incorporate repressive notions into their sense of sexual selves and they use metaphors of "play" and "fire" to express bodily pleasure. That is, in discussing their intimate relationships, playing was a recurring metaphor, which signified women's experiences of teasing, testing or pushing the boundaries of social convention. In women's discourse, fire had dual meanings: the repression of desire, where sanctions were "too hot," and the uncontrollable force of the erotic where passion consumed them. Women, then, sometimes "got burned" in transgressing social conventions, even as they sought sensations and experiences of the body enflamed. (Forthcoming)

Some of the most prolific Chicana feminist writers openly claim their lesbianism. They also are the best known in mainstream circles. Writers like Cherríe Moraga, Gloria Anzaldúa, and Emma Pérez have been pivotal in making sexuality a central part of Chicana feminist theorizing. Chicano communities have been as homophobic as white mainstream communities. Chicana feminists who expose and defend lesbianism profoundly challenge the status quo (Saldívar-Hull 1991, 214). It is important to highlight the fact that progressive politics in Chicano communities are practiced by individuals deeply committed to maintaining the cultural integrity of Chicano culture as a counterchallenge to the dominant hegemony of cultural, linguistic, and economic assimilation. Most lesbian Chicana writers have an intense loyalty to their communities of origin, to Chicano culture, to the Spanish language, and to working-class issues. As such, to propose that homophobia should be challenged even among the working class is a deeply courageous act.

Many Chicana lesbian writers have also written eloquently about their loyalty to their mothers (Córdova 1994, 193) and to female Catholic deities like the Virgen de Guadalupe.[1] These writings highlight the intimacy, love, and caring provided by women, even when many of them disapprove or do not understand their daughters' commitment to lesbianism.

The writers' loyalty to their mothers was born out of Chicanas' shared condition as women as well as their recognition of their mothers' struggles to survive. Many Chicana feminists see in their mothers unnamed feminists and unsung heroes who, through their daily lives, map what Chicana feminists want to capture in their writings (Fregoso forthcoming; Hurtado forthcoming). Although it can be tense, the relationship between mothers and daughters in Chicana feminisms is overwhelming in its solidarity in political struggle.

Claiming a Discourse

> Foucault transcribes historical documents to ventilate the power of discourse. He argues that through discourse power-knowledge is realized. Language, after all, is power. Third World people know that to learn the colonizer's language gives one access to power and privilege, albeit controlled, qualified power. —Pérez 1991, 165

Discourse is still yet another meaning for *lengua*. Chicana feminisms use a Foucauldian definition of discourse, in which "groups of statements and rules exist historically and change as the material conditions for their possibility also change" (Childers and Hentzi 1995, 84–85). Furthermore, "discourse informs and shapes subjectivity, including the possible activities and knowledge of the individual" (ibid.). Chicana feminisms proclaim that creating and controlling their own discourse are essential to decolonization. Passive silence has been the enemy that allowed others to construct who Chicanas are, what they can and cannot do, and what they are capable of becoming. Claiming discourse is claiming power to construct themselves.

> If discourse reveals the history of sexuality, then women of color face an obstacle. We have not had our own language and voice in history. We have been spoken about, written about, spoken at but never spoken with or listened to. Language comes from above to inflict us with western-white-colonizer ideology. (Pérez 1991, 175–76)

The lack of access to academic writing erased Chicanas from the white feminist intellectual landscape. They did not exist as intellectuals because, from a dominant white hegemonic feminist perspective, they had not acquired the "master's tools" (Lorde 1984). Chicana feminists recuperated the wisdom of their foremothers by reconstituting what was considered valid discourse in the academy. As Lorna Dee Cervantes claims, "I come from a long line of eloquent illiterates / whose history reveals what words don't say" (1981, 45); Sonia Saldívar-Hull exhorts us to go beyond the "dominant discourse" and look in "nontraditional places for our theories" (2000, 46); and Alvina Quintana advocates the use of literary texts written by Chicanas as "cultural self-ethnographies" (1996, 34).

Chicana feminists struggle to decolonize language, to burst open discourse to allow for the possibility of a liberatory consciousness (Sandoval 2000). They reject the dichotomization of discourse between "high" theory and everyday discourse.

> We speak our history to each other now just as our ancestors used oral tradition. A tradition which is minimized. We must write in accomplished English to legitimize our work. We must master the language of the colonizer before our studies are read. *Gringos y gringas* censure our real language which is often born from rage. (Pérez 1991, 175–76)

Chicana feminists claim women's discourse within their communities. They assert that women's bonding, through shared stories of defeat and resistance within their families, is worth recording and writing about. No longer is women's gossip outside the purview of academic theorizing. It was through the sharing inherent in "gossiping" that women subverted the silence around abuse by husbands, lovers, parents, and other authority figures. If it was spoken about, it existed in the memory of others. Accountability was at least possible if not viable.

Chicana feminists have self-consciously fashioned a rhetoric that integrates different genres—poetry (Cervantes 1981; Cisneros 1994; Villanueva 1978), spoken-word (González and Habell-Pallán 1994), *teatro* (theater) (Broyles-González 1994; Yarbro-Bejarano 1986), *declamación* (oratory) (Cantú 1995), short stories (Viramontes 1993; Serros 1993, 2000), artistic performance (Broyles-González 2001; Nájera-Ramírez forthcoming)—to explicate the content and form of their feminisms. Many Chicana feminist writers align themselves with cultural theorists who examine discourse to uncover the dynamics of power (Fregoso 1990; Chabram 1990; Alarcón 1994; Sandoval 2000).

Chicana feminisms talk back to white hegemonic feminism, to the colonizing discourses of the academy, and to parts of their cultural practices in their own communities that are politically regressive. The targets of their speaking back include the progressive men in the Chicano movement who have not been willing to acknowledge women's issues. Because the silent, passive woman who is willing to sacrifice everything on behalf of her family has been the ideal of womanhood in Chicano communities, there was a backlash when Chicanas claimed their outspokenness against the men in their communities. As the poet Elba Sánchez (forthcoming) proclaims, Chicanos want their women "mute" because "así eres mas bonita" (you are prettier that way):

Woman's Word

> *woman*
> *her story*
> *I sustain in my memory*
> *the want you want*
> *to erase*
> *to domesticate*
> *with your alphabet*
>
> *you have wanted me mute*
> *since childhood*
>
> *once*
> *my silence*
> *carved the place*
> *you call smile as*
> *your frothing words*
> *spilled out*
> *your eyes sternly*
> *warned*
> *—don't think*
> *you're prettier that way*

once
I would hide
my forbidden voice
in the pleats of my conscience
entire cities trapped in my throat

that was then

now
my tongue
has birthed the words
challenging
what is
no longer accepted.

Chicana feminisms' emphasis on class issues (Pesquera 1991; Romero 1992; Segura 1994; Zavella 1987) stems from the high participation of Chicanas in work outside the home as well as their association with the Marxist-infused Chicano movement of the 1960s and 1970s (Córdova 1994, 175, 188–89; Segura and Pesquera 1992). They have appropriated a discourse that challenges multiple constituencies and that consciously allies itself with progressive political causes in the United States and internationally.

Sitios (Spaces)

Claiming a Historical Space

> Here [the conquest of Mexico], the sexual, political, social, and psychological violence against *la india*—the core of the Chicana—is born. This core has been plundered from us through conquest and colonization. We reclaim the core for our woman-tempered *sitio y lengua*.
>
> —Pérez 1991, 168

Chicana feminisms openly fight the "loss of memory" (Pérez 1991, 174) through the recuperation of history—not only of women but of their ethnic and racial group as a whole—to carve out a geographical and philosophical space where their complexities are not ignored or elided. A central part of the project is debunking the stereotypes that portrayed Chicanas as non-agents in the creation of history, especially in political struggles around labor issues (Córdova 1994).

An integral part of the recuperation of history was to revise the official narrative of the historical events surrounding the colonization of Mexicanos. Chicanos, as a group, originated from an act of war and eventual conquest codified in the Treaty of Guadalupe Hidalgo, which ended the Mexican American War of 1848. The treaty formalized Mexico's defeat by the United States and the loss of over 50 percent of Mexico's territory. Overnight the people residing in what had become the southwestern United States had a new government that imposed a different language, a different culture, and a different political order (Almaguer 1991; C. García 1973). This history of colonization affects all Mexican descendants whether they were part of the conquered territory or not. Mexico as a nation still feels the loss of its former territory. Much of the Southwest still bears signs of having belonged to Mexico: city and street names, the presence of Catholic missions and other historical buildings, and the vibrant cultural practices that are very much alive.

This, however, was not the first experience of conquest. La Malinche, an indigenous woman, was a pivotal figure in the conquest of the Americas in 1519 by the Spanish. La Malinche was the ultimate traitor of Mexico because she allegedly facilitated Hernán Cortés's conquest of the Aztec empire by acting as translator between the Spanish and the different Mixteca tribes. Norma Alarcón notes that "Malintzin [La Malinche] comes to be known as *la lengua*, literally meaning the tongue. *La lengua* was the metaphor used, by Cortés and the chroniclers of the conquest, to refer to Malintzin the translator" (1989, 59). Modern Mexico was born from this betrayal, both figuratively and literally, since La Malinche converted to Catholicism *and* bore the children of Hernán Cortés's soldier Jaramaillo (Pérez 1993, 61). Although Chicana feminists did not choose La Malinche as the defining figure in their feminism, many male writers made her and her betrayal iconic (see Paz 1961 as a prime example of this tendency). All Mexicana/Chicana women are potential Malinches capable of betrayal if they are not under the watchful eye of patriarchy. Chicana feminists have engaged the polemics around La Malinche either to redeem her, to commiserate with her, or to appropriate her as a feminist hero (Alarcón 1989). Other female historical and legendary figures have been embraced as potentially mapping a specifically Chicana feminist consciousness, including La Virgen de Guadalupe (Castillo 1996), Sor Juana Inés de la Cruz (Gaspar de Alba 1992), La Llorona (Cisneros 1991; Mora 1996, 91; Saldívar-Hull 2000), and Frida Kahlo, among others (Córdova 1994, 193).[2] These historical and legendary figures engaged with gender struggles and also with struggles around labor and social revolutions against repressive governments.

The historical experience of conquest by the Spaniards and the imposition of Catholicism on indigenous people produced culturally specific definitions of womanhoods—what cultural theorists have called gendered subject positions for Chicanas. According to Chicana feminists, Marianismo and Malinchismo dichotomized women's womanhood into the "good woman" and the "bad woman" according to their sexuality (Hurtado 1996a). Marianismo is the veneration of the Virgin Mary (Nieto-Gomez 1974, 37). Her Mexican version, La Virgen de Guadalupe, is the role model for Chicana womanhood—she is the mother, the nurturer, the one who endures pain and sorrow, the one who is willing to serve (ibid.). These values form the basis for the construction of Chicana womanhood (Córdova 1994, 175) and are rooted in the practice of Catholicism. To be a "good woman" is to remain a virgin until marriage and to invest devotion, loyalty, and nurturance in the family, specifically Chicanos' definition of family, which includes extended networks of kin as well as friends and parts of their communities (Baca Zinn 1975, 13).

Other ethnic and racial groups have similar models of idealized womanhood (members of the Christian Right are a good example). For many Chicanos, however, commitment to these values has been a source of solace and strength to fight racism and resist oppression by the dominant group. Women's dedication to their families and many men's commitment to upholding their side of the bargain by hard work in the agricultural fields, dehumanizing work in factories, and low-paid, unskilled labor have made it difficult for Chicana feminists to challenge them. Chicana feminists critique the inherent sexism in a system that dichotomizes their womanhood between Malinchismo and Marianismo; at the same time, they strive to recognize the courageous work of women and men who have fought to preserve their families against brutal racist state intervention—a challenge that has not always been successful. Among the critics are Chicanas who do not see the advantages of challenging patriarchy and others who consider it a betrayal to join *any* feminist cause.

The debates around deconstructing these subject positions were especially heated during the Chicano movement of the 1960s and 1970s. When Chicana feminists questioned their roles in the Chicano movement, they were perceived by both men and women as not only attacking unequal gender practices but also as questioning the Catholic underpinnings of *all* Chicano culture. Consequently, the emerging Chicana feminist consciousness was perceived as a betrayal, and Chicana feminists were labeled "anti-family, anti-cultural, anti-man and therefore an [*sic*] anti-Chicano movement" (NietoGomez 1974, 35). Ironically, they were called Malinchistas and attacked as "selling out" to white feminism; they were also labeled lesbians, because they were supposedly privileging their sex above the unity of the Chicano movement in its struggle for social justice.

There are rewards for women who comply and punishments for those who rebel against the model of a "good woman." As in white mainstream culture, the power of patriarchy to enforce norms can occasionally be expressed by the father or husband with little or no accountability. Women who rebel openly pay the price. Punishment, which can include banishment from Chicano communities, has been especially harsh for women who openly declare their lesbianism. To sexually prefer women is viewed as the ultimate rejection of patriarchy. Furthermore, the strong Catholic underpinnings of Chicano culture make it a "mortal sin." Many Chicana lesbians find refuge in white lesbian communities and in activism on behalf of gay and lesbian issues. These gay activists, however, never completely disengage from their Chicano communities or from political work on behalf of Chicano issues (Trujillo 1991). The political and theoretical sophistication gained from participation in this broader political base has infused much of the theorizing about Chicanas' gender issues.

White women, as well as other non-Latina women, are not held accountable to the demands of these subject positions, because they are not the descendants of La Malinche. White hegemonic feminisms have not helped Chicana feminists deconstruct subject positions that had historical specificity and were based on the material conditions of Chicanos as a group.

Claiming a Geographical Place

> I have rights to my space. I have boundaries. I will tell you when you cross
> them. I ask that you respect my request.
>
> —Pérez 1991, 178

The site of colonization also had geographical specificity—the southwestern United States. It was in *la frontera* (the borderlands) that Chicanas situated their feminisms to highlight a particular border culture and language that stood between two nation-states—Mexico and the United States—but not belonging fully to either. Chicana feminists have been at the forefront of theorizing from *la frontera* as their *sitio* (space) (Anzaldúa 1987; Mora 1993), as Emma Pérez reminds us:

> My boundaries. El Río Bravo was once a life-giving stream that my ancestors
> crossed to travel north or to journey south. Back and forth, completing cy-
> cles. The river was not a boundary. *Gringos/as* built boundaries, fences, for
> themselves while they invaded our space, our boundaries. (1991, 175)

The geographical area represented by *la frontera* has become the guiding metaphor for all the borders Chicanas negotiate on a daily basis—class, race, ethnicity, sexuality. They have to fight different battles because of the multiplicity of boundaries they have to cross. Maintaining a core self and preventing others from invading their boundaries are constant battles.

> The boundaries that I draw sustain my sanity. We cannot be friends as long
> as you think you know every part of who I am, as long as you think you can
> invade my space and silence my language, my thoughts, my words, my rage.
> *Mi sitio y mi lengua*. Invasion, a deceitful intimacy. The Perpetrator wields
> power over the victim. The colonizer over the colonized. Sexual-racial vio-
> lence mired in language, in words. A speculum of conquest to "penetrate"
> further. (Pérez 1991, 175)

The history of conquest, which basically layered another country over a preexisting nation, gave Chicana feminists the knowledge of the temporality of nation-states (Klahn 1994). The political line dividing the United States from Mexico did not correspond to the experiential existence on the border. Many Chicana feminists declare the border the geographical location (*lugar*) that created the aperture for theorizing about subordination from an ethnically specific Chicana/*mestiza* consciousness (Anzaldúa 1987). It was at the border that Chicanas/*mestizas* learned the socially constructed nature of all categories. By standing on the U.S. side of the river they saw Mexico and they saw home; by standing on the Mexican side of the border they saw the United States and they saw home. Yet they were not really accepted on either side. Their ability to "see" the arbitrary nature of all categories but still take a stand challenges Chicana feminists to exclude while including, to reject while accepting, to struggle while negotiating. Chicana feminists variously called this *facultad* (ability) a *mestiza* consciousness (Anzaldúa 1987), differential consciousness (Sandoval 1991, 2000), and conscientización (Castillo 1995, 171). The basic concept involves the ability to hold multiple social perspectives while simultaneously maintaining a center that revolves around concrete material forms of oppression.

More recently, some Chicana feminists have pointed out that the *facultad* to cross "borders" is not easily exercised, nor is it often without pain and retribution by authority figures (Lamphere et al. 1993) who require a "false" unified self. True enough—those who exercised *la facultad*, especially in writing, were the outliers (Hurtado 1996b) who by definition ran the risk of expulsion from their communities. There were, however, those who exercised *la facultad* without writing and without calling it a feminist consciousness, who imparted their lessons to younger women, and who resisted gender subordination through everyday acts of rebellion (Steinem 1983) and guerrilla warfare of the mind (Hurtado 1989; Sandoval 1991, 2000). Chicana feminists' commitment to work across differences, finding dimensions of similarity through strategic suspensions (Hurtado 1996b), allowed them feminisms that defied "geopolitical borders" (Saldívar-Hull 1991, 211).

La frontera is also the geographical area that is most susceptible to hybridity that is neither fully of Mexico nor fully of the United States. As Gloria Anzaldúa claims, *la frontera* is where you "put chile in the borscht / eat whole wheat tortillas / speak Tex-Mex with a Brooklyn accent" (1987, 195). The borderlands denote that space in which antithetical elements mix, not to obliterate each other or to get subsumed by a larger whole, but rather to combine in unique and unexpected ways.

The combination of colonization and the location of their feminisms in *la frontera* makes Chicana feminisms deeply aware of their racial mixture—their *mestizaje*. The borderlands are a space of *mezclas* (mixtures, hybridity) of all kinds, including racial. Chicana feminists address issues of racism within their communities based on skin color and Indian heritage as determined by phenotype (Anzaldúa 1987, 21; Broyles-González 1994; Castañeda 1990, 228). Male scholars have as well (Arce, Murguía, and Frisbie 1987; Forbes 1968; Telles and Murguía 1990, 1992). Expanding on this work, Chicana feminists specifically analyze how racialized physical features are used to define desirable standards of beauty and womanhood (Anzaldúa 1981). They reclaimed *mestizaje*—the mixture of European, African, and Indian "races"—to resist the racist standards adopted in Chicano communities in preferring lighter skin and European features, especially for women (Saldívar-Hull 1991, 214–15). Exposed also were the negative racist judgments of darker-skinned, Indian-looking women and the derogation of their womanhood even by otherwise progressive men (Broyles-González 1994; Anzaldúa 1987). By speaking to the internal racism of Chicano communities and of progressive Chicano men, Chicana feminists turned the critical lens inward. Their use of standpoint theory reveals how the dynamics of prejudice influence relations in Chicano, as in all other, communities (Ochoa and Teaiwa 1994, ix). Importantly, the analysis of *mestizaje* was *woman-centered* rather than relying on male scholars' paradigms for studying racism.

Claiming a Philosophical Space

Ya no me van a robar mi sitio y mi lengua. [They will no longer steal my space and my language.] They live inside my soul, with my mother, my sisters, mis hermanas del tercer mundo [my sisters of the Third World].
—Perez 1991, 179

Chicana feminists agree with white feminists that patriarchy oppresses them. They diverge, however, from white feminisms, because their analysis of patriarchy does not focus on *individual rights* denied to them by men. Instead, Chicana feminisms propose that their subordination is the result of the intersection of multiple systems of oppression that include gender, race, ethnicity, class, and sexuality. It is from this *bocacalle* (intersection) that they situate their feminisms. The interlocking systems of oppression stem from the historical specificity of colonization, first of native peoples by Spain and second by the conquest of Mexico by the United States. Chicana feminisms take the history of the Americas as the bedrock on which they theorize their condition as *mestizas* (hybrids, mixed-race women). Unlike Virginia Woolf, who claimed "a room of one's own" as the means to liberation, Chicanas claim a space to congregate with others like them as liberatory. The space envisioned is a nurturant space where cultural and language differences do not have to be constantly explained. It is also a space of replenishment, a respite from the daily interactions in which Chicanas negotiate a fragmented self. Chicana feminisms theorize about *collective* liberation against all kinds of oppression. Chicana feminisms focus not so much on men as individual potential oppressors, but on systems of oppression that converge into what Emma Pérez calls the "subject" who holds "sociosexual-racial power" over marginalized others that include her and others like her: "I see you, who hold sociosexual-racial power, as the subject who objectifies the marginal other—me. . . . I sense you as invasive, conquering and colonizing my space and my language. You attempt to 'penetrate' the place I speak from with my Chicana/Latina *hermanas*" (1991, 178). The "subject" oppressing Chicanas is sometimes white men, other times white women, and still other times men of Color and other members of their communities. Regardless of this *relational* analysis of power, Chicana feminists still put Chicanas and Third World women at the center of their analysis.

> I prefer to think of myself as one who places women, especially Third World women and lesbians, in the forefront of my priorities. I am committed to women's organizations because in those spaces we revitalize, we laugh, we mock the oppressor, we mock each other's seriousness and we take each other seriously. This is a process of support, this is living the ideal, if only momentarily, to give, to nurture, to support each other in a racist, sexist, homophobic Western society. I speak at this moment of historical consciousness as a Chicana survivor who has survived much more than I speak of here, just as we, women of color survive daily. (Pérez 1991, 178)

Chicana feminists think of themselves as multiply positioned because of the interlocking nature of their oppression. It is from this philosophical space that they develop political proposals for coalitions to accomplish social justice. Chicana feminists' commitment to coalition politics stems theoretically from their knowledge that "women of Color," or "African American women," or "Chicana women" are racialized subjects that have been constructed through historical events and material conditions (Davis and Martínez 1994). Rather than adhering to an essentialist notion of racial or gender identity, Chicana feminists struggle to implement standpoint theory through coalition building. Ultimately, Chicana feminisms' main goal, to accomplish social justice by building successful coalitions, is part of their theoretical and political agenda.

Future Directions in Chicana Feminisms: The Current Study

In the next fifteen years, the challenge for Chicana feminist scholars will be similar to the crisis facing contemporary white feminisms—how to fully engage young women when many of the barriers that were the impetus for feminist theorizing are slowly melting away (Frith 2001). Chicana feminists' common working-class origins, the predominance of Spanish in their backgrounds, and the persistence of sexism, heterosexism, and racism have fueled much of their activism and scholarship. Younger Chicanas will have had much more varied social and class experiences than current writers. The question is whether our present feminisms will capture and enlighten emerging social formations. The amount and types of interethnic contact have increased in the last twenty years. Although race and ethnic relations in the United States remain extremely contentious, nonetheless, they are a far cry from the early days of the Chicano movement, when interethnic contact was scorned and interethnic mating was frowned upon. The children of the intermarriages of the 1960s have grown up and require us to rethink "Chicana identity" (González and Habell-Pallán 1994, 81–82). In the past, intermarriages were not only few in number but primarily between Chicanos and whites; in contrast, the 1960s provided a broader context for intergroup mating. "Mixed" heritage has come to include every possible combination of ethnicities and races; many of these are unions between members of subordinate groups. Especially important for Chicana feminist theorizing, which was based on Mexican history and nationality, was the increase of intermarriage between different Latino groups, whose children will increasingly identify with a Latino "pan-ethnicity" rather than a specific Latino national group.

These emerging social formations will also be characterized by an increase in social and economic mobility, which granted, is likely to remain very small, but which will still diversify class. To be sure, those with increased economic and educational opportunities will be the ones most likely to join the academy and be the next generation of writers.

Sexuality will also continue to be prominent as we explicitly study the range of sexualities and their relationship to patriarchy within Chicano communities. Lesbian writers have made enormous contributions, but the study of heterosexuality has just begun (most notably Zavella 1997, forthcoming). Another area for future elaboration will be the study of Chicano gay issues and how they subvert the power of patriarchy within Chicano communities. How is homosexuality handled by members of Chicano communities? (There have been some promising starts in this area as well, most notably Almaguer 1991 and L. Cantú 1999, 2001.) Addressing sexuality issues in Chicano communities is an especially delicate subject for the same reasons that addressing women's issues was in the early 1970s. There exists a risk that these issues could divide the political struggle to gain some basic necessities of life. Another concern is that addressing sexuality could potentially subvert the Catholic underpinnings of Chicano culture. Scholars writing about issues of sexuality confront the next frontier in Chicano studies and will be especially important in furthering our paradigms of how we address gender issues from a feminist perspective.

The Study: How, Where, and with Whom: Methods and Sample Characteristics

I situated this study directly in the framework provided by the Chicana feminist literature. I interviewed a total of 101 Chicanas who had some education beyond high school and were between twenty and thirty years of age. "Chicana" was defined as a person who had at least one parent of Mexican descent. The literature on Chicana feminisms grew directly out of the history of conquest of the Southwest, first by Spain and later by the United States. Immigration from Mexico had also predominated in the

United States; only since the late 1970s have immigrants from other Latin American countries come to this country in substantive numbers. Mexican immigrants' motivations for coming to this country were predominately economic, though some also came to escape political persecution, particularly oppression based on sexual orientation (Arguelles and Rivero 1993; L. Cantú 1999, 2001). Political persecution and upheaval were more prominent motivators for other Latin American immigrants. Furthermore, Puerto Ricans' history and political relationship to the United States were different from those of people of Mexican descent, and all of these differed from the Cuban experience in this country. Chicana feminists addressed the specificities of the Mexican-descent experience in the United States while expressing solidarity with other Latinas (Saldívar-Hull 2000). There are also important feminist writings that address different Latino communities in the United States. Most recently, Chicana feminist writers have begun collaborative intellectual efforts to weave together the commonalities and differences between women of different Latino ancestries (Latina Feminist Group 2001).

The *mezcla* (mixing) of different ethnic and racial groups has always existed in Chicano communities. Although historically intermarriage has occurred primarily between Latinos and whites, most recently *la mezcla* has increased among different Latino groups. This unfolding *mestizaje* has gained prominence in scholarly literature as non–Mexican-descent Latino immigration increases. I wanted to capture the diversity of the Chicana population in my study. Fourteen respondents were part of this *mezcla*. Table 1 lists the mixed respondents, detailing their parents' ethnic backgrounds and whom they lived with while growing up. Of the fourteen respondents, six had mothers and two had fathers who were white (of various ancestries). The remaining six respondents had mothers and fathers of various ancestries.

Diversity of Ethnic Labeling

Latinos have many ethnic labels available to them for representing their different histories and the complexities of their social, cultural, economic, and political existence in this country. While my respondents were subject to these complexities and used a multiplicity of labels, I located this study in the Chicana feminist literature that self-consciously labeled itself

Table 1

Mixed-Heritage Respondents

Respondent's Name	Respondent Lived With?	Parents' Ethnic Background
Nicole Rodriguez	Parents	Mother—Armenian; Father—Mexican
Mariposa	Mother	Mother—White; Father—Mexican
Sonya K. Smith	Mother	Mother—Mexican; Father—Anglo
Jessica Delgado	Mother	Mother—Mexican; Father—Colombian
Hilda[a]	Mother	Mother—Mexican and White; Father—Mexican
Misty	Mother[c]	Mother—Irish; Father—Mexican
Gabriella Gonzalez	Parents	Mother—White; Father—Mexican
Mieka Valdez	Mother	Mother—White; Father—Mexican
Jennifer Dominguez	Parents	Mother—White; Father—Mexican
Bianca	Parents	Mother—Mexican; Father—Italian-American
Ramona Perez	Parents[b]	Mother—Mexican/Jewish; Father—Mexican
Dorian López	Parents	Mother—Mexican; Father—Puerto Rican
Nicolasa I. Sandoval	Parents	Mother—Indian; Father—Mexican
Tonantzin	Parents	Mother—Italian; Father—Mexican

a Her grandmother on her mother's side was Mexican and her grandfather was Anglo.
b Parents divorced when she was eighteen.
c Lived with her mother and her step-father (who is white). Her parents divorced when Misty was 8 and her mother remarried when she was 9.

Chicana. Claiming the label *Chicana* was a political move to highlight its "in-between" position in the interstices of multiple social, economic, and cultural systems. *Chicana* has come to signify the celebration of hybridity and the claiming of what Gloria Anzaldúa called *El Mundo Zurdo*, the queer world that hybrids inhabit because they offend purists on all sides. *Chicana* therefore became a political assertion through the restitution of self, a self that was constructed in the interstices. My respondents "felt" this rejection from the purists, but some had not yet decided what it meant. They knew they were violating cultural expectations by not marrying young, by leaving home before marriage, or by having premarital sex, but they were also not accepted in the "white" world they were joining through their educational achievement. To paraphrase Lani Guinier (1998, 66), they were "border people," fully accepted by few. At the same time, my respondents acted as the "bridge called their back," to paraphrase Cherríe Moraga and Gloria Anzaldúa (1981), between all the different social worlds they belonged to. So even if not all my respondents claimed the label "Chicana," inadvertently they were claiming, through their lives, the cultural, intellectual, and political space created by Chicana feminist scholarship.

Parents' Educational and Class Background

Chicana feminist writers have squarely situated themselves as coming from working-class perspectives and being deeply influenced by the political movements of the 1960s, especially those with strong Marxist leanings. Their writing has been much less relevant to the experiences of middle-class Chicano communities. Most Chicana college students still come from predominantly working-class backgrounds, have parents who did not finish high school, and are likely to be the first generation born and raised in the United States. This was certainly the case with my respondents. Half of them identified their class background while they were growing up as "poor" (18 percent) or as "working-class" (32 percent) (see table 2).

It was interesting to hear respondents explain the basis on which they made their class assessments. For example, even though almost a third of the respondents thought their families were middle-class (30 percent), they based this judgment primarily on their parents' job stability and on the amount of money they made *in relation* to Latino families around them. It was not uncommon for self-proclaimed "middle-class" respondents to have parents who did not finish high school but had a union job, or to live in situations in which both parents and other members of the

Table 2

Respondents' Views of Their Social Class Background

Class Identification	Number of Respondents
Poor	18
Working-Class	32
Lower-Middle-Class	16
Middle-Class	30
Upper-Middle-Class	4
Rich	1
TOTAL	101

Table 3

Work Status of Respondents' Parents

Work Status	Percent of Mothers (N = 101)	Percent of Fathers (N = 101)
Stays home	18.9	3.0
Works outside the home	75.2	72.3
Attends school	1.0	0.0
Retired	1.0	6.9
Deceased	3.0	5.0
Parent not present	1.0	11.9
Not reported	0.0	1.0
TOTAL	100.0	100.0

family worked to obtain a total income that they considered "middle-class." Only one respondent considered herself "rich." Even in this case, the respondent's father had barely finished grade school. He had become a "self-made millionaire" by buying land in South Texas and "making parcels" for development. Her mother finished high school, had "taken a couple of college courses in computers," and worked as a computer programmer.

Both of the respondents' parents had a high degree of participation in the workforce: 72 percent of the fathers and 75 percent of the mothers worked outside the home. The majority of the respondents' parents who were working were either unskilled or skilled workers: 66 percent of the mothers and 61 percent of the fathers (see table 4). They were factory workers, farmworkers, housekeepers, receptionists, pattern makers, and so on. Many of the respondents spoke about their parents' harsh lives and their economic vulnerabilities. Many came from large families and their parents' small incomes caused considerable hardship (see chapter 5). There were also a sizable number of parents who had attained some kind of higher education, although not all had obtained their degrees (twenty mothers and twenty fathers). Many of these parents were the first in their families to obtain a college degree, and my respondents had a substantial amount of contact with their less-well-off relatives. Eight out of nine white mothers and both white fathers in the study were professionals. The remaining white mother worked as a manager for the family-owned business and was part of a small number of mothers (8 percent) and fathers (12 percent) who had their own businesses. As mentioned above, with the exception of one father who was described by his daughter as "rich," most of the businesses, such as upholstery shops and small catering businesses, were modest. All these businesses had existed in my respondents' families for only very short periods of time. None of the respondents came from inherited wealth.

Feminisms in the Academy

Women who had had the benefits of higher education produced Chicana feminist writings. Even for those writers who did not remain in the academy and chose creative writing as a means to make a living, such as Sandra Cisneros, Cherríe Moraga, Ana Castillo, and Gloria Anzaldúa, university life provided fertile ground for their early development. Many of my respondents were attending the institutions that had produced the Chicana feminist writers reviewed in this book; as such, they could be considered

Table 4
Occupations of Respondents' Parents

Occupations	Percent of Mothers (N = 76)	Percent of Fathers (N = 75)
Unskilled (e.g., factory worker, housekeeper, farm worker, day care worker, cafeteria worker, dishwasher, laborer, truck driver)	28.9	36.0
Skilled (e.g., pattern maker, receptionist, postal worker)	36.8	25.3
Professional (e.g., teacher, social worker, lawyer, professor)	26.3[a]	26.7[b]
Owns Business (e.g., catering, upholstery, sign company, real estate)	7.9	12.0
TOTAL	100.0	100.0

a Of the twenty professional mothers, eight were white.
b Of the twenty professional fathers, two were white.

the second generation of Chicana intellectuals produced in these institutions of higher education.

I chose to interview Chicanas who had some kind of higher education—one of the constituencies Chicana feminist writings are theorizing about. Young educated Chicanas were the most likely to gain exposure to Chicana feminist ideas either directly by reading the work or indirectly from professors familiar with this literature. Chicana feminisms, like white feminisms, have not "hit the streets" in any significant way. Our feminist theorizing has remained mostly within the academy, and it is here that we can assess its utility to its most direct inheritors, young Chicana students and professionals.

There is a recurrent concern in Chicana feminist scholarship about asserting the heterogeneity of Chicanas based on a multiplicity of factors like geographical diversity, language differences, and variation in social and economic class status. I took this concern seriously and wanted the final sample of respondents to reflect the richness of this variation. The Mexican-descent population in this country resides primarily in the five southwestern states of Texas, California, Arizona, New Mexico, and Colorado, with a sizable number in the city of Chicago. In addition, the majority of this population has been concentrated mainly in two states—California and Texas. To accurately represent the areas where Mexican descendants reside, I had to interview respondents from all these states, with an oversampling of respondents in California and Texas. Heeding the warning of Chicana writers, who argue that our theorizing should take into account the "atypical" case to avoid essentializing "the Chicana experience" as residing primarily in the southwestern United States, I interviewed respondents in the East Coast and Midwest as well. The final sample of 101 respondents reflects a broad scope of experiences on many levels, as respondents were attending a wide range of institutions (see tables 5 and 6).

At the time I interviewed them, most of my respondents were still attending institutions of higher education (74 respondents) (see table 6). Twenty-seven percent had already graduated (some with a bachelor's degree and most with a master's degree or other advanced degree) and were working or seeking employment. Of those who were in school, some had already been in the workforce before returning to obtain advanced degrees. Of the total number of respondents (N = 101), 15 percent were married and of those, 7 percent had children. There were a few part-time

Table 5
Place of Interview

Cities and States of Interviews (N = 101)	Number of Respondents
Arizona	
Tempe	8
California	
Los Angeles	2
Oakland	7
Palo Alto	2
San Diego	1
Santa Cruz	8
Watsonville	3
Colorado	
Colorado Springs	6
Illinois	
Chicago	13
Massachusetts	
Cambridge	7
Michigan	
Ann Arbor	6
New Mexico	
Albuquerque	9
New York	
New York City	7
Texas	
Austin	1
Edinburg	8
McAllen	1
San Antonio	8
Washington, D.C.	4
TOTAL	101

students who juggled school, work, children, and family. Most, though, were single and did not have children (80 percent). A few had children as teenagers and remained single (5 percent). Only one respondent had children and was divorced. The average age of my respondents was twenty-four, only two were under twenty (they were both nineteen), and only two

Table 6

Respondents' Institutional Affiliations

Institutions	Number of Respondents (N = 101)
Arizona State University	
Master's Program in Education	4
California State University, San Diego	
Undergraduate	1
City University of New York	
Doctoral Program in Psychology	1
Colorado College	
Undergraduate	6
Columbia University	
Master's Program in Counseling	1
Master's Program in Education	1
Law School	1
Doctoral Program in Sociology	1
DePaul University	
Undergraduate	1
Farmingdale University	
Undergraduate	1
Gillian Community College, Tempe, Arizona	
Undergraduate	1
Harvard University	
Master's Program in Education	3
Master's Program in Business	1
Doctoral Program in Sociology	2
Loyola University	
Undergraduate	1
New Mexico Highlands University	
Master's Program in Social Work	1
New York University	
Doctoral Program in Anthropology	1

(Table 6 Continued on next page)

were over thirty (thirty-one and thirty-two).[3] All in all, my respondents were extremely heterogeneous.

Situating Chicana Feminisms

Chicana feminist writings have argued powerfully that the *sitio* from which they theorize is *la frontera. La frontera* has become the metaphor for both

Table 6 *(Continued)*
Respondents' Institutional Affiliations

Institutions	Number of Respondents (N = 101)
Stanford University	
Master's Program in Education	2
University of California, Berkeley	
Boalt Law School	3
Doctoral Program in Social/Cultural Studies	1
Doctoral Program in Urban Planning	1
Doctoral Program in Sociology	1
University of California, Los Angeles	
Doctoral Program in Education	1
University of California, Santa Cruz	
Undergraduate	8
University of Chicago	
Undergraduate	8
University of Michigan	
Doctoral Program in American Studies	1
Doctoral Program in Sociology	3
Doctoral Program in Education	2
University of New Mexico	
Undergraduate	2
Master's Program in American Studies	1
Master's Program in Sociology	1
Doctoral Program in Political Science	1
University of Texas, San Antonio	
Undergraduate	2
Master's Program in Bicultural Studies	2
Medical School	2
University of Texas, Pan American	
Undergraduate	4
TOTAL NUMBER STILL IN SCHOOL	74

real borders, like the U.S./Mexico border, and cultural, socioeconomic, and political borders that Chicanas were forced to negotiate on a daily basis. Nonetheless, regardless of all their border crossings through *sitios* and *lenguas*, Chicana feminisms situate themselves within a U.S. experience. The connection to Mexico is an ancestral one as well as a political one, but Chicana feminisms are a U.S. phenomenon and claim their U.S.-based "Americanness." Chicana feminist writers did not claim a foreign

Table 7
Respondents' Professions

Professions	Number of Respondents (N = 101)
Bachelor's Degree, no job yet	3
Bank Worker (e.g., branch assistant)	2
Bookkeeper	1
Caregiver	1
Community Organizer	1
Cultural Arts Administrator	1
Elementary School Teacher	1
Freelance Writer	1
Government Employee	3
Lecturer at a University	1
Medical Assistant	1
News Assistant (e.g., Reuters News Service)	2
Owner of Advertising Firm	1
Program and Graphic Designer	1
Recruiter for a University	1
University Administrator	6
TOTAL NUMBER OF PROFESSIONALS	27

status but rather inserted themselves in the U.S. debates around gender while remaining in solidarity with working-class Mexican women and the rest of Latin America. The majority of respondents also felt this way. Most were born in the United States (92 percent) or, if born in Mexico (8 percent), had been raised in largely Chicano communities.[4] They fully acknowledged their Mexican background but claimed their rights and privileges as U.S. citizens.

Chicana feminisms also claimed "lived experience" as their *sitio* for obtaining knowledge. It was on women's flesh that you could find history, love, politics, and liberation. Abstract theory was suspect because it often appeared irrelevant to the daily experience of traversing borders and its consequences (Anzaldúa 1987). Chicana feminisms basically posed the challenge, as some other feminisms did, to seek truth not only in abstract categories but also in what women lived and "told in their stories." As Sonia Saldívar-Hull advocated,

We have to look in nontraditional places for our theories: in the prefaces to anthologies, in the interstices of autobiographies, in our cultural artifacts, our cuentos [stories], and if we are fortunate to have access to a good library, in the essays published in marginalized journals not widely distributed by the dominant institutions. (1991, 206)

That was why I chose to do open-ended interviews rather than using other kinds of social science methods only and to interview women in groups of two or three to best re-create the experience of sharing in a circle of women, an experience that was part of the daily lives of many of my respondents. I did not ask them about Chicana feminist theorizing, but it was my challenge to *translate* that theorizing into a set of questions based on my respondents' lived experience. I asked them about dating when they were growing up, about whether their parents placed value on their virginity and why; I asked them about doing household chores and whether their brothers were treated differently; I asked them about menstruation, premarital sex, and who taught them about these issues; I asked them about marriage, kids, and partnering across ethnic and sexual lines; I asked them about their future plans and their political commitment. My respondents resonated with this approach. As is true for many young women in this society, nobody besides very close women friends had asked them to reflect on their lives. It was unusual in my respondents' experience to have older people, especially educated older people of Color, listen to them talk about their lives. I was overwhelmed by my respondents' need and desire, even yearning, to talk—to me, to each other, and to a wider audience. They had no shame in their defeats, great joy in their triumphs, and a sense of hope that was inspiring. My interviews were full of laughter, reflection, incisive insights, loving memories, pain, hurt, tears, and redemption. I *felt* I was not only capturing Chicana feminisms *in the flesh* but simultaneously *living* them in the company of these extraordinary women. Our interviews lasted between two and three hours; afterward, my respondents could ask me anything they wished. Many asked very kind questions about my own upbringing, marriage, children, opinions, and career. Most of the time, however, respondents chose to talk about life, racism, and politics. We had "conversations with power" about how authority was imposed on them on a daily basis—about why their lives turned out the way they did, why their parents raised them the way they did, why whites treated them the way they did, why lovers mistreated them. It was during this part of the interview that we soared as equals—Chicanas who had succeeded beyond what anybody had expected of us and could reflect, theorize, and articulate from the interstices of the many places we occupy in this society. I am deeply indebted to my 101 respondents for how much they taught me. Equally important, these young women poured a balm of hope over my soul as I realized our collective potential to achieve social justice. I walked away from my interviews amazed at the magnificent creatures our communities had produced.

A Short Methodological Note

I contacted most of my respondents in institutions of higher education through counselors, professors, student organizations, and personnel of student affairs offices. I usually sent an electronic message describing the study and outlining the age and ethnic requirements for potential respondents. I had no difficulty obtaining responses and setting up interviews, which took place mostly in hotel rooms. Focus groups had two or three respondents, although occasionally I interviewed respondents individually. I audio- and videotaped all interviews. The audiotapes were transcribed by bilingual and bicultural research assistants and cross-checked with the videotapes. The transcripts were coded and entered into a computer.

In addition to the interviews, I also mailed out a questionnaire to all my respondents and shadowed thirty-five of them by spending one or more days with them. As part of the shadowing, I met their parents, siblings, and other relatives. I attended respondents' graduations, weddings, baptisms, and professional presentations. I received notes, letters, electronic mail, pictures, cards, and books from many of my respondents. I got to know many of them well.

A Short Personal Note

After I finally got over my apprehension described in the preface of this book, I began writing with an enormous amount of joy, so much so that I would often cheat my family for extra time to write; I would talk to my classes about my book instead of composing new lectures; I would skip family dinners, friends' birthdays, faculty meetings, invited talks, and numerous other activities to remain at my desk and write. I felt like a kid after my bedtime with a lamp under the covers reading an exciting novel. I enjoyed every single word of it. When I finally sent a complete draft to the editors at New York University Press, I almost clicked my heels in anticipation of their reaction, which I expected to be nothing less than absolute enthusiasm (with the usual editorial cautions) at hearing my respondents speak. Two weeks later I received a long, detailed letter that hit me right between the eyes, basically challenging me for the very personal tone I had chosen in writing about my respondents. Later that same week, by coincidence, I began reading AnaLouise Keating's new book, a compilation of interviews with the Chicana feminist Gloria Anzaldúa, and it became clear to me that writing from a feminist perspective is personal. To avoid one's perspective in clear and explicit terms is to hide. And I have hidden well—behind multiple regressions (Hurtado and Gurin 1994), behind structural equation modeling (Hurtado, Gurin, and Peng 1997), and behind theoretical analyses (Hurtado 1996b). Only through the urging of feminist friends and scholars like Michelle Fine, Patricia Zavella, and Abby Stewart have I been forced out of the intellectual closet to say who I am *as I write*.

The fear of being out of the closet is not ungrounded. Gloria Anzaldúa urged AnaLouise Keating to leave the protection of academic writing behind. Keating's fears in reaction to Anzaldúa's suggestion were not unlike my own as I began this book:

I am a product of the U.S. university system. I have learned to mask my own agenda—my own desires for social justice, spiritual transformation, and cultural change—in academic language. . . . Because it [theory] seems to hide private feelings, desires, and deeply held beliefs behind rational, objective discourse and abstract thought, theory can be more persuasive for some readers. . . . My academic training, coupled with my love of privacy, make me fear self-disclosure. If I incorporate the personal into my words, perhaps I won't be respected as a scholar. Or maybe you'll think that I'm vain, egocentric, and selfish. . . . Or maybe I'll sound stupid, unsophisticated, naïve. (2000, 1–3)

To respond to these fears, Keating returned to Gloria Anzaldúa's writings to find the answer to her dilemma.

But one of the most important things I've learned from reading and teaching Anzaldúa's works is the importance of risking the personal. Throughout her writings, Anzaldúa draws extensively on her own life—her early menstruation; her campesino background; her childhood in the Rio Grande Valley of South Texas; her experiences as a brown-skinned, Spanish-speaking girl in a dominant culture that values light-skinned, English-speaking boys; and her sexual and spiritual desires. (2000, 2)

So I, too, take Anzaldúa's challenge to disclose at the risk of sounding biased, unsophisticated, unscholarly, and lacking in objectivity. I have chosen a style of writing that communicates to the reader that I admire my respondents, that I do not take their struggles for granted, and that I do not feel I have the authority to judge them. I let them speak for themselves rather than only analyzing their words to make theoretical points. I have chosen to follow Gloria's advice to "put myself into it more," not to glorify myself or to decenter my respondents. I do so in spite of the fact that this may lead some readers to exactly those conclusions, when, in fact, I am trying to enhance my respondents' life stories by not denying my own.

■　■　■　■　■　■　■　■　■

The Development of Self

Existing within a Family

Part I

■　■　■　■

SANDRA CISNEROS begins her short story "Woman Hollering Creek" (1991) with the transfer of Cleófilas Enriqueta DeLeón Hernández from one owner, her father, to her new owner, her husband, whom she is to follow to "el otro lado" (across the border to the United States).

> The day Don Serafín gave Juan Pedro Martínez Sánchez permission to take Cleófilas Enriqueta DeLeón Hernández as his bride, across her father's threshold, over several miles of dirt road and several miles of paved, over one border and beyond to a town *en el otro lado*—on the other side—already did he divine the morning his daughter would raise her hand over her eyes, look south, and dream of returning to the chores that never ended, six good-for-nothing brothers, and one old man's complaints. (43)

In this short paragraph, Cisneros outlines many of the central concerns in Chicana feminist writings regarding the restriction of young women's freedom. Young women in Chicano/Mexicano communities are closely monitored by their parents, their mothers in particular, until they are handed over to their next "keeper," ideally a husband. The socialization of these restrictions occurs in families as parents enforce curfews and instill the values of respect, obedience, and sacrifice on behalf of the family. Included in women's commitment to family are "the chores that never ended," from which male members of the family are exempted, as were Cleófilas's "six good-for-nothing brothers." A major motive for women's restriction is the concern over the preservation of their virginity until marriage.

In this study I asked about all these issues. In essence, what is it like to grow up female in Chicano/Mexicano families? I knew that all these issues were important when I was growing up in South Texas, regardless of my educational and professional achievement. However, I was as much as twenty-eight years older than the youngest of my respondents. It wasn't unusual, in fact, for me to be the same age as their parents and, in several instances, actually older. A few of the respondents also had college-educated parents, so I assumed that many of these issues around restriction of freedom and the importance of virginity had decreased in importance. There was also the issue of the respondents' current class status. All the respondents had achieved much more than was usual in families of Mexican descent in the United States. In fact, many of the respondents had already achieved more than the most accomplished citizens of this country. So I expected dramatic changes in socialization practices from when I grew up, especially because I assumed I was dealing with the most "assimilated" and "acculturated" women of the U.S. Mexican-descent population. I was in for a very big surprise.

Overview of Chapter 2: Growing Up Female

Long before Cleófilas left her parents' home "intact," she had undergone a series of biological transitions that had insured that her husband was the recipient of her prized virginity. Cleófilas had to be protected from birth so that each biological development resulted in the properly gendered enculturation, ensuring that Cleófilas would know her role as she stepped across her father's threshold.

The first significant biological transition for Cleófilas, as for other women of Mexican descent, was menstruation. This marked the end of a carefree childhood with relatively few gender-based constraints and the beginning of a stage of vulnerability and parental (especially motherly) surveillance to ensure at all costs that she did not become "illegitimately" pregnant. It was a dramatic transition because of the silence surrounding menstruation and the taboo on talking about anything sexual. For most of my respondents, this biological transition of becoming a *señorita* (young woman) happened as early as the age of nine or as late as fifteen.

As Cleófilas developed physically and began to look more like a "woman," her family's surveillance intensified. The goal of their policing was the transfer of Cleófilas from her previous owner, her father, to her new owner, her husband, with her hymen intact. This, for the most part, was the framework almost all my respondents negotiated as they developed physically. As restrictive as their lives were, many of my respondents were able to expand their families' views on what was acceptable or not for young women. Their efforts paved the road for younger siblings and expanded the horizons for their mothers and for other women in their lives.

My respondents weathered their physical transitions well and were deeply involved with another aspect of their development—becoming family with those around them.

Overview of Chapter 3: Becoming Family

One is not born a member of a family but becomes one through everyday struggles and joys. Being female involves biological processes and changes that one feels "in the body." In contrast, family is a set of social relations revolving around intangibles such as privileges and responsibilities. Certainly for my respondents "growing up female" involved their physical development, including menstruation, their loss of virginity, and (for some) motherhood, within the context of familial relationships. Becoming family, however, involved an ever-changing set of social relations. This was especially the case for respondents who were the first generation in the United States (59 percent of the mothers and 63 percent of the fathers were born outside the United States, mostly in Mexico). Many of their parents had been temporarily separated, as men (or in some cases women) came alone first to the United States and eventually sent for the rest of their families. In some instances, the respondents were left behind with relatives in Mexico, while both parents came to the United States and eventually sent for them. At times, family members were strangers to each other until they became reacquainted in a new and strange country. In a few instances, respondents grew up with no parents present at all (as in the case of Lucha; see chapter 2), so they created family with siblings and friends. Being a family was not preordained from the womb but evolved according to the socioeconomic circumstances of respondents, their history of migration, the birth of siblings, and the respondents' own social development. In some instances, my respondents sought fathers who were absent so as to reconnect and "become family." In others, respondents deliberately rejected fathers (and, in a few rare instances, mothers) to "become family" with those more suitable than their families of origin. In most instances, my respondents had developed a deep connection with both parents—a connection that was imbued with tension but also a great sense of love, affection, and respect. "Becoming family," however, was definitely a "gendered" process: the mothers did most of the emotional work to develop the "bond." Only in a few instances were fathers equally involved. Nonetheless, fathers' different relational style, although not as central as that of the mothers, was still essential to many of my respondents as they sought their fathers' presence, love, and *apoyo* (support). Many of my respondents tried and continue to try to shape their fathers with the goal of becoming closer to them and being able to connect with them at a deeper level. It is within these complexities that my respondents learned to "become family."

2

■　■　■　■　■　■　■　■　■

Growing Up Female

Dating

I FIRST ASKED the respondents, "Was there a particular point in your life when you were allowed to date? That is, when a boy could come to your home, pick you up, and go out to a movie or something?" Most of the respondents would giggle and joke. As Rita put it, "I'm still waiting for an answer to that one!"[1] That is, regardless of the respondents' age, most parents did not approve of them going out with a boyfriend. In fact, many of the respondents stated that the assumption, however unrealistic and nonsensical on the surface, was that, like Cleófilas, they would go from living in their household under the supervision of their parents directly to some mythical husband who had never crossed their home's threshold before. Victoria laughingly recalled, "The day that my dad met one of my boyfriends was the day that Rafael went over to ask for my hand in marriage."[2]

Many of the respondents circumvented the issue by going out (or saying that they were going out) with a group of friends and then meeting a date at a mall, movie, football game, or some other social event. For some, family restrictions were modified, allowing, for example, a boy to come and watch television with the respondent or sit outside on a porch and talk. However, someone else always had to be in the house to chaperone. Many respondents were astute about desensitizing their parents, especially their fathers, to the presence of their boyfriends by first having them stand outside their homes, until finally they could enter the house and sit and watch television (but usually with someone else present). Nonetheless, several of the fathers did not budge and often gave the respondents' boyfriends the "cold shoulder" by refusing to talk to them. Most mothers, unlike most fathers, were understanding and treated the boyfriends cordially.

Most respondents, however, agreed with their parents' view that it was wiser to wait and see whether a relationship was serious before introducing a mate to the family. Most respondents never experienced dating. Familial proscriptions regarding dating served in many instances to ensure that respondents' sexuality developed according to a culturally sanctioned framework. Furthermore, many of the respondents described themselves as "late bloomers" and not particularly popular in high school. It was unclear whether respondents' lack of one-to-one dating was because of their parents' unusual strictness or because of their academic inclinations and disinterest in boys in comparison to their peers. Also, their socializing took the form of having strong friendship networks and going out with groups of friends.

Even when not dating, most respondents had strict curfews, which they rarely disobeyed. Respondents continued to have curfews when visiting from college or moving back home after graduation. In contrast, most male children in these families had few, if any, restrictions. Gloria recalled how her brother, who was nine years older than she, "had a totally different set of rules. He was allowed to date when he was in junior high and to stay out at all hours of the night. He never had a curfew. He lived in the basement so he had his own door to come and go."[3]

Most respondents raised under these social restrictions did not perceive them as particularly punitive, as most of their friends had similar rules. A few also saw their parents' socialization practices as reflecting cultural differences between their families and those of white students in their high schools. Most did not admire white students' freedom to come and go as they pleased and preferred their parents' concern over their whereabouts.

Family Responsibilities

Most respondents had specific household chores that started with age-appropriate tasks when the respondents were relatively young. As they grew older, their responsibilities increased. Many respondents stated that every Saturday was "cleaning day." They, their sisters, and mothers cleaned the entire house. As Soledad stated, "We'd wake up very early on Saturdays. We thought we were the only family in America that woke up at 6:30 to clean house."[4]

Only a few of the respondents did not have any chores or had parents who were lax about enforcing compliance with their duties. Several of these mothers wanted their daughters to focus on their schoolwork and others felt that they were going to be saddled with housework when they married, so they wanted to spare them from the burden of "women's work." Sara stated that her mother "cleaned and cleaned. She made my bed, she washed dishes. I didn't wash dishes."[5] Sara was well aware that her mother was providing a "privilege" that would be short-lived, although Sara's mother was only partially right, as Sara's "husband does most of the housework."

In the majority of families, however, respondents' only viable excuse for not doing housework was to say they had homework. Most mothers deferred or suspended household chores for the sake of their daughters' schoolwork. Soledad, for example, could escape the Saturday morning cleaning rituals by saying that she "had lots of homework; that was the tactic I came up with."

In many of these families, brothers were exempt from household chores as they were from curfews. In the most extreme cases, economic resources were unfairly distributed according to the children's gender. Soledad recalled how her brother, who was the youngest in the household, was not required to follow the rules, although she and her sisters had to. Soledad was raised in Chicago; her father was a sergeant in the police department and her mother was a secretary for an insurance company. Her brother Ben was an extreme example, albeit not the only one, of the privileges males had in these families. Ben was allowed to come and go as he pleased, he did not have a job during the school year, and he was not required to perform household chores. During the Saturday morning cleanings, Soledad's mother told her daughters, "Hush, [because] your brother is asleep," and to not "run the vacuum yet." After he woke up and left his bedroom for the living room to watch television, by now clean and tidy, his sisters would enter his room and clean it for him. Soledad recognized that "the freedom that my brother has, even as a twenty-year old, is incredible to me."

Through high school Ben simply announced, "Mom, I'm doing this," not "Mom, can I do this?" Everybody in the family indulged Ben, "the baby," including Soledad's father, who routinely gave him spending money because he empathized with a young man "wanting to go do things and not having money." When Soledad jokingly challenged her father, "What about me and Molly [her sister] when we ask for money? You didn't say, Here's fifty bucks. You said, Go get a job!" He replied, "Well, you're going to end up taking care of Ben anyway, so I need to groom you to be independent 'cause someone's going to have to take care of him." "And I was like, Oh!"

The privileged position of the respondents' brothers also existed in ethnically mixed families. Mariposa, who was raised by her white mother in San Francisco, recalled that her brother had all the "privileges that my father would have had if he lived in our house. My mom surrendered everything to my brother."[6] Mariposa was well aware that "it definitely had to do with the fact that he was a boy and I was a girl." Like Ben, Mariposa's brother did not have "a curfew that stuck. He pretty much had freedom." Mariposa picked up the slack by doing chores usually assigned to boys and "mowed the lawn out of embarrassment. He had his own room—the works."

Most respondents' perceptions about their brothers were extremely nuanced and recognized both their brothers' privileges and vulnerabilities. They tried to be patient with their brothers' shortcomings, they worried about them, but they also were perfectly capable of getting "pissed off" at them when they acted irresponsibly. Patty exemplified these complex views by expressing exasperation about her brother's lack of family responsibilities.[7] He dropped out of college twice, even when Patty's mother had obtained loans so he could attend private schools. Patty told her mother, "You know what? Can I be like Max and sit around at home, have you give me money, and not work? Why would you leave?" In contrast to Max, Patty "went to college right away, graduated early to save money. I did all that so that Max could be at home for a year watching MTV. It pisses me off, because it seemed like he had no motivation." Patty concluded that her discipline in comparison to her brother's was "maybe a female thing. I don't know."

Although Patty resented her brother's behavior, by the end of her narrative she also recognized that her "brother has it hard, because he's gay" and their parents refused to acknowledge it. Patty knew that her brother could never "bring his boyfriend home," because her mother was "in denial." Her brother was twenty-one and he had never "talked about a girl." Patty's father was seventy-one, twenty years older than her mother, and even less likely than her mother to come to terms with Max's homosexuality. The only hope Patty held was that her family would change their views on her brother's gayness when her "dad passes away and my mom is older and she finally accepts it." So at the same time that Patty recognized her brother's privileges, she also felt "bad" for her brother.

Respondents gave several justifications for gender differences in privileges: brothers were the youngest in the family, or the oldest, or the only boys in the family, or there were all boys in the family and the respondent was the only girl. Whatever the justifications, many times male privilege remained unchallenged.

Other respondents, however, did not accept gender differences within their families. After years of struggle, many of them succeeded in changing the family dynamics, making their brothers accountable. Gloria, whose brother José had the same privileges as the brothers described above, did not remain silent in her family. "I was constantly telling my parents, 'Why are there these separate rules for José?'" Her parents replied, "Well, he's a boy. Girls have different rules." Gloria persisted, "Why?" And her parents said, "'Well, you guys could get pregnant; you can ruin your lives.' That was always the big issue. It didn't get me anywhere, but I wasn't silent, I was very defiant—verbally—not in my actions." Nonetheless, "I obeyed my parents despite their wacky beliefs." Gloria even turned for help outside her family to change her parents' views. She talked to the priest, called her godmother, and contacted relatives to "talk to them about how irrational my parents were."

The patterns of dating and restriction I described above applied to about half of the respondents (48 percent were not allowed to date in high school), but others (51 percent) were given permission to have boyfriends and date at around the age of fifteen or sixteen. For example, Ruth N. Lopez Turley, who grew up in Laredo, Texas, was allowed to date boys as long as her parents knew them.[8] But her mother questioned her extensively after she went out by probing, "*¿Y que hicieron? ¿Y a donde fueron?*" (What did you do? Where did you go?), which resulted in Ruth "rarely coming home past eleven." However, unlike other families, her brothers were also treated the same way in terms of curfews and household chores. According to Ruth, "The expectations were pretty much the same for all of us as far as the household work. My mother had this cause that she was going to fight against machismo.[9] She was very into not going along with the typical Mexican practice of expecting the women to do the housework from a very young age. My mother kept insisting that her boys were not going to grow up like that."

The egalitarian families were not necessarily the most educated. Ruth's mother, for example, was born in Mexico and had become an orphan when she was nine. She lived in the streets of Mexico for a while before she ended up in an orphanage in Laredo, Texas, where she remained until she got married at the age of fifteen.

Adolescent Transitions: *Quinceañeras*, Menstruation, and Virginity

Quinceañeras

> Wherever it is celebrated, the *quinceañera* remains a cultural marker for La-tinidad, and for the honoree it remains a coming-of-age ritual. . . . From a feminist perspective, the performance of the ritual is in of itself an act of womanist theology and of the necessary rendition of a female ritual in a par-ticular space, at a particular time in a woman's life. However, one can also argue that in its socializing fervor the celebration is anti-feminist in intent, for instead of acknowledging the young woman's self-determination and po-tential, it can become a way of constricting and limiting her choices. Even as she moves from childhood to womanhood, she remains bound by the ex-pectations of the church and the community.
>
> —N. Cantú 2002, 18

A *quinceañera* is a celebration that takes place when a young woman turns fifteen. *Quinceañera* comes from the Spanish word *quince* (fifteen). *Quinceañeras* are often compared to "debutante" parties but have certain cultural and religious specificities that give the celebration a different meaning (N. Cantú 1999, 74). For example, *quinceañera* parties include a Catholic mass, a series of gifts such as a *libro y rosario* (missal and rosary) and a *medalla de la Virgen de Guadalupe* (a medallion with the image of the Virgin of Guadalupe), and *padrinos* (sponsors to offset the costs of such a celebration). There are many similarities to debutante parties: the *quinceañera* wears a formal dress, dances a waltz with her father where she is introduced as a young woman, and has a dinner as part of the celebration. There are many variations to this general description (see N. Cantú (2002) for a discussion of these variations and their significance).

Chicana feminist writers have analyzed "cultural rites of passage" as an important aspect of Chicana womanhood and ethnic identity (N. Cantú 1999; Dávalos 1996). Baptisms, confirmations, *quinceañeras*, and weddings, are all communal events that affirm the Chicano community's values and culture (N. Cantú 1999, 77).[10] The rites of passage also serve as markers for appropriate behavior for women; for example, the wedding ceremony sanctions sexual intercourse, procreation, and freedom from parental control (at least theoretically). *Quinceañeras*, therefore, are an especially significant ritual in Chicano/Mexicano communities. When I asked my respondents whether they had had *quinceañeras*, the majority had not (73 percent), but all of them knew about the celebration and its significance.

The lack of economic resources was one of the top two reasons respondents gave for not having a *quinceañera* (13 percent). This was especially the case if there were several sisters close in age in their families; sometimes only one of the girls—usually the youngest—in the family would enjoy the celebration. The second most frequent reason was that the respondent chose to go on a trip, purchase a car, or receive some other large gift in lieu of the party (15 percent). A small number of respondents were given a choice to use the resources for educational purposes instead of having a costly celebration. For example, Belinda Martínez took a trip with her mother from Los Angeles to Northern California to visit the University of California, Berkeley, campus.[11] Belinda treasured this trip. "My mom was really good about knowing that she had five daughters and it could be hard sometimes," and it was Belinda's turn to "spend time" with her mother alone. They "stayed at a hotel." And her mother "bought me a chain and gave me money, and I bought myself a ring at the L.A. jewelry district."

Similarly, Soledad's family didn't have a lot of money while she was growing up, so her father gave her a choice. He said, "You can have a *quinceañera* or we can take the money and do something else." Soledad said her parents were very "focused on us going to college. They had sent me to a very expensive private school." So instead of a *quinceañera*, Soledad's parents suggested that she apply the money "toward a Stanley Kaplan SAT prep course." Soledad's extended family, including "my aunts, my uncles, and my grandma, said she's got to have a *quinceañera*; everyone's got to have one." Her father did not give in to the pressure. He replied, "That's not the way she's going to enter society. I want her to enter society with a degree. That's more important."

The *quinceañera* parties varied from small family gatherings to elaborate celebrations very similar to large weddings. The celebration is "a living tradition," so there are elements that change, others are added, and still others "have fallen by the wayside" (N. Cantú 1999, 73). Nayelli made changes to her *quinceañera* celebration to accommodate her cousin's mixed ethnicity: her cousin's father was African American and her mother was of Mexican descent.[12] Among the changes was the elimination of "*chambelanes* and *damas* [escorts]."[13]

The number of generations the respondents have been in the United States did not seem to influence whether they had a *quinceañera* celebration or not. In fact, many of the first-generation respondents also had the lowest income, severely restricting their ability to finance a *quinceañera*. Geographical distance from the U.S./Mexico border was also not a determining factor.[14] For example, two respondents who grew up in Brooklyn and Queens, New York, had *quinceañeras*. Jocelyn Solis's *quinceañera* mass was celebrated in the Virgen de Guadalupe Church in lower Manhattan and her party was at the Centro Español in Queens.[15] Dorian López, the only mixed-heritage respondent to have a *quinceañera*, had a small family gathering at her parents' home in Queens.[16] Her mother was from Mexico and her father was from Puerto Rico. Her grandmother and mother were both seamstresses. Her mother had advanced to the prestigious position of pattern maker in the garment district in New York City. Both Dorian's mother and grandmother wanted to make her *quinceañera* dress, so they each designed and sewed their individual creations. Dorian wore her grandmother's dress first, then, later during the party, she changed into her mother's dress. This is how Dorian described both of her dresses: "My mother's dress was so elegant. My grandmother's dress was more of the traditional dresses that flip open in the front—it was more traditional but my mother's was very modern; it was very beautiful. I know she really loved what she did, so I had to have that party to make her feel good."

Fig. 1 and 2. Dorian López at her *quinceañera* celebration, first wearing the dress made by her grandmother and then wearing the dress made by her mother. Reprinted by permission of the López family.

The celebrations, no matter how elaborate or small, did not result in any significant transition into womanhood. Most respondents still could not date in the U.S. mainstream sense of the word or have any other kind of significant freedom or responsibility because of a *quinceañera* celebration. Although in many families the *quinceañera* celebration indicates that a young woman can wear makeup and heels and is allowed to date (N. Cantú 1999, 90), most of my respondents did not experience this transition but rather saw their *quinceañeras* as "cultural affirmation" (Dávalos 1996, 116–17)—they enjoyed and cherished their *quinceañeras* as an opportunity to spend time with their families and have a good time.[17]

Mixed-heritage respondents were the least likely to celebrate *quinceañeras*. In fact, although they knew about the tradition, only Dorian celebrated a *quinceañera*. There were several explanations for this. Most of the mixed-heritage respondents did not live in predominantly Latino neighborhoods, although they did keep contact with their Mexican-descent relatives and were highly identified with their Mexican ancestry. *Quinceañeras* are communal celebrations and therefore did not make sense in non-Latino neighborhoods. From this perspective, it was reasonable to expect these respondents not to participate in the *quinceañera* tradition.

A few of the mixed-heritage respondents, however, wished they had had *quinceañeras* because they identified with their Mexican American heritage, but either their mothers did not agree with the tradition, they did not have enough economic resources, or both. This was the case with Mariposa, who was raised by her white mother. Mariposa wanted a *quinceañera* but her mother was reluctant to recognize Mariposa's identification with her "dad's side of the family," as well as her "identity as being Latina or Mexican American." Lack of money, coupled with her mother's attitude, prevented any discussion of a *quinceañera* celebration.

Menstruation: Becoming *una Señorita*

Aída: Do you remember when you started menstruating?
Carolina: It was April Fool's Day and I thought someone was playing a joke on me.
Aída: The Goddess was playing a joke on you.

A more significant transition than the ritual passage celebrated by a *quinceañera* was the respondents' onset of menstruation. For many of the respondents this was a traumatic experience they had obviously gotten over, as they recalled with great senses of humor their first encounters with "becoming *una señorita*" (a young lady). When I asked Patty, "Do you remember when you started menstruating?" she replied with a laugh, "How can you forget!" Many respondents' views about the onset of menstruation revolved around the lack of information and simply the physical discomfort of dealing with the bodily aspects of the entire process—from severe cramps to lack of knowledge about sanitary products. Desireé recalled that when she got her period she said to herself, "Oh God! What happened?"[18]

> I was sooo embarrassed. I remember mom being on the phone and sitting there going, "How am I going to tell her this?" I remember exactly, saying, "Mom I think I need one of those pads." I totally knew everything about it. In my classes they'd show you "the film." [Everyone laughs.] It was just gross to me and I was just like, "What is the point of this?" My mom came and gave me a sanitary napkin. She's like, "Oh *mija*" [*cooing*]. It was so embarrassing, and I was like, "Don't tell dad, please don't tell dad." That was my first reaction.

Most respondents never had an explicit talk with their parents about menstruation (55 percent) or sexuality in general (64 percent).[19] When discussions happened, however, it was with mothers (43 percent talked to them about menstruation and 29 percent talked to them about sex) rather than fathers (only two fathers talked to respondents about menstruation and the same two fathers spoke to them about sex). Most respondents relied on older sisters or relatives (like aunts) and the infamous "movie" that many respondents mentioned.

The silence around menstruation included the use of euphemisms for sanitary products and elaborate rituals for disposing of them to avoid detection, especially by their fathers and brothers. According to Belinda Martínez, in her family sanitary napkins were referred to as "cookies."

> My older sisters obviously had their periods before I did, but when they needed pads, they'd ask my mom to "go get them cookies." It was just a

code word and there was only one male in the household, my dad, and I'm sure he could have dealt with it. There was a family joke because one of my sisters said, "Oh, are you going to the store? I need cookies." And I was little and said, "Yes, please chocolate chip."

Some of the mothers gave the respondents elaborate instructions on disposing of sanitary napkins. Sara recalled the instructions she received from her mother. Sara quoted her mother as saying,

> "Make sure you wrap it [the sanitary napkin] up, you put it in a bag, and you throw it away. Don't throw it in the dumpster!" It's like you have to be totally discreet about [menstruating] when you begin because you don't put the Kotex where everyone can see it. [Her mother would say] "You put it in the closet, always at the bottom, where no one can see it. And you don't leave them hanging out in the bathroom. And when you're finished using it, you don't throw it in the toilet; you throw it in the bag! Wrap it up in the bag and then . . ."

Sara and the other respondent in the focus group concluded that disposing of sanitary napkins was more complicated than making *tamales*.[20]

There were also respondents' mothers who sat them down and explicitly explained the biological aspects of menstruation. Most of these mothers had had a high school or college education. The respondents did not necessarily appreciate the explicitness, especially because many of their peers did not go through that kind of experience. They felt embarrassed and a few begged their mothers to stop by saying, "enough already!"

Many of these families had severe economic constraints, so the only open reference to menstruation was to not be wasteful with sanitary products. Nayelli, who started menstruating when she was eleven, stated laughingly that her mother "got mad 'cause I would change my pad like twenty times a day." Her mother "never had the talk with me, she was just like, 'Stop using so many pads 'cause they're not cheap!' And that was it."

Menstruation was also mentioned when respondents suffered from severe physical side effects, like cramps, because of their period. Many respondents' mothers prepared *remedios* (home remedies) like *té de hierba buena* (mint tea). In some instances the home remedies were more archaic and the respondents recalled with amusement the most unusual ones.

Christina J. Reynoso recounted her mother's favorite remedy for cramps: "I used to have really, really, really bad cramps. Before we got heating pads, my mom would tell me, 'I'm going to go heat some tortillas up and put them on your stomach.'" Christina would reply, "I don't want tortillas!" As we discussed this, Rita jokingly interjected, "Are you supposed to eat them afterwards?" Victoria, another focus group member, added, "But it was their way in Mexico of putting heat." Christina continued by quoting her mother as saying, "You're lucky, I used to have to wear rags [during menstruation] and go to the river and wash them out!" At the end, Christina told her mother, "Just give me the Ibuprofen!"[21]

Respondents also had great fun recounting how their mothers required them to wear outmoded sanitary pads that were so thick that Rita felt like "*a caballo* woman" (horsewoman). They also had to wear garter-like contraptions, girdles, and other types of underwear that were extremely uncomfortable. Rita 's mother never gave her any clear instructions about how to use sanitary pads, so she used the pad for two months with the "sticky side up. I mean, think about it, where is the stuff coming out of? It's coming out of you, so you want to make sure it stays there. I lost I don't know how much hair. It was such a secretive thing." By this time, the respondents in this group were rolling around laughing, each contributing their outrageous stories about their biological transition into adulthood.

The communication patterns in most of these families consisted of mothers speaking directly to children, especially daughters, and then reporting back to fathers. Fathers rarely spoke directly to children about sensitive topics, especially sex or menstruation. When I asked Patty whether her father had ever spoken to her about menstruation, she laughed and replied,

No, I mean, now he probably knows. The thing that sucks is, like I'm sure mom would tell him everything, but never when I'm there. I guess it's kinda nice; it's less embarrassing for me. I know he knows everything; he just never talks about it. [He never says,] "Gee honey, how was your period this morning?"

Several respondents experienced physical restrictions imposed by their mothers after menstruation, especially pertaining to such activities as swimming and horsing around with their brothers or other neighborhood kids. Although, with two exceptions, none of the fathers spoke to their daughters about menstruation or about sex, they still were aware of their daughters' physical changes. In several instances, respondents described their fathers as "freaking out" or treating them differently after they found out they had started menstruating. Most fathers got over it, but in a few instances the relationship between father and daughter changed irrevocably. As Victoria indicated, her father, who was very loving and close to her and used to take her on all his projects around their ranch, all of a sudden stopped relating to her. This "abandonment" made her feel sad.

> When I was little, I was really close to my dad. He would take me with him everywhere. I would go with him to the hardware store and I would try to help him when he would put up walls. I was always getting in his way, but he didn't mind. As soon as we [Victoria and her sisters] hit puberty, everything changed. He wouldn't talk to us.

Her father never recovered from Victoria "becoming *una señorita*" and Victoria and her father were never close again.

Valuing Virginity

There was no doubt that Cleófilas was a virgin when she was transferred from her father to her new husband, Juan Pedro Martínez Sánchez. Loss of virginity before marriage could have condemned Cleófilas to a life of shame and possible banishment from her father's home and rejection by her six brothers as "damaged merchandise" (Hurtado 2000, 278). As extreme as these actions may seem, they are not unheard of in Chicano/Mexicano communities. Could virginity, in fact, be as relevant for the group of respondents I interviewed as it was for the fictional Cleófilas, who, after all, lived in Mexico in a rural area, had little or no education, and was from a working-class background? Again, I was surprised to find that on issues of virginity my respondents were, overall, not very different from Cleófilas.

Overwhelmingly, my respondents stated that "virginity was a big deal" in their families. Their parents communicated to them, many times in oblique ways, that virginity was the only way they could ever secure husbands and happy futures. Still, the silence that surrounded menstruation also surrounded sexuality (64 percent of respondents reported never talking to their parents about sex). With a few exceptions, parents simply did not speak about sexual matters. Whereas almost all my respondents had learned about menstruation in school, such was not the case with sex. Most found out about sex from their sisters, friends, and occasionally relatives such as aunts and cousins. Belinda Martínez considered herself particularly lucky. Her older sister, who was the first in her family to attend college and obtained her bachelor's degree from the University of California, Santa Barbara, and her master's degree from Syracuse University, was a principal at a school in Cochella Valley. Belinda used to spend a lot of time with her older sister's family. In one of the car trips to visit her, they talked openly about sex and contraception. Belinda's sister told her, "If you are thinking about sex, you can talk to me." When they arrived at her sister's home in Palm Springs, she showed Belinda "a diaphragm and she showed me a condom and that was really interesting." At age sixteen, Belinda had already learned some of the biological aspects of sex, but she still very much appreciated the conversation with her older sister because she was very "excited. I didn't know what was going to happen. I wanted it to be the right person." Belinda thought engaging in sex was very "serious," but "it was nice also" and "it was definitely a relief to be able to talk to somebody." When Belinda finally had sex with her boyfriend in college, her older sister "was one of the first people I told." She wouldn't even tell her "other sisters—there's no way," and "my mother definitely not."

The onset of menstruation provided the mothers the occasion to talk to their daughters about pregnancy. Most respondents were not told about the biological workings of the menstrual cycle, nor did most of them discuss sex with their parents. The focus, instead, was on admonitions to avoid pregnancy at all costs. Although sexuality was not talked about openly, there were definite expectations about proper behavior. Euphemisms were often used (just as they were for menstruation) for keeping virginity until marriage, as were cautionary tales about what befalls women when they do not follow these rules. Ironically, the warnings given by most mothers had not been followed in their own lives, as a substantial number of them got married because of pregnancy. Others were single parents.

For example, although Nayelli's mother did not talk to her about menstruation or sex, she did tell her, "*no te enamores*" (don't fall in love), meaning that passion would cloud Nayelli's judgment. "Letting yourself go" could result in a lack of respect on the part of men. According to Nayelli, her mother told her "*que te respeten* [they should respect you] and have your self-respect, too." She told her "wait to have sex till you get married 'cause look what happened to me, look what happened to your sister, look what happened to your cousins." According to Nayelli's mother, if a woman "got pregnant before they got married" she would be at the mercy "of the guy and if he didn't want to get married and was forced into it, then it wouldn't be a happy marriage."

Silence on sex also led to silence on contraception; implicitly, sexual transgression was equated with pregnancy or, in Nayelli's words, "getting pregnant and messing up your life." Christina Santana, a fellow respondent in the same focus group, confirmed, "It was like once you made that step, *ya arruinaste tu vida*" (you ruined your life).[22]

Many of the respondents did not abide by restrictions placed on sexual intercourse. Only eight of the respondents explicitly stated that they were virgins. Most respondents who were sexually active, however, thought their parents, especially their mothers, knew about it, although they never talked about it directly. According to Christina Santana,

> I think my mom does know I had sex. But it's not because I've told her; it's not because anybody has told her. The only thing she tells me is "*Cuídate mucho*" [Take care of yourself] and "*Cuando te vas a casar?*" [When are you going to get married?]. Things like that, which make me think that she knows. I would never tell her. I could not sit down and tell her, "Oh mom, guess what, you know, *ayer* [yesterday] I had sex, whatever!" She would be upset because all of my younger sisters have left with their boyfriends. So it's only me. My sisters are sixteen and eighteen. My mom tells them, "*Ustedes ya se fueron del nido.*" [You already left the nest.] So it's only me, so if I were to tell her that I had sex, she'd be like, "What! *Tú también!*" [You too!] You know what I mean? She'd be really disappointed. I don't think I could do that to her or to me.

Cuídate (take care of yourself) was the euphemism used most often to refer to birth control—a euphemism used in Mexico as a caution about not getting pregnant. "Take care of yourself" means "Use some kind of birth control so you do not get pregnant." When women have an unplanned pregnancy, it is not unusual for female relatives to comment, "*no se cuidó*" (she did not take care of herself). Several respondents joked about not knowing exactly what that meant. According to Marie, "I had already heard all about the pill 'cause of my sister but never had a sex talk. I mean the only thing my parents said was 'just be careful, *cuídate,*' which I never knew what that really meant. Be careful of what? [*Everyone laughs.*] Crossing the street? Natural disasters—what?"[23]

Although most of the respondents' mothers were relatively young—mostly in their mid- to late forties—the respondents spoke about them as if their major life decisions had already been made and they, as their daughters, embodied all of their mothers' unfulfilled dreams. Nayelli, whose mother was forty-seven, explained, "I was holding all her dreams. I was going to be a teacher, I was going to school, I was still a virgin, I wasn't going to get married until I had my career set. Those were her dreams. I was holding all that up for her."

Many respondents eventually did tell their mothers (not so much their fathers) they had become sexually active. While their mothers did not approve, they did not threaten to disown them either. The mothers, however, did express sadness and loss when their daughters did not follow what they considered the proper way to conduct themselves sexually. As Nayelli recalled, "The time came when I told her that I had sex. I don't know, it's hard to explain. She was disappointed, very disappointed. It's like, she believed in me completely. Now I've put her down in a big way! So it's like, what else is next?"

On the other hand, Nayelli could not bring herself to tell her father. When I asked her what she thought her father would do if he found out about her loss of virginity, Nayelli stated,

> Oh my God, I don't know. He still cries about my sister getting married. I guess because to him, like, we're still *sus niñas* [his little girls]. The way my sister left *también* [also]. She was pregnant at seventeen and got married. Now she's twenty-six and it was ten years ago practically. It's still sad for him so he still has me, up there [she raises her hand over her head]. No way my mother is going tell him. I can't either.

Many of the respondents adhered to their parents' rules because of their deep love for them. My respondents were very connected to their parents;

they were not isolated individuals who made decisions about their lives independent of their families' judgments. Christina Santana eloquently explained the support she had received from her mother, who raised her and her two sisters as a single parent, and why she could not disappoint her by telling her that she had had sex:

> Just coming to the university, every accomplishment that I've made. I'm like, OK, I'm going to go tell her. She'll cheer me on. Her approval makes me feel really good. So, of course, a lot of what she taught me has helped me more so because she's a single mom. Growing up, she was the only person that I could say *es mi mamá* [she's my mother]. My dad wasn't there.

The downside of carrying their mothers' expectations on their backs was that when my respondents finally decided to have sex, their decisions were not well planned and some did not use contraception, putting themselves at risk of pregnancy and sexually transmitted diseases. Christina recounted when she finally decided to have sex: "I think it just happened! Throughout the whole thing, I could tell you that I felt really guilty. I kept saying, Ah, my mom, my mom, my mom. My God, what am I doing?!" Eventually Christina did use contraception but still felt guilty about having sex when her mother's potential disapproval was clear.

Cristina represented a more drastic example than Christina Santana of the consequences of the lack of information about menstruation and sexuality.[24] Cristina married at the age of fourteen and had her first child at the age of fifteen. At the time of the interview she was twenty years old, a junior in college; her daughter was five years old, and Cristina was eight months pregnant with her second child. Cristina was the youngest of five children, considerably younger than her siblings. Her parents were older when they had her, and by the time she was in elementary school, her sisters had already left the house. In addition, her mother was diagnosed as schizophrenic and was often heavily medicated. Cristina had never heard about menstruation or anything about sex, so it was a shock to her to learn about it in elementary school:

> The only way that I found out about menstruation was because a teacher in fifth grade told me. My mom didn't tell me anything and I don't think my sisters did. I would see [sanitary] pads, and I'd ask, What are they for? And

my mom and my sisters never told me. I didn't know where babies came from! I didn't even know what the word sex was until third grade when the number sextillionth was on the chart and everybody was like, Is that sex? And I was like, What is that? And everybody was like, That is what your mom and dad did to have you. And I was like, My parents didn't do that!

Cristina was ten years old when she found out about menstruation. Four years later, she still did not know much about the mechanics of reproduction. "I just thought once you had sex and you didn't use protection that you'd get pregnant." After Cristina and her boyfriend had sexual intercourse, they started living together and shortly after got married, although they did not get pregnant until two months later. Although Cristina loved her children dearly, she was well aware that she only agreed to get married because she thought she was pregnant after the first time she had intercourse.

Most of the sexually active respondents, however, were conscientious about using birth control and openly discussed it during our interview. It was in the beginning of their "transgression" that some of them were reluctant to actively seek information. Eventually most did take precautions.

My respondents were also very secretive about living arrangements with boyfriends prior to marriage. Many of them at one point or another had a "live-in" companion, but most had not told their parents. They developed elaborate schemes to avoid detection. For example, Gloria stated, "My fiancé and I moved in together last May and we got caller ID so my parents think I live alone and his parents think that he lives alone. When the call comes in, we know who's calling."[25] In addition, she used a friend's address to avoid detection. Other respondents mentioned moving entire apartments around when their parents came into town either for a visit or for graduation. They had their boyfriends and their belongings moved out. Even in situations where respondents were engaged to be married, premarital cohabitation was generally taboo. The only exception, for the most part, was with mixed-heritage families. For example, Bianca, whose father was white and mother was Mexican, stated,

I was pregnant when I first moved in with my boyfriend. My parents were very accepting that he wanted to take care of me. They didn't care. Marriage is not on the plate for my parents. It's important that Phillip supports me and supports our son. My parents live with us right now.[26]

Similarly, Sonya K. Smith, whose father was white and mother was of Mexican descent, received a bouquet of yellow roses from her mother when she found out that Sonya had "lost her virginity" by "finding condoms in the garbage."[27]

> I was in high school, and I was petrified because I thought, What is she going to think of me? I'm not a virgin. I was very nervous about it but then it turns out everything I feared that she would do, it was completely the opposite. She was like, "I just want to make sure you are safe. I'm glad you are using condoms. Let's get you on the pill." The next day I woke up in the morning and I had a dozen yellow roses from her. I was just like, "Oh, OK. Why didn't I tell her earlier?" But in terms of telling my dad, he has never been told, but I think by now he knows.

Although her father was white and had a master's degree in business administration from the University of California, Berkeley, supposedly making him more open-minded about sexual issues, Sonya was very reluctant to speak to him about her sexual behavior. Sonya's mother was raised by her mother until she was nine years old and her mother had "a nervous breakdown," and through "some heavy manipulating by her doctor" she "checked herself in [a hospital]." The doctor told Sonya's grandmother that "if she didn't do it herself, he would demand it under doctor's orders and then she wouldn't have control over when she got out" there was a high probability she "would lose her children." In spite of her compliance, Sonya's grandmother "never got her kids back anyway" and at that point, Sonya's mother went to live with her father and stepmother. According to Sonya, "That was a whole new area and my mother was really Americanized then. She was told not to speak Spanish because she would have an accent and would be discriminated against. She went to a pretty much all-white school." Sonya's mother was molested by her father until she was nineteen, when she ran away from home and married Sonya's father. Consequently, Sonya's mother did not have close ties with her family until very recently, and her views on sexuality were not as closely connected to her family of origin. However, the liberal views held by Sonya's mother were the exception among my respondents.

Protecting the Hymen: Restrictions on Tampons, Premarital Sex, and Pregnancy

I did get a talk. I got the tampon talk, which is, "Nice girls don't use tampons. *Los tampones son para mujeres casadas.*"[Tampons are only for married women.] Mother did not want us to use tampons.

—Lucinda, thirty-two-year-old respondent, San Antonio, Texas

You could always tell us Latinas. We hid when we undressed, modestly facing a wall, or, in my case, dressing in a bathroom stall. We were the ones who still used bulky sanitary pads instead of tampons, thinking ourselves morally superior to our white classmates. My *mama said you can't use tampons till after you're married.* All Latina mamas said this, yet how come none of us thought to ask our mothers why they didn't use tampons *after* getting married?

—Cisneros 1996, 46

The "cult of virginity" in these families included a taboo around using tampons. In fact, although there was little discussion about menstruation or sex, mothers often cautioned their daughters against using tampons "because they would lose their virginity." According to Patty, her mother told her shortly after she started menstruating, "For girls who are virgins, it's not very good to use a tampon." Patty replied, "I heard that isn't true, mom." Patty proceeded to tell her mother that the nuns at her Catholic high school had demonstrated a tampon in a glass of water. "You could watch it expand just in case you had any doubts that it wouldn't absorb it." When the rest of the respondents in the focus group were incredulous, Patty replied, "We had radical '60s nuns from Berkeley. They were totally renegade nuns." Patty's mother was not convinced and continued to buy her pads. "And I'd buy tampons, but she never gave me a full talk about menstruation."

The value placed on virginity reached a fever pitch for many mothers who were extremely concerned about keeping their daughters "intact." Sara's mother illustrated how extreme this concern could become when Sara was supposedly seen in a car with a "guy I was dating": "I think I was fifteen or sixteen . . . and she took me to the clinic to see the nurse to make sure I still had a hymen." Sara's mother asked the nurse, "Is she still a virgin?" The nurse asked Sara, "Honey, did you have any penetration?" and Sara said, "No! No!" "And she told my mom, 'Yeah, she's a virgin.' It was my first pelvic exam and it was such a traumatic experience. So yeah, for my mother virginity was a big deal. It was really sad."

Sara's mother tried to justify her drastic actions by telling Sara that if she got pregnant, her mother was going to be the person at fault. "I didn't want to give her more stress than she was already going through. She was like, 'I do all of this for you. Please can you at least do that for me?' It was sort of framed in that way."

After that experience, Sara said, "I had a negative attitude about my sexuality, something that held me back to the point that I totally denied that aspect of myself. So I just avoided sex by avoiding boys, because they could get me into trouble." Sara eventually got over her negative feelings about sex. She and her mother became very close when Sara took care of her during the last months of her mother's life as she succumbed to cancer (see chapter 3). Sara missed her mother tremendously and held no resentment toward her because of the experience detailed above.

In several situations, the obsession with virginity reached Kafkaesque proportions because of incest and sexual abuse. Carina García Guzmán lived in a family that valued virginity, but, at the same time, her father was committing incest with her and her three sisters.[28] When I asked Carina whether virginity was important in her family, she responded by saying, "I was sexually abused as a little girl and all the way up until I was fifteen. So when my mom found out she went psycho for a little bit. Actually all three of my sisters were [sexually abused] too. So the only one that was a virgin was the little one, Mellie." When Carina's mother found out about her husband's abusive behavior, she threw him out of the house. Still, Carina's family took great pride in Mellie's virginity. This had recently changed when Mellie's boyfriend called Carina and told her "they had started having sex. And I'm just like, 'Mellie, my God, she was the only one.'" Carina's mother was so upset that she "just never believed her. She was like, 'Not my little baby!'" Carina's mother wanted so badly for at least one of her daughters to remain a virgin until marriage that, according to Carina, when "my mom found out that Mellie was doing it, she told her don't do it again. Just don't tell anybody, and don't tell your [future] husband."

Even though Carina was no longer a virgin, her mother did not want her to live with her current boyfriend.

I kind of do live every summer with the guy I have been with for the past two years. Just because he is white and he's thirty, so of course he expects to live with his girlfriend when she has her own place. And I've told my mom too. We've talked about when I'm going to get married. And I told her that I want to live with someone before I get married, because I don't want to get married and find out that he snores and is a nasty old guy that doesn't clean the restroom. So I told her and she wasn't too happy. She was like, "How can you do that? No, you have to have a church wedding." And I've told her that this summer we are going to officially move in together, because I'm finished with school and I have nowhere else to go. So, she's not too thrilled. If I were dating a Mexican guy she would be like, "You have to get married." But since he is a white guy and he doesn't understand the culture and he's a lot older, I think that's why she's letting it slide.

Although Carina's mother was "letting it slide," she still was distressed that Carina was moving in with her boyfriend without the benefit of marriage.

At the same time that virginity was such a strongly held value, respondents' complete compliance with the restrictions against premarital sex also led to families suspecting them of being lesbians. When she was twenty-five, Desireé brought her first serious boyfriend home to attend a cousin's wedding. While she was dancing the "dollar dance" with the groom, who was her cousin, he told Desireé, "I thought you were gay all this time."[29]

Parents also worried about their daughter's sexuality if the respondent had lesbian friends. Patty's mother and her relatives suspected her of being a lesbian, because she never really talked about boys and because during college one of her closest friends was a lesbian.

My mother told my cousin that she thought I was a lesbian because I never talked about guys. When Megan and I were going to go to Europe for two months, in her eyes, that was it—I was a lesbian. [Her mother said,] "Oh honey, I just don't think you should go on this trip." And I'm like, "But why? I've been saving up for this. I graduated from college. I want to do this." And she's like, "Are you sure that you and Megan aren't seeing each other." And I'm just like, "Mom, I'm pretty sure." She's like, "So why are you guys going on this trip?" And I'm like, "Because we're going to go back-packing through Europe. We're going to meet friends."

Patty's mother's suspicions about her daughter's sexual orientation were exacerbated by her sense of failure because she suspected her son's homo-sexuality. Patty related her mother's fear that both her children were ho-mosexual: "*Como si no fuera suficiente con tu hermano*" (as if it's not enough with your brother), "*me tocaron dos*" (I've got two). Patty's mother felt it was "her fault" and asked herself, "What did I do wrong?"; at the same time, "she didn't blame my father. It was always her fault."

Many of these respondents felt themselves in a catch-22. On the one hand, they were potential "sluts" if they dated men; on the other hand, they were potential lesbians if they did not. Surprisingly, many of these re-spondents, although hurt by their parents' distrust, handled the situation through humor and through the process of head-on engagement with their parents, mostly their mothers. Many respondents were able to par-tially shift their parents' rigid ideas to more flexible views of their daugh-ters' sexuality.

Sexual Orientation

Of the 101 respondents, three stated that they were lesbian and three stated that they were bisexual or had had relationships with women.[30] These respondents' socialization was very similar to that of the rest of the sample. That is, they had very firm curfews and were not allowed to date or go out with boys without a struggle with their parents. They also had chores and were held responsible for helping the family, especially in com-parison to their brothers. The differences, however, emerged when the re-spondents' families learned that their daughters were either lesbian or bi-sexual. Jessica Delgado, who was raised by her mother, had dated boys in spite of her mother's disapproval.[31] But by the age of sixteen she was "outed" as a lesbian in high school, an experience that Jessica described as traumatic. By the age of eighteen, however, Jessica was ready to tell her family that she was a lesbian. Her mother did not react well to the news and distanced herself from her. There was a period of estrangement, but after a while they worked through it. At the time of the interview, Jessica was twenty-eight and had had several serious, long-term relationships with women. Her family, including her beloved *abuelita* (grandmother), had met and accepted Jessica's lovers. Jessica didn't have much contact with her father, whom her mother left when Jessica was twelve because of his abusive behavior.[32] Consequently, he did not have much influence in the conflict Jessica had with her mother over her relationships with women.

Frida had experiences similar to Jessica's in that she dated boys and had a very strict family.[33] However, unlike Jessica, Frida did not start a relationship with her current girlfriend until she was in her early twenties. Until that point, she had only dated men. Frida was not very close to her mother and stepfather while she was in high school because of their strictness and because her parents had serious marital problems. After several years in college, however, Frida had become closer to her mother, especially because her mother started to assert herself in her marriage, requiring Frida's stepfather to stop battering her. However, Frida still could not bring herself to disclose her lesbianism (or bisexuality—she was still trying to figure it out) to her mother.

> In the past couple of years our communication has increased and she's begun to understand how I feel about women and women's rights and my rights as a woman. And also her rights, because she's a woman, and because of the transition that she's been through with her husband. But I think that homosexuality is on the edge. It's too way out there, and I think she would be devastated—literally.

Frida was not ready to tell her family about her lesbianism, especially because of her girlfriend's experience with her own family. Frida's girlfriend, who was Chicana, had come out to her mother as a lesbian when she was fourteen. Her mother refused to believe it and told her, "No, it can't be. You'll change. And I'll pray for you." According to Frida, her girlfriend's mother "never liked any of the girls that she used to date, but when I went to visit my girlfriend's family in Hollywood, her mom and I got along, just naturally." The fact that her girlfriend's mother liked Frida made her daughter's lesbianism real and, according to Frida, "something got to her," and her girlfriend's mother "actually tried to commit suicide. It was really horrid. And she did it in front of her younger daughter. It was during finals last semester." So both Frida and her girlfriend decided not to tell Frida's mother because "the consequences can be harsh. I think that stopped me from telling my mom, too, for at least a while."

In comparison to these very difficult family relationships, Mieka Valdez called her divorced parents separately when she was a freshman in college.[34] "Guess what? I just told both of my parents. I felt like I needed to tell them so I could talk about my life. . . . I was different in high school and I did not know why, and I didn't want to see why." Although her mother was surprised by Mieka's call, Mieka was quick to remind her that when she was in high school, her mother had told her, "If you ever feel you're lesbian, I'll still be here for you." Mieka just responded, "OK, but why are you asking me that?" "And it was weird 'cause at the time I didn't feel comfortable with it." When Mieka phoned her father, he failed to respond. "It was just silence and that hurt me a lot, even though for a lot of other people that would be great. At least they're not saying anything negative. So I talked to him about that, and I think both of them have learned a lot just through me talking about things."

According to Mieka, "My brother's been cool. He's more like, 'Hey, what do think about that girl?' My parents have been pretty open; they haven't made a judgment about me." By the time Mieka was a senior, her parents were completely aware of her relationships with women and spoke openly about them. In Mieka's case, it is important to point out that both of her parents were college educated. Her mother was white and a therapist, while her father was of Mexican descent and a professor in Chicano studies at a junior college. In many ways, although they were still somewhat surprised by Mieka's sexual orientation, they had the skills and intellectual framework to understand their daughter's development. This was not the case with other respondents whose parents were first generation in the United States, did not have very much formal education, and were extremely religious. Nonetheless, none of the respondents' parents who knew about their daughters' lesbianism had rejected them completely to the point of not relating to them. They struggled together.

Changes in Socialization Practices

Although most of the respondents' parents were relatively young, their socialization practices had changed through time. Respondents had siblings who were not teenagers yet and parents who, for the most part, were in their forties. Usually the parents were most strict with the first children, becoming more flexible as they grew older and had more children. Many of these families were very large, so it became practically impossible to enforce rules on them. However, in no instance did these families shift from a strict mode to a completely laissez-faire style.

Another cause of changes in parenting styles was children's behavior. Firstborns tended to "break in" their parents by violating curfews or engaging in taboo behaviors like living with boyfriends. Ironically, if the eldest child's behavior was particularly disruptive, the younger children complied more with their parents' rules because they did not want to hurt them. As Gloria recalled,

> I have two older siblings—I'm the youngest. My sister moved out of the house when she was seventeen with her boyfriend because my dad was so strict. Having watched what that did to my family, it was just a terrible time for us. So I said I'm never going to do that to my parents. So I had respect for them. I just let them believe what they wanted to believe and I just kept my life separate because I felt I was the youngest one and I couldn't screw up. The rest of my siblings did awful things, but not me.

Major life events in these families also caused parents to change their values and normative practices. For example, as respondents became older and moved away from home, especially if they married, their relationships with their parents became more egalitarian. As Victoria explained,

> At this point I don't think that anything can shock them anymore, because my youngest sister got pregnant. She's twenty now. She was nineteen when she had my niece. I was living with Rafael and we were keeping it a secret from my parents. I mean we had the total system down. And then I had my appendix taken out and so my sister had to come down to our apartment, take all his things out. It was a crazy ordeal. So my sister, when she decided that she was going to live with her boyfriend, she just told my parents. My parents had the shock from me getting married, my sister having a baby and getting married, and Raquel living with her boyfriend. But I don't think anything can shock them anymore.

Even though silence around sexual issues between mothers and daughters and certainly between daughters and fathers was common, sometimes a daughter's marriage, the discovery that a daughter was having sex, or the occurrence of a divorce in the family led to more open discussions. A number of the respondents stated that such newfound honesty, although exciting, was not easy. In spite of their trepidation, respondents embraced the possibility of having a more open relationship with their mothers.[35] Leticia Sedano explained that her forty-three-year-old mother all of a sudden was very willing to discuss sex when her sister got married: "It was weird. We talked about sex more at home, my other sister, my mother, and me. All summer we had conversations about sex, in detail, it was like, 'Mom, why are you talking to us like this?'"[36]

The changes for parents were not easy as they struggled with their children's new ideas, behavior, and values. Many of these parents coped by making the changes in small increments. In Julissa's family it was unacceptable to bring dating partners home unless it was a serious relationship.[37] Her family's rationale was that when "you bring someone into your family, they're seeing everything. There is nothing that's hidden." If the relationship did not work out, that person would "walk away with that family's intimate knowledge. They see your family when it's a bad day. They're taking something with them." If the relationship was lasting, then the person would also "bring something in. So, for my parents it was very emotional to bring a boyfriend into the family."

Recently, however, Julissa's brother was allowed to bring his girlfriend on a family camping trip although it was not clear whether this was a "serious relationship." According to Julissa, this was "a big thing in my family." Nonetheless, when Julissa asked whether her brother and his girlfriend could sleep in the same tent, her mother replied, "Not the same tent yet." Julissa replied, "OK, mom." Julissa understood that her mother was willing to change her views but could only do it slowly. Julissa felt her parents' willingness to change was "exciting because they always believed that a good parent is strict and never changes." Julissa felt that her parents' strict views were related to her parents' own family history, because her "dad was homeless and my mom was orphaned and did not have a family." Julissa felt that her parents were struggling to "understand what having a family was like." Julissa, like other respondents, saw her parents as full human beings with faults but also with many admirable traits, including the willingness to change. But most of all, almost all the respondents felt a deep love and commitment toward their parents and their struggles.

Diversity of Socialization Practices

Chicana feminists have been adamant that scholarly writing recognize the diverse experiences and histories of Chicanas in this country (Blackwell forthcoming; Ruiz 1998; Hurtado 1998; Zavella 1991). At the same time that we recognize normative patterns of behavior, we should be aware of different segments of the population, with special emphasis on the atypical cases. Following this strategy, Chicana feminists believe we can avoid essentializing the "Chicana experience" and perpetuating stereotypes like those promoted in the early literature on Mexican Americans (Madsen 1964; Heller 1966). In addition, by showing the diversity of the experiences of Chicanas, we can have a more accurate picture of the reality of Chicana/Mexicana communities. And by including the atypical cases, we enrich our theorizing and research practices by becoming aware of what is hidden because it is unusual.

In my own study, there were a few respondents whose family life was so exceptional that many of the questions covered in my interview did not apply to them. I will provide a case study of one such atypical case. I will return to Lucha at the end of each chapter to illustrate her similarities to and differences from the rest of the respondents.

Empieza la Lucha (Lucha's Struggle Begins)

When I asked the respondents the first question about dating, most reacted by laughing as they recalled their adventures with asking their parents' permission to date and many times getting refused or postponed indefinitely. Lucha's focus group had two other participants, who started answering the question with lively stories of their "dating escapades." Lucha joined in the fun but looked rather sheepish when it was her turn to answer. She said, "Right now I am wondering how good I would be in this interview." Lucha was concerned that her family was so atypical that many of the questions I was asking did not apply to her and that somehow it would ruin my study. I assured her that she belonged in the focus group regardless of the composition of her family and, in fact, I was looking for diversity in Chicano families. I said, "I think that it is really important to see the diversity of experiences and to see how complicated life is and how people make sense of their lives and try to put together a life. The questions do not a priori assume you grew up with your biological parents." Lucha interjected, "What if they were really screwed up?" I replied, "Well, then you say that. I think that it speaks very highly of you that you were able to sort that through. You should just answer how it is relevant to you and to your experiences." With my assurance, she proceeded to tell us her story.

Lucha came from a family of eleven. Her parents were born in Mexico and immigrated to the United States. "I'm number seven in the family and my older brothers and sisters were born and raised in Mexico. And then my parents came here and my mother was pregnant and she had a miscarriage and all this stuff happened and then they came out with my sister and I and then the rest of the family."

Lucha's father had a severe alcohol problem that led to extremely abusive behavior toward his family, especially his wife. Lucha's mother also had a drug problem and was eventually diagnosed with schizophrenia. When Lucha was five years old, Child Protective Services removed all the children from the home and placed them in different foster families, except for Lucha and her younger sister Fuerza who were placed in the same foster home. Nonetheless, Lucha and Fuerza continued to have contact with their siblings. "When I was younger, and even when we were in foster homes, we [all the siblings] would have contact on major holidays. We would get together."

Lucha and Fuerza lived in several foster homes until Lucha was nine, when they were placed in a group home with fifteen other girls of various ages. That's when Lucha started menstruating. Lucha recalled how Fuerza, who acted like a mother rather than a sister, did "research" on the topic by reading magazine articles on menstruation and tried to instruct Lucha on how to use a tampon. Lucha remembered that she was

> nine years old. I have learned about that kind of stuff [menstruation], because when we were growing up in foster homes, we were older and it was hard to place us. We were in a group home and that's how I learned. We were in a cottage living with fifteen girls. This was in Chino [California]. I learned from them and my sis. My younger sister always had played the

mother/father/brother/sister role and she had started to do research. So when I started [menstruation], I remember being in the bathroom trying to put on a tampon and I came out and I said, "Fuerza this hurts! I can't believe women do this!" So she's like, "hmm." She's trying to figure it out. "What is it? What is it?" And she said, "Well did you leave the applicator in?" I'm like, "What do you mean?" She was like, "Well you're supposed to take something out" and I'm like, "Really?" After that I was kind of scared, so I used Maxi pads for a while. But then Fuerza would make fun of me because they'd crinkle; they were the older kind—real big. Fuerza would giggle with her friends, "Look you can hear it; you can hear it!"

At this point Nicole Rodriguez, another respondent in the focus group, offered, "It felt like it was a diaper or something."[38] "Right!" Lucha replied.

A few years afterwards, when Lucha was twelve, she and Fuerza were adopted by a couple. The mother was white and the father was of Mexican descent. The adoptive parents did not want Lucha and Fuerza to have any contact with their siblings. According to Lucha, "Our adoptive family said no. You can't see them anymore. That won't be good for you. And we were like, OK, whatever. I was twelve years old. What did I know?"

As the girls grew older, they did not get along with their adoptive parents until, finally, Lucha and Fuerza decided to become legally emancipated. They left their adoptive home.

We just started going to different friends' houses because we were at a crisis point. And then we tried going back with our adoptive family and that wasn't working. And we just realized that we should go our own way. So my sister got a job working as a nanny at this house, and she was also doing bookkeeping on the side. So that's how we earned a living. At that point I think I was like seventeen. And I was working at the In'N'Out since I was fifteen and a half. So that's how we survived, just working and hanging out with friends. And then we got in contact with my sister Martha and my sister Lilia and I went to live with my sister Lilia. This is all down south [in Los Angeles]. Both my sister and I started at Cal State and we got scholarships to go because we couldn't afford to go to college; we really did not know too much about it. Then Fuerza transferred to Stanford and I transferred to a college in the East Coast. I graduated then came straight here to Boalt Law School [at the University of California, Berkeley]. My sister actually graduated from Stanford University. Then she worked as an investment banker for a while. She's brilliant. She's a brainiac. And then she decided she wanted to try the law, so she applied to law school. She just started her second year at Stanford Law School.

At the time of this interview, Lucha was in her third year of law school. By the time I was writing this chapter, Lucha had passed the California bar exam and was applying for a position as an attorney at the San Francisco public defender's office.

These two young women raised themselves with almost no contact with their family of origin. They nurtured and supported each other and their success in life came through strength (Fuerza) and struggle (Lucha).

3

■ ■ ■ ■ ■ ■ ■ ■ ■

Becoming Family

Introduction

IN THE MIDST OF WRITING this chapter, I visited the National Gallery of Art in Washington, D.C., and saw the Mary Cassatt exhibit, which portrayed upper-middle-class Victorian visions of motherhood. Although the paintings were exquisite, the images were disquieting. I left the museum a bit depressed but not quite knowing why. Later the same day I came across the following quote from the book *The Unknown City*, which helped me understand why I found the Cassatt exhibit disturbing.

[We set] out to analyze the micro-politics of child rearing amidst poverty. The story we tell comes from interviews with over seventy-five women, black, white, Latina, across two cities, trying to raise up the next generation with insufficient financial resources, often surrounded by violence on their streets and in their homes. . . . rearing children under any conditions is tough work. Alone, very difficult. Without money, excruciating. Within violence, near impossible. . . . "good mothering," or what passes for good mothering, happens in a particular context; a context of money, time, and excess. And that in the absence of these, it is far too easy to "discover" bad mothering. As a society, we scrutinize the least equipped and least resourced women, holding them to standards of mothering that most of us could not and do not achieve. (Fine and Weis 1998, 186–87)

The quote articulated my fears that my respondents' mothers did not meet the hegemonic standards of mothering as represented in Cassatt's images. Furthermore, I feared the potential misunderstanding by many readers of not only my respondents' mothers but their fathers as well. After all, for the Cassatt images to be possible, for example, the woman tenderly bathing a young child in a context of opulence and peacefulness required the unrepresented father to have enough economic power to provide his family with the resources necessary for this lifestyle. So my respondents' fathers were also implicated in these images, because they were inadequate providers. With these fears in mind, I gingerly stepped into this chapter hoping against hope to do my respondents' families justice.

Parenting Together:
The Discourse of Personal Responsibility

The most important familial relationship for respondents was with their parents. Most came from very loving families, the majority with both parents present (81 percent) and others from single-parent households (17 percent, all respondents lived with their mothers).[1] Although mothers and fathers had different parenting styles, most parents emphasized what Michelle Fine and Lois Weis (1998) call a "discourse of personal responsibility."

I asked respondents, "What important things have you learned from your mother?" and then asked the same question about their fathers. Many respondents teared up as they recalled the powerful lessons they learned from their parents by direct verbal commands and by example. The values mentioned most often revolved around morality, work ethic, and, above all, education. These values were not ranked in any manner but rather represented a worldview. Parents, especially mothers, constantly told their daughters that they could accomplish "things in life" and that they were responsible for their own livelihood. In fact, many respondents began working as soon as they entered high school, if not earlier. When I asked Nicolasa I. Sandoval if she had chores at home while growing up, she replied,

> Oh yeah, absolutely. Not only chores, but also I started working when I was twelve, and my other sisters started working when they were about thirteen.

My first job was cleaning motel rooms for one summer when I was twelve. Then the following summer, I did that but then I also got a job at a bakery. I worked at a bakery all through high school and my first year of college. Part of the deal was that before we were eighteen we gave 25 percent of our earnings to the household. After eighteen, if we decided to live under my mother's roof, we paid $100 a month for rent.[2]

The notions of "personal responsibility" were deeply ingrained in most of my respondents. At the same time, most of the brothers in these families were not socialized in the same way.[3] In many ways, my respondents were already being socialized to work a "double (if not triple) shift" (Hochschild 1999; Fine and Weis 1998), in that most were required not only to work but also to do well in school and attend to family obligations. Brothers were not necessarily held accountable for all these aspects of "personal responsibility."

My respondents felt very maternal toward younger brothers and wanted to help them succeed. Julissa, a third-year doctoral student, had her brother live with her while he finished his bachelor's degree in biology.[4] They shared an apartment, saving in living expenses to send money to their retired parents, who could no longer work in the agricultural fields. Julissa's parents felt "bad because they don't consider it our responsibility to help them out financially, but that's what family is for."

Nayelli, during the last two months of her senior year in college, brought her fourteen-year-old brother to live with her during his summer break from middle school.[5] Nayelli took care of her brother and helped him get a job at McDonald's. Nayelli did not have a car, so she taught her brother how to use public transportation to go to his job, grocery shop, and do other household errands. Nayelli made sure her brother attended a few of her classes to gain exposure to college; all the while Nayelli never considered him a burden or felt he was not her responsibility. This, of course, was in the middle of her own final exams, while she was working as a research assistant fifteen hours a week and making preparations to move to New York City to attend Columbia University to begin a master's program in education. Furthermore, she was one of the main organizers for the Chicano/Latino graduation ceremony on her campus.

Many respondents also manifested the "discourse of personal responsibility" in meeting other family obligations. Most respondents' parents were in their forties and fifties, but several respondents had already assumed responsibility for parents, mostly mothers, who had fallen terminally ill. Sara's experience with her fifty-eight-year-old mother was one of the most dramatic instances.[6] Her mother was diagnosed with cancer at the end of Sara's first year in a doctoral program. Sara left school and went to take care of her. Her brothers, who never left the area, were not required to nurse her mother. Sara's mother admitted that she initially disapproved of Sara going away to school so far from home. "But now I realize how important it is." Her mother came to appreciate Sara's skills gained through education. "I helped her through the whole medical ordeal—the language for her to understand things like chemotherapy." Sara was also able to ask the appropriate questions from doctors and other hospital personnel.

Sara took her mother on one last vacation to San Francisco before she became extremely ill. "We went to the fanciest hotel, and went to the fanciest restaurants. We went shopping at Macy's, we were just walking around, we had a lot of fun. I told her, 'Anything you want.' I spent a lot of money. I didn't care. I charged up the credit cards." She felt that taking care of her mother was "the right thing to do" and that "we had a chance to talk and resolve past issues."

Besides illness in families, respondents were also called upon to help family members in legal troubles. Many of my respondents were the first in their families to attend college and also, at times, the only ones fluent in English. Families relied on their knowledge about predominantly white institutions and their ability to translate whenever family members needed help. Generosa, like Sara, also left her doctoral program during her first year to help her family cope with her twenty-two-year-old brother's impending incarceration.[7] Although her family had been in the United States for four generations and was fluent in English, Generosa was the first to attend college. She faced criticism by several faculty in her graduate program because of her commitment to helping with family problems.[8] Her stress did not come primarily from her feelings toward her family—she was very clear she wanted to help. The stress came from the strain of juggling two different worldviews—the familial and the academic.

The commitment to personal responsibility sharpened my respondents' understanding of how structural factors—be they economic, legal, educational, or others—restrict individual agency. Many respondents were keenly aware that their individual discipline was always constrained by their social class, gender, race, and ethnicity. They felt it most poignantly when they saw their parents' work ethic often go unrewarded. Their compassion extended to the men in their families and their experiences of harassment by police and other authority figures. Respondents who had brothers affected by the criminal justice system had an especially well developed critique of the limits of "individual responsibility." The ability to "see" freedom within restriction and the commitment to "struggle" within "constraint" were examples of Chicana feminists' proposals that women of Color develop a "*mestiza* consciousness" as a result of the arbitrary nature of social interaction when one is poor, a woman, and racially and ethnically different from the white majority.

The Centrality of Mothering

I was very close to my mom. The neighbor across the street used to call us "*un par de aretes*" [a pair of earrings] because we were always together. We were never apart.

—Conchita, twenty-eight-year-old respondent, San Antonio, Texas

A principal theme in Chicana feminist writings is the centrality of mothers in the lives of their daughters (Moraga 1981, 1983, 60–61; Anzaldúa quoted in Keating 2000, 23, 78). An example is Rosa Linda Fregoso's (forthcoming) critical analysis of the portrayal of the "phallocentric mother" in the character of Mercedes Cruz in *Lone Star*. In this film, Mercedes crossed the U.S./Mexican border illegally, married, and then was widowed. She eventually became an entrepreneur who owned a Mexican restaurant called Santa Barbara. Mercedes raised her daughter, Pilar, who did not abide by her mother's political and social values and did not follow in her mother's career path. While Mercedes became a financially successful businesswoman who sacrificed her Mexicanness to obtain the "American dream," her daughter chose the less lucrative profession of elementary school history teacher and defied the school board by teaching Texas history from a Chicana perspective. Objectively, Pilar was extremely successful and even admirable: she was raised by a single mother in conditions of poverty in the racist environment of South Texas, yet she became a professional with a political consciousness. Mercedes, however, did not necessarily see Pilar's success or admire her political values. In fact, she claimed she had nothing to do with creating this rebellious daughter with whom she disagreed in many areas. Rosa Linda Fregoso posits that "Nowhere is the subordination of women of color in history more evident than in the racialized mother-daughter relationship, embodied in Pilar and Mercedes Cruz's estrangement, their conflicts and unresolved tensions." Fregoso continues, "It is not so much that I was disturbed by this, for their mother-daughter conflicts triggered memories of my own conflictual relation as the link in the motherline chain. I too have had similar conflicts on both sides of the chain—as the daughter of an assertive, strong-willed, vocal and independent mother and as a mother of an equally assertive, strong-willed, vocal and independent daughter." In Fregoso's analysis, the conflicts and tension between mothers and daughters are not uncommon between those "who share similar personality traits." She agrees with Brown-Guillory, who states that

> "when a mother looks at her daughter, she sees herself. She is constantly re-minded of her mistakes, yearnings, dreams, successes and failures. When a daughter looks at her mother she often sees herself and rejects the image in the mirror." . . . Such has been my own experience with these two "don't-take-no-prisoners" kinds of women in my life. (Fregoso forthcoming)

Many of my respondents experienced this tension in their relationships with their own mothers—the pulling away while simultaneously feeling the need for connection. They were also aware of the "mirroring" between their own lives and the lives of their mothers. They spoke often of "carrying their mothers' dreams" and of living their mothers' yearnings for "independence and accomplishments." Alejandra Dominguez's mother, who was married at the age of fourteen, used Alejandra's *quinceañera* as a fulfillment for her own frustrated dream because of an early marriage.[9] However, my respondents' mothers' dedication to their daughters was not simple psychological projection; they were also excellent mothers, a fact most of my respondents vehemently emphasized. Respondents' mothers supported their daughters' dreams as well as provided them with the discipline, skills, and material goods to succeed beyond their wildest dreams.

Many of the women in my respondents' families came from the long "motherline" of women learning from each other how to resist their subordination. Soledad stated that her mother had "a subtle, subtle strength," which she had learned from her own mother.[10]

> I've got some crazy uncles and they come over and they always drink beer. They'll get themselves into crazy jams. My grandmother takes care of them in this traditional way, and yet, there's a certain line you cannot cross with her. And if one of my uncles is getting loud with her or they're getting obnoxious or disrespectful, she just ends it right there. She just says, "That's it. I've had enough!" And she leaves. Some people would say that's walking away from conflict. But in her case, it's not. I can't really put my finger on it exactly. But she has a way of letting you know who's in charge. My mom is very much the same way. My dad thinks the person that shouts the loudest wins the argument. She will sit and she will wait for him to have what I call his tantrum. And then she'll say, "You know you didn't have to go there. And this is what we're going to do whether or not you want to do it." Nine times out of ten he just folds. [*Everyone laughs.*] My father just goes, "OK!" So it's very subtle. It's not this defiant in your face sort of strength.

In addition to their mothers' strengths, many of the respondents also spoke about their mothers' failed dreams of going to school, becoming teachers or artists. Jessica Delgado's mother made attempts to become a singer.[11]

> My mother finished high school in Santa Fe [New Mexico]. She wanted to be a singer, so she moved to Hollywood around 1964 when she was in her early twenties. She's got an amazing voice and she was able to do some vocal work in studio background singing. There's a picture of her with the Supremes in the studio. But then she met my dad.

Her mother's story turned tragic when she married Jessica's father and was severely abused by him. When Jessica was twelve years old, she and her mother fled in the middle of the night from Los Angeles to Texas. At the time of the interview, Jessica's mother was a secretary at the University of Michigan and had given up singing.

Religion became an outlet for many of the mothers whose dreams of attaining higher education had been frustrated. Several of them took religion as an intellectual endeavor and carefully studied the Bible. For example,

Christina J. Reynoso refused to discuss religion with her mother, because their discussions inevitably turned into arguments, which her mother won, because "she has read everything, the entire canon of religious writings throughout history."[12] Christina's mother had so much intellectual passion for religion and no outlet that she "invited Jehovah's Witnesses into the house" just to debate them. Once they were in the house, Christina's mother "whipped out her Bible. She knows her Bible inside and out," as well as other religious writings, like those of St. Thomas Aquinas and St. Augustine. It was no secret in Christina's family that her mother's dream was to be a "theology teacher," a dream that Christina completely supported.

What became obvious from the respondents' tales of their mothers' frustrated dreams was that ambition, intelligence, discipline, and self-efficacy were not enough to succeed in this society. My respondents' mothers' stories confirmed my colleague Mary Romero's observation, made in reaction to my presentation of my respondents' success stories, that in a racist, sexist, classist, heterosexist society personal virtue is not enough—the structural scaffolding cannot be climbed by will and talent alone.[13] Rather, there have to be opportunities provided by hard-won political victories against a structure that is relentless unless otherwise provoked. I am convinced that as talented and disciplined as my respondents have been in their young lives, and as much as their families supported them, few would have succeeded without special programs throughout their education to insure their success.[14] The unanswerable question is whether my respondents' mothers (and fathers) would have accomplished as much as their daughters had they been born later rather than sooner.

Mothering for Empowerment

Even though I was raised as a girl . . . I was raised like a man too.
—Agustina, twenty-one-year-old respondent, Chicago

According to my respondents, many of their mothers saw their mission as giving their daughters as much education as possible, so they would not be economically dependent on a man. At the same time, most mothers assumed that marriage was not only inevitable but also desirable. They simply felt that education was insurance against a bad marriage. Agustina stated that although her mother raised her very traditionally, keeping tight curfews and emphasizing virginity until marriage, she simultaneously insisted on the importance of education to insure economic independence:

> Even though I was raised as a girl with certain traditions and not having a boyfriend until you're eighteen, in a sense I was raised like a man too. Ever since I was little, my mom told me, "You're going to get an education. You're going to become independent and one day when you get married and you're not happy, you'll leave him and you'll still be making money. You will support your children and you won't need anyone's help." So that's basically what she's ingrained in my mind. That's the reason why I'm getting an education. You never know what's going to happen *y para proteger el porvenir de mis hijos* [to safeguard my children's futures]. I want to be able to make money in order not to depend on anyone for anything.[15]

Most respondents' mothers indeed could be characterized by Rosa Linda Fregoso's (forthcoming) assessment of her mother: "don't-take-no-prisoners" kind of women. Their desires for their daughters were well articulated, and they often left little room for deviation from their expectations. Therefore, it was not surprising that they produced, for the most part, extremely strong daughters. Alicia Granillo stated, "What I learned from my mother is determination and perseverance. She's a very determined woman. Once she puts her mind to something, *lo va a hacer* [she's going to do it] no matter what and it's got to be done now [*snaps her fingers*]. I'm very much like that. Why wait until tomorrow if you can do it today?"[16] But like Mercedes Cruz in *Lone Star*, my respondents' mothers did not necessarily get what they thought they had bargained for. Many of these respondents spoke of rebelling against their mothers at least verbally if not in action. Their rebellion sometimes caused tension between mothers and daughters. Mariela, with regret in her voice, talked about how she was both close with and distant from her mother.[17] Mariela thought she had learned a lot from her mother. "I speak my mind. If I don't agree with something I'll stick up for it." Their defiant attitude, according to Mariela, "unites us because we're so similar. At the same time it separates us, because we have such opposing points of view, and neither of us will stand back on what we believe in."

But, as Fregoso surmises, "If both mother(s) and daughter(s) are fortunate enough to weather the frictions, hang in there and work through some of the resentments, blames, ill-feelings, guilts, and judgements, their relationship usually blossoms into a life-long, indissoluble bond." Unlike Mariela and her mother, many of my respondents had arrived at the "blossoming" stage of their relationship with their mothers. Most respondents spoke to their mothers often, and many referred to their mothers as their "best friends." Carolina was not unusual in saying that she and her mother had "a great relationship. I talk to her about four times a week."[18] This was while Carolina was in Cambridge, Massachusetts, and her mother was in Los Angeles. Although respondents spoke to their mothers about their romantic relationships, the only area that was consistently taboo, however, was extensive details about respondents' sex lives. As Carolina put it, "When it comes to sex, it's zero communication."

Nevertheless, the respondents' closeness to their mothers was palpable; many of them grew teary-eyed when they related the enormous sacrifices their mothers had endured on their behalf and on behalf of their entire families. Tomasa's mother worked very odd hours as a maintenance worker in a bank so that she could be home when the children arrived from school.[19]

> The arrangement was that my father would work during the day so that my mom could be home to take us to school or pick us up. Then she'd make dinner and my father would come home and my mom would work at night. She would get home at 2:30 in the morning and wake up at 4:00 to make my father's lunch, then take a half-hour nap before she woke us up and get us ready to go to school. She's strong in that sense that she worked nonstop; she slept maybe three or four hours a day until I was 18. I could see that she was really tired because she did maintenance at a bank—she vacuumed rugs and carried heavy equipment, which she was way too small to do. [Her mother was four feet, eleven inches tall.]

As a result of carrying such heavy equipment, Tomasa's mother suffered from a hernia but refused medical attention because, as she told Tomasa, "I can't quit work because if I get operated [on], I have to recuperate at home and we can't afford that right now. We need to work."

For the respondents' mothers, the reward for their sacrifices was to see their daughters succeed. Most fathers were also supportive of their daughters' endeavors, but their presence was mostly in the background. The mothers were the ones who did the day-to-day hand-holding, who knew if their daughters were doing well in school, or if their daughters were worried about a test. Several respondents spoke about "standing on their mothers' shoulders" and of their mothers telling them, "I don't want you to have my life." Many wanted their daughters to have the choices they never had. In essence, the opportunity to choose their lives was the gift these mothers were giving their daughters.

It is not unusual for research about mothers—regardless of ethnicity, race, and class background—to portray them as controlling and domineering and to read of daughters trying to escape their grip. Ramón Gutiérrez's analysis of Chicana mothers is not unusual in its tone:

> Mothers came to be despised by their Chicana daughters in large part because of their subordination/accommodation to patriarchal power. As mothers who often favored assimilation, they urged their daughters to learn English, to get educated, to marry well (to wealthy Anglo men all the better), and, if necessary, to abandon their cultural past. (1993, 58)

There is resonance of these conflicts in my interviews. However, such contentiousness, when found, is not the defining element in the relationships between my respondents and their mothers. Many reflected that what they saw as too restrictive when they were in their early teens, they later reassessed in a more favorable light. As Norma I. Garza concluded about her own mother's disciplinary practices, "It's not that it's without conflict. It's not that she's controlling. It's just caution. She just doesn't want me to have her life."[20] As respondents became older and educated, many encouraged their mothers to pursue their own goals and to follow the dreams they thought were lost to them. Many times, the relationship between them turned into mutual support, a collaboration to make each other's lives better.

Fathering in the Background

My dad doesn't talk. My dad is just an onlooker.

—Tonantzin, twenty-two-year-old respondent, Edinburg, Texas

The relationships between my respondents and their mothers were extremely complicated, as were the fathers' positions in the respondents' emotional lives. With few exceptions, most respondents expressed great love for their fathers. It was not uncommon for respondents to refer to themselves as "daddy's girls." However, most respondents mentioned that they did not have an emotionally intimate relationship with them. When I asked, "Are you close to your father?" invariably most respondents would hesitate and respond, "It depends what you mean by close." Without hesitation most said they loved their fathers and that their fathers loved them. But immediately they clarified that it was not the same type of relationship they had with their mothers.

Unlike the almost daily contact respondents had with their mothers, they spoke less often with their fathers. Conversations between them were often loving but superficial. Christina J. Reynoso spoke to her mother on the phone "a few times a week," but "as far as my dad is concerned, he is not a very talkative man." When I asked Christina whether she was close to her father, she replied, "In some ways we are. There's an emotional bond there. We have had real conversations, but he doesn't talk. He is more likely to bottle up and not say anything or if he has to say something to me, he will tell my mom and have my mom tell me."

Fathers were exempt from the day-to-day socialization necessary to maintain a family, and they were especially distant during crisis situations. In the case of Victoria, it was her mother alone who accompanied her to counseling sessions after she was raped.[21]

The counselor asked me, in front of my mom, what if I got pregnant. My mom was like, "She would keep the baby!" And I'm like, "No I would not!" At that point, she asked me if it was my first sexual experience. I don't know what on earth I was thinking. I admitted to my mom it wasn't the first time I had had sex. As if my mom wasn't already traumatized enough! At that point, I thought I had nothing to lose. I wasn't going to lie, and I told her, "I'm glad that wasn't my first time." She didn't say anything to me, but she was yelling at my sister, "What kind of girls have I raised!" But she never said anything to me directly.

Victoria's mother kept all of this information from her husband. Both the pain of her daughter's rape and the discovery of a transgression that was of paramount importance to her were traumas she handled by herself.

Fathers still had a significant amount of authority in the family, regardless of the mothers' influence over my respondents and on the overall direction of their families. Although mothers were "the movers and the shakers," on the surface many deferred to their husbands' authority in parenting. My respondents were cognizant that their fathers were the "figureheads," and emphasized that it was really the mothers who ultimately made many of the family decisions.

The fathers' authority derived from cultural norms of *respeto* (respect), but also from the respondents' knowledge of how much their fathers worked on behalf of their families. It was not unusual for the fathers to work as many as three jobs, especially when they were committed to sending their children to private schools. Many of the respondents also felt that their fathers' work demands, often in underpaid, unskilled jobs, explained the distant relationship with their children.

Consequences of Divorce

Fathers' authority was disrupted when there was a divorce, in which case most respondents became intensely loyal to their mothers, often cutting off contact with their fathers afterwards. A total of 16 percent of respondents had parents who were divorced, and in all cases, the respondent was raised by the mother or by the mother's relatives. With the exception of one respondent, the divorce was difficult for the respondents. In most cases, regardless of when the separation happened, the respondents did not have consistent contact with their fathers. Only Mieka Valdez had a regular visiting schedule, according to which she lived with her mother during the week and she saw her father on most weekends and often during the week.[22] In other instances, visits with fathers were irregular and fraught with tension, making it difficult for respondents to have a close relationship with their fathers. Hilda's father picked up her brother and her "on the weekends, and he would pretty much not say anything. I felt really uncomfortable, just sitting there. My brother was fine with that; he didn't mind. But I'm a talker and my father wouldn't say anything."[23] Her father's silence was in stark contrast to her mother, who talked to them and asked them about everything in their lives.

Most of the respondents who did have contact with their fathers after a divorce tried to understand their fathers' emotional distance and to see them within the context of the fathers' own upbringing. For example, Hilda stated, "I try to be close to my dad. I think my dad came from an abusive situation and so I think that he has a lot of emotional scars and things that have happened to him in the past. He doesn't know how to be close." Hilda felt that her father didn't appreciate "the real value of having children" when they were young because her parents had gotten pregnant while they were in high school. As was the case in most of the unplanned pregnancies in my study, the mothers rose to the occasion, and the fathers remained uninvolved in the raising of their children. Exacerbating Hilda's relationship with her father was the fact that she did not like the way her father had treated her mother.

> He said a lot of things that were hurtful and I think that that's why it makes it difficult to be close to him. And, even with him walking me down the aisle [Hilda was engaged to be married], my mom doesn't really feel comfortable about that. I don't feel so great about it either. We were watching *The Father of the Bride*, that movie with Steve Martin; I was thinking, "Gosh I wish my dad was like that. I wish." I mean, who probably doesn't? I know that there are some people who do have that.

In spite of her father's faults, when I asked Hilda whether she had learned anything from her father, she tried to recall his acts of kindness and his good qualities. Hilda knew that her father had "a good heart." "I know that he loves me, and he does show that."

Understanding their fathers' context and own emotional history was one way my respondents tried to get close to their fathers.

Fathering for Empowerment

In spite of the difficulties many respondents had with their fathers, they also spoke eloquently of their fathers' contributions to their sense of independence. Instead of providing direct guidance, like most mothers were, fathers emphasized very practical activities that were independent of the daily chores usually assigned to women. For example, Victoria remembered how helping her father around the ranch, putting up fences and building things, influenced her into adulthood, when she still "liked building things and doing things with tools. If we had to put something together at home, I'd do it. My husband doesn't." She truly "loved spending that time with my dad and watching him work. That is probably where I learned the value of working hard and seeing an accomplishment."

Empowerment sometimes came from respondents' resistance to their fathers' abusive behavior, mostly verbal and mostly directed at their mothers, not them. Guadalupe did not approve of her father's verbal abuse toward her mother nor of his flaunting the fact that he "ran around with other women."[24] Although her parents were married, she was not close to her father and was extremely critical of him. However, when I asked her what she had learned from him, she replied,

> From my dad I learned to be as strong as he is—a strong woman. I really had to put [up] a fight against him. If I could speak up to my dad, I'm not going to be intimidated by any guy—I can tell them anything. If I didn't allow the only man that's really in my life to tell me what to do, I don't think anybody else can tell me what to do. So it just taught me to be strong and independent. He really doesn't touch, no hugs. He's changing with his grandchildren, but I don't look at that. I guess I still hold grudges and I don't want to [let go] right now. I still want to savor my grudges.

Magdalena, unlike Guadalupe in the previous example, had a very close and loving relationship with her grandfather, whom she referred to as her father because he and her grandmother raised her.[25] Her father taught her the valuable lesson of speaking up against male authority. Magdalena and her father were watching the television show *Cristina*, the Oprah Winfrey of Spanish-language television, and they disagreed about a social issue presented in the show and "we got into this huge argument about it." Her father left with her mother in the middle of the dispute to go to the movies. Magdalena stayed at home crying, and when her father returned home, "He kissed me. He's like '*Ay mija*, I really love you, 'cause you really stand up for what you believe in even if it's against me.'" According to Magdalena, "Ever since then, I knew that I had some power if I held on strongly to my beliefs even to my father who was the almighty of the house! I guess I felt like a stronger person because my dad did respect that. I was an independent person who was my own person and no one is going to change me."

One of the most consistent messages many of my respondents received from their fathers was that education was important. Even if the fathers were not intimately involved in teaching their daughters the skills necessary to succeed in school, many worked two or three jobs so their children could attend private, mostly Catholic schools. There was only one exception, in which a father vehemently opposed his daughter's plan to obtain higher education. In this case, her mother fought and won her daughter's right to go to college. Of course, there were also fathers who were completely absent from my respondents' lives, and in these cases, they had nothing to do with their daughters' educational success.

Parenting: A Family Affair

Although less common, I did find tri-generational families, in which fathers were old enough to be the respondents' grandfathers and in which respondents' mothers had children when they were well into their forties. The larger number of siblings also meant that in many of these families the age range among the children could be as large as twenty years. In these circumstances, the older siblings, more specifically the older sisters, became like second mothers and did a substantial amount of parenting. A few of the older parents became like pseudo-grandparents and were not as involved with their youngest children. For example, Nina A. Perales's older sister, who got married when Nina was five, essentially raised her and was like her "mom."[26] Nina's older sister "moved away to California," but Nina would go and "stay with her every summer." She was the "one who told me about menstruation. She had the birds and the bees talk with me."

Some respondents, the children of very young parents, had been relinquished to grandparents, who took primary responsibility for raising them. Magdalena's mother had her when she was just seventeen. Magdalena was raised by her grandparents after the age of nine, together with her cousin, whom she considered her brother. Magdalena's mother remarried and had two more children who, at the time of the interview, were fifteen and eleven. Magdalena was twenty-two. Magdalena lived with her grandparents until she left for college, although her mother lived close by and had consistent contact with her and her half-brothers, whom Magdalena considered "like full-blooded brothers."

On the other hand, she had inconsistent contact with her father, although he lived in the area. According to Magdalena, "I lost contact with him, my dad. I studied abroad last year in Paris, and right before I left I called him. But I lost his number when I was gone and he moved. So I have no idea where to contact him. So unfortunately I haven't talked to him for a while." I asked Magdalena whether her father contacted her. She shook her head "no" and said,

> Well, until he wants to, he will. I stopped seeing him when I was three years old. He didn't reappear until I was nine. He disappeared till I was twelve. And then from twelve up till last year I saw him constantly and that's when I met all my four brothers and two half-sisters. Ever since two years ago, I haven't seen him.

Magdalena had been raised and nurtured by her grandparents, whom she felt were, for all practical purposes, her parents.

Parenting across Borders

Several respondents were separated from their parents for long periods of time, because the parents immigrated to the United States first and then later brought their families over. In these instances, relatives or older siblings took care of the children so that parents could forge ahead economically.

Sandra's parents came to California to work and brought over only Sandra's oldest brother, leaving behind Sandra and five other siblings.[27] Sandra was a year and a half when her parents left and remained in Guanajuato, Mexico, for about six years in the care of Sandra's oldest sister, who was twelve years old. Sandra did not see her parents after their departure and grew up thinking that "my sister was my mom, and I don't remember it, but my mom says that there were times I'd call my sister 'mom.'" Sandra and her siblings did not reunite with her parents until she was seven. "My mom didn't really have a role in my upbringing." Sandra's mother felt "she didn't have the right to tell me stuff because my older sister raised me for about five or six years. It was always my older sister who took the mother role."

Although Sandra became distant from her mother, Blanca Gordo was forced by hers to confront their emotional distance once Blanca rejoined her in Los Angeles after living with her grandmother in Mexico for ten years.[28] Blanca remembered thinking as the reunion approached, "What am I going to call her? Mami? Mom? What?" Blanca also did not want to leave her grandmother and "didn't want to come to the United States." Blanca "would cry and cry." Blanca was really dependent on her grandmother because, although Blanca's "grandmother was outspoken, she still was very traditional in some ways and did everything for us." When Blanca arrived in the United States, there was a power struggle between her mother and her grandmother over her upbringing, and Blanca recalled exactly the moment when it was resolved. She was going on a field trip and "My mom and my grandmother were sitting in the living room and I walked in and I'm like '¡*Ah, no encuentro mis huaraches*!'" (I can't find my sandals!). Blanca's grandmother promptly got up and offered: "Oh honey, I'll go get them for you!" Blanca's mother also got up and said, "No! Let her look for them." Blanca's grandmother "started crying and I started crying. I thought, 'Oh my God, my grandmother can't do this for me and here is this woman [her mother] who is taking over.' I realized, shit, this is going to be different."

The Social Context of Parenting

There were very few families that were not connected to larger Mexican American/Latino communities, especially to relatives who lived close by. Most of my respondents were essentially raised in a "village" rather than in isolated nuclear families. Patricia Alvarez had lived her entire life in the south side of Chicago, and most of her family, especially her father's side, lived within a five-mile radius.[29] The families got together often at her uncle's home and all three floors would fill up with Patricia's relatives.

Having a network of adults responsible for their upbringing was especially helpful for these respondents, because many of their working-class neighborhoods were not particularly safe. Furthermore, many respondents felt accountable to various adults, and this helped guide their behavior in appropriate ways. The greater availability of adults also provided many respondents with mentors to turn to with questions too intimidating to pose to their own parents. Agustina's uncle, her mother's brother, was both a friend and father figure after her own father left the family "for another woman" when Agustina was thirteen. Agustina felt that her uncle was "like a father to me because when my father left us he took over the father role." At the same time, he was also "like a best friend" and she could "tell him anything." Agustina attributed her closeness partially to the fact that he was forty and single, so Agustina felt "like he is more my age." Agustina could broach any subject with her uncle, especially taboo topics like sex, and he would "sit down with me and he's very open."

Extra-parental figures became especially important when strong disagreements emerged, especially ones between my respondents and their mothers. Magdalena had a younger aunt, who was the only person she could discuss birth control with and the trouble she was having regulating her period when she was on birth control pills:

> I did go on birth control pills at age seventeen. And I was paying for them and it was tough. I was working at Baskin Robbins. I could barely afford them and my boyfriend was helping me, but it was still tough. I remember I got my period twice in a month. My grandma and I don't talk about sex very much. And I remember asking my aunt, "Like tía [aunt], why did I get my period two times in a month?" And she knew. She's like, "*Mija*,[30] are you taking the pill?" And I was like, "Yeah." I was really embarrassed. But my aunt has always been the cool one, you always have like a "cool aunt," and she's like, "Well, have you been skipping pills?" And I'm just like, "Yeah." She's like, "You know, be careful because obviously it's messing up your menstrual cycle and you can also get pregnant."

Magdalena's aunt worked for a county agency and was able to refer Magdalena to their Planned Parenthood services, "where they give you pills for free. So she actually set me up there."

Magdalena's "cool aunt" helped her to use contraception effectively and also was an important liaison between Magdalena and her grandmother when, by accident, Magdalena's grandmother found her birth control pills. According to Magdalena, her grandmother came to her and asked, "Are you having sex?" "And I was just like, 'Yeah.'" Her grandmother was furious and said, "Don't talk to me," and proceeded to give Magdalena the "cold shoulder" for a few days. Magdalena "felt really bad and I called my aunt right away." Her aunt spoke to Magdalena's grandmother, who would not budge until Magdalena's aunt finally said, "Would you rather have her pregnant at seventeen like us?"[31] Magdalena's grandmother finally replied, "That's true." Magdalena's aunt continued, "She's still getting good grades and she's going to go to college. So what are you worried about?" Magdalena's grandmother ultimately got over her granddaughter's transgression, thanks largely to her aunt's intervention.

Sigue la Lucha (Lucha's Struggle Continues)

Lucha's parents were from Mexico: her mother was from Guadalajara and her father was from Durango. They met in Guadalajara. Lucha had never gone to Mexico to meet her mother's relatives, although she had a brief encounter with them when she was around nineteen at her mother's fiftieth birthday party, held in the halfway house where she still lived. The "village" failed Lucha and Fuerza, and they were not happy about it. Lucha bitterly remembered how nobody in her very large extended family took responsibility for her and her siblings when their family fell apart. According to Lucha, "they really didn't react too well with what happened [when Child Protective Services took all the children]. Most of my mother's family was in Mexico at the time. No one was here and they just never stepped in to help when things were going on. So I think that pissed me off."

When Lucha was five, she and her sister were placed in a foster home and they never saw their father again. She explained, "When the whole split-up happened, both my parents got taken away into police custody for child neglect. I haven't seen my dad since." I asked her whether she knew anything about her father, and she related what she had learned through her mother and her siblings, whom she saw sporadically:

> I know that he beat my mom, that he was a philanderer. I know that when
> they met in Mexico, that her family came from a better family than his and
> that they didn't like that she was going with him. My mother's parents had
> a store, and my father went in and they really didn't like her hanging out

with him. He fell in love with her legs. [*Everyone laughs*]. That was the thing. They were like, "the García family has great legs."

In spite of Lucha's clarity about her father's faults, she talked about how at times, when she looked at his picture, she would think, "if I lived in a fantasy world I'd be like, 'Oh, it's my dad. Look at him. He's handsome.'" However, aside from these fantasies, Lucha felt that "he's nothing."

Lucha used her mother's life as a model against which to fashion her own life.

> The driving force behind my life is I do not want to be like my mom. She came to this country, couldn't speak English, and couldn't get a job. My father would not let her out of the house. I mean, having eleven kids one after another! Basically she lost her mind and her body! Right now she's down in Los Angeles in a home and she's schizophrenic. I've thought, "I am so angry at her!" I guess maybe she is the model I did not want. Like, "How could you let this happen? How could you let him do that?!" I always thought growing up, "I am not going to be that." I'm not getting married, I'm not having children, I'm not going to feel like that. I'm going to have a career, I'm going to be somebody. I never had a strong woman like that [the other respondent's mother] in my life. The only other woman I've had even close to that is my sister.

Conclusion

Children learn in many ways how to become family. They learn from what they are told, from what they see, from how they are treated. But they also learn from what they are told and do not believe, from what they see and do not want to repeat, and from how they are treated and want to avoid. Sadly, Lucha and Fuerza might have learned to become family not from all the affirming things that families can be but from all the things they wanted to avert. Nonetheless, they embraced each other and other kind people around them, proving that family of origin is not destiny and that human beings learn from what is good but also from what is bad.

Review of Part I

Implications for Feminist Theorizing

I HAVE THEORIZED elsewhere that the core of Chicanas' subordination is the control of their sexuality (Hurtado 1996a, 2000). Chicano/Mexicanos' cult of virginity allows only a restricted number of acceptable subject positions for women—virgin, mother, daughter, sister, and grandmother—which are largely determined by a woman's virginity and conformity to culturally acceptable standards for sexual behavior. In one way or another, women have to be supervised by representatives of patriarchy—a father, brother, uncle, and older female authority like a mother or grandmother.

In contrast, the unacceptable subject positions—whore, unmarried but sexually active woman, divorced woman—are those in which women dictate the terms of their sexuality. Lesbianism is especially undesirable because it is the ultimate rejection of patriarchy.

The enculturation of sexuality happens in the social context of family relations. As Sonia Saldívar-Hull (2000) proposes, patriarchal messages around the desirability of these subject positions are certainly transmitted and to a large extent enforced by mothers and other women in the family. Almost all my respondents experienced restriction and were policed constantly as they developed physically. The fathers, when present, were largely symbolic in their enforcement of patriarchy.

These were certainly the "cultural templates" (Zavella forthcoming) my respondents were socialized into in their families. But there were many other "templates," some conscious and others not quite so, that were also available to them. At the same time that many female folk in the family were pushing marriage and children, others were not. Still others would verbally approve of these cultural templates but live their lives differently. They "wore the pants" in the family or otherwise dominated family decisions. My respondents were absorbing all of these complexities. Above all, many of these families inculcated in their daughters an understanding that they should obtain an education and be economically self-sufficient. Chicana feminisms have been able to capture these complexities, whereas these negotiations of compliance and resistance have not informed white hegemonic feminisms (Sandoval 2000, 42; Holvino 2001). Rather than only analyzing the surface of women's lives, Chicana feminists have taken their entire context, history, economic structures, and cultural orientations to theorize a feminism that allows us to see both the regressive elements in these cultural templates and also the places of resistance and potential liberation. Emma Pérez (1999) calls them interstitial feminisms; I call them underground feminisms (Hurtado forthcoming), because they are based on how poor women of Color *live* without labeling it feminism, in contrast to academic definitions that have not captured fully the complexities of these women's lives (Behar 1993).

Hegemonic feminisms, largely produced by white writers, did the same for middle-class white women. They were able to articulate their oppression amid what appeared to be an otherwise privileged life. They named the "problem that had no name" (Friedan 1963) and from that positionality deconstructed the gender dynamics that took place in the intimacy of white middle-class existence. Patriarchy is enforced through the intimacy of family socialization. All feminists have claimed this, in opposition to male-centered analysis that looks at structures outside the family as the sources of oppression. Hegemonic feminisms (Sandoval 2000) have done a brilliant job of shifting the site for analysis to the everyday interactions between women and men: the way women and men occupy physical space (Henley 1977), power dynamics in conversations (West 1992, 1995; Zimmerman and West 1975), physical abuse (Dworkin 1987), body image issues (Orbach 1997), and control over reproduction.

What all feminisms have failed to do is to describe *theoretically* the process I call relational dovetailing—how each feminist theoretical advancement *dovetails* into our existing knowledge of women's oppression. To dovetail means "to fit into each other, so as to form a compact and harmonious whole" (*Shorter Oxford English Dictionary*). Previous knowledge does not have to be approached from an adversarial standpoint; rather, newly articulated knowledge can move in and out of previous analyses describing in *relational* terms what is true for different groups of women and what is not.

Another significant theoretical oversight is the construction of feminist theory that does not take into account the fact that women's sexualities are constructed *in relationship* to ethnic, race, class, and sexuality groups existing within specific contexts. White hegemonic femininity exists only in relationship to other raced and classed femininities. Lesbians, from a hegemonic perspective, are not considered "feminine" at all. Toni Morrison's (1992) brilliant analysis of the construction of whiteness *in relationship* to the "Africanist other" proves the point well.

> The fabrication of an Africanist persona is reflexive; an extraordinary meditation on the self; a powerful exploration of the fears and desires that reside in the writerly conscious. It is an astonishing revelation of longing, of terror, of perplexity, of shame, of magnanimity. It requires hard work *not* to see this. . . . What became transparent were the self-evident ways that [white] Americans choose to talk about themselves through and within a sometimes allegorical, sometimes metaphorical, but always choked representation of an Africanist presence. (16–17)

Power is defined in relationship to the powerless—it is from this *sitio* that we can best unknot the nature of oppression and liberation. It is not in opposition to white hegemonic feminisms and other feminisms, but in the *relational dovetailing* that we can best understand the similarities and differences between women.

In part 2 of this book I examine how differences outlined in part 1 around socialization practices and my respondents' ethnicity, race, class, and sexuality get played out in the predominantly white world outside their largely segregated Latino communities. Many respondents entered the white mainstream with very different cultural templates for acceptable sexual and social behavior *as women*. Encountering systematic oppression because of their social group memberships resulted in my respondents' emphasizing their social rather than their personal identities. The theoretical section of part 2 addresses the implications of these differences for our constructions of feminisms.

Multiple Group Identities

Existing in the World

Part II

The Story of Three Women

Patty

Patty was a lively twenty-something who embodied the Los Angeles style—pierced nose, pierced tongue, and an almost encyclopedic knowledge of popular culture. She spoke with a "valley girl" tone sprinkled with Spanish words for emphasis. She rarely went for more than a minute without a quip punctuated with a reference to some rock group, television show, or current buzzword. And, of course, every sentence ended with the rhetorical question of the 1990s, "You know?" She was a delight to interview and her focus group was one of the ones that laughed the most, given Patty's playfulness.

Cristina

Cristina was reserved. She was eight months pregnant and it was the middle of *la canícula* in South Texas, where I interviewed her.[1] She seemed to carry the weight of the world on her slender twenty-year-old shoulders. She had difficulty stealing away for two hours, because her twenty-four-year-old husband did not want her to participate in an interview without his presence. He also was not pleased to have to watch their five-year-old daughter while Cristina reflected on her life. As the interview progressed,

Cristina slowly calmed down and was very thoughtful and articulate in her answers. She was honest and forthcoming and her face would occasionally light up when she spoke about her daughter, her sister, and the days prior to her marriage at age fourteen. She was about to have her second child and she was weary. There was also a resoluteness in her demeanor that at times was betrayed by the slight clenching of the jaw and a depth in her dark brown eyes that seemed misplaced in someone so young.

Alejandra Dominguez

Alejandra Dominguez was a whirlwind that I could anticipate. I heard her cackling laugh in the hallway of the old hotel as she approached my room. I opened the door and saw a petite, stylishly dressed young woman with the most voluminous hair I had ever seen besides my own. She had blonde streaks in her auburn hair à la Jennifer López and she flipped it as she threw back her head in a belly laugh at the slightest provocation. Every question I asked was answered with an elaborate story that often included incredible adventures and mishaps, because her contagious joy for living always placed her in precarious and interesting situations. She came with her best friend, Zulma Rodriguez. Together they behaved like two frolicsome puppies that pawed and nibbled at one another, while they related their daily contact in their student life at the University of Illinois. Their interview lasted into the night as they took great delight in talking to me and to each other, and in reflecting on their own ideas and lives. Close to midnight Alejandra and Zulma left the hotel to go out and eat and then drive to a suburb of Chicago. They left behind in my musty old room a whiff of youth, sweetness, and hope.

In my previous work I elaborated the distinction that many psychologists make between *personal* and *social* identity (Tajfel 1981; Deaux and Ethier 1998; Gurin, Hurtado, and Peng 1994, 524). Tajfel posits that *personal identity* is defined as an aspect of self composed of psychological traits and dispositions that give us personal uniqueness. Personal identity is derived from intrapsychic influences, many of which are socialized within family units (however they are defined) (Hurtado 1997, 309). From this perspective, we have a great deal in common as human beings precisely because our personal identities comprise certain universal processes, such as loving, mating, and doing productive work, what are considered in psychology universal components of self. Personal identity is much more stable and coherent over time than social identity. Most individuals do not have *multiple personal identities*, nor do their personal identities change from one social context to another (Hurtado 1996b).

On the other hand, *social identity* is defined as those aspects of the individual self-identity that derive from one's knowledge of being part of categories and groups, together with the value and emotional significance attached to those memberships (Hurtado 1997, 309). Tajfel argues that the formation of social identities is the consequence of three social psychological processes. The first is *social categorization*. Nationality, language, race and ethnicity, skin color, or any other social or physical characteristic that is meaningful in particular social contexts can be the basis for social categorization and thus the foundation for the creation of social identities. *Social comparison* is the second process that underlies the construction of social identities. The characteristics of one's group(s), such as status or degree of affluence, achieve significance *in relation* to perceived differences from other groups and the value connotation of these differences.

The third process involves psychological work, both cognitive and emotional, that is prompted by what Tajfel assumes is a universal motive—to achieve a positive sense of distinctiveness. The groups that are most problematic for a sense of positive distinctiveness—ones that are disparaged, memberships that have to be negotiated frequently because they are visible to others, ones that have become politicized by social movements, and so on—are the most likely to become social identities for individuals. Moreover, it is these identities that become especially powerful psychologically. They are easily accessible, individuals think a lot about them, they are apt to be salient across situations, and they are likely to function as schema, frameworks, or social scripts (Gurin, Hurtado, and Peng 1994). Unproblematic group memberships—ones that are socially valued or accorded privilege, those that are not obvious to others—may not even become social identities. For example, until very recently, being white was not the subject of inquiry and is still not widely thought of as a social identity (Fine et al. 1997; Hurtado and Stewart 1996; Phinney 1996).

The three descriptions above of Patty, Cristina, and Alejandra were my *subjective assessments* of who these three respondents were as *individuals*.[2]

They were three very different people, and one could say that each one of my respondents was indeed unique. That is, each respondent's *personal identity* was as complex and varied as it is in all human beings. What gave them commonalities, however, were their shared *social identities*.

Social Identity and Multiplicity

Nobody
Can talk to anybody
Without me
Right?
I explain my mother to my father my father to my
little sister
My little sister to my brother my brother to the white feminists
The white feminists to the Black church folks the
Black church folks
To the ex-hippies the ex-hippies to the Black
separatists the
Black separatists to the artists the artists to my
friends' parents . . .
Then
I've got to explain myself
To everybody
I do more translating
Than the Gawdamn U.N.
                    —Rushin 1981

In the writings of women of Color, the overriding metaphor for women's consciousness is multiplicity. Like Marcel Duchamp's painting *Nude Descending a Staircase* (Feldman 1967, 264), many women of Color have been forced into cultivating multiple social identities. Donna Kate Rushin's "Bridge Poem" illustrated the situation of many of my respondents, who were indeed the bridge between their family members, between different communities of Color, and between different communities of Color and white communities. From an early age, they were compelled to juggle multiple social groups while still maintaining, in fact needing, a strong coherent individual self to prevent the relationships around them from colliding.

Social Identities: Believers, Workers, and Lovers

All individuals possess many social identities as they belong to multiple groups. However, social identities gain particular significance when they represent "master statuses" and when they are stigmatized. Race, social class, gender, and sexuality are the significant social identities that are considered master statuses, because individuals must psychologically negotiate their potential stigmatizing effects. In the United States, as in many other countries, master statuses are used to make value judgments about individuals' group memberships. In my interviews, I asked respondents about three areas related to significant social identities: their religious beliefs, their social class when they were growing up, and their views on mating and raising children.[3] These questions asked respondents to think about how their social identities (their religion and class, their identities as spouse, partner, and parent) affected their functioning "in the world."

In part 2 I begin each chapter with a poem that illustrates the issues covered in the chapter. Chicana feminist writers urge us to use the arts directly in our academic writings and analysis to present a holistic view of people's lives. For Chicanas/os (as well as other oppressed groups) who have had less access to the academy, poetry, song, and art have been the tools used to "theorize" their existence as well as to restore their sense of self. Art has salvaged Chicanas/os' humanity.

Chapter 4, "Believers," examines my respondents' and their families' religious beliefs. Chicana feminisms have integrated and critically assessed the importance of Catholicism in the cultural practices of Chicano communities. They have made important theoretical interventions by seeing religion not only as institution but also as cultural practice. In other words, many Chicanos grow up Catholic but do not necessarily attend church or abide by religious rules. Instead, Chicana feminists have examined the folk practice of religion in the form of noninstitutional worship of saints (Mora 1997), the integration of indigenous beliefs into everyday life, and the appropriation of religious symbols by Chicana artists to raise consciousness about gender and sexual issues in their communities. Chicana feminisms have also placed emphasis on the practice of noninstitutional religious beliefs to develop a spiritual framework for politically progressive work. Amalia Mesa-Bains constructs altars, not to honor the Catholic religion but to spotlight the importance of women artists and leaders; Gloria Anzaldúa recuperates indigenous beliefs and Aztec Goddesses to highlight the multiple channels of perception and knowledge available to Chicanas; and Ana Castillo compiled an anthology on La Virgen de Guadalupe to provide a comprehensive overview of the significance of her appropriation in Chicana feminist thought. My respondents resonated with these views of Catholicism and of other religions as they mostly considered themselves spiritual and believed in a higher power but did not practice according to religious dogma.

Chicana feminisms situate themselves squarely within a working-class experience, with special emphasis on the plight of farmworkers and other unskilled laborers. Many of the current writers came from working-class backgrounds and had families that participated in the annual ritual of leaving their homeland to harvest the crops in the U.S. Midwest, West, and South. Many of my respondents also resonated with this class background and readily identified themselves as having working-class origins. Chapter 5, "Workers," examines the intricacies of my respondents' class identifications to gauge how they affect their feminisms.

Chapter 6, "Lovers," looks at my respondents' views of themselves within romantic relationships. Chicana feminisms advocate a holistic approach to theorizing women's condition to include love, sex, and emotion. My respondents, regardless of sexual orientation, claimed their need for emotional support, family, and children. They also had specific demands for their romantic relationships and a clear view of the conditions under which they would marry. Almost without exception, my respondents wanted children and had resolved to have them with or without a partner.

Overall, my respondents had a clear sense of the significance of their social identities and how they operated in the world to facilitate or restrict their individual desires.

4

■   ■   ■   ■   ■   ■   ■   ■   ■

Believers

San Martín de Porras
Can I sing you, Brother Martin,
saint whose hands know work, like mine?
Would that we could sit together,
tell our cuentos, sip some wine.

Soon I'll close the church till morning.
Please guide me walking home alone.
Not a safe place for a woman.
Justice this old world postpones.

. . .

Bread you gave to those in hunger,
kindness to the child alone,
held the trembling hand that suffered,
kindness from a man disowned.

. . .

Brother Broom, with just a handshake,
you could cure a soul in pain.
Oh, I wish that you could touch me,
Make these old joints fresh again.

. . .

How we come, the dark-skinned faithful,
comforted to see you here,
able to confide our sorrows
to a black man's willing ear.   —Mora 1997

My *Virgen de Guadalupe* is not the mother of God. She is God. She is a
face for a god without a face, an *indígena* for a god without ethnicity, a
female deity for a god who is genderless, but I also understand that for
her to approach me, for me to finally open the door and accept her, she
had to be a woman like me.   —Cisneros 1996

CHICANA FEMINISMS do not deny or reject the Catholic undergirding of Chicano/Mexicano culture. Instead, Chicana feminists embrace
many Catholic rituals and practices to fulfill their spiritual needs. At the
same time, they have provided a powerful critique of the role of institu-
tionalized religion in women's oppression. Chicana feminists' dovetailing
in and of Catholicism aptly reflected my respondents' approach to religious beliefs and practice.

Religion as Cultural Practice

Strong values and a sense of morality characterize many of my respondents
and their families, which are largely attributable to their religious faith. The
majority of the respondents were raised as Catholic (67 percent), although
they were more culturally Catholic than practicing Catholics.[1] They were
baptized and took First Communion, but most were not confirmed, nor
did they attend church every Sunday or adhere to many of the church's restrictions. However, they felt a close affinity with the communal events
sponsored by their churches and attended mass on special holidays and
family occasions. Bianca referred to her practice of Catholicism as the
"mall approach" to religion.[2]

I grew up Catholic, but now I consider myself as religious as I am like a shop-
per. I go to church and to the mall to the same degree. I only go to church

for holidays, baptisms, anniversaries, or weddings. I go to the mall to buy gifts for the weddings, to buy gifts for birthdays, or because there's a big sale on Christmas, Easter, or Thanksgiving.

In spite of Bianca's practical approach to religion, she still felt a deep spiritual connection with the church, modifying it to meet her own emotional needs. When she became pregnant she made "a commitment to attend mass for an entire year" and she "stuck to it."

I felt I needed religion in my life again when I got pregnant. Phillip [her fiancé and the father of her child] comes from a very religious family. His mom wanted me to walk down the aisle six months pregnant and I'm like, "No, I don't think so." But they're very religious. My fiancé's mom is a member of the Catholic Daughters [a women's organization within the church in Bernalillo, New Mexico] and they read at church. They used to be the *mayordomos* [foremen] of the church so we go to church with them on special occasions. Phillip doesn't push church on me, whereas I think he was raised in a more religious family than I was.

Bianca still had a critical perspective on Catholicism, as she had a "major conflict with priests. I think women should be allowed to be priests. I don't think that I need to confess to a man in a box. I can talk to God directly." The only reason she still attended church occasionally was that she "liked to sing in Spanish. [*Laughter.*] I can practice my Spanish at Spanish mass and I love it." At the same time, Bianca stated, "I'm not disrespectful of the church, so although I don't feel like I can fully participate in prayer or in the entire mass, I'll be quiet. Sometimes I won't say a prayer unless I feel like it. So if my fiancé's parents invite us to mass, I'll go out of respect for them and out of respect for the values that are somewhere deep inside me." She concluded, "That's the role that religion has in my life; when I'm feeling bad or when I need that safety net, it's there."

Like Bianca, many respondents saw participation in religion not only as spiritual practice but also as cultural expression. They valued rituals in the Catholic Church that made use of Spanish and allowed them to enjoy the company of other "Mexicans." Several respondents prayed or attended mass only in Spanish, because otherwise they did not feel they belonged in the church. Tomasa "loved going to church, but only Spanish masses. I disliked English masses. But my Spanish masses . . . the music, like, everybody sings. Oh, it's just beautiful."[3]

Similarly, Irma Martínez, who was living in the Washington, D.C., area at the time of the interview, did not consider herself "a devout Catholic" but rather saw her participation in religion as a cultural practice that she hoped to instill in her future children.[4]

> I don't go to mass every Sunday but when I do, it definitely gives me a sense of *paz* [peace]. It's a very familiar place because when I was growing up I went every Sunday. [*Laughter.*] My mother is very religious. When I go home to Los Angeles, I go with her, which I actually enjoy. I think it's more cultural because it's what I knew growing up—something that I could do with my family, my mother, my *madrina* [godmother]. I told my boyfriend that if we have children, I wanted them to go to church. So I guess I am religious, but I'm definitely not a devout Catholic.

Religion as Devotion and Spirituality

The majority of the respondents' families were religious but not consistent in practicing many of Catholicism's organized rituals. They participated in their own personalized way and adapted the rituals to their daily lives. For example, many of the respondents and their families expressed devotion to the patron saint of Mexico, la Virgen de Guadalupe. La Virgen, as most Chicanos and Mexicanos refer to her, is the protector of the downtrodden and is "a fusion of Aztec, indigenous Catholic, and folkloric world traditions, who made her first miraculous appearance on American soil in 1531" (Castillo 1996, book jacket). Respondents and their families expressed their dedication to La Virgen and had personal rituals to demonstrate their commitment. Tomasa recalled that her father routinely stayed after Catholic mass to spend a few moments alone with La Virgen:

> My father has this unbelievable love toward La Virgen. Of course the whole family does. For him, it's like, "*Esta ofrenda es para Lupita.*" [This offering is for Lupita.][5] I remember when we went to church, the mass would end and my father would say, "*Me esperan aquí*" [Wait for me here], and he'd go

to the front to La Virgen's altar and he'd sit there and he'd talk to her. For
him, La Virgen is almighty and great.

A minority of respondents' families were extremely religious in the traditional sense of attending religious services and following the church's
rules. The more common pattern was for one individual in the family to
be extremely religious, usually the mother, but in certain families it was the
father. They in turn influenced the entire family. However, Catholicism
was very important to many of my respondents as an avenue to spirituality
in general. For example, although Tomasa's father was devoted to La Virgen, she did not consider him religious in comparison to her mother. According to Tomasa, "My mom is unbelievably religious. She takes her
rosary and Bible to work.[6] Maybe that's one of the reasons I think she's so
strong. She has undying faith in God and her religion."

Several spoke about attending different churches, some Catholic, others not, when they moved away from home to cultivate a spiritual life. Valerie, who considered herself "spiritual more than religious," attended
Catholic school at her mother's insistence, although her father did not
agree with the decision.[7]

> My dad wanted us to be streetwise because he was like a *cholo*.[8] So he
> thought we should go to public school. And my mom was like, "No! I want
> something better." That was always the debate. The only reason my mother
> worked was to pay for the tuition, because my dad didn't want to pay for
> Catholic school. Even until this day, my little brother just graduated eighth
> grade and my mom was fighting with my dad to enroll him in a Catholic
> high school, but it's so much money. It's impossible now.

Ironically, although Valerie's mom made enormous sacrifices to send her
to Catholic school and Valerie fully appreciated it, she recounted with a
laugh that her mother "got a bad deal," because all her hard work to pay
thousands of dollars in tuition "had gone to hell." In spite of Valerie's religious upbringing, she had developed "such a critique of Catholicism and
I think my husband joins me in that so it makes it harder to go to church."
Instead of attending one particular church, Valerie and her husband followed

this one priest who's very atypical. He's what I think the Catholic Church should be. He talks about AIDS; he talks about the war. My brother was in Desert Storm and that's what really got my mom turned on to him. Now we travel to try to find him wherever he goes, because the good ones they always ship them out. Right? So we found him and we go when he's giving mass, because his sermons are so simple and yet so great and I cry through them. I think that spirituality is more than Catholic practices. For example, the Catholic Church is anti-homosexuality; I have a problem with that and other things as well. So I can't say attending mass is a religious commitment, because I'm not affiliated. My commitment is not in the traditional sense of religion. But my husband and I try to pray at least three or four times a week.

Valerie and her husband decided to marry outside the Catholic Church because of their intense ambivalence toward it.

I didn't want to be a hypocrite. So we wanted that one priest [described above] but in an outdoor ceremony. He couldn't do it because of the archdiocese and their rules that he has to be inside a Catholic church. So we got married by a minister because we wanted to have some religious figure there to make it a more spiritual ceremony.

Both families were scandalized by Valerie's and her husband's decision to have such an unconventional wedding. In Valerie's case it "was an issue with my family," because they could not believe the wedding did not include the Catholic ritual of dispensing Communion. Her family kept asking, "There is no Host?"[9] They kept repeating to her, "You know, you're supposed to get the Host when you have a wedding."

Religion as Solace and Inspiration

Many of my respondents were made to attend religious services as children and recalled not having quite understood the significance of the rituals. Tomasa remembered, "We would go to church every Sunday and, at first, like any other kid, you start falling asleep and your mom taps you, '*Despiertate!*' [Wake up!] So I never really saw any importance in church other than to fall asleep and take a nap." As adults, especially in times of crises, these same respondents used religion as a source of solace. Tomasa had recently gone through a difficult breakup with her long-term boyfriend. She had found refuge in prayer as a way to cope with her loss.

> This year I've been through a lot and I've been depressed. So I felt a need to talk to God, which I actually do at night. I pray every night and I don't really go to church that often now because of school, but I make sure to pray. For me, you don't necessarily have to be inside the church to speak to God.

Religion was also a source of strength for many of the respondents' parents, helping them cope with the vicissitudes of their lives and find inspiration for pursuing their goals. Hilda's mother's Catholic religion provided spiritual support while she pursued a college degree, worked full-time, and raised her children by herself.[10]

> I remember when I was growing up we lived in a little town called Puerto Vaca [Texas], and my mom had just finished junior college. She became a dental hygienist and she started working. It was just me, my brother, and my mother. She really got involved in a charismatic type of Catholic movement that was going on at the time. Me and my brother thought that was so strange and so silly. We were singing and clapping our hands and laying hands on each other.

Hilda's mother's religious commitment helped her pursue a master's degree "in psychology and philosophy at Our Lady of the Lake [a Catholic college]. She goes on weekends." Her mother was thinking of continuing her education and pursuing a "Ph.D. in psychology or maybe in law."

At times, family traumas could serve either to make family members find even more solace in religion or turn away from it because they felt abandoned by God. Blanca Gordo's mother "was really into church," especially "liberation theology."[11] Blanca considered her mother an activist "who got the Spanish mass to be instituted" in their local parish in Los Angeles. She stood up to "the monsignor." She told him, "You can't treat Latinos the same way you treat the rich English-speaking population." Blanca's mother continued to explain the differences between the two populations of parishioners: "You can't expect Latinos to come to church events and restrict them from coming with their children. They can't afford baby-sitting. And even if they did, they are not going to do it. It's just culturally different." As part of her participation in her church, Blanca's mother was also very "involved in the community." Her mother tried to live by her Catholic principles and participated with organizations "to feed the poor at the Plaza Olvera [in Los Angeles] where there's a lot of undocumented people." Blanca's mother fell ill with cancer when Blanca was an undergraduate at the University of California, Los Angeles. Her mother had a very painful death. "When my mom passed away and when my aunt passed away is when I really changed my closeness to God. I went through this stage where I was really furious at God. Here is my mom who went to church, was thankful for everything in her life, and a model Samaritan, she acted like she was supposed to be a saint or something." Blanca had directly witnessed her mother's decline. "My mom died a very painful death. I was with her all along. I was one of her caretakers. And I was really angry. So I think ever since then I rejected God because I felt like what good did it do her."

On the other hand, Nina A. Perales, whose mother was Catholic and whose father was Presbyterian, started out in early childhood by attending Catholic "church because I thought it was more traditional and that was kinda cool. Everyone's standing up and singing and I liked the rosary."[12] However, after her father

> got into a really bad car accident from drinking and driving when I was about five, he's been very, very religious. Always going to church, and so he always made me go to church. I got grounded if I didn't go to church with him. I'd get so mad 'cause my mom and my sisters didn't go to church.

At the end, however, Nina appreciated having her Presbyterian religious background: "But now I like to go to church but only when I'm home in Austin [Texas]. I feel like that's my church, those are my people—what I consider my religion. I like to go to my church because it's Spanish and it's all a Latino community." Magdalena, the other respondent in the focus group, chimed in, "It's just the culture behind it, I think, and you get attached to it." "Exactly," Nina said.

> So when I can't find that same feeling somewhere else I can still be religious. I can still be faithful on my own without having to go to church. Religion really does affect me. I feel peaceful after I pray at night, and I can't go to

bed without praying either. Even if it's just like, "Thank you, Lord, for letting me get through this day. I'm really tired. Good night." It's really comforting and I'm glad that my dad did give me that push and made me go to church.

While most respondents were at least nominally Catholic, some belonged to other religions or had experiences with other religions. Sandra Saenz, who did not consider herself religious, "was baptized, I had my First Communion, I had my *quinceañera*, everything Catholic but we were never actually Catholic."[13] Her family became Jehovah's Witnesses when Sandra's father was incarcerated in Mexico, because "the only way my mom could control her five children was to bring religion into the home. And it was nice. But I think I was twelve when I decided that I didn't want to study the Bible anymore." Sandra felt she learned from being a Jehovah's Witness, but the restrictions and the time it took away from studying made her decide ultimately to leave it. Sandra "didn't like the fact that there were so many prohibitions—the kinds of clothes that you can wear, the kind of stuff that you can study at school. I wanted to study psychology, and it was not one of the approved subjects because it conflicts with God. I just wasn't happy." She told her mother, "No, I'm not going to study the Bible. I have too much homework."

Unlike some other respondents who returned to Catholicism as adults, Sandra felt alienated from organized religion. "Ever since I left the Jehovah's Witnesses, I haven't been into a religion." However, Sandra still followed some of the moral tenets of her religions and "prayed every single night." Although she never went to church, "when things go wrong I always pray to God and ask for help. So in that sense I do believe that there's someone or something out there. There is a force in nature that has to keep some balance in life." Sandra also did not rule out the possibility of instilling at least the cultural aspects of Catholicism in her future children.

Religion as Community

Respondents who did not live in predominantly Latino communities tended to see Catholic religious practice as a way to connect with other Latinos.[14] Many times congregating with other Latinos led respondents to mobilize politically around social issues affecting their communities. In this case, the practice of Catholicism created a sense of "common fate" (Lewin 1948), which then led to group political action. For example, Gloria grew up in Battle Creek, Michigan, which did not have a large Mexican population.[15] According to Gloria, the only time she saw other Mexicans was when she attended Catholic services. Even though her mother was skeptical of the Catholic Church, a skepticism that Gloria incorporated into her own assessment of organized religion, she still saw the Catholic Church as having enormous potential for organizing the "Latino community."

> I consider myself very Catholic. But like all things in our life, everything's up for debate. So my mom would always tell me, "You should believe in God but realize that the Bible was written by a bunch of men, and men just want to keep women down so you don't have to believe everything the priest tells you." So there was always this arbitrary sort of religion. We went to church every Saturday. But it was more like there were no other Mexicans in town other than at church. So it was the only time I saw other Hispanic people. For me it's very much a cultural thing and it was also a migrant parish. So we had a priest that would come in and do the regular mass and then they'd go out to the labor camps. It was more of a religion of trying to improve the life of this very impoverished community. Some Catholic churches I walk in, I'm like, this is not the Catholic Church I know. It was always very much about improving your life, treating your wife with respect, being nice to your children, and encouraging education.

Gloria used her Catholicism to dovetail into her political activism as she saw the Catholic Church as a site to organize around issues of social justice.

> I'm very active in my community as well, and I really see the church as a way to reach the Latino community, especially in the Midwest. It's the one place—if you're organizing something, that's where you're going to go. I see the church within our community as a vehicle to improve our lives; if you're committed to our cause, you will always be involved in the church.

Lucha as Believer

Lucha was baptized Catholic before she and her siblings were placed in foster homes. After that, their religious upbringing varied according to the foster family they were living with. According to Lucha, "I definitely went through so many different religions." One particular foster family Lucha remembered was very "Christian—out of control strict!" When Lucha and her sister lived with them, the family insisted that they join a children's group called Primroses. The foster family closely monitored everything Lucha and her sister did and wore. This experience made Lucha question religion and the notion that individuals were either entirely "bad" or entirely "good" depending on whether or not they accepted Christ in their lives. Lucha felt there had to be some in-between and that nothing could be all bad or all good.

When Lucha was sixteen, she and her sister became emancipated from their adoptive parents and they lived with various friends and eventually went to college (see chapter 2). Lucha attended church occasionally with her friends and enjoyed the services. Then she became seriously involved with a boyfriend who was Jewish and was engaged for a year. She began the process of converting to Judaism before the wedding, and although she and her fiancé broke off the wedding, Lucha continued the process of conversion, because she found spiritual fulfillment in becoming a Jew.

Regardless of her religious trajectory, Lucha felt that she was religious and that it was "through education that I really started questioning religion and tried to find my own way with it." Throughout her life she always "felt that there was a God. I felt that God was watching over me and Fuerza." Even though Lucha and her sister's lives have been difficult, she never "asked God for anything." Instead she "thanked him for giving me a great life. I'm right here." Lucha felt that the God she believed in was more understanding than the one she had encountered in her foster homes, so that although she "always prayed," she "didn't feel guilty if I forget because I feel like God's cool."

5

■　　■　　■　　■　　■　　■　　■　　■　　■

Workers

"Woman" of Color

> I have stepped
> > Outside of my robes
> > > Of femininity
> I have clenched around my body
> > for so long
>
> Because I wanted
> > *Machos* to be *machos*
> > and *hembras* to be *hembras*
>
> I wanted to raise Chicanos
> > to change the world
>
> I wanted my womb
> > to be the place of revolution
>
> But I was a woman to no one
> > > But myself
> > to the world I was
> > > a beast of burden
>
> So, slowly, very slowly, *cuidadosamente*
> > I let go.

—Hurtado 1990

A RECENT STUDY by the American Association of University Women Educational Foundation made national headlines as it documented that Hispanic women and men had the highest dropout rate from high school (30 percent) in comparison to Blacks (11.1 percent for males and 12.9 percent for females) and whites (9.0 percent for males and 8.2 percent for females).[1] Newspapers attributed the high dropout rates of Latinas to "cultural values."

> Schools must do more to recognize cultural values that saddle Hispanic girls with family responsibilities, such as caring for younger siblings after school, that take away from educational endeavors. . . . "Many Latinas face pressure about going to college from boyfriends and fiances who expect their girl-friends or future wives not to be 'too educated' and from peers who accuse them of 'acting white' when they attempt to become better educated or spend time on academics," the study said. (Gamboa 2001, 1A)

The reports of this study failed to mention or recognize in their analysis of Latinas' "school failure" the poverty conditions many families live in, the inferior school facilities, the overcrowded classrooms, the inferior teaching in many minority schools, and the constant threat of violence many poor students have to negotiate on a daily basis. By relying on a cultural explanation for the school failure of Latinas, the reports appearing in newspapers fell prey to what the anthropologist Virginia Dominguez (1992) calls "culturalism," that is, overrelying on "cultural" factors in attributing causation and ignoring other equally powerful structural influences like poverty on Latinas' behavior. Chicana feminisms avoided the pitfalls of culturalism by examining Chicanas' lives from a standpoint of intersectionality. That is, Chicanas' lived experience is a product of their stigmatized multiple group memberships that operate *simultaneously* in the world to produce negative outcomes. Chicana feminisms were influenced by the Chicano movement, which had a strong Marxist undergirding. As such, the feminisms developed by Chicanas were deeply rooted in the material conditions of Chicanos as a whole. Chicanos became U.S. residents either through conquest after the Mexican American War or as a result of unskilled and semiskilled labor migration from Mexico. Chicana feminisms assert that social class is as important as gender, race, ethnicity, and sexuality; all of these factors contribute to negative social economic out-comes in their communities.

My respondents had a complex view of their social class standing in this country. They were deeply aware of where they stood on the economic ladder, as many saw their parents work endless hours in ill-paid jobs with few benefits. They also made very nuanced judgments of their class stand-ing *in relationship* to others around them. When these "others" changed, as they inevitably did when they moved from their mostly segregated neighborhoods to more affluent communities when they moved away to college, they accordingly reassessed their class standing. Overall, however, most did not feel "deprived" or "disadvantaged" by the fact that they had grown up in what most would consider poverty conditions.

Social Class

A large number of my respondents' parents had less than a high school ed-ucation and had working-class occupations: factory workers, farmworkers, housekeepers, secretaries, receptionists, and pattern makers (66 percent of the working mothers and 61 percent of the working fathers). Many of my respondents spoke eloquently of the economic hardships they and their families had endured. Of the parents who had college educations and pro-fessional jobs (26 percent of the working mothers and 27 percent of the working fathers), most were the first in their families to achieve this level of economic and educational achievement.

There were no respondents who came from several generations of wealth. The most educated and highest-income respondents had parents with advanced doctoral and law degrees, which gave both parents a rela-tively high income. In these instances, according to standards in the United States, they could be considered solidly middle-class. There was only one respondent whose father, although he had never finished grade school in Mexico, had become a "millionaire" through his entrepreneurship.

Social Comparison
in the Construction of Social Class

Class assessments did not depend solely on education or income levels. Most respondents made relational judgments about their class backgrounds based on what others around them had or did not have. Claudia Rodriguez, who was living with her parents while she was completing her undergraduate degree in communications at the University of Illinois in Chicago, asserted with assurance that her family, which consisted of her parents and her brother, was middle-class.[2] This was a rare response, so I was interested to hear what her parents did for a living. When I asked about her parents' occupations, she replied, "My mom works labor, at a factory where they make parts for automobiles. Since my dad got to the United States he has been working at a meatpacking plant for almost twenty-five years." I did not understand how, given their occupations, Claudia categorized her parents as middle-class, until she stated, "I think what has gotten us to be middle-class is the overtime!"

Patricia Alvarez also considered herself middle-class because everybody in her family was working, although her "mother does not earn much at all working at Jay's Potato Chips in a factory packing chips and my dad also works at a packing company."[3] Like Patricia, many respondents saw their class status drop dramatically from "solidly middle-class" to "working-class" to "poor" depending on layoffs and the number of family members who were working at any one point. Patricia, for example, stated, "Dad's gone from one meatpacking company to another. A lot of them started closing down and he would jump from one job to the next. When we were smaller, of course, I would have definitely considered us probably working-class."

Many respondents' fathers safeguarded their families from economic instability by always keeping a second job on the side that they stepped up during hard times. These jobs were kept alive as an economic safety net even when they worked full-time. When Patricia's father "didn't have a regular job, he'd just spend more time in the garage fixing transmissions," although when "he had a regular job," he still "came home and went into the garage and fixed transmissions," but not as many.

My respondents did not define belonging to the middle-class necessarily by their parents' income, the prestige of their parents' jobs, or the number of years of education their parents had, but rather by job stability and job security. Carolina thought of herself and her family as middle-class.[4]

I thought I was middle-class until I got to college and then realized we weren't. I just figured, compared to East L.A. [Los Angeles], we were middle-class. We moved from East L.A. to a suburb of Los Angeles when I was five. My father's a truck driver and he graduated from high school. My mother also graduated from high school and she's a secretary. My father has always been lucky enough to have very good union jobs, so there was rarely a time where money was wanting because they made enough. They bought their house in 1972, so their mortgage is like $230. I always had this middle-class mentality. But now I say that I'm from a working-class background.

Home ownership contributed to my respondents' families' sense of economic stability. As Carolina indicates above, owning their homes meant that they had passed the threshold from "working-class" to "middle-class."

Alicia Granillo claimed middle-class status on grounds similar to Carolina's.[5] "It's funny because I always said I was middle-class too," because "my mother's a property owner," although "we always took the bus everywhere!" Alicia continued,

When I was born, my mother took me home from the hospital on the bus. [They lived in East Los Angeles.] And I always thought I was middle-class. I think it was relative because you compare yourself to other kids at school and the people renting our garage. So you're like, "Woo-hoo! I'm rich!" But now I realize that we were pretty poor.

Alicia's mother had immigrated to Los Angeles from Durango, Mexico, in 1970 with four children; she eventually became pregnant with Alicia. Her father was a farmworker. Her parents separated later and her mother and Alicia, who was fifteen at the time, moved to Las Vegas. Her other siblings were already grown. Alicia's mother was very frugal and had an entrepreneurial spirit. She had the foresight to buy small properties that she rented to other large Mexican immigrant families (even at times renting her garage).

It's funny because now I realize that we were poor. Maybe between working-class and poor. There was not really any profit from renting my mom's properties, because we just broke even to pay the mortgage. It goes back to my mom's experience about providing the opportunity for other people that they didn't provide to her when she first arrived to the United States. Now she's sixty-five and she still wants to work. The last job she had was as a dish-washer at a casino [in Las Vegas]. It's funny because at Harvard [which Alicia was attending at the time of the interview], people are talking about their parents, "My mom's a professor or teacher," even a teacher's assistant or truck driver. It's like, "Oh, my mom's a dishwasher," because she doesn't have the language skills.

Regardless of these relational judgments in defining social class, respondents had been aware of their parents' economic hardships since they were children. Rita recalled that even as "a little kid [I was] so conscious about the lack of money, that I never straight up asked for a toy. I would just hint by saying, 'Wow, this is really nice!' But I would never ask for anything directly."[6]

As children, some respondents had felt that their parents' working-class origins were a source of embarrassment, especially if they had to tell others about their parents' jobs. However, not a single respondent still held these feelings of ambivalence toward their class origins. Instead, they were very proud of how much their families had accomplished, especially when they started with so little. For example, Tomasa's early feelings of embarrassment at her parents' occupations turned to deep-seated pride as she grew older and understood the full range of their sacrifices.[7]

My mom was born in a little *ranchito* (ranch) and they were very very poor. She only completed fifth grade in Mexico. When she was ten years old, she had to start working as a live-in servant for a rich family to give money to her family. She had this little dark hole of a room that she slept in. My mother might not be the most educated person, but I think she's a very wise person in life experience. I am proud of her. I don't see her and think I'm ashamed to be her daughter. Maybe when I was small and people would ask me, "Oh, what do your parents do?" I was in a sense, not ashamed, but I didn't like people to know that my mom was a janitor at a bank or that my father was an elevator operator. It was not so much shame but just embarrassment. Now, I want everybody to know what they do and what they have accomplished. They raised three children. Two already graduated from college. I'm almost finished with college. They struggled so much in life, especially when we were little, and look at what they gave us. It's great and I'm proud of them. But when you're small, you don't see it that way, you know?

Tomasa's family had attained a certain amount of economic stability with the purchase of their home. They no longer struggled to pay the "$700 a month mortgage," because "my sister has a real job and so does my brother." But Tomasa recognized that "when we were young, dang we struggled just to put food on the table."

Precarious Economic Lives

Many respondents spoke with great emotion about the economic instability suffered by their parents. Many told stories of parents who worked as many as twenty-five years in factories and at other unskilled jobs only to find out unexpectedly that they had been "downsized." Many of these parents did not have retirement or medical benefits and spent the last years of their lives seeking other employment. Irma Martínez recalled with tears in her eyes that her father collapsed after he tried to go back and work in the farm fields when all other avenues had been closed to him because of his age and his lack of formal skills.[8]

> He worked as assembly line worker, air conditioner installer, and he lost that job in April of '82 because the company moved to Ohio. Since '82 he just struggled endlessly, never getting a permanent job. For a long time when he was younger, he worked in the fields in California and Texas. He tried that again but couldn't do it. My father was not lazy. He just couldn't. He literally collapsed the last time he tried it. He was over fifty [*begins crying*], but he tried.

Irma continued with rancor in her voice, "That's what makes me mad about us Mexicans. We think that by working our asses off we are going to make progress and that's not the way!" Irma felt that instead of working oneself to death, as her father had, the key to securing an economic future was to go to school—a fact lost, in her opinion, on many in her extended family and in her community. Irma's mother held the family together after Irma's father died prematurely: "My mom continued to work in an elementary school cafeteria although now she's about to retire. She'll be sixty-seven this year."

Carina García Guzmán also spoke about her family's struggles to survive in South Texas on a farmworker's income of $3,000 a year for a family of seven.[9]

> We were migrant workers so the only thing we ever had was a truck, which was what we needed to get from place to place. But we never owned a house, we just stayed with whoever we knew in whatever town we were in.[10] I remember missing school because we couldn't afford shoes, and staying home the day there was supposed to be a field trip because we didn't have five dollars to pay for it. I never did any of the school events because of money.

Carina's father left, or, more accurately, was thrown out by Carina's mother, after she found out that he had been sexually abusing Carina and her sisters. Her mother had to go "on government aid." Carina still had one brother who was under eighteen. "Christy [her sister] is working and sends my mom a couple hundred every month. With that, my mom buys my brother school clothes."

Single Mothering

The economic position of single mothers, often raising sizable numbers of children and helping extended kin, was very difficult. In my sample, there were 17 percent of the respondents who were raised by single mothers. Most were unskilled workers (twelve single mothers), although a few (three single mothers) had obtained college degrees. Rosa Lazo's mother often had two jobs after she was left to raise her daughter by herself, because shortly after the divorce, her "dad went out of the picture completely, although he was rarely there, even when he was married to my mother."[11] According to Rosa, "Our economic situation kept changing from bad to worse. But my mom and I always came through, because she would do whatever was necessary." Rosa's mother had only gone to "fourth grade in Mexico," and had started working at age fourteen in "*los cines*" (the movies). Rosa's mother's early experience working helped her cope when Rosa's father left and never paid child support. "My mom has done everything. She's been a seamstress, an *avañil* [construction worker]—you name it. Right now she is a cook at the Patio Café [a local

Mexican restaurant]." Rosa recognized that her mother "has always taken care of us. It wasn't that plentiful but we got by."

Relatively Undeprived Children

In spite of the precarious economic situation of her family, Guadalupe echoed many of my respondents' assertions that they never felt "disadvantaged" or "deprived."[12] Guadalupe stated that although money was so tight for her family that her parents and her five unmarried siblings lived in a one-bedroom mobile home, she never felt "poor."

> My parents have always worked in the fields during the season or *florerías* [greenhouses where flowers are grown] in the off season. They have no savings or extra money. But I never realized we were poor, because we've been low but we always had food and a roof over our heads. We didn't have toys or anything, but my mom is the greatest. She always made up for everything. I don't know where she got food, but she always had food. She always made flour tortillas every day because we couldn't afford to buy them. Regarding toys, she would just play marbles with us or anything. I didn't realize how deprived we were until you go out and start comparing yourself with other people. But still, I don't feel deprived in any way in regard to food or toys or anything, although we didn't have very much, really. [*Laughs.*]

Guadalupe continued by describing her family's cramped living situation.

> We lived in a one-bedroom mobile home. It was with all of us [her siblings]. My parents slept in an unfolding couch and then there was a bed next to it so it would turn into a whole huge bed. [*Laughs.*] Between the bed and the couch, it was my parents and my little sister, myself, and my other sister. The two guys, they slept out in the living room. But yeah, there were a lot [of us].

Aside from her mother's efforts to make Guadalupe and her family feel loved and taken care of, another reason Guadalupe did not feel deprived was that she started working at the age of twelve as a maid in a local hotel. She continued to work throughout her adolescence in various jobs. "I always worked so I always had my own money. I guess that's why I didn't feel deprived. I bought my own clothes."

Maritza C. Resendez remembered with amusement how she thought the way people lived and worked in her neighborhood was the way everybody lived.[13] She was surprised at the extraordinary wealth she encountered when she left the Los Angeles area to attend college at the University of California, Santa Cruz, in the northern part of the state.

> It's funny how you don't realize how deprived you are until you see how others live. I remember seeing my parents and all the people in my community, like our neighbors, waking up at five in the morning to be at work by six, and thinking it was like that for everybody. It wasn't until I came to Santa Cruz and saw the differences. I saw how people take time to have lunch and go out to eat at some café. I'm thinking, aren't they supposed to be at work? I thought everyone woke up in the morning to be at work at six. That was my reality.

Although most respondents readily recognized their families' economic hardships, even at an early age, they simultaneously felt that being poor did not necessarily imply being "less than rich people" or "being less than white people." Irma Martínez, who "grew up in housing projects" in Los Angeles, found out when she went to Princeton that she "was categorized as disadvantaged. But I never felt disadvantaged. Looking back, yes, we didn't have lots of things other people did, but I never felt disadvantaged."

Contrary to the research literature, which emphasizes the negative internalization of the stigma of being poor, many of my respondents did not perceive themselves as hampered by their economic background. On the contrary, they very much preferred the communities and values they grew up with. Carina García Guzmán could not believe the contrast between the way she grew up as a poor migrant worker in South Texas and what she encountered when she went to Colorado College, a private elite liberal arts college in Colorado Springs.

> We're still poor compared to some people, but I never thought we had it that bad growing up. I always thought, we're doing really well. And compared to everybody else where I went to school [Elsa, Texas] it's all migrant, so among all of my friends, we were doing about average. Then getting to CC [Colorado College], oh my gosh! Students just write a $100,000 check and give it to the school to pay for four years of tuition.[14]

Many respondents also felt that white students were spoiled and very unappreciative of their economic resources, often creating confusion and "messed up values." Respondents felt that their own upbringings, in which family and community were so valued, were superior to most white students'. The majority of respondents felt that their families, as complicated as they were, did not lack anything in comparison to their white peers. Carina expressed this passionately:

> Coming to CC [Colorado College] I've learned that that's not the life I want. I really miss my life at home, I really do. I really miss having your neighbors to count on and all of you sharing. If you know of a little kid that needs a pair of shoes, we all pitched in for them. And everyone here is so self-centered: "Only if you're my family do I care." I really don't like that. I like the communal way of living.

The Tolls of Poverty

Regardless of their positive views of their families and communities, being poor took a definite toll in my respondents' lives. Maritza C. Resendez described how hard her parents' life had been in the United States. In fact, she came from a long line of cross-border workers that started when her grandfather joined the Bracero Program in the 1950s.[15]

> I always remember my mom and dad working real hard, having to leave early in the morning. It's sad because my mom has been working in the same factory for twenty-five years as a sewing machine operator and uses her vision a lot to make quilts and bedspreads. She's diabetic and has arthritis. A lot of the arm movement is really repetitive and it tires her out. She only gets paid six something an hour. My dad is a painter. So they've just worked real hard all their lives. I remember when I was little saying, "When I grow up I'm gonna be rich and I'm gonna buy you guys a house and you won't have to work anymore."

In fact, after Maritza described her parents, it was startling to find out that her mother was only forty-six and that her father had only recently turned forty-three.

It was not unusual for respondents to describe their parents as if they were much older than their actual ages. (Most parents were in their forties.) The parents' premature aging could be the result of the combination of the stress caused by their economic lives and physically demanding jobs. Respondents spoke often of the physical toll that, at times, resulted in premature death—mostly by heart attacks and cancer—or in disabilities due to accidents on the job. Some of my respondents' parents were forced into early retirement because of ill health or physical disabilities with few, if any, sources of income. Another reason many respondents saw their parents as old was the fact that many of them did not have an education or a career. Whereas most professionals spend their twenties obtaining degrees and their thirties building their careers, by the time they reach their forties they have just hit their stride. In comparison, these working-class parents were most economically viable when they were young and could work long hours and hold multiple jobs. As they grew older, their bodies no longer were as physically strong and their children, whom they had at a relatively young age, were grown and gone. It was surprising to hear some of my respondents, whose mothers were in their late thirties and whose fathers were in their early forties, refer to them as if their lives were over.

Economic Adjustments

Many of my respondents' families made attempts to offset financial difficulties by creatively pooling their resources. A number of respondents (23 percent) lived at home with their parents and helped with the family expenses. However, there was enormous flexibility in this arrangement. Rarely was there a set agreement about how respondents contributed to the household. The most common way was for respondents to live at home while they were attending school and use their earnings to pay for their schooling.

In a few rare instances, families were under such economic duress that respondents lived with their families while they attended institutions of higher education and gave their families the money they would otherwise spend on living expenses. This was more likely to occur in single-parent households. For example, Agustina received a high level of financial support from the University of Chicago, mostly in the form of academic scholarships that she directly contributed to the family because her mother was a single parent.[16]

> I was born and raised in the Little Village [a large Mexican neighborhood in Chicago] and in the summertime, four, five months out of the year, my mom works at this ice cream shop—taking care of it and ordering stuff. In the winter, she's at home 'cause my parents divorced when I was thirteen. We took my father to court so we had child support and alimony checks coming in every week. Thank God! So we basically lived out of that and plus everyone works. My brother works, I work, my other brother works, so we pitch in money here and there. Then I got scholarships for college so I have $3,000 dollars coming in. I call it *mi papi* [my daddy]. It's like the check from my dad. [*Laughter.*]

Other respondents helped their parents once they graduated and started working. Guadalupe surprised her mother with a gift of $300 when her mother returned from her yearly trip to Mexico. Her mother was both surprised and grateful and promptly proceeded to pay bills with the extra money. Guadalupe was not unusual in fearing that her parents were "not going to be there after I'm finally settled to help them. My mom's fifty-six and my dad is fifty-seven, but they feel tired because they have worked in the fields all their lives."

Irma Martínez's sister, Adriana, graduated with a bachelor's degree from Stanford University, worked in Washington, D.C., for a couple of years, then returned to Los Angeles to work and help her mother buy the first house her family had ever owned.

> Last November Adriana and my mother bought a house. My mother finally moved out of the projects to West Covina. The other day I talked to Adriana, and she said, "My mom spoils me. Every day *me tiene cena*!" [She has dinner for me!] I'm like, that's the way it should be. My mother is happy doing that. Adriana is working in L.A. [Los Angeles] for a public relations firm. She's living with my mother until she applies to business school at UCLA.

Families had to make various economic adjustments to survive. Sometimes the responsibility for managing the finances shifted from one family member to another. In some instances, the mothers started out trusting their husbands to run the household income, only to find out they were in trouble. Zulma Rodriguez asked her mother why she and Zulma's father did not have a joint banking account.[17] According to Zulma,

> After arriving in the United States, she always gave her paycheck to my fa-
> ther. They were saving to buy a house, the whole big American dream. A
> year had gone by. One day my mom got home early from work and she
> found the checkbook. She opened it and there was only five hundred dollars
> in the account! My mom wanted to cry 'cause she was like, Where did all this
> money go? She didn't tell my dad that she saw the checkbook and my father
> goes, "Where's your check?" 'cause it was Friday and she got paid. My mom
> goes, "I'm not giving you the check until you show me the checkbook." And
> that was that. My mom never gave him money from then on. So now my
> mom has her own account and my dad has his own account. But when they
> want to do something together, like the house that we live in, they bought
> it together. They each paid half.

Respondents' mothers often decided to work outside the home, no matter how humble the jobs, to have control over their earnings. Many felt that earning their own income entitled them to make decisions independently of their husbands. Gloria's mother worked "in the schools as a classroom assistant." Prior to these jobs, when Gloria and her siblings were young, "she cleaned different teachers' houses on weekends, worked as a waitress, and took care of people's children." Gloria felt that her mother had "always had a very strong work ethic and thought it was very important to have her own money without having to go through my dad for getting money."[18]

It was not uncommon for my respondents to state either that their mothers controlled all household spending or that when their mothers worked, whatever they earned was under their absolute control. Of course, much of what they earned went to their children or to pay for household expenses, but it was the ability to control how resources were spent without having to consult their husbands that was extremely important to respondents' mothers.

Respondents' parents also made economic adjustments by following jobs wherever they could get them. Many respondents spoke about their parents' loyalty to their employers and their work ethic, which included not missing work even when they were ill or had family emergencies. Their loyalty did not always pay off, as many saw jobs disappear as a result of company relocations or downsizing, which forced them to move, sometimes across the country, to find employment.

Entrepreneurial Spirit

Aside from the economic adjustments these families made, many also had an entrepreneurial spirit that helped them survive and, in a few instances, even thrive economically. Maritza C. Resendez related how her mother supplemented her income by taking sodas and snacks to her job in a sewing factory and selling them to her coworkers.

> I think I learned from my mom how to be strong, because she's the one that's always pushing the family to move forward when my dad was unemployed forever. Aside from working in the factory she'd buy chips and *dulces* [candies] that and she'd sell them at work. So she had two incomes. She doesn't let anything bring her down. She had to push my dad and motivate him: "*Andale viejo, haz algo, no nomás te quedes allí sentado.*" [Come on old man, do something. Don't just sit there]. That was always the message— don't ever just sit, *no te quedes sentado.* Always try to do something, because otherwise you're not gonna get anywhere.

María del Rosario Santos' mother had ten children, so she spent a great deal of time driving them to school and sundry activities.[19] It occurred to her that she could provide a driving service for the families in the neighborhood. According to María del Rosario, her mother drove for "three neighborhoods—for the elementary school, middle school, and high school—because they were located right there in our neighborhood." Her mother started out by driving a van, but soon enough "she started saving up to buy her own school bus." People in their working-class neighborhood paid María del Rosario's mother with "cash or food stamps." She became the "official driver," because "there were so many of us in school. Whenever a teacher needed transportation for field trips or they wanted to go down to the beach, they'd call my mom." Her mother's "bus service" provided María del Rosario's family much-needed cash as well as allowing her to insure "that her kids were safe. She was in charge of all of the Mexican kids in our neighborhood. She used to have the car seat in the bus for my little brother right by the shift gears. We were always with her."

María del Rosario's mother, like Maritza's mother above, kept pushing her husband to leave his job painting signs for someone else and finally convinced him and her son to open up their own sign company. They don't have a really nice building but they have their *taller* [workshop] where they work and they have workers too." Once the children were grown, María del Rosario's mother also opened her own business, "a flower and bridal shop. She sells flowers, tuxedos, and wedding dresses."

Relatively Privileged Children

There were ten respondents whose parents were both professionals, five of which had one parent not Latino. There were also three single mothers who had a college degree. (None of the respondents were living with their fathers alone.) In all of these instances, the Latino parents themselves did not have parents who attended college. In families where both parents were Latino, my respondents were the second generation to attend college. In these families, the recency of college attendance meant that even when parents were middle-class, as measured by their income and their years of education, their class privilege was only relative. For example, Aixa's father, who had recently died, had obtained his bachelor's degree and master's degree from Saint Mary's University in San Antonio, Texas.[20] He then received his doctoral degree in education from the University of Houston. He taught at Southwest Texas State University in San Marcos, Texas, and her mother had "worked in civil service all her life." Aixa had "very heated, spirited debates about class background" with a friend, who felt that Aixa was solidly middle-class and, therefore, privileged as compared to other Chicanos. Aixa felt that the issue of privilege was more complicated than her friend made it out to be, especially because her family still suffered economic stress and worried about money often.

I understand the kind of cultural currency that comes with the education that my father had and, to a certain extent, with the job that my mother has. That puts us in a certain class. I won't deny that. That is really important to acknowledge. But my father had this way of life of wanting to have the trappings of the upper class, so we really lived beyond our means. We had a nice car, but we were so behind on payments that there were times we couldn't eat. It is this fresh memory that has opened this place inside me. We used to call it being in the *seca* [in the dry season]. My mom would say, "Girls, we are in the *seca* this week. All we have is some rice and we have to figure out what to do." My dad worked at the university, so he was friends with all the janitors that were *raza* [other Mexicans]. When they had big catered receptions, they'd give him all the leftover food. So my dad would come home with trays and trays of food. That is how we would eat, because we got it free from the university. How weird is that? Again, these contradictions. I know what it meant to have a family where the primary emphasis was on education and getting your degree. I knew what it was like having in your social circle professors and very literate, well-read, erudite and educated people. Then to have the daily reality of "Well, no, we can't buy you shoes this month." So it's really very complex. So in terms of social class, I don't know what I really classify myself as.

The majority of the most educated respondents echoed Aixa's views of not feeling solidly middle-class and not having economic security.

College-educated parents were more common among respondents who had one white parent. In these cases, the white side of the family was usually, although not always, well-to-do and had attended college. Mieka Valdez, for example, definitely saw a difference between her mother's social class background and that of her father, although both had a college education.[21] Her mother, who was white, was a psychotherapist and had a master's degree in counseling. Her father, who was Chicano, had a master's degree as well and taught Chicano studies in a community college. Mieka's parents met in the dining hall while her father was a graduate student at the University of California, San Diego. They married and had Mieka and her brother and divorced by the time Mieka was three years old.

I think my mom's parents were definitely more upper-class. I saw where they used to live, and they said that was a normal middle-class neighborhood. I was like, "Damn! These are mansions!" Even my older brother was like, "What! They're wealthy!" My grandfather was an executive head of advertising for May Company [department store]. I remember seeing a newspaper article on him, so I know that they definitely had some kind of wealth.

In comparison, Mieka's grandparents on her father's side of the family were service workers. "My Grandma worked in the Lemon Grove cannery and my grandfather was a janitor and groundskeeper for a church."[22]

As a consequence of Mieka's mother's remarriage to a school psychologist, her family's class had gone from "middle-class to upper-middle-class, especially moving to the rich side of town." When her mother moved to an affluent neighborhood, Mieka told her mother, "I don't want to live there!"

Mieka was not unusual among my respondents who came from professional families in maintaining frequent contact with the Mexican side of her extended family. Respondents of mixed heritage saw their Mexican relatives often and were especially close to their grandparents, leading them to be keenly aware of the recency of their parents' poverty.

Many of the respondents whose parents were educated and/or those who had one white parent expressed deep love for their less well-to-do, usually Mexican, extended family members like grandparents, aunts, and uncles. Many of these respondents often sought a connection with them, especially by learning Spanish, many times as adults. As Nicole Rodriguez, whose father was of Mexican descent from San Jose, California, and whose mother was Armenian from Fresno, California, stated:[23]

> I love my grandmother. She's my favorite woman. She is a U.S. citizen. She was born and raised in this country, but she doesn't speak any English. I always thought that she was a remarkable woman. I learned how to speak Spanish so that I could communicate with her. She means a lot to me.

There were several respondents whose parents were white and had a college degree but did not come from an educated or affluent background. For example, Misty's mother was of Irish descent, but not all of Misty's white relatives had a college education.[24] Misty's mother had grown up on a farm in Nebraska, which the bank repossessed because of defaulted loans. According to Misty, relatives on her mother's side of the family "all got married before they were nineteen and twenty and they all have at least three kids, and none of them completed college. My mom was the only one." All Misty's aunts worked in the farm fields "side by side with their men." Yet "when they get home, they also cook and take care of their kids. As far as getting out into the workforce and seeking a professional position with a $200,000 salary, no, they are not interested." Misty's aunts thought that a "woman's place is in the home and that the first thing is family. That's both on the Mexican side and the Irish side. Family is the most important thing." Family was so important that nobody on her mother's side of the family was "without kids. I'll probably be the first. I want kids but not for a long time."

Only one respondent considered her family wealthy. Tonantzin's sixty-three-year-old father was born in Mexico and came as an undocumented worker to the United States when he was in his teens.[25] He was deported but then returned legally and went directly to Chicago to work in a factory. Tonantzin's fifty-six-year-old mother, whose parents had emigrated from Italy, was the first one in her family to be born in the United States. Her parents met in Chicago, where Tonantzin and her brother grew up. As Tonantzin said, "I am right off from the suburbs of Chicago—WASP [white, Anglo-Saxon, Protestant]." Tonantzin, unlike her younger brother, was considered the "black sheep" in her family. She and her father had never gotten along. "My dad and I have not talked since I was very little. We always clashed. My mom says it's because we are too much alike—real bull-headed, stubborn, and opinionated."

When Tonantzin was sixteen, her father moved to be close to his nine siblings in McAllen in South Texas, a predominantly Mexican American area. Tonantzin's mother stayed in Illinois until Tonantzin finished high school and then joined her husband in Texas. After high school, Tonantzin stayed to attend Northern Illinois University. While attending college, Tonantzin got pregnant by her African American boyfriend, which further distanced her father from her. According to Tonantzin, her pregnancy was "icing on the cake," and even though she interacted with her father, he had "disowned" her and never spoke to her directly even if she was in the room. When Tonantzin had her son, she moved to McAllen to be close to her father's extended family, hoping they would support her even if they did not know her very well. Indeed, they embraced her and Tonantzin's aunt became her son Marcos' primary caregiver while Tonantzin continued her education in a local college.

In spite of his distance from Tonantzin and her three-year-old son, Tonantzin's father bought her a car and a house so that she and Marcos had reliable transportation and did not have to move from apartment to apartment. Tonantzin paid her parents "rent" for the house, but she fully understood how generous her parents had been in spite of their emotional distance, especially her father's. Tonantzin also recognized how hard her father had worked to achieve his economic wealth.

> My dad was dirt poor. I know that his family was poorer than poor. My dad stayed in the same company in Illinois for over twenty-five years. He started out boxing things. By the time he left the company, he was the consultant. They couldn't even keep him as a manager anymore, 'cause he was so high up. They paid him to be a consultant making real good money, and he got stock dividends. He is really good with money, so he just let the dividends just sit there, and they kept accumulating. My parents are worth millions now, but more in land than actual cash, more in property than capital.

Tonantzin's father had only attended grade school in Mexico and learned English on his own. He was adamant that his children not learn Spanish.

> When I was little, he never taught us Spanish, because I grew up in a white neighborhood. I never saw a Mexican person until I was in college. From kindergarten to college, I never met another Mexican. So I always thought that being Mexican was a bad thing because my dad would never teach us Spanish. He just refused. I found out recently through my mom that my dad refused to teach us Spanish 'cause he was always trying so hard to learn English. He didn't want to confuse the two languages. When you are little you don't understand that. You just think that they are keeping you away from Spanish for a reason. He taught himself everything. He is totally self-taught. I give him props for that.[26] He is really incredibly smart.

Regardless of her parents' financial success, Tonantzin admired her extended family on her father's side more because of their ability to be close as a family.

> I see my cousins with their parents and I get real jealous because they are so close. It just freaks me out. They like to give big parties and get the whole family together. My dad has never been like that, and my mom doesn't either. All of my aunts and uncles think that my family is just freaky: What is wrong with you people?

Tonantzin was by far the wealthiest respondent in my sample. Although she had grown up in a white suburb not interacting with any "Mexicans" until she got to college, by moving from Illinois to South Texas she had reconnected with her extended family and lived only eleven miles from the Mexican border. By the time of this interview, Tonantzin was twenty-five years old and was completely steeped in Mexican American culture. Her son was being brought up as bilingual and bicultural largely due to Tonantzin's extended family. Her father's wealth, ultimately, had not completely insulated Tonantzin from his humble origins.

Lucha as Worker

Lucha's parents were very poor when they immigrated to the United States. They were both unskilled workers and they had eleven children. She did not know the whereabouts of her father, and her mother did not work as she was battling schizophrenia and living in a halfway house in Los Angeles. Lucha and her sister had started working in early adolescence, which facilitated their decision to leave their adoptive parents when the situation became intolerable. Lucha's started her first job, at the In'N'Out, when she was fifteen and a half, and Fuerza started working as a nanny when she was sixteen. By the time she was seventeen, Fuerza had an additional job doing accounting.

Both Lucha and Fuerza worked to put themselves through college—Fuerza at Stanford University and Lucha at a private liberal arts college in the East Coast. Fuerza graduated from Stanford before Lucha and "worked as an investment banker for a while." According to Lucha, "She's brilliant!" But Fuerza decided she wanted to try law school, applied, and was accepted at Stanford. Eventually Lucha also took the same course of action, but at Boalt School of Law at the University of California, Berkeley.

Between her second and third year of law school, Lucha recalled how she reacted when she received a job offer from a very prestigious law firm in San Francisco, where she had worked for a summer.

> I had been working for a law firm and I got an offer to go back to the law firm. They took me to a fancy dinner. After dinner, it was the only time I have ever in my life felt my accomplishments. I was in my car by myself and I just started bawling—crying. It was the first time that I was like, Wait a

minute. I think I've done something here! I think I've done something good. It was the first time I was in a position where I could recognize it for myself rather than wanting to have someone else say, "Oh, good job!" because I know that's not coming. It's not happening.

Lucha and Fuerza graduated from law school. Lucha eventually worked in the Office of Public Defenders in a large city and Fuerza worked in a corporate law firm in the same city. They had been workers from an early age—first to survive and later to fulfill their dreams of being economically self-sufficient and doing meaningful work. However, at times, it had been difficult not to have a parent to tell them, "good job" when they had achieved such extraordinary accomplishments. It was a void that Lucha readily admitted was difficult to overcome.

6

■   ■   ■   ■   ■   ■   ■   ■   ■

Lovers

You Bring Out the Mexican in Me

You bring out the Mexican in me.
The hunkered thick dark spiral.
The core of a heart howl.
The bitter bile.
The tequila *lágrimas* on Saturday all
through next weekend Sunday.
You are the one I'd let go the other loves for,
surrender my one-woman house.
Allow you red wine in bed,
even with my vintage lace linens.
Maybe. Maybe.

For you.

You bring out the Dolores del Río in me.
The Mexican spitfire in me.
The raw *navajas*, glint and passion in me.
The raise Cain and dance with the rooster-footed devil in me.
The spangled sequin in me.
The eagle and serpent in me.
The *mariachi* trumpets of the blood in me.
The Aztec love of war in me.

The fierce obsidian of the tongue in me.
The *berrinchuda, bien-cabrona* in me.
The Pandora's curiosity in me.
The pre-Columbian death and destruction in me.
The rainforest disaster, nuclear threat in me.
The fear of fascists in me.
Yes, you do. Yes, you do.

You bring out the colonizer in me.
The holocaust of desire in me.
The Mexico City '85 earthquake in me.
The Popocatepetl/Ixtaccíhuatl in me.
The tidal wave of recession in me.
The Agustín Lara hopeless romantic in me.
The *barbacoa taquitos* on Sunday in me.
The cover the mirrors with cloth in me.

Sweet twin. My wicked other,
I am the memory that circles your bed nights,
that tugs you taut as moon tugs ocean.
I claim you all mine,
arrogant as Manifest Destiny.
I want to rattle and rent you in two.
I want to defile you and raise hell.
I want to pull out the kitchen knives,
dull and sharp, and whisk the air with crosses.
Me sacas lo mexicana en mi,
Like it or not, honey.

You bring out the Uled-Nayl in me.
The stand-back-white-bitch in me.
The switchblade in the boot in me.
The Acapulco cliff diver in me.
The *Flecha Roja* mountain disaster in me.
The *dengue* fever in me.
The ¡*Alarma*! murderess in me.
I could kill in the name of you and think
it worth it. Brandish a fork and terrorize rivals,

female and male, who loiter and look at you,
languid in your light. Oh,

I am evil. I am the filth goddess. Tlazoltéotl.
I am the swallower of sins.
The lust goddess without guilt.
The delicious debauchery. You bring out
the primordial exquisiteness in me.
The nasty obsession in me.
The corporal and venial sin in me.
The original transgression in me.

Red ocher. Yellow ocher. Indigo. Cochineal.
Piñón. Copal. Sweetgrass. Myrrh.
All you saints, blessed and terrible,
Virgen de Guadalupe, diosa Coatlicue,
I invoke you.

Quiero ser tuya. Only yours. Only you.
Quiero amarte. Atarte. Amarrarte.
Love the way a Mexican woman loves. Let
me show you. Love the only way I know how.

—Cisneros 1994

CHOOSING WHOM TO LOVE embodies in the fullest sense an individual's history, language, culture, passion, and *anhelos* (desires). In this most intimate relationship is where we can see an individual's social projection of self. For my respondents, it was this choice that "brought out the Mexican" in them. As Sandra Cisneros's poem illustrates, all those "Mexican" aspects that seem hidden (perhaps even obliterated) are brought out when one expresses the passion of love. Loving is not only an individual choice but also an enactment of all that has gone into creating a person. In the case of Chicanas, it is the cross-border existence between two countries that hybridizes all expression—popular culture (Dolores del Río, *mariachis, Alarma* magazine),[1] cultural narratives (dance with the rooster-footed devil),[2] and religious beliefs (*Virgen de Guadalupe, diosa*

Coatlicue).[3] It brings out the expression of passion in two languages—
"*Quiero ser tuya*" (I want to be yours), "*Quiero amarte*" (I want to love
you), "*Atarte. Amarrarte*" (tie you up)—as well as in two cultural views
of love. The expression of love is affected by what women have survived
and by the strength required to exist in a colonized space at the same time
they attempt to create a decolonial imaginary (Pérez 1999). These women
are fierce in their expression of love—"The raw *navajas*" (blades), "*bien-
cabrona* in me" (the "fuck you over" in me), "stand-back-white-bitch in
me," "the switchblade in the boot in me"—a fierceness that can be understood only in the context of Chicanas' larger political and social struggles. Many of my respondents did not know how "Mexican" they were
until they fell in love.

Marriage

Most of my respondents were very close not only to their parents and their
siblings but to their extended family as well. For most, marriage was also a
very high priority. Regardless of sexual orientation, the majority of respondents wanted to be married (79 percent) and have children, either biologically or by adoption (82 percent). Many referred to their own families as models of what they thought the ideal family was—a large number
of children and extended kin living close by. Of the 101 respondents, 15
were already married and 7 had children. In addition, there were five single parents and one respondent who was divorced and raising her daughter by herself.

Regardless of the laws against gay marriage, several respondents who
were lesbian had marriage arrangements. Jessica Delgado had just broken
up with her girlfriend of five years, whom her family treated as if they had
been married.[4] I asked her whether she would ever have another committed relationship with a new partner and she replied, "I probably will. It was
as close to a marriage as I can imagine. I knew it was, because my family
certainly treated it that way. And they're very upset by our breakup."

A few of my respondents reported getting married to move away from
their parents. In some cases, that worked well; in others, their marriage was
limping along. For example, Maria Villa was twenty-six years old, had been
married for eight years, and had a six-year-old daughter.[5] She was the oldest of three children and had a very difficult adolescence with her parents,

particularly her father, who was very strict. Maria developed an attraction for boys "in fifth or sixth grade" and became "boy crazy." Her father did not want her "to date or for boys to call" until Maria turned sixteen, which "caused a lot of conflict between us." According to Maria, her father wanted her "to stay his little girl forever." Maria was rebellious and wanted to be very independent. "My parents were really clingy."

Maria finally moved out while she was still in high school and her then boyfriend and now husband helped her lease an apartment. Maria still went to school and got good grades. "That was very important to me. I was an honor graduate." Initially, she did not want to get married and preferred to live with her boyfriend. Her father was vehemently opposed, and so she got married shortly after she moved out rather than risk completely alienating her father.

In spite of these difficult circumstances, Maria's marriage was the best thing to happen to her. "From the moment that I met Joel, I knew he was my soul mate." She felt very lucky because she and her husband "really love each other. We were able to grow together and not grow apart, which was certainly a struggle for me." Once Maria was married and had a child, "her family calmed down a lot."

Cristina was not as fortunate as Maria.[6] She married Mario before her fifteenth birthday because she thought she was pregnant. At the time, she was also having difficulties at home because her father was very strict and old enough "to be her grandfather," a situation that, in her opinion, created a generation gap difficult to overcome. Cristina's mother was diagnosed with schizophrenia and had to take very heavy medication, a condition that, according to Cristina, negatively affected their relationship.

My mom is about fifty-six and my dad's fifty-nine. My dad works at a factory right now but he's a temporary worker. My parents are really old-fashioned. First of all, they're older and they act like they're ten years older than their age. They have morals and rules that they followed when they were young. You couldn't talk to boys or go out on a date. When I was a teenager they were already forty-something, so they didn't really understand me at all. There was a big age gap and my mom acted like my grandmother rather than my mother. It was real hard growing up with that age difference, because we had nothing in common. We couldn't talk—the language barriers.[7]

Cristina's marriage had been tumultuous, and the last time she separated from her husband, at the age of nineteen, she swore not to return. However, shortly before her heartfelt resolution, they had a brief reconciliation and she became pregnant. Reluctantly, Cristina returned to her husband. At the time of the interview, Cristina was twenty years old, had a five-year-old daughter, and was eight months pregnant with her second child. She was determined to make her marriage work, but as described in the introduction to part 2, she still seemed tense about her decision.

Although Cristina felt distant from her father, he insisted on talking to her about the importance of staying in school. He posed himself as the example of the consequences of not obtaining an education—hard labor, long hours, job instability. According to Cristina, her father, who only received a third-grade education, "always stressed staying in school." He asked her, "Do you want to be like me?" He urged Cristina "not to give up school regardless of what else was going on" in her life. Her father's words persuaded Cristina "that education was what I needed not to have the same hardships as my parents." Cristina took this message to heart and continued school after she became pregnant a second time, especially because her twenty-four-year-old husband "works at the same factory with my dad. He wants to go to school eventually but right now he's supporting us. I just have work-study and we have a house payment."

Cristina was a junior in college majoring in occupational therapy and hoped that "later on, if everything goes right, I may go to medical school as a second career." First she wanted to be with her "kids while they are growing up." Cristina figured that by the time her children started school she would still be young enough to start medical school.

Preferring Latinos, Rejecting Whites

What I've learned about myself, being away from my home, is that being with someone who is Latino or Indian in a sense makes me feel home.
—Nicolasa I. Sandoval, twenty-eight-year-old respondent,
Washington, D.C.

The majority of respondents (60 percent) and their parents preferred that they marry Latinos and even more specifically Mexican descent Latinos.[8] The reasons cited most often were that respondents wanted to maintain their culture and language; they wanted to avoid tensions with their families, especially when their families did not speak English; they were afraid of class differences, as they assumed that most whites were better off than Latinos; and they believed that Latinos were more likely to "understand" them better without needing them to "explain everything." Alicia Granillo summarized what she expected in a future partner after she had divorced her first husband, who was white.[9]

> He's got to know what *menudo* [tripe soup] is, eat with *tortillas*. I don't care if we're active in the Catholic Church or not but he has to know what the *posadas* are, to know what to do in church.[10] So yeah, it is very important for me to marry a Latino because I want my [future] children to be able to maintain their culture.

Part of the reason Alicia wanted to "get married to a Chicano or Latino" was that "he's got to speak Spanish! My mother doesn't speak English." The same concern was voiced by many respondents that having non-Latino partners increased the potential for language barriers between them and their non–English-speaking parents and relatives.

Respondents were also concerned about potential language barriers between them and their partners. Although my respondents were all English-dominant, many valued and cherished the use of their second language and wanted the freedom to code-switch spontaneously between English and Spanish. Several of them, like Agustina, gave examples in which using Spanish with non–Spanish speakers became awkward.[11]

> I went out to lunch with Chris, this guy from school [the University of Chicago]. And while we were talking, I found myself using some Spanish words. Sometimes Spanish words just come out and the other person is Latino so they understand. They don't make a big deal about it. I told him something in Spanish and he gave me a strange look, and I'm like, "Oh, sorry!" That's why I want to get married with a Latino, because that way we can speak English and Spanish, it's interchangeable.

Many respondents stated that marrying a white partner entailed the risk of not being able to transmit Mexican culture to their future children. They especially did not want their households divided along linguistic and cultural lines, such that a child would be taught "Latino culture" by one parent and "white culture" by the other. Tomasa felt that "if I were to marry a white man, I can see our house. [Her husband would say] 'Well, speak Spanish to your mother, but speak English to your father.' I wouldn't want that."[12]

Although many respondents had strong critiques of the ways they were brought up by their parents, especially their strictness, they still thought their parents' socialization practices were best. In fact, many respondents admitted that when their turn came to raise children, they would probably use their parents as role models. They speculated that if they married a non-Latino it could result in conflicts over parenting styles. As Agustina said,

> I want to raise my daughter the way my mother raised me, because I like the way I turned out. If my husband was white, he would have a difficult time trying to understand that because many white people usually date at an early age, and they don't have the same values and principles as we do. There would be constant conflict over that.

There was also a concern that a white partner was more likely to come from a higher social class and not understand the economic struggles many respondents' parents had experienced. As Tomasa explained,

> I think I would feel much more comfortable just being with somebody who's Latino because you can relate better. It would be difficult for somebody who is not Latino to understand our background, where we came from. How can they imagine our struggles? How can they imagine our parents' struggles, which are twice, three times as difficult as the ones we've had? It would be very difficult for me to see how they can understand that because white people's lives have been much easier than the struggles we've had.

Very few respondents spoke about social class considerations in making their mating decisions. Instead, like Tomasa above, they equated "whiteness" with a higher social class than their own. But even if a white partner did not come from a privileged class, some respondents felt that the differences in political consciousness around race and ethnicity would lead to disagreements.

Most respondents of mixed heritage and/or their families also expressed a preference for marrying Latinos. According to Sonya K. Smith, whose mother was of Mexican descent and whose father was white, her mother's parents urged her to consider finding "a good Mexican man; not even a Latino would do, but a good Mexican man."[13] Although Sonya didn't necessarily agree, she understood her grandparents' views as related to the fact that "all their kids out-married. I'm half [white and half Mexican]. They are always telling me I want you to marry a Mexican. Marry your own kind."

Finally, several respondents felt that many white men racialized their womanhoods and saw Latinas either as unattractive mammies or as sexual objects to be "played with." According to Agustina,

> To me, many white men look at us like we're not good enough for them. Like you're just a Latina and you're here [at the University of Chicago] because you're on financial aid; you're not that smart. I was raised to believe that I'm wasting my time going out with white men, because they don't take Latinas seriously. They only want Latinas *para divertimiento* [for diversion]—to have sex. They think Latinas are easy. So I'm thinking why even bother with white men? He's only going to want me for sex and I'm not like that. So all the guys I have dated have been Latino.

Regardless of sexual orientation, respondents felt it was important to mate with a Latina/o. Jessica Delgado's family changed their views on her sexuality when she brought home Kathy, who was a Chicana from El Paso, Texas. It was the first time that Jessica's family agreed to meet her partner. Kathy's cultural knowledge about how to behave with Jessica's family allowed her to win them over.

> My relationship with Kathy had a lot to do with my family shifting to become a lot more tolerant [of her sexuality]. Prior to that, they hadn't been overtly hostile, but they certainly didn't want to hear about that part of my life. When Kathy came along and I brought her home, they loved her. I think a lot of it had to do with her being Chicana, but it was also the way she interacted with them. She was incredibly deferential, very respectful; that really mattered to them. She knew how to interact with my grandmother and the rest of the family.

Many of my respondents were willing to make compromises and were unconcerned with finding someone of "equal status" in order to find a Latino partner. They wanted someone to love them, respect them, "not cheat" on them, and, above all, not hamper their educational and professional aspirations.

Rejecting Their Own

When I dated Latino men I felt that I always had to look my extra best. I had to shop for clothes. When we went to parties, I noticed they looked at all the girls with real short-short skirts and it just bothered me. Whereas Keith [her fiancé, who is of German descent], I can be wearing sweats or whatever and he's like, "You're so beautiful!" I go look in the mirror and I'm like, "Oh God, I look like hell!"

—Gloria, twenty-seven-year-old respondent, Albuquerque, New Mexico

A few respondents' parents were actually anti-Latino, with mothers the most likely to caution their daughters against marrying within their own ethnic group. Gloria laughed as she remembered her mother telling her, "never marry a Mexican man."[14] Gloria's mother, however, made a distinction between someone "from Mexico" and someone born in the United States. According to Gloria, "She thinks the ones from Mexico are *machistas*. They cheat on you, they'll beat you. She has this awful image of Mexican men." She held these views in spite of the fact that Gloria's father "isn't like that. But she said that all the men back home in Mexico are like that. She thought she would never marry until she met my father, who was a decent man."

Several respondents also mentioned that Latino men were too controlling and did not support their efforts to obtain an education or have a profession. These concerns stopped respondents from pursuing relationships with Latinos. Although Agustina stated that she was not "physically attracted to white men" and she was very committed to marrying a Latino, she was having difficulty finding a suitable mate. The Latinos she dated resented her "going to the University of Chicago and my ambition of becoming a lawyer." She related how one of her boyfriends "actually proposed that I quit school, that he'd be willing to financially support me if I stayed at home [when they married] and be a homemaker with the kids. I'm thinking, I'm sorry but I can't do that because that's not how I was raised. So that failed." Another boyfriend felt she "was too good" for him and "dumped her." Agustina still wanted to "marry a Latino, but the Latino principles that they have, they want to wear the pants, they want to be the *macho*, they want to be the ones who are superior to the woman."

Although this was not the predominant view, several of my respondents had concluded they were not going to mate with someone of Latino descent.

Living Together

Many of my respondents had premarital sex as well as "live-in" relationships with romantic partners. Few, however, had told their parents. It was only when they were on the verge of getting married that they finally would "confess their transgression." In these instances, the mothers were much more accepting than the fathers. For example, Valerie had been living with a female roommate.[15] After the roommate moved out, Valerie's mother suggested that Valerie and her boyfriend "get an apartment." Valerie was completely surprised and said, "OK!" However, Valerie still misled her mother about the actual sleeping arrangements. "I told my mom that I wasn't going to sleep with him. I told her, 'Don't worry, OK? I'm not going to get pregnant.' I still felt the pressure even though I had gone away to college, I was older, I was independent, and living away from home."

Valerie felt fine about living with her boyfriend prior to marriage, but emotionally she still needed her grandmother's approval. "I still called my nana, my dad's mother, and said, 'I'm going to be moving in with him.'" Her grandmother told her, "It's OK. He's going to take care of you. He's going to be there for you. You're going to be safe with a man in the house. Don't worry about it!" Valerie "felt such a relief, even more than when my mom approved, because my nana is of that generation that is stricter and the most judgmental in my family. Her blessing meant a lot to me."

Many of the fathers refused to acknowledge their daughters' living arrangements as did Valerie's father who refused to visit Valerie and her boyfriend. Once respondents married, their families changed dramatically.

In Valerie's case, "Three years into the marriage, it's great. My dad now comes over more. It's really different, very loving."

It was not uncommon for the boyfriends' parents to be unconcerned that their sons were living with their girlfriends prior to marriage. Valerie's boyfriend's parents not only visited them but also spent the night and did not feel uncomfortable. Valerie fully acknowledged the "double standard." Her boyfriend's parents "didn't mind at all. They trusted him and respected his choices. But, you know, he's a guy, right?"

Children

Almost all respondents either had children (14 percent) or wanted children (82 percent). Lucinda responded in a way similar to most respondents when I asked whether she wanted to have children: "I definitely do."[16] Her fiancé's sister had recently had a baby, and this made Lucinda even more desirous of a child. "He's only four months and he's a wonderful miracle." However, Lucinda felt that having a baby was "such a wonderfully selfish thing. When I really think about having a baby, it's about me." But as soon as she put the child at the center of her analysis, she began a long litany of concerns that were shared by many other respondents.

> What scares me about having a child is the environment they're going to grow up in. Should we put them in a public school or private school or home school? What if he turns out to be a mass murderer? Do I take responsibility for that? Yet I think it's a wonderful gift to be able to give life. What if my baby ends up being the first Chicano president or creating world peace or defusing a nuclear bomb? [*Laughing.*] Maybe my genes have something to offer.

In addition to these large existential questions about bringing new life into this world, Lucinda had some practical concerns, which again were commonly expressed by my other respondents.

> If I get pregnant, will I be able to lose the weight? [*Laughing.*] My fiancé, Antonio, is wonderful with kids and he's a musician, so we talk about the different roles we would take. I want to continue my professional career, but I

also want to breast-feed. I'm thinking about the craziest things. Let's see, how would I do it? Antonio would bring the baby to the office every two hours. [*Laughing.*] He said he'd be "Mr. Mom," which is great, but it's a total switch of gender roles. I would be the one earning the income and he would be staying at home taking care of the baby. Then, I think, wait a minute! I wanna stay at home and be part of the baby's day-to-day growth. I want to experience that. But then, how do we pay the bills?

Lucinda felt that she obsessed about all these details because she was "too damn intellectual about it." She pointed to Mexican families with seven or eight kids. "I'm thinking, Get over it!" Her fiancé's cousin has "six kids and they are not financially in any position to have one, much less six. I'm thinking, God, how do they do it!" Lucinda took inspiration, as did many of my other respondents, from the success stories of large Mexican families around them surviving with much fewer emotional and economic resources and felt confident that she and her future husband, too, would make good parents.

Accepting Children, Rejecting Marriage

A number of my respondents were very committed to having children but not to getting married. They considered adoption and artificial insemination as alternatives. Frida had relationships with both men and women.[17] I asked whether she saw herself having a marriage-like arrangement with her current girlfriend. Frida replied, "No." She proceeded to explain with a laugh, "I need a lot of space." She had also made her position clear to her partners. According to Frida, "I've never envisioned myself with any kind of partner. I've always seen myself with my own house, even in my seventies." At first, Frida thought she was rejecting marriage as a reaction to the difficult relationship between her mother and her stepfather. But as she grew older, she recognized "that it's just because I like being by myself. I love my independence, my autonomy, my agency, my space, all of that. Most of the relationships that I've had that resemble a marriage crowd me. That's why I don't want to get married."

Nonetheless, Frida wanted to raise children, but "I don't want to have kids. If anything, I'd want to adopt a child." Frida was also an environmentalist, so was "into zero population growth." Her mother struggled with and finally accepted Frida's desire not to marry. More difficult for her mother to understand, however, was not having a biological child: "Just have a child, your bloodline. You don't have to marry the guy. Who cares?" Frida understood that "It's very important for my mother," but "I just think there are too many kids in the world already."

There were other respondents who had not completely rejected the possibility of marriage, but were skeptical of finding a partner, in which case, they were willing to parent by themselves. Sobeida definitely saw herself "surrounded with children," although she didn't "see marriage till ten years down the line."[18] She had already told her mother, "If I don't get married, I'm going to have children, even if I adopt. But I still want to have children."

Large Families

Many respondents viewed their own large families as ideal and wanted what could be considered a large number of children: on average three, although a few mentioned as many as twelve, and many viewed fewer than four as a relatively small family. Many justified their preference by recalling the happy times their families spent together regardless of the economic hardships.

Although most respondents wanted a large number of children, they also expected to have full-fledged careers in highly competitive fields like law and medicine. It was not clear how they expected to accomplish these goals given the demands on their time. Many respondents recognized this dilemma, but at the same time they expressed confidence that when the time came, they would figure it out somehow.

Not surprisingly, respondents who already had children were much more realistic about the tensions between the demands of child rearing and the demands of school and work. They were also very aware of the economic constraints on having a large number of children. Rosario was twenty-eight and in her first year of a doctoral program in education.[19] Rosario had been married for eight years and was having difficulty deciding when to have a second child because of the demands of graduate school.

> I want to be a professional but at the same time I'm torn, because I have one four-year-old. If I wait till I finish school before I have another child, my

kid's going to be almost ten years old. Those are very difficult issues that I haven't resolved. I know that I want to finish school. I can't get pregnant immediately after graduation because I have to work and start making contacts. It's really hard. I feel like I'm being torn in different directions.

Rosario and her husband kept going back and forth. "No, we don't want to have any more kids." "Well, honey, maybe we could adopt." "Maybe I can get pregnant." Rosario concluded, "It's just hard because I never wanted to be a yuppie, those women that wait till they are forty-something years old to have another baby." In addition to the logistics of when to have another child, Rosario and her husband had recently bought a home, prompting Rosario to take another job to make ends meet. All these demands made Rosario feel that "everybody wants a piece of us." At the same time she recognized that "my son is the most important thing, and it's hard for me. I don't want to bring another child into this world that I can't tend to." Rosario kept asking herself, "Do I want a family or do I want a career? It's like, at this point, right now, I can't have both. I can't do both, I can't! I'm having a nervous breakdown. [*Laughing.*]"

The difficult issues being confronted by Rosario and her husband were not being seriously considered by many of my respondents who did not have children yet and who confidently asserted that they wanted as many as twelve children.

Rejecting Marriage and Rejecting Children

My mother would always talk about children as just being a strain and I think I got that from her. That's why I haven't had children. [Her mother would say,] "Don't do it. If you get pregnant, you can have an abortion. We can do it. You need to get the pill. Don't do what I did."

—Christine Granados, twenty-nine-year-old respondent,
Austin, Texas

Many of my respondents' mothers had a deep commitment to family and especially to their children. However, there were a few mothers who were openly opposed to their daughters having children. Alicia Granillo spoke about her reluctance to have children because of her mother's views.

I grew up thinking that I wasn't going to have any kids because my mother always described kids as "*es una desgracia. Te vas a arruinar toda tu vida.*" [It's a calamity. You are going to ruin your life.] To this day, José and I have been engaged for two years and we've been living together for two more years. So we've been together for about five years. I finally decided that I was going to marry him. For a long time I put up these walls because of my experience with my first marriage, and also coming from very strong-willed women, a women-dominated family. So I finally said, "Okay, we'll get married."

Alicia felt the pull between her mother's views on marriage and children and her fiancé's insistence that they get married. "I could be perfectly happy not getting married and having children but he wants to get married. You have to give in a little bit. So we're going to get married this summer."

Once Alicia and her boyfriend decided to get married, she was reluctant to break the news to her mother. She called all her siblings and her friends before she finally called her mother. "*José y yo nos vamos a casar este verano.*" (José and I are going to get married this summer.) Her mother replied, "*Bueno, tú sabes lo que haces. Yo no tengo ninguna opinión.*" (Well, you know what you are doing. I don't have an opinion.) Alicia tried to reassure her mother that her fiancé was more psychologically stable than her first husband and told her, "*Mami, no está loco como el otro.*" (Mami, he's not crazy like the other one.) Her mother replied, "*Pues, tú sabes lo que haces, mija, porque los hombres están locos en varias otras partes.*" (Well, you know what you are doing, my daughter, because men are crazy in multiple ways.) According to Alicia, she and her mother never had the type of idealized conversation in which mother and daughter fantasize together about "*Que bonito cuando tenga un niño, y tú me ayudas a cuidarlo.*" (How wonderful when I have a baby and you can help me take care of him or her.)

Alicia's mother was so adamantly against her daughters marrying and having children that she would stop talking for months to Alicia's married sisters when they became pregnant. Alicia's mother associated having children with "reduced freedom, reduced opportunity. Anything that can be negative, she equates it with having children." Alicia concluded that her mother's aversion to motherhood was related to "her own experiences. That although she loves her children very much, at the same time, she's had a lot of resentment because she didn't get past the second grade. She's always loved education. She had this passion for education but was never able to attain that goal."

In spite of her mother's resentment, Alicia and her mother were extremely close, especially because Alicia was the "baby" in the family. Alicia described herself as "mami's little girl" who was "spoiled rotten" within the confines of her mother's economic resources.

Only one respondent definitely did not want to have children. Jocelyn Solis felt that she was raised to think she should get married and have children, but as she became older, she realized that she could not realistically have both children and a career.[20]

> I used to hold on to the belief that I could have it all. I wanted to be the superwoman who had the career, the children, and the husband. Everything that women are supposed to have. Now I feel like I don't necessarily want all that. I've invested so much in building a career. Maybe I'm overly selfish, but I don't want to share that. I don't want to split myself, and I don't think that I could do a good job with all those demands.

Jocelyn thought that "women who try to have it all end up messing something up. I don't want that. If I am going to have a family, I want to do it right. And if I'm going to build a career, I want to do that well. So I don't always see how the two could be combined so easily." As clearheaded as Jocelyn was about her choice to emphasize a career rather than a family, she still admitted that "it's pretty scary. I don't know, maybe I'll change my mind. But at this point, I don't see myself wanting to have children."

Jocelyn had told her parents how she felt. "They think I don't know what I'm talking about and that I'll come around eventually." Her family would "joke around about it," because they thought that Jocelyn was taking an extreme position. "They are not expecting me to get married and have children anytime soon." Jocelyn also knew that her parents were "really invested in my education and my career. They don't want me to jeopardize that at all, so they wouldn't insist on me getting married at this point."

Mothering Their Own

Of the respondents who had children, six were single mothers and seven were married. None of the respondents who identify themselves as lesbian or bisexual had children. One respondent, who had a four-year lesbian relationship, became pregnant with an old boyfriend just as she met her current husband. She and her current husband were raising her daughter as a family.

Coping with raising their own children helped respondents appreciate their own mothers. Many mothers helped their daughters achieve their educational goals by providing child care and helping them with household chores. Several of the respondents who were married made an effort to live close to their parents and in some instances in the same household. For example, Rosario spoke of how much closer she became to her mother when her child was born with a rare skin disorder that forced him to remain in the hospital for almost a year. Her mother, who worked as a receptionist, missed work for an entire month when Rosario's son was ill.

> My mom was always there. She's like a rock for me. The first year of my son's life was very traumatic for me. Gosh, I'm going to start crying now! I was still in school and the hospital was three and a half hours away. My mother, bless her soul, was always at the hospital with my son when we were going to school. My mother is a very strong woman. She would do anything for her family. She made a lot of sacrifices. I wished she had finished school. I think she would've been an excellent teacher.

Degrees of Transgressive Mating

Interethnic and Interracial Mating

Many of my respondents' parents made explicit how much transgression they would accept in their daughters' choice of romantic partners. The different levels of acceptance varied, depending on the romantic partner's ethnicity, race, class, and sexuality. Overall, parents preferred that their daughters partner with Latinos, although most were equally accepting of whites, broadly defined as being of European descent. Tomasa recalled how her mother would joke by telling her, *"Ay, espero que encuentras un Italiano con ojos azules, güero, alto, con dinero."* (I hope you find an Italian with blue eyes, blond, tall, and with money.) With few exceptions, most parents rejected African Americans as partners for their daughters. This was even the case when respondents had already had children with African American men. For the most part, parents did not have a well-developed opinion about other ethnic and racial groups.

Like most of my respondents, Rita stated that it was important to her parents that she marry a Latino, although "they would be OK if I married a white man."[21] On the other hand, if she were to bring home an African American boyfriend, it "would rock their world." Rita's parents' acceptance of whites was not based on interracial and interethnic contact, which was uncommon in most of these families. In fact, Rita commented that when her sister dated a "white guy," it was the first time a white person had ever entered their home. The potential for interracial couplings came mostly from the respondents' social contacts in college.

Even in families where parents had accepted respondents' lesbianism, they still harbored racial and ethnic prejudice. Like most of my respondents, Jessica Delgado felt that if she brought an African American woman home to meet her family, "they'd be very uncomfortable" because "I think they're racists." Jessica concluded that her "upbringing was very anti-Semitic, very racist." Her family made a distinction between "who's dark-skinned in the family and who's lighter-skinned. My grandfather from Mexico is very *moreno* [dark], and so that part of the family was really treated as sort of crazy." The other side of Jessica's family was from "Santa Fe, New Mexico, so there's always this rush to identify with the Spanish blood." Jessica felt she had experienced "a lot of racism growing up, because my mom, of all the siblings, looked like my grandfather the most. So she was always teased because she was darker, even though I don't think she's that dark." Jessica concluded that part of her family had very skewed "judgments about skin color." Nonetheless, Jessica thought her family's views had become "a lot less racist because of so many years of me taking them on about it."

Some families' ethnocentrism extended to other non-Mexican Latinos. Several respondents were surprised to find out that their Mexican-descent parents actually did not approve of their Latino partners. Nicolasa I. Sandoval thought that her father, who recently had moved back to Mexico to live, would be "thrilled that I was bringing home a Latino."[22] To her surprise, her father had very negative stereotypes of Puerto Ricans, which he was quick to express when Nicolasa announced "that we were going to Puerto Rico to visit my boyfriend's family." He said, "Well, you be careful Nicki, because the women down there run around half naked! Just turn on the television and you'll see." Her father was also quick to warn her to "be careful because he might turn out to be a *mujeriego* [womanizer]. He's good looking. The women are always going be after him, so you just gotta watch it." Nicolasa's father did not confine his negative views to Puerto Ricans. He was equally prejudiced toward African Americans. According to Nicolasa, her father had already warned all his daughters that marrying an African American was "the worst thing that any of us girls could ever do to him. He says that marrying or being with a Black man is unforgivable." Nicolasa was prompt to press her father for an explanation when she asked, "Why is it unforgivable? What if he's good to us?" Her father wouldn't budge; he replied, "It doesn't matter." According to Nicolasa, her father gave her the usual reply, "The whole thing of we should think about what a hard time our children would have." Her father did not convince Nicolasa. She simply concluded that "he's very racist."

My respondents' mothers and fathers often disagreed about their daughters' potential choices of spouses. In some instances, the father was the most unbending and the mother was the most supportive that their daughters be free to choose their partner. For example, whereas Nicolasa's father was adamantly against his daughters marrying anybody but "Mexicans," Nicolasa's

> mother wouldn't have a problem with any of us marrying outside our ethnicity, she just wants us to be happy. My sister dated a Black man for a while, and everyone really liked him. She was even gonna take him to Sacramento [California] to visit my father [before he moved to Mexico]. I said, "Are you crazy!" She said, "Well, Poppa can have a cow if he wants to but this is my life. He's not gonna tell me what to do. If he doesn't like it, I won't visit him. That's his problem. What do you think he's going to do, tell me I can't come in with this Black man?" I said, "No, you're right, he's going to want to see you. He's not going to slam the door in your face."

Latino parents were not the only ones who had negative views of African Americans. White parents were also not shy about expressing their racist views. Bianca's father was Italian American and grew up in Chicago; her mother was Mexican American.[23] Bianca had dated African Americans but her parents remained unconcerned because they were not "serious boyfriends." In spite of this apparent acceptance, Bianca stated,

> Both of my parents have very deep-seated racial hatred in them, and it's just bizarre. It comes out in weird ways, for example, when they [African Americans] are on the news. They'll say, "Those freakin' Black people!" My dad uses the term nigger a lot. But it's circumstance. My dad grew up in Chicago at a time when Italians and Blacks were battling each other for land and for housing and for jobs and for everything.

Bianca felt she understood her father's views and she did not "blame my dad for having those feelings, but I try to help my dad understand why that's not true anymore or tell him, 'Look, they do their share too.' We just have very heated political discussions about race."

Gay Mating

It was not unusual for respondents (42 percent) to report that they had gay family members. Sometimes a family member's homosexuality was handled with great sensitivity and acceptance. In other instances, there was rejection by some family members and acceptance by others. Another response was complete silence—everybody in the family "knew," but nobody openly addressed the issue. Jennifer Trujillo's nineteen-year-old brother was extremely homophobic to the point that he told Jennifer, "If I had a son who was gay, I would beat the gay out of him."[24] However, one of Jennifer's cousins "is gay and in a way everyone accepts it. It's similar to the whole sex thing. We just don't mention it. We'll still love the individual no matter what, because that's what family does, but you just don't talk about it."

I asked all the heterosexual respondents to predict their families' reactions if they were to get involved in a lesbian romantic relationship. Most respondents predicted that their families' initial shock would turn to acceptance. Others predicted that their parents would blame themselves for their daughter's sexual orientation. Still others had discussed the possibility with their parents, either because other family members had "come out" or because they had close friends who were gay, bringing up questions about their own sexuality. For example, Christine Granados had talked to her mother "about that because I was in sports. It just happens that sports attract a lot of lesbians and they became my friends."[25] Christine speculated that her mother was more likely to accept lesbianism than Christine's decision to marry "a white man." At the same time, Christine was certain that if she had a relationship with a woman, she could never discuss it with her father because "It would be really hard for him. There are just some things that you can't tell a father."

In Gloria's estimation, "My parents would not be happy if I brought home a woman." Upon further reflection, however, she continued, "But to tell you the truth, I don't know, because if my mom just envisioned her as my roommate, a companion for the rest of my life, and if she had a degree too, and I had my separate bank account, I was well cared for, I think they would have gotten over it." The major impediment that Gloria could foresee was that if she and her hypothetical "lesbian lover decided to have a child, then that would be a problem. Even though in the beginning it would be a terrible shock, I think eventually they would have gotten over it. Although they wouldn't disown me."

Aside from the respondents who were openly lesbian or bisexual, all reported that if they were to bring home a woman it would definitely cause a ruckus in their families. However, almost all felt that their families would "get over it" and eventually accept their choice. Also, when I asked the heterosexual respondents about bringing home a woman, almost all respondents remained unfazed by the notion of shifting their sexuality. They had enough exposure to lesbianism that they found the question, albeit somewhat startling, not inconceivable or inappropriate.

Cultural Adjustments to
Interracial and Interethnic Mating

Many respondents did not plan to mate outside their own group, it just happened. In several instances, respondents started out adamantly against intermarriage and had to reverse their previous views when they fell in love with a non-Latino. Carina García Guzmán called her mother in South Texas from Colorado Springs, where she was attending college, to tell her she had "started dating Mark," her new boyfriend, who was white.[26] Carina's mother "started laughing hard, I could picture her crying. And she told my sister, 'Guess, what? Carina's dating a white guy!'" Carina's sister also started laughing. Both were very amused, because Carina had always said, "I'm never going to date a white guy. Like never, ever in my lifetime! I'll die before I date a white guy. So when I did, they just thought it was hilarious."

Carina took her boyfriend Mark to South Texas to meet her family. Everything was a culture shock for Mark—from the extreme heat so prevalent in the region to the type of food Carina's mother made for the family.

> When he got off the plane, the humidity just hit him! He went back a couple of steps. Then when we got home, he tried to be nice and play football with my little brother. In less than two minutes he came back into the house covered in sweat, completely red! I think he got sunburned in a minute. My mom kept asking, "What do these people eat?" [Carina replied], "Buy him a hamburger, he'll be happy." Still, he got sick from the food because my mom made him salsa. She used two pounds of tomatoes and put one little chile, and it was too spicy for him. He's like, "This is really hot!" And I'm like, "this is ketchup!" [*Laughter.*]

In addition to these cultural clashes, Carina's mother did not speak English and Mark didn't speak Spanish.

Carina was a senior in college, and she and Mark were planning to move in together after graduation; they were also trying to get pregnant, so Carina was seriously thinking about their cultural differences and their influence on raising their future children.

> I was raised in Mexico for the first five years of my life and I want that for my kids. I want to go back every summer to the house in Mexico and raise them there. Mark is not too thrilled about that, and I think that's where the problems come in with dating a white guy. We don't have the same values, we don't have the same dreams, and we don't have the same anything.

Nonetheless, Carina was committed to working things out with Mark, and she planned to move to wherever he found a job after she graduated from college.

At the beginning of her relationship, Gloria had "a lot of issues" with becoming seriously involved with her "German American" boyfriend. Although her involvement with Keith "was never a cultural issue for my parents, it was for me." One concern was that Gloria's siblings were married and had "children with Anglos. So for me it was a big source of pride that I would be the only person in my family to bear a brown child [*laughter*]." Gloria's political activism also made her feel uncomfortable choosing a "white boyfriend. It was embarrassing to be the chair of the *fiesta* committee, to be doing the *tamalada*, and then here I am with my white, blond, blue-eyed boyfriend." The way Gloria resolved it was "for many, many years we just kept our lives separate and he wouldn't go to *quinceañeras* with me, he would never participate in my life because I was embarrassed, plus I danced salsa and I've been doing *ballet folklórico*. I'm very much into my culture." Finally, they broke up "a couple of times and I dated Latinos, because I was looking for this perfect Latino male. They were always jerks who treated me awful. We'd go out to dinner and they'd be looking at some girl who walked by. Keith would never have done that to me. Just like the stereotypical thing my mom told me about. They were just *mujeriegos* [womanizers]. It just never worked out." However, Gloria made a distinction between the Latinos she dated and did not like, and their families: "I loved their moms and their sisters and I really wanted that kind of family. As individuals, the sons were awful and creepy." Gloria finally resolved her ambivalence about Keith's ethnicity. At the time of the interview, she was just a few weeks away from marrying him.

Christine Granados, like Carina above, had never planned to marry outside her ethnic group. As Christine put it, "I think I lucked into this relationship and just stumbled into it." Christine was extremely happy in her marriage to Esten, and they lived close to her in-laws in a small town outside Austin, Texas. However, there were cultural differences between their families that required adjustments from everybody.

> Every time we go to El Paso to visit my family, my husband has to gear himself up. We are with my family the whole time we are there or else we don't tell them we are coming. A few times he asked me, "Can't we just go to the movies without everybody?" I said, "No! Are you kidding me? What's wrong with you?" And then he realizes, "OK, it is the whole family or nothing." So he's had to learn a little bit about how our family is different.

Christine also had to adjust to his family, who acted so differently from hers. "There are still little things about his family. For example, I have to knock before I walk into their house." One of these "little differences," which Christine found "real hard" to understand, was why her in-laws were "not at my house every day. We live in the same town and we can walk to each other's houses. His mother just doesn't come over. That has just been the strangest thing for me."

These "cultural adjustments" did not dampen Christine's happiness in her marriage. She felt they had learned a lot from each other:

> What I like about being married to a white man is that he's teaching me a lot about his culture and I'm teaching him a lot about mine. He is realizing how disadvantaged minorities are. It just amazes him that I live and breathe being Mexican and not being white. It just didn't occur to him. I think he is realizing all the obstacles that Latinos face, and he's in a very good position to do something about it, especially in the small town that we live in. He's looked up to and his family owns the newspaper. He's effecting a lot of change. That's just the way he is too. But he's a little more sensitive and he's putting more minorities on his front page, and I'm writing a column. All the Latinos there are just like, "Wow!" They can't believe that there is a Latina writing a column in that small paper. He's become more aware, and he teaches me a lot about the white world.

Accepting Difference

> My mom's friends tell her, What if your granddaughter comes out half Black and half Spanish? What kind of hair is she going to have? My mom tells them, I guess I am going to have to learn how to make *trensitas* [little braids] and that's it—end of discussion.
> —Dorian López, twenty-year-old respondent, New York City

There were a few parents who wholeheartedly accepted all racial, ethnic, sexual, and class differences. Although they were in the minority, they were very clear about their open-mindedness. Usually only one parent in a couple felt this way, and several were single parents. Parents' lack of prejudice did not appear to be related to years of education, religious affiliation, or number of years in the United States. These were unique individuals who focused on judging their daughters' partners mostly by how well they treated them and by the individuals' personal qualities. For example, Carina García Guzmán stated that her mother "didn't have a problem when I dated several Black guys my freshman year." Carina's "sister is dating a guy from Haiti. And my mom doesn't have any problems with it."

It's important to note that these accepting parents had strong opinions, but they told their daughters up front that they were willing to change for the sake of their children's happiness. Dorian López, who grew up in Queens, New York, with a Mexican mother and a Puerto Rican father, reported that her mother was very aware of Dorian's attraction to African American men.[27] According to Dorian, "My mother would prefer that I marry somebody of my own race, of my own cultural background, but if it didn't happen, then I think that she'd be OK with it." Her grandmother, who was Mexican, was not as accepting. Therefore, Dorian's mother's acceptance put her at odds with her own mother as well as with her friends in the neighborhood who, for the most part, did not accept interracial marriage. According to Dorian, her mother's neighborhood friends "snickered" at "young women dating African American men." In turn, Dorian's mother was not shy about rebutting her friends' views, but at the same time, she admitted it "wasn't a bed of roses to marry an African American man. You have to deal with having mixed children, but it's not anything you can't technically overcome." Nonetheless, Dorian's mother would tell her, "'It's your life. Just meet somebody that treats you fine. And if you are OK with it, then it's OK with me.' I feel that my mom is very understanding." Dorian felt affirmed by her mother, who simply said, "they will be my grandchildren" and "I'll just learn how to make *trensitas* [little braids]" so she could comb her future grandchildren's hair.

Bucking Family Prejudice

Almost all my respondents rejected their parents' homophobic and racist views. They had grown up in a different world, where, regardless of their expressed sexual, ethnic, class, and racial preferences for their partners, respondents were still open to different kinds of relationships not only for other people but for themselves as well. Most respondents had dated interracially and interethnically.

Respondents worked hard at moving their parents toward more reasonable positions. Sometimes they were successful and other times they were not. Almost all respondents, however, did not relinquish hope in their parents' capacity to change and grow, expressing great compassion for their parents' opinions by taking their parents' life experiences as partial explanations for their narrow views.

Accepting Mating Decisions

Overall, almost all respondents expressed confidence that their parents would ultimately accept their mating decisions regardless of how transgressive their choices were. Most parents simply wanted their daughters to have a partner who "loved them," who would "not cheat on them," who had "a good job," and who would not "mistreat them." As María del Rosario Santos's mother told her, "As long as he's not an alcoholic, he doesn't drink or do any kind of drugs, and if he works, that's all that matters."[28]

Lucha as Lover

Lucha very much wanted a family of her own, especially because she wanted to build what she had never had—a loving home with two parents and children. "Deep down, the most wonderful thing that I could possibly have or do with my life is to have a family and have children."

She did not always feel this way. At one point in her life, she did not want to consider children. "Based on my own family, I feel like, oh my God, that is never going to happen. Or it's not possible for me." She did not want to re-create the family she came from and was afraid she would end up "messing up" her children. "Sometimes I do feel like—OK, this is kind of embarrassing to admit—God wants to break my family's cycle of violence and so maybe I'm not supposed to be a mother. I'll just have a career. I won't have a family and kids. And I want it." Eventually she changed her mind and was even engaged for a year to a Jewish man after a seven-year relationship that started when Lucha was first an undergraduate. Her boyfriend proposed "the day after my birthday, in February" and they were supposed to "get married the following year in April."

In preparation for her marriage, Lucha had started the process of conversion to Judaism (see chapter 4), which she continued after her boyfriend broke off the engagement a year later. She realized, however, after her marriage plans fell through, that marrying a Latino was more important to her than she initially thought. Reflecting on her relationship with her Jewish boyfriend, she commented,

> I feel like it is a dynamic that happens a lot in going out with white guys. You get exoticized. It makes you feel like you are less of a person. There are some simple things that they don't understand and you can't explain. If you are around their family, every time someone starts talking about brown people they get quiet and look at you like you're supposed to suddenly teach all of them about the brown population. [*Laughing.*] So, I started to think that it is important to be with a Latino. Also it's really important to me that my husband speak Spanish. That was hard because I tried to teach my ex-fiancé to speak Spanish and he said he'd learn, but he never did. I'd get very frustrated and upset because I love hearing Spanish and I want my [future] children to speak Spanish, especially if they were going to be mixed. I thought, I want them to have some sense of identity through language.

Lucha's current boyfriend was Marcos, who was "half Mexican and half Jewish." According to Lucha, "just saying his name" made her feel more comfortable than she did with her previous boyfriend.

Lucha's sexual exploration began at an early age, when she "was living in a group home and there were a lot of older girls around so they experiment sexually on younger girls. So I had these experiences with them, and I wasn't sure what they were about or what they meant for me." When Lucha was in high school she found out that her older sister Alicia, with whom she did not have close contact, was a lesbian. Lucha thought that homosexuality was inherited, so she said to herself, "Oh my God, I'm lesbian. And then I had a pretty difficult experience the first time I had sex. So then I kind of switched, like I'm going to be completely heterosexual." When Lucha was in college, she slowly realized that she did not "feel one way or the other. It was just kind of whomever I encountered. I've had sexual experiences with women and men. I don't feel like you have to be one or the other necessarily [heterosexual or homosexual]. I feel like you find something in someone else and if it happens to be female, then it's female; if it happens to be a male, then it's male."

Lucha was still ambivalent, however, about whether she could see herself in a long-term relationship with a woman, primarily because, as she stated, "I want to have children," although she had entertained the "possibility of having children with a woman." She felt "that a woman would understand" and "be willing to take on more responsibility for co-parenting than a man." In Lucha's experience, "I don't care how liberated the guy is. The woman is the one doing most of the work. So I definitely thought about that." Lucha had "two women in particular that have been around for a while and that I love." "I think about them," she said, chuckling, "but I don't know."

At the same time that Lucha had a very strong desire for a family, she realized the difficulties of raising children and at the same time having a successful career as a lawyer.

> I have a good friend who just had her second baby. I spent so much time with them and their kids, and it wasn't just a guest visit. I got this very realistic view of what it is to have kids. I'm thinking, How could I do that and have a career? And you definitely need to find a good man to support you.

Nonetheless, Lucha had a clear view of her ideal marriage.

> I want my husband to be my best friend. Somebody really understanding and good with kids. I'd want him to definitely have a job. [*Laughing.*] There is one part of me that would like to have three or four kids. I've always wanted to have a big family, to have lots of kids around, and have them bring their friends or just have this really warm home with an open door and like lots of hugs and stuff.

Lucha wanted all those things that many of us take for granted and that she had never experienced growing up.

Conclusion

Most of my respondents, like Lucha, were still in search of a partner to love, create a home with, and raise children with. Many did not know whether this would happen or with whom. Unlike Lucha, who grew up in foster homes, many respondents had loving memories of their own families with all the difficulties that families involve. What they seemed to remember most was the love of their parents and siblings. They did not hold idealized pictures of what families were but were quick to point out all the conflicts, stress, and vicissitudes of growing up mostly poor, sometimes with only one parent, and even with abuse in their backgrounds. But many still remembered the small gestures of love—the fathers who brought their mothers flowers for no reason, the grandmothers who soothed scrapes, the brothers who defended them against neighborhood bullies, the pride of their farmworker fathers as their daughters crossed the stage to graduate. All these memories gave them hope and spurred them to look for love and to fantasize about their future children.

Many of those who had found their mates were grateful and cherished their partners and offspring. As they raised their own children, they came to appreciate their parents even more, as many relied on them to help them as they handled the multiple demands of wife, mother, student, and professional. They recognized themselves in their mothers as they too began their journey of worrying about the next generation more than they worried about themselves.

Some had also started the wearisome road of raising children by themselves as their marriages did not happen or did not work. They too depended on relatives, friends, and parents to help them raise their children, as they struggled to finish school and become professionals. Single parents seemed the most beleaguered of all the respondents, and yet they also seemed the most focused, because they had a mission—to safeguard the future of their children, who were left, many times, to their sole care.

Overall, respondents, regardless of their life experiences, still believed in love and in sharing their journey through life. They were just beginning to find out how it would all turn out.

Review of Part II

Implications for Feminist Theorizing

ALTHOUGH PATRIARCHY is enforced on all women, it is not enforced in the same way. Different groups of women have different value in the service of patriarchy, differences that are largely determined by race, ethnicity, class, and sexuality. Lesbians are the group of women least useful to patriarchy: they do not reproduce offspring who are direct descendants of any male line. If they procreate, they do so with their own concerns and desires in mind, using artificial insemination, which makes men irrelevant to the decision. Women of Color serve the white patriarchy largely as workers, as they are not able to reproduce racially pure offspring to inherit the race privilege of whiteness (Harris 1993). White women, especially those of the middle and upper classes, serve white patriarchy most directly as the biological producers of the next generation to inherit the status quo (Hurtado 1996a). All women, however, exist under patriarchal systems that value men more than women, and all pay a price for being women. The question is how the different forms of patriarchy imposed on women affect their sense of self and their social identities.

Women across different ethnic, racial, class, and sexualities can relate to each other because of commonalities based on their social identity as women. The differences, however, often emerge out of the value attached to the intersection of other stigmatized *social identities*, largely constructed through historical events (such as colonization), and how this intersection further complicates a woman's access to power beyond being a women does. White hegemonic feminisms have identified as a site of struggle the restoration of white women's sense of self primarily on the basis of gender alone. Feminists of Color have emphasized the deconstruction of privilege based on stigmatized multiple group memberships. The *sitio* of Chicana feminisms is social identity, *not* personal identity. Sonia Saldívar-Hull (2000) squarely delineates *el territorio* (the territory) covered by Chicana feminisms: "since there is no recognized nation-state 'Chicana' or 'Chicano,' when we invoke *Chicana* as a self-identifier, we invoke race and ethnicity, class, and gender in their simultaneity and in their complexity (45)." Saldívar-Hull further elaborates that it is through shared social identities created by colonization and oppression that women of Color in and outside the United States can stand in solidarity with each other.

> The writers whose works I examine present themselves as Chicana feminists, all conscious of their working-class origins. They all reside in that other borderland between professional writer, seasonally employed academician, and community activist. As mestizas, they acknowledge their political and ethnic relationship to African American feminists as well as their indigenous ties to Native American traditions. They find the term *Latina* acceptable because of its implicit solidarity with other similarly politically oriented Spanish-speaking people in the United States. . . . For Chicanas, *women of color* is a *political* designation that expresses our solidarity with Asian American, African American, and Native American women who share similarities in our histories under racism, class exploitation, and cultural domination in the United States—a kinship that extends beyond sharing a national language. (2000, 45–46)

My respondents reflected this emphasis on social identity in their discussions of self. In many ways, the discussions around their religious beliefs, class backgrounds, and choice of mates were impersonal and focused on the social and political aspects of these choices. Although many times they would begin by relating a personal anecdote around lack of resources, for example, not attending school activities because they could not pay the fees, they would quickly shift to a larger framework for their narrative, for example, how other people in their community suffered similar deprivation and how it was related to structural barriers imposed on them by their lack of education and their poverty. It was very difficult for them to completely personalize their narrative without any reference to the social and political world. It is when social identities are nonproblematic—for example, whiteness and middle-classness—that individuals can stick to a purely *personal* narrative of self. When white women students in my feminisms class write about themselves, they do not begin by saying, "As a white person" or attribute their success or failure to having college-educated parents. For the most part, my white feminist students focus on personal psychological assets or shortcomings to explicate who they are and where they stand in the world. The only time they explicitly connect their personal identities to larger social structures is when they discuss their gender and sexuality if they are lesbian. It is being a woman and lesbian that connects them to the broader social world, because it is here that they have to do the "psychological work" (Tajfel 1981) to rid themselves of the stigma of sexism and heterosexism.

My respondents even "historicized" and "socialized" religion beyond individual ritual. Religious practice and beliefs became tools to create community and reconnect with Chicana/Mexicana culture and to resist negative assessments of Chicano/Mexicano culture. It was a basis for "positive distinctiveness" (Tajfel 1981) and allowed them to repel negative views of their social group memberships. Tajfel and his colleagues speak of this process of reassessment of negative group characteristics to transform them into positive views of self. Tajfel and Turner (1979) argue that when the motive to achieve positive distinctiveness is threatened by membership in stigmatized groups, two psychological strategies are likely to be used. One, called social mobility, involves cognitive, affective, and behavioral processes that help a member exit, psychologically or physically, from the group. These processes include denying membership in the disparaged group, identifying with the more powerful, privileged groups, and actually "passing" into them. The other strategy, called social change, also involves various cognitive, affective, and behavioral processes—for example, shifting bases of comparison so that the derogated group becomes superior, altering the meaning of the derogated attributes so that pride can be felt, denying the legitimacy of the derogation, and acting with others for social change (Gurin, Hurtado, and Peng 1994, 524). An integral part of the strategy for social change is taking the characteristics used in the construction of social identities (e.g., skin color, language, culture) and using them as badges of honor rather than sources of shame. Political movements like the Black civil rights movement, the women's movement, the Gay Pride movement, and the Chicano movement were critical in reassessing negative group characteristics as positive emblems of self rather than of degradation: "Black Is Beautiful," "Brown Power," "The Personal Is Political," and "Silence Equals Death" all helped group members reappraise their social identities in a more positive light.

My respondents' strong preference for mating with Latinos was related to their sense that this intimate decision would affect the maintenance of language, culture, history, and worldview—the elements that constituted their social identities as Latinas. My respondents were some of the most educationally successful Latinas in the country, and yet 60 percent were adamant that they wanted to mate with Latinos/as, retaining their ties to their communities and "passing on" their heritage to their offspring. Among the respondents who had intermarried (4 percent), several required their spouses to become knowledgeable about their ethnic heritage and expected to pass it on to their children. As predicted by Tajfel and his colleagues, many of my respondents' social identity as Latinas became more salient to them through the process of social comparison the more exposure they had with out groups—they did not know how Mexican they were until they had extensive exposure to non-Mexicans. The more exposure, the more they wanted to preserve what many times they had taken for granted in their highly segregated communities of origin.

Chicana feminists have been an integral part of this political project of reassessing negative group characteristics; they have provided the analysis and the raw material through cultural production that enable individuals to have an alternative perspective to the negative hegemonic narrative of "Mexicans." For example, religion was critically reconstructed by Chicana feminists to emphasize spirituality—especially the recuperation of cultural and indigenous ritual—to provide psychic healing and empowerment (Hurtado 2000). White hegemonic feminisms (Sandoval 2000) were only partially able to provide this alternative narrative for Chicanas. Although reassessments of the negative characteristics attributed to women helped Chicanas, white hegemonic feminisms were not helpful in reassessing what it meant to be Chicana/Mexicana, poor, and Catholic. Sexuality is a mixed bag; white hegemonic feminisms partially responded to this diversity, but not entirely.

White hegemonic feminisms emphasize the restoration of self through the delineation of the downside of the privileges acquired through their filial relationship to patriarchy as the daughters, sisters, and wives of white men. They brilliantly exposed the victimhood within their class and race privilege. Theirs was a subtle and nuanced analysis of everyday interaction and naturalized social arrangements that resulted in white women feeling less than white men. Even when white women were given access to education, many times it did not diminish their sense of insecurity and doubt about their abilities. In the process of this deconstruction, they built entire areas of scholarship that educated the academy about the nature of manmade social categories and language (Spender 1980; West 1995). What started as an analysis of the personal as political ended up being the impetus for a social, political, and intellectual revolution.

On the other hand, the rallying cry for Chicana feminists was that the political was personal (Hurtado 1996a). They took the personal responsibility socialized in their families to the public sphere. Many Chicana feminist writers claim a working-class background in their writings and in their theoretical assertions about gender subordination (Córdova 1994, 175, 178, 182). Chicana feminisms privileged the primacy of material conditions and advocated strongly for the "basics" required for human existence: adequate jobs, decent wages, good working conditions, child care, health care, and public safety. The differences in what white hegemonic feminisms and Chicana feminisms saw as the site for intervention have had enormous repercussions for how we define feminism within the academy, for the general public, and most important, for young women who should be its beneficiaries. Part 3 of this book engages the polemics around the definition of feminism and its implications for engaging the next generation of young women who will advance the following phase of the feminist political agenda.

Living and Speaking Feminisms

Part III

Sara's Story

I took a leave of absence from graduate school for my second year in the doctoral program. I came back to California when my mother was diagnosed with cancer; she was fifty-eight.

My mother called me in Michigan. She told me, "I need you." That's when I knew it was serious, because my mother was a very strong woman; she did her own thing; she never said that she needed me.

When I got home, that's when I started taking care of her. I was responsible for keeping track of all of her medicines, helping her go to the bathroom, and changing her bed sheets. At the same time, I read the Bible to her, prayed with her, gave her support. It was really hard. I was on the clock twenty-four hours a day, making sure she had her pain medicine. I only got a break every three or four days. My dad would come and help when he had his break from work. My two sister-in-laws helped tremendously. She had the worst body breakdown. I saw the whole thing. But we had a chance to talk, resolve issues.

The reason why my mom didn't get an early diagnosis was because the various doctors she saw didn't do a full medical exam. It all goes back to the class and race issue. The doctors told her, "What kind of work do you do?" She told them she stacked boxes at the chili processing plant. They said, "Oh, that's why you have that back problem, because you're already in your fifties. You probably have osteoporosis, and you're twisting a lot, so that's why you're having back pain." They never did any x-rays or anything. By the time that she couldn't stand the pain any more, the cancer had already metastasized. When she finally saw a specialist, he did a full checkup and told her, "You have cancer." By that time it was already the size of a quarter around her aorta and pressing against her spine. I could not believe that my mother tolerated that pain for so long.

In mid-October, it was like four o'clock in the morning, *se cayó* [she fell] in the bathroom, and she couldn't urinate, but felt pressure like she had to pee. And that's when we took her to the emergency room that was fifty-six miles away. It was so ironic. I was driving, and it was around 5:30 in the morning by this time. We saw the helicopters spraying in the fields. We lived in an area where there was a bunch of *files* [farm fields]. The ranchers always sprayed early in the morning at 6:00. My mom would walk in the mornings to do her exercise at 6:00 or 6:30. First, she'd fix the *lonches* [lunches for her husband and sons] in the morning, and then she'd go do her little exercise afterwards. I was just thinking this is just killing me. But I didn't show a lot of emotion. I'm known for not being very emotional. I'm not touchy-feely, none of that. But I wanted to cry at that point because I was thinking I know this has a lot to do with her having cancer. I knew that there were so many other people who are still being affected by the spraying. Even one of her doctors told her it might've been because of the pesticides.

I took her to the hospital, and the doctors told me they had to put a catheter inside of her. And the catheter stayed from there on out. She could not urinate by herself. I brought her home after that. Then the doctor called and said, "Look, they shouldn't have let you go out of the hospital. You need to bring her back." So we went back home, fifty-six miles, and then we drove back again, another fifty-six miles, carrying my mom now. By this time, we had to get a wheelchair to carry her into the hospital. In a matter of days, she lost the ability to walk and became paraplegic by the end of the week. They did everything they could. They gave her radiation to stop the cancer from growing, but it just didn't stop. I had to stay in the hospital with her in the cancer ward.

During this whole time, Emilio, my fiancé, was very supportive. He said, "Sara, you got to do this. This is the right thing." . . . I said, "We can't afford to hire somebody to take care of my mother. Not only that, you can't even think of hiring somebody when you have a daughter who's not married, has no kids, who can come and help."

My mom was in and out of the hospital several times. The second time she was in the hospital was because she suddenly began to bleed through her rectum. I noticed that it was like a blob of blood, just coming out, oozing out. I called an ambulance. I was so scared to drive fifty miles to her oncologist so she went to the local town hospital. The doctors were such assholes that they said, "Well, there's basically nothing wrong with her. She just has a problem with constipation." I said, "No, a lot of blood came out, a lot of blood." But my problem was that I cleaned it up before the paramedics came and they didn't see how many feces and blood there was. I told them, "No, it was a lot of blood." The doctor told me, "Oh, for a layperson a little blood is a lot of blood." I said, "Excuse me, but you're not talking to a layperson. I'm an educated woman, in a Ph.D. program, and I do understand the difference between a lot and a little!" I was really pissed off. All of my brothers and my dad told me, "*Cálmate Sara! No seas tan grosera!*" [Calm down Sara! Don't be so vulgar!] Back to the *grosera, malhablada* [vulgar, foulmouthed] accusation. But then I explained to my dad, "*No tenemos que decir que sí, cuando no estamos de acuerdo o no entendimos algo!*" [We don't have to say yes when we don't agree or when we don't understand!] All of a sudden my dad said, "Yeah, you're right!" I don't know where that came from. He goes, "Tell 'em, tell 'em!" But my older brother was kind of pissed off, because I always had a big mouth, always challenging people.

She went in the hospital at the end of October. We were going to have a little celebration at home for *Día de los Muertos*.[1] We always had some *mujeres* [women] come over a *rezar el rosario para mi mamá* [to pray the rosary for my mother]. I remember the women always telling me, "*Ay, tú eres tan buena hija. Dios te va a repagar.*" [You are such a good daughter. God is going to repay you.] I was like, Where is *Dios* [God] right now? I need my dishes washed and I have to clean and cook and I have to do all these things!

We took her home. The doctor didn't want to give us a transfer to her oncologist's hospital fifty miles away. He sent us home with a prescription of Zantac. The next day she was hemorrhaging again, and she was bleeding so much she was really pale. The ambulance came, firemen came. They took her out in a stretcher and I went with her in the ambulance. I've never ridden in an ambulance before. I kept thinking it's like a dream, like, This is not real. This is not happening to me. My mom was lying there; they were doing all these things to her, sticking needles all over her. That was it. She never came out of the hospital.

The doctors examined her and they couldn't find what was wrong. I think what happened was that her blood no longer was clotting; it was like just water. That week she was also saying good-bye to everybody. We knew the end was near. She stayed in the hospital for a week before the doctor gave the "OK" to go home. But she was experiencing a lot of pain. I asked her, "How's the pain, mom?" She goes, "*Ay, se siente como una mecha que me está quemando atrás de la espalda.* [I feel like a match is burning me on my back.] And it doesn't go away, Sara." She wanted me to request the machine that injected the morphine at the push of a button so she could self-dose herself instead of taking the pills because she was in excruciating pain. She didn't want to bother anybody. I told her, "If you want that machine, we'll ask for it. It's easier and more convenient. Let's do it." So she said, "OK."

The day before she was getting ready to leave the hospital, she began to bleed again. I noticed she started to lose her blood pressure and I told the nurse. They started to give her a blood transfusion but the blood didn't enter her veins. She started to lose her breath and they resuscitated her and put her on a respirator. Three weeks later, my mother passed away. She died in December.

MANY CHICANA FEMINIST WRITERS have argued that women of Mexican descent gain their consciousness about discrimination through "lived experience" (Trujillo 1991; Moraga 1983; Hurtado 1996b; Anzaldúa 1987). Chicanas' awareness of discrimination stems in part from being mistreated as members of stigmatized groups based on gender, race, class, and sexuality.

The difficulties Sara experienced with her mother's illness highlighted for her the unequal treatment she received in multiple social contexts. As she drove her mother at the crack of dawn through rural California, she realized that perhaps it was her mother's daily walks exactly at this time of morning, when the fields were sprayed with pesticides that might have caused her cancer. Sara was primarily the one coping with her mother's illness while her father and brothers continued to work. As the unmarried daughter, Sara was in charge of physically taking care of her mother, fighting with the doctors, and being chided by her family for her "outspokenness."

The doctors, Sara believed, gave her mother second-class treatment, because she was a poor Mexican woman. And yet it was Sara who was accused of being *malhablada* (foulmouthed) because she defied authority. Sara also saw her mother's acquiescence to authority figures and her reluctance to "bother anybody" with her pain. It was Sara who urged her mother to seek the medicine that would make her last few weeks bearable. Sara had no roadmap for all these actions. She was reacting to her "lived experience" and finding forms of "resistance" as she went along. Yet, toward the end of her mother's illness, she was redeemed by her family's recognition that if it hadn't been for her transgressiveness, her "talking back" and demanding respect, pushing the male members of her family to cooperate, and protecting her mother's dignity, nobody would have noticed her mother's pain and nobody would have stepped up to make her last days as loving and as comfortable as Sara did. Sara learned to be a feminist through the sheer force of confronting her daily experience and finding out that she had the right and skill to refuse to accept what was, to her, unacceptable.

Part 3 examines respondents' lived experience as a basis for their consciousness about gender, race, and political solidarity with other oppressed groups. Chapter 7 examines respondents' negotiations around their color and phenotype within their families and communities and with members of dominant groups. Chapter 8 delineates respondents' commitment to feminisms and chapter 9 looks at respondents' understanding of other political issues besides gender in their efforts to make sense of their lives.

7

■　■　■　■　■　■　■　■　■

Negotiating the Color Line

In my country, I am not exotic,
I do not have Asian eyes, I
was not raised on a reservation.
I do not go artificially blond.
The sun that gravitates to my dark
pigmentation is not my enemy.   —Castillo 1982

The Color Story: Lani Guinier and Lucha

Sometimes their [her grandparents'] comments betrayed their profound confusion about having a darker-skinned grandchild. Even though he made his considerable living as a shopkeeper, a businessman, a man who worked with money rather than ideas, my maternal grandfather, Grandpa Phil, fancied himself an intellectual. His father had been a rabbi; he was much better educated than my grandmother, who had dropped out of elementary school. His Russian heritage was superior in his mind to her Polish roots. Grandpa Phil was well-read, even cosmopolitan. He always challenged me to recite the populations of California and New York, to show off what I had learned in school. . . . When I was little, Grandpa Phil, a funny, outgoing, and very proud man, would sometimes give me baths. He inevitably would end the bath by saying, "Lani, I don't know what it is; I scrub and scrub. You are still dirty. I scrub your elbows and knees, but I can never get them clean." He wasn't being malicious. He was making an observation from his limited perspective, but it hurt, nevertheless. I loved him, but his ignorance defined our relationship for me much more than his witty banter about statistics. . . . My maternal grandmother, Grandma Molly, a quietly assertive, dignified woman, would offer me fashion advice. She used to tell me that I should never wear black. "You are too dark, Lani, to wear dark colors," she would admonish me. Black, especially, would only accentuate my darkness. . . . The daughter of a Jewish mother and a black father, I was only about eight or nine at the time. I didn't call myself "black" then. I would say, if asked, "My mother is white and my father is Negro." Or "I come from a 'mixed' family." My sisters and I were "bridge people," my mother would tell us. We were children who lived in two worlds, but came from no one place. We spanned the experiences of two families of immigrants—Eastern European Jews and West Indian blacks. We were neither black nor white then: we were interracial. (Guinier 1998, 65–66)

When I was younger I associated being white with being educated and with being somebody. My sister would tease me because I'd tell her, "Don't go in the sun!" I used to rub my skin to try to be white. . . . In one of my foster homes, my foster mom would always scrub us, and so I thought being dark meant I was dirty. So I thought, "I have this dirt on me and so I have to get it off." You know? And just try to be white that way. It wasn't until I was a little bit older that I started to realize that brown is pretty, brown is beautiful. But it took me a long time. My [adoptive] mother was white and even she would never touch me, never. It was like being dark was a really bad thing. I had to actively pursue people in my life and find dark people and be around them because they're beautiful and if I'm with them, then I'm beautiful and I'm just as brown.

—Lucha, twenty-five-year-old respondent, Berkeley, California

IN THE TWO STORIES ABOVE, Lani, the older, more experienced woman of Color, seems to be speaking to Lucha, the younger and less experienced woman of Color, telling her, "Yes, I have experienced white people who didn't know how to deal with my color." "Yes, these were relatives of mine, just as your foster parents had difficulty adjusting to your darkness." "Yes, I still loved my relatives in spite of their ignorance." "Yes, they showed me and my family enormous kindness and love in spite of the distance created by color." "Yes, you do survive and even thrive." "Yes, color does color your existence at all levels." "Yes, we do have this color bond that makes for political alliances." "Yes, confusion about 'race' labels is natural because 'race' is unnatural." "Yes, you will endure and above all come to terms with who you are."

"Race," made visible principally through skin color and facial features, is what Stuart Hall calls a "floating signifier": it gains significance in relationship to other signifiers in particular social contexts. And yet its floating nature means that it will always matter—at least in this country at this particular historical time. I did not ask respondents about "race" as an abstract category even though, given their education, they were quite capable of engaging in the latest rhetoric around racial identification. I did not ask them how they "identified ethnically," because, again, it would have rarified something that is lived literally "in the flesh." I knew that no matter how privileged or how educated my respondents were, their skin color and facial features mattered. I also knew that for women, assessments of womanhoods are entwined with racialized sexualities largely based on color and facial features; race matters because it is something we experience on a daily basis in others' reactions to us.[1] I also knew that assessments of "beauty" and "attractiveness" depend on skin color and conformity to white hegemonic standards of beauty. Ultimately, all my respondents were racialized subjects who had to negotiate the color line on a daily basis.

The Color Line and Beauty:
Con el Nopal en la Frente

My sisters were real *güeras* [fair-skinned] and I got called *morena* [dark-skinned]. I looked more Mexicana than my sisters did. My sisters did the whole highlight, blond streak thing and my other sister wore blue contacts for a while to get away from the fact that they were Mexican. Of course, they had the *nopal* [cactus] right on their foreheads![2]
  —Norma I. Garza, twenty-two-year-old respondent, Edinburg, Texas

My respondents were deeply aware of the arbitrary nature of beauty standards. Sometimes assessments of beauty varied according to geographical location, as in the case of Anna Reyes, who went from being unpopular and thinking of herself as ugly because she was "dark," had "hair on her arms," and a "big nose," to being eagerly sought after when she moved after high school graduation from South Texas to the more cosmopolitan city of Austin to attend the University of Texas.[3] Similarly, Patricia Alvarez talked about how her weight was perceived by different colleagues: African American coworkers did not think that she was too heavy, but when she compared herself to coworkers who were white and in her words "anorexic," she thought of herself as obese.[4]

Although most of my respondents did not directly define themselves exclusively vis-à-vis white hegemonic standards of beauty and femininity, they did side-glance at themselves through this prism. They were not oblivious to the images in white fashion magazines, the standards by which they were being judged. At the same time, they often mentioned their own communities' beauty standards, which deviated from whites'. Although they could not fully articulate this alternative aesthetic, they would use such euphemisms as "we take care of ourselves," "we are not afraid to look like women," "I like my long hair and high heels," and "I like my red lipstick and hoop earrings." Regardless of the description, other respondents in different focus groups echoed statements such as those above. Many perceived that it was their different beauty aesthetic that many times racialized them and made them appear different from the white women around them.

An integral part of my respondents' assessments of beauty was the degree of darkness or lightness of their skin color, and the degree to which they were indigenous-looking. Whether dark- or light-skinned, all respondents measured their skin color against whiteness as the norm. There was not a single respondent who stated that she had never thought about her skin color, which is often the case with white respondents (Frankenberg 1993). Even respondents who had one white parent, and who phenotypically could have passed as white, still had experiences with "being considered mixed" or "nonwhite." The racialization process was set in motion as soon as there was recognition of any kind of ethnic identifier, like a Spanish first or last name, or self-identification with any of the ethnic labels available to Mexican descendants in this country, and/or self-identification as "mixed." As a result of any of these identifiers, acquaintances "saw" respondents as racially different even when phenotypically they could pass as white. Growing up in Mexican environments, speaking English with a slight Spanish accent, and acting culturally Mexican also triggered racialization in very explicit terms.

Equally influential in my respondents' developing awareness of race, were wide ranges of phenotypes in many of their families. Respondents often referred to either lighter or darker siblings, uncles, and cousins. They often had one parent that was fair skin and a parent that was darker. Harsh judgments were made in families along color lines. Many respondents reassessed these color dynamics in college when their awareness was raised through classes, readings, and exposure to a diversity of people. Many times respondents with dark skin began, for the first time, to value their *mestiza* [mixed] racial heritage.[5] In other instances, many fair-skinned respondents began to wish, for the first time in their lives, to be darker so they could appear more "Mexican." All respondents had to negotiate their racial identification depending on their skin color and their facial features. In other words, they were all "racialized subjects" within the colonized context of the United States.

Succumbing to Hegemonic Standards of Beauty

Body image is just such a touchy subject for me.
—Claudia Rodriguez, twenty-four-year-old respondent, Chicago

I think it is for any woman.
—Patricia Alvarez, twenty-four-year-old respondent,
Chicago, in response to Claudia

Normative white standards of "beauty" influenced my respondents' body image. Several felt that their weight kept them from feeling "physically beautiful" and that if they could "just lose another twenty pounds," they would be happy. They explicitly pointed to images of white women as influencing their assessments of how much they should weigh and believed that that standard was applied to all women regardless of race and ethnicity. Claudia Rodriguez answered a definitive no when I asked whether she thought she was physically beautiful.[6] Asked why, she said,

'Cause I'm fat! That's why. A couple of years ago I gained a lot of weight and I have lost sixty pounds. [She interrupted herself and gave herself a cheer: "Yeah me!"] I've maintained it, but I just wish I could lose another twenty pounds and I'd be happy. It's a fact of life that society is there with the images of what is acceptable. I don't want to be anorexic. I just want to lose twenty pounds.

Many respondents who assessed their appearance negatively usually described something else about themselves that they truly liked. For example, Claudia said, with a giggle, "I like my hair."

Belinda Martínez's problems with her body image between the ages of twelve and fourteen were severe enough to be considered "the beginnings of anorexia."[7] Belinda went to a doctor, who "threatened to put me in the hospital if I didn't start eating." Eventually Belinda got better because "like any good Mexican family, they fed me, and once I got chubby again they said, 'Oh she's fine now.'" Belinda believed that she had "recovered physically," but "mentally it took me time to deal with it."

María del Rosario Santos felt that the problems with women's body image came from the media and that women had to confront these issues on a daily basis: "It's hard looking through magazines. Everything caters so much to white, mainstream beauty standards. There's nothing wrong with you when you have breasts and hips. But when it comes at you every single day, especially on this campus, it's very hard."[8] The feelings of inadequacy several of my respondents felt were very similar to those experienced by many other women across ethnic and racial lines (Pacheco and Hurtado 2001).

Family Affirmation/Family Negation

Many respondents mentioned that somebody in their families, usually their mothers, constantly told them they were physically beautiful. Although Claudia Rodriguez felt she was too heavy, her "dad tells my mom, '*Nuestra niña es tan tan chula.*' (Our little girl is so so beautiful.) Similarly, once Patricia Alvarez "started blossoming," her mother told her, "*Ay mija, estás tan bonita.*" (My daughter, you are so beautiful.) Her mother's positive comments "reinforced the feeling that I'm pretty, but sometimes I look in the mirror and I'm like, I'm so ugly, I'm so fat. Ughh!"

There were also instances in which parents were extremely critical, causing respondents great anguish until they were able to develop their sense of self-worth, mostly by excelling academically. In some of these families, parents, especially fathers, drew comparisons between their daughters and ranked them according to their looks. Norma I. Garza realized early on that she was not "as thin as my sisters and I was never going to be."[9] "Growing up, that was a real hard thing for me to say." She used to "worry about it and then it was like I cried about it because I couldn't lose weight and I didn't have the right physical frame." This self-assessment was aggravated when her father paid for her older sister's modeling lessons but refused to pay for Norma because she "wasn't thin enough." According to Norma, her father told her with a skeptical tone in his voice, "*Mija*, I don't think that you're ever going be thin enough, so just stick to your books. You're good at that." Norma's father's comments "hurt" her "so bad," especially because her father was also willing to pay for modeling lessons for Norma's younger sister, who "was also pretty, thin, and a cheerleader." Norma felt like the odd person out, because her sisters "were all excited and had something they could do together." Norma felt that the message from her father was "Don't even try to be a model," which hurt Norma and "lowered my self-esteem." Norma decided to fight these negative assessments by doing well

> in school and bringing home good grades. Eventually I started to fill out and guys were calling the house and then my ego just shot right up and it hasn't come down. [*Laughing.*] I put on weight since I've been with my boyfriend, because we are real comfortable with each other and we eat all the time. But I still feel beautiful. I feel people watching me when I walk down the street, maybe because they can feel the ego, maybe it's just an air about me. I've come to believe that I am beautiful.

Transnational Beauty Standards

Many respondents visited Mexico on a regular basis and talked about enjoying going there because the beauty standards were so different from those in the United States, where many were not considered attractive and were not pursued romantically. The situation changed when they went across the border. Claudia Rodriguez loved going to Mexico, where she received quite a bit of male attention. Even "walking through the plaza, men were always whistling." Her aunts told her, "They're talking to you." Claudia responded, "No, they're not!" She could not believe the male attention she received in Mexico, where many would tell her, "you're so pretty!" and she "dated a lot."

Similarly, Carina García Guzmán recalled how she met the "love of [her] life" in the little *ranchito* (farming village) where her parents were from in Mexico.[10]

> When I was fifteen I met the first guy that liked me. I was like, How could you like me? I had ultra short hair. So ugly! I just didn't feel very pretty, but then he came up to me and told me that he had to threaten people to stay away from me. I was like, Wow! this guy likes me! Cool! I don't want to ever leave Mexico. I felt so beautiful there.

The experience of a "cross-border" standard of beauty alerted many respondents to the contextual nature of beauty judgments. When I asked María del Rosario Santos whether she thought she was physically beautiful, she replied, "it depends where I am." Upon further probing, she explained,

> My freshmen year at CC [Colorado College] I looked like the traditional Mexican from Texas, really long, curly hair, wearing the red lipstick and black mascara. I did fit in back home in Houston, but I didn't fit at CC. Now I just cut my hair and I don't fit in at home. Then when I was home for the summer working on my thesis, I was dressed like this. I was like, Damn! I look terrible. I've been at CC too long! But when I returned to Colorado College in the fall, I was overdressed.

Many respondents' awareness of the arbitrariness in beauty standards both restricted and liberated them. On the one hand, they could readily see the social construction of those standards, giving them the freedom to negotiate them between countries and across situations. On the other hand, because they had knowledge of multiple definitions of beauty, they were also aware that they were held to many standards and did not quite fulfill any one of them. María del Rosario was underdressed in Houston and overdressed in Colorado College. Patricia Alvarez's weight was acceptable to her African American coworkers but unacceptable to her white coworkers. Claudia Rodriguez and Carina García Guzmán were actively pursued by men in Mexico but had difficulty dating in the United States. My respondents used all this information to construct their sense of self—sometimes feeling inadequate, other times feeling beautiful, and many times laughing at how ridiculous and vagarious the construction of beauty was everywhere.

Substituting Personhood for Beauty

I think that I'm beautiful because I'm beautiful inside. I have a good heart. I treat people well.

> —Norma I. Garza, twenty-two-year-old respondent, Edinburg, Texas

My sister is definitely the type, where she is like, "I'm not beautiful, but I'm number one in my class!"

> —Lucha, twenty-five-year-old respondent, Berkeley, California

Many respondents expressed the view that beauty was socially constructed and extremely subjective. They knew that women's energies were distracted from other endeavors because society rewards women for their physical appearance. The realization that their looks were not going to be the avenue for their success made respondents develop other assets that would help them achieve in the world. As Gloria put it,

I've never prided myself on my looks. I know I'm not homely, but I've also come to terms with the fact that I'm never going to be the prettiest person in a room, and decided, "Well, I'm going to be good at political organizing. I'm going to put together this *fiesta* [party]. I'm going to be good at other things." So I get my ego stroked different ways. I think that makes me more of a rational person.[11]

Gloria concluded as did other respondents, that is was better to cultivate their personality, social skills, and sense of humor to overcome the fact that they weren't noticed for their appearance alone.

Many respondents did not attempt to appear traditionally "feminine" and reported not using makeup until later in their teens, not paying much attention to the way they dressed while in high school, and generally refusing to "be a cheerleader type." As they grew older and came into their own, many reassessed their physical beauty. By then, they had already developed a very strong identity as intelligent and as high achievers rather than as "lookers" or as particularly "feminine."

Most respondents did not date much when they were in high school and had their social needs met through friendships with women, a practice that they continued through college and beyond. Almost all respondents referred to a longtime female "best friend" with whom they spoke on a daily basis. They also joked about sometimes wishing they were sexually attracted to women to capitalize on their affinity with their best friends; a romantic relationship with them would solve all their problems with men. Respondents often felt their friendships would last "forever" and spoke about becoming *viejitas* (little old ladies) and retiring together. Many respondents also had a network of female friends that they socialized with on a regular basis, relying on them when they went for long periods of time without romantic involvements. Similarly, married respondents also maintained strong friendships with women beyond their immediate families.

An Ethnic Aesthetic

You are brown and you are beautiful.
—Cynthia Duarte, twenty-four-year-old respondent, New York City

Respondents were well aware of the hegemonic standards of beauty that divided women according to race into "an exotic" version of womanhood and a "white" standard, in which women of Color's racial and cultural characteristics, like dark hair, dark skin, "big" lips, large hips, and "loud" clothing, were considered less desirable. Respondents were also aware that their self-perceptions did not diminish categorization into an "exotic" other. According to María del Rosario, white students in Colorado College saw her as "not being attractive but exotic." She thought that the perception stemmed from "two different standards" of attractiveness applied to women according to race. María del Rosario thought that the term "exotic" was used "to identify women of Color" and to "differentiate their beauty from that of white women." Jennifer Trujillo, another respondent in the focus group, chimed in: "For example, women of Color represent the sexual. 'Oh, you have curves!'"[12] Both respondents agreed that dichotomizing beauty standards according to race did not result in separate but equal valuations of women because the ethnic aesthetic "isn't accepted into the white mainstream."

Several parents tried to instill in my respondents a beauty aesthetic based on their culture and history. Cynthia Duarte's mother tried to inculcate positive messages about her appearance very early on when she enrolled Cynthia at the age of three "in a preschool that was very political and very oriented toward children who were low-income and on public assistance. It was located in East L.A .[Los Angeles]. All of us were children of Color and they very specifically taught us, 'You are brown and you are beautiful!'"[13]

Although parents were not always successful in displacing dominant images of beauty with an ethnic aesthetic, their attempts helped respondents in their struggle to resist hegemonic standards of beauty. Cynthia recalled how early messages of racial pride helped her: "when I was starving myself by dieting, my mother tried very hard to make me aware that there is an indigenous type of beauty that I have and that although it's different, it's still very beautiful."

Several parents also took the opportunity to talk about an ethnic aesthetic when respondents as children asked questions about their skin color and phenotype. Camila Fuentes noticed that she was "the darkest one in my family."[14] This was especially the case when "we used to go swimming, I'd get black and my family used to say, 'Eres la negrita.' (You're the little black one.) This led Camila to ask questions "because on my mom's side of the family, they all have blond hair and blue eyes. My mom is the only one that has light brown hair and brown eyes." Camila's mother used the questions to talk to Camila about why she looked different from the rest of the family. Camila "was just being curious about why there's different shades in my family." Her mother told her that "on my grandfather's side, they are Irish and Spanish. She told me more about our heritage and history. That's how I learned that Mexicanos are *mestizos*."

For other respondents, college afforded the opportunity to discover the origins of their phenotype, helping them place themselves historically and connecting with a past that had not been taught to them previously. Alicia Granillo found out in a class in college that, even though she was fair-skinned, her facial features had indigenous origins, a realization that opened up a new way to view herself and to connect to her Chicano community.[15]

It's funny because people have always told me, "*Tan güerita*" [You're so light], but I didn't feel attractive when I used to see other *güeras* [light-skined women] because my nose is different and I knew that my cheekbones and the shape of my eyes were different. When I took a class in college, "Spanish for Bilinguals," we read about Chicanos and *mestizos* and our Indian heritage. I was like, Dang! I've got their features, bold jaw and big nose. I started feeling more in touch with my indigenous side.

Racialization

Mestizo *Families: The Fuzziness of the Color Line*

Academic writings on "race" tend to focus on the process by which people choose to self-identify with particular groups. This is certainly an important aspect of racial identification, and one that has implications for a variety of behaviors. Less examined, however, is the process by which others, especially those who belong to different racial groups, impose "race" on a person. That is, regardless of an individual's desires, wants, needs, and preferences regarding their racial identification, others, particularly those in dominant groups, can project *their ideas, desires, fears, and misconceptions* of what a racialized subject should or should not be (Morrison 1992). My respondents spoke poignantly of how they were racialized by their family members, lovers, friends, and even complete strangers.

Mexican descendants exhibit a range of racial characteristics, from African to European, to indigenous. Many times my respondents' phenotype was related to their parents' geographical origins in Mexico and that region's particular colonization history. The color line, therefore, is not easily demarcated. My respondents' racial and ethnic allocation, especially by non-Latinos, varied from context to context. Most, however, were racialized into a general category of "people of Color"; a few were linked to other European ancestries (e.g., Italian, Spanish). It was not uncommon for my respondents to be approached in public spaces by complete strangers, for example, while standing in line in a grocery store, and asked, "What are you?" Many respondents constantly negotiated this public assertion of the "color line," which taught them the fuzziness of ethnicity and race in U.S. society.

Misty learned about the inconstancy of the color line while growing up in rural Nebraska, where she and her brothers "stood out, being dark-skinned."[16] Misty was "mixed"—her mother was white and her father was Mexican. In fact, her "dad was the only Mexican" in the community where they lived. Her parents divorced when Misty and her two brothers were very young, and her mother remarried a high school principal who was hired for the specific purpose of "cleaning up troubled high schools." Misty's step-father relocated every couple years because "he was excellent at his job." Misty's family usually moved during the summer and when they first arrived at their new homes, many people thought Misty and her brothers were "Black, because we got dark-dark." There were no other people of Color in her environment, so she gained her "race" conscious-ness through her color, which shifted according to the season.

Tomasa's indigenous features and her petiteness led people to believe that she was Asian.[17] Even when she was a child, people in her Chicago neighborhood told her, "'Oh, you look Chinese.' Little kids made fun of me because my eyes look Chinese." Her mother counteracted the racial slurs by telling Tomasa, "*Tus ojos son lo mas bonito de tu cara, son* 'almond shape.'" (Your eyes are the most beautiful part of your face. They are "al-mond shape.") Tomasa eventually became "very proud" of her eyes.

The fluidity of the color line made the racialization process unpre-dictable. At times respondents felt assaulted when racialization occurred in unexpected situations. For example, Gloria had a speech impediment as a result of her overbite. She sought medical advice from "a surgeon and an orthodontist, two white males." After the initial consultation the surgeons asked her, "Have you thought about what you're going to look like when your jaw surgery is done?" Gloria replied, "No." The surgeons proceeded to scan a picture of Gloria's face into their computer to show her. They "started adjusting my lips a little bit because they were going to be a little fuller." After this initial adjustment, they asked Gloria, "Well, what do you think?" Gloria asked, "Am I going to be able to eat and talk right?" They said, "Oh yeah!" Gloria replied, "Well, it looks fine." The surgeons were not satisfied with Gloria's pragmatic approach to the results of her surgery and persisted in asking her, "Well, is there anything else about this picture you'd like to change?" Gloria replied again, "No." The surgeons then asked Gloria directly, "Well, did you ever wonder what you would look like with a different nose?" The surgeons then manipulated the computer image to "straighten out my nose. They made my nostrils bigger; they took the top part and rounded it more and then they showed me the picture." After they were finished, the surgeons asked, "What do you think?" Gloria was startled, and the first thing to come out of her mouth was, "I've got a white person's nose on my face!" Both of them went silent. Gloria said, "You know, this would make a very good sociological study. How many ethnic people come into doctors' offices just like this one and walk out with a nose that doesn't fit their ethnicity?" Gloria told the surgeons that their suggested adjustments to her face "wouldn't be me. I wouldn't be Mexican if I had that nose on my face. It's been interesting but no thank you. I'm never going to get my nose done."

Gloria was caught off guard by her surgeons' suggestions to modify her racial phenotype, although she was also slightly amused because the individuals involved did not know her well. In other cases, the racialization encounter was more intimate and so unexpected that respondents did not fully grasp the racial comments until years later. Jessica Delgado recalled that when she was nineteen one of her old girlfriends, "who was white," said "some pretty provocative things. She had this nickname for me, 'little brown wench.' I didn't register that it was a racialized comment until years later."[18]

Attraction and "Race"

Respondents' phenotype often correlated with others' attraction to them. Alicia Granillo's fiancé, José, explicitly told her, "I was attracted to your skin color because it's so beautiful, so light." Alicia replied, "Ugh! What if I was *prieta* [dark]? Then what?" This assertion was very disturbing to Alicia, but she felt that José had many other desirable qualities.

During adolescence several respondents preferred the hegemonic standards of beauty; for example, they wanted to be "blond and blue-eyed." As they grew older, however, their views changed. Lucinda recalled that "during my teenage years I sat out in the sun with lemon juice in my hair so I could get blonder and get a tan because I wanted to have blonde hair and dark [skin]. But as I got older, I always thought, you know, brown people sure are pretty. When I see a Latino man versus a *gringo* man, I'm immediately attracted to the Latino. I'm attracted to the dark skin, to the dark features, and I wish I was brown. I do."[19]

A few respondents had partners who explicitly appreciated the physical characteristics of *mestizas*. Camila Fuentes's boyfriend told her she was the perfect size, even though in her estimation, she needed to lose weight: "My boyfriend thinks I'm beautiful and he likes my body, and I'm like, hmmmm? I joke around and say, '*Te gustan las gorditas.*'" (You like women who are a little overweight.) Camila received further reinforcement when she lost a bit of weight and her boyfriend said, "Oh my gosh, you're getting so skinny; you're becoming a supermodel." Camila concluded that her boyfriend's "view of skinny is distorted!" "Maybe that's why I like him so much."

According to Camila, her boyfriend's unusual beauty standards were influenced by his political commitment to Chicanismo.[20] Camila's father made fun of them because Camila and her boyfriend wore matching t-shirts with an Emiliano Zapata emblem on the front.[21] Her father told them, "*Para que necesitan eso? Tienen el nopal en la frente.*" (Why do you need those shirts? You have the cactus on your forehead.) Camila's boyfriend often used terms of endearment that highlighted their *nopales* as an act of racial affirmation:

> My boyfriend is very romantic and likes to say, "*Eres mi India*" [You are my Indian], or make references to me being *mestiza*. Like the color of my skin— *café con leche* [coffee with cream]—to him that's most beautiful. He has lighter skin than me, but he is *más* [more] Indian looking. His father was full-blooded Native American, but my boyfriend doesn't know his tribe because he was adopted by a Mexican family. We're really into looking the way we do and being proud of it.

Marketing the Body

> The agencies were very specific, "Don't get dark. You cannot be a dark Mexican and get acting jobs."
>
> —Cynthia Duarte, twenty-four-year-old respondent,
> New York City

Several respondents had tried acting as a profession and developed an acute awareness of the "viability" of their phenotype in the acting marketplace. Lucinda, who still took acting jobs although acting was not her primary profession, had a well-developed analysis of her beauty assets and skin color:

> I don't think I'm physically beautiful. Looks ain't my forte or my strength. I came to terms with that a long time ago. See, I used to do a lot of acting. Well, I do still. You have to see yourself as a product and it's like, OK, what about me can I sell? And you realize, number one, I can't sell myself as a Hispanic because I don't look Hispanic. But it's like, Am I the knockout? Am I Mary Anne or am I Ginger?[22] I'm Mary Anne and I'm gonna have an affair with the professor! I have always been real *güera* [fair-skinned]. When I was little I always wore my hair in pigtails and they used to call me Buffy from Buffy and Joey from the TV series and that stuck with me.[23] It was like, Oh, she's so cute, because I have dimples. So I was like cutesy. It wasn't like, Oh, she's beautiful. And I never really got the football players, so I learned early on that I wasn't beautiful but I was cute.

Cynthia Duarte had tried acting while she was in high school and living in Los Angeles. She continued when she started college at the University of California, Los Angeles (UCLA), where she "started off as a theater arts major." Cynthia had an agent and "acted professionally for a few years." The first thing her agent told her was "wear sunscreen every day. Don't get too dark. Casting agencies don't like you too dark." Cynthia concluded that, unlike Lucinda, who was not viable to be cast as "Hispanic," she "looked Mexican. "I knew I didn't look 'too Mexican' and that was considered a good thing in the entertainment industry."

Cynthia learned the euphemisms used in audition calls to avoid attracting actors who looked "too Mexican" and were "too dark." According to Cynthia, a typical casting call would ask for "a girl with long dark hair, olive skin but not too dark, who was half Spanish and half indigenous." The "half Spanish" requirement insured that the actors responding would not be "too dark."

In addition to the color requirements, Cynthia's weight was also scrutinized and she was asked directly, "'can you drop five pounds?' Straight up! That was really rough." Cynthia commented that if she tried to get "a job now, I'd have to lose ten pounds."

Cynthia's views on her physical beauty were influenced by her foray into acting as she still "wears sunscreen every day." However, she had grown beyond the "whiteness standard" and had come to appreciate her "darkness":

> It's only been in the last maybe few years that I've gotten comfortable enough to allow myself to get darker—where I actually like myself darker. Over the summer I will make a point of getting tanned, because I spent so many years avoiding it—staying away from the sun and wearing a hat—all that kind of stuff to stay lighter for acting jobs. To be honest, though, I did have it in my head that lighter was better. I knew that was the wrong thing to feel, but I felt it.

Cynthia finally decided to change career paths because

> to be an actor, to be an artist where there's a lot of rejection, it has to be so much a part of your identity that you feel like you couldn't do anything else. I felt I could do academics and I do them well and liked it. It has to be in your soul to be an artist. I don't think it was in my soul enough to pursue acting.

Cynthia acknowledged that her decision was also influenced by the fact that she could only get limited roles because of the way she looked: "Competition is stiff. If you don't feel so much confidence that you could beat out the competition, you're already dead. So definitely racism influenced my decision."

At the time of the interview Cynthia was in her first year of the doctoral program in sociology at Columbia University in New York City.

"The White Sheep in the Family": The Color Dis/Advantage

My Italian coworkers are always saying how white I am, which I am. I tell them, "Well, I'm the whitest Mexican that you are ever going to meet. I'm the lightest in my family."

—Christina M. Cota, twenty-seven-year-old respondent, Washington, D.C.

There were respondents who, for all practical purposes, "looked white." These respondents resented people's assumption that they were not Mexican. Patty and another friend who was also often confused for white thought of writing a book to document the vicissitudes of looking white.[24] It would be called "The White Sheep of the Family." White-looking respondents were met with skepticism when they disclosed that they were Mexican or displayed knowledge of Spanish. Patty recalled that she was speaking Spanish at work and someone commented, "Wow, you learned that in college? That's really good! I'm like, 'Hello—no!'"

Similarly, Desireé was called "little white rich girl" by her cousins, because in her rural community in California, her mother's job as an elementary school teacher and her father's job as a laborer at a local chemical factory made her family "rich" in the eyes of the farmworker families living around them.[25] Desireé's "cousins said they thought I was white for a lot of years. I was the only light-skinned one out of thirty cousins. Ten of us that were about the same age grew up together, and I was the fairest one." According to Desireé, "It didn't help that my mom called me Desireé. My nana [grandmother] couldn't even say it. Everyone called me Wee. They just gave up, like, 'Wee's your nickname.'"

Desireé was also "teased" by her extended family, who told her she was not her parents' daughter because her "dad is very dark, very curly hair. Some people think he's black and my mom's lighter-skinned, but I'm still lighter than her and they both have brown eyes." Desireé called her father by his first name, Bobby, because as a child she heard her mother use his name, further compounding the teasing by her extended family, who told him that even Desireé "knows you're not her father. [*Laughter.*] She's this little *güerita* [fair-skinned] with light eyes and light hair."

Desireé's whiteness continued to be an issue when she attended college, where she was confused with other ethnicities. Fellow Latino students asked her, "Are you Jewish? Are you Persian?" When Desireé clarified that she was Mexican, "They're like, '*Pues* [Well], say something in Spanish.' [*Laughter.*] And I'm like, 'I can't. I'm *pocha*.' [*Laughter.*][26] They're like, 'Get out! You're not as Mexican as us.' It's just like, damn! Got the name against me, got the skin against me, and now I'm supposedly against the language."

Desireé also had to negotiate her whiteness with boyfriends. Some criticized her complexion and antagonistically asserted, "You don't know what it's like to be Mexican because you look white." Others were attracted to her skin color and said, "You're so different from other girls. Look at how light you are and you're Latina." Whichever way it went, she did not feel comfortable with the comments made about her skin color.

There were a few respondents who had always considered themselves beautiful and this assessment was intricately related to their coloring. For example, Leticia Sedano told me, "Yes, I do consider myself beautiful. I have very high confidence in myself. I was a cute baby. And I was only one year old, and I was very light-skinned with red hair and colored eyes."[27] From the time Leticia was born, she held a special place in her family because of the color of her skin and her "light eyes." All of Leticia's family told her she was beautiful explicitly because of her phenotype. In addition, Leticia was told when growing up "that I would always have it much easier because I was lighter, compared to my sisters who are darker." In particular, Leticia's sister told her, "When you go to college, you're going to have more privileges because of the color of your skin." Leticia's entire family repeated this message. Leticia's experiences verified her family's predictions. According to Leticia, her cousin, who was only two weeks apart in age from her and was quite beautiful, was treated differently from her simply because she was darker. Leticia did not agree with the privileges of whiteness and thought, "There are a lot of people who are darker-skinned, beautiful. Their color is just beautiful." At times, Leticia wished she had darker skin because "*se me ven las arrugas.* [You can see my wrinkles.] I love dark skin."

Lucha's Looks

Like some of my other respondents, Lucha had succumbed to dominant views of beauty. "I definitely grew up feeling like I wasn't pretty, because I was dark. I always wanted an Anglo nose. As far as my physicality goes, I definitely had people in my life say too much, too often, and too strongly that I was ugly." Unlike the majority of my respondents, who had at least one family member telling them they were beautiful, Lucha did not have any adults affirming her. Instead, her adoptive mother, who was white, openly expressed dislike for Lucha's skin color. "In my adopted home, Pat [her adoptive mother] definitely was calling me like a sloppy slut and dirty.

She would literally not touch me. I'd take really good showers to make sure that I wasn't dirty and so that I wouldn't be too dark. I've had tons of therapy to help me with this."

Her adoptive mother's rejection was especially difficult, because Lucha was only twelve at the time and still very dependent on the approval of adults. Her adoptive father "was Mexican American and definitely more affectionate and nice." Nonetheless, her adoptive mother had an enormous influence over Lucha and her sister and was in charge of disciplining them. Pat was very religious and wanted Lucha and her sister to dress and behave modestly. According to Lucha, Pat would tell them,

> "Don't show your legs!" The one thing I always felt kind of proud of was my legs. My older sisters talked about how my mom had beautiful legs and how that's why my father fell in love with her. That was something that I could feel proud of. But Pat would always be like, "Don't show your legs! Don't wear shorts! Don't wear skirts!"

Lucha's ex-fiancé had always been very affirming: "he always was saying how beautiful my skin was. He definitely always made me feel beautiful. He gave me compliments such as 'you have this great figure,' saying really, really nice things." However, Lucha had difficulty accepting the compliments. "Oh, he's just saying that because he thinks that's what I want to hear." However, part and parcel of his admiration for Lucha was his tendency, in Lucha's eyes, to "exoticize" her. Lucha explained why she felt this way. "Well, one way it was sex. He thought that sex with me was so much more great and adventurous because I was Latina." In addition, her ex-fiancé put Lucha "into this role of being the entertainment."

> In a way it was cool for him to walk into a room with all his lawyer friends (he was a lawyer) or white friends and be like, "Oh, look at my dark girlfriend" or "she's hot!" It was kind of complex, and I didn't like it. Honestly I hated seeing pictures of us together where I was really dark next to this really white guy. I couldn't stand it.

Lucha felt a need to still be told that she was attractive, because she had many past injuries to overcome.

In my relationship now, he doesn't say things like my ex-fiancé did. Never. And I don't know if it's important to me, but it's different. Whether their compliments are sincere or not, I like to hear them because it still makes me feel good. Sometimes I feel like I want to hear nice things, because I have a lot of "you're ugly" to make up for.

Conclusion

One of the most painful questions for most respondents was whether they were physically beautiful or not. Certainly, there were respondents who felt they were physically beautiful (49 percent), but many did not, and it was a painful admission, one that many had negotiated with themselves and with the world. All respondents explicitly stated that beauty was socially constructed through arbitrary standards reinforced in mass media, and that it was highly dependent on artificial accouterments like cosmetics. As Cynthia Duarte stated,

> My beauty so much for me depends on makeup, a blow dryer, and a curling iron. So I really, really need those things to feel beautiful. Without those things, I would walk with my head down. So that's why I think whether I'm beautiful or not is a hard question for me to answer. You know? I'll answer yes but I mean depending on whether I have a curling iron or not. [*Laughter.*]

Respondents were fully aware that a predominantly white standard of beauty, defined by blond hair, blue eyes, and thinness, was preferred by most people and most did not meet this standard.

Many respondents had their own criticisms about the way they looked. For many, these negative assessments started fairly early in life. For example, Jessica Delgado answered no when I asked her whether she was beautiful. She felt this way because "it's all about size for me," which she had worried about even as a child, when she "found a box with all of my elementary school papers" that her mother had kept for her.

> I found this essay that I wrote in second grade while I was in Catholic school. The assignment was to write the things you liked about yourself and the things you didn't like. Mine was mostly about the things I didn't like. There

were three things you had to say and mine were I didn't like my skin color,
I didn't like my weight, and I didn't like the hair on my arms.

Jessica was "just mortified" to find out how long she had been carrying
these assessments about herself, when, in fact, she "was an average size kid.
So, yeah. I don't have any tangible memory of those messages about race
or gender or body image at that time, but obviously they were there."

Assessments of color and facial features were an integral part of my respondents' daily lives. They were ignored or paid attention to depending
on their looks and their skin color, regardless of whether they agreed with
these norms or not. Many rejected the *nopal* they carried on their forehead
and wished at different points in their lives that they were lighter, thinner,
taller—"less Mexican looking." After years of struggle, however, many
came to embrace their *nopal* and wore it as a sign of pride. Others who
were less identifiable as Chicanas wished they had a *nopal* so they too could
be part of this community that they belonged to but that at times rejected
them because they could be potential "color" traitors to their group. Regardless of all these variations, my respondents dealt with the color line on
a daily basis and had learned to be tightrope walkers, always negotiating
the potential pitfalls of their color, ethnicity, class, gender, sexuality, and
looks. Many of them had learned to dance on a very thin surface.

8

■　■　■　■　■　■　■　■　■

Chicanas Speak Feminisms

I keep before me the memory of Esperanza's laughter breaking the
evening stillness whenever I would get too serious about trying to analyze what she was telling me. My aim is to work the dialectic between
Esperanza's no-name feminism and my feminism of too many names, to
go beyond the search for heroines on either side of the border.

—Behar 1993, 276

IN WRITING ABOUT a Mexican street vendor in *Translated Woman*
(1993), Ruth Behar notes that Esperanza acts, lives, and speaks as a feminist without ever calling what she does feminism or even being aware that
her actions could be construed as feminist. The exclusion from scholarly
attention of the lives of women of Color, as well as the exclusion of the
analysis of many scholars of Color, has resulted in the paradoxical dilemma
identified by Behar, in which mostly white academics have put forth many
definitions of feminism but have failed to substantively capture the experiences of poor women of Color (Pesquera and Segura 1996, 231). Our theoretical definitions need to be expanded to include the full diversity of
women's lives and actions. The resulting feminisms might look different
from those developed and defined in the academy, helping us to answer
why there is an apparent lack of feminist identification among young
women today (Griffin 1989).

In this chapter I begin by showcasing respondents' replies to the question of whether there were any women in their families who considered themselves feminists. I wanted to demonstrate how gender, class, race, and ethnicity affected women's lives, and how women both accepted and resisted their subordination. Respondents learned from listening to these women's stories how to "resist subordination through their activities in everyday life, whether in renouncing the cultural prescriptions that control their bodies or rejecting pejorative self-perceptions" (Lamphere, Ragoné, and Zavella 1997, 6).

"No-Name" Feminisms: Women's Stories

I asked, "Do you think there's anybody in your family that's a feminist?" Alicia Granillo reply:

My mother, she had a very difficult life. Her father was very *macho* and used to abuse his children mentally and physically, not sexually. My mother was the oldest of fourteen so she was in charge of helping her mother with all of her brothers and sisters and was only able to go up to second grade. She knows how to read and write and do a little arithmetic. Only seven of her siblings survived. She had to take care of the kids and see them die.

When she was fifteen, my mom met Ricardo, who was seventeen, fell in love, and got married. Ricardo came by himself to the U.S. to work. On the way back to Mexico to pick my mom up, he was killed and she was absolutely devastated. Years later she met my father, who is about twenty years older than she is. I've always known that she married him just to get out of the house, not because she loved him.

My mom was always ahead of her times, even in Mexico. *Me cuenta que vendía quesos y tenía ganado.* [She tells me that she would sell cheese and had a few cattle.] She worked for the postal office and at the same time, she used to sew and sell things. Just very much an entrepreneur.

She came to the states by herself because she had a couple of her sisters living here. So there's another source of strong women. Out of my four aunts, only one of them is still married. One of my aunts owns a restaurant, and she's been married like three or four times. My other aunt, she does crafts and has a booth at the swap meet. She's been married a couple of times. My other aunt is very independent also. So I've always seen these women on my mother's side of the family as very strong, doing what they want to do. My mother and my aunts have definitely been a source of empowerment for me.[1]

Marissa's reply:

I think my mom is definitely a strong feminist and her views overall are feminist. She's always made me really happy to be a woman and not think of it as a negative thing.

My mom had me when she was in high school. When she graduated, she went to the U of M [the University of Michigan] and got her bachelor's degree. She had to leave me with my grandmother in South Texas for a year to go to U of M and get settled with my dad. After she got her bachelor's, she went to law school and she had me throughout the whole thing. I think that takes a very strong woman. She definitely made a better life for me by going to school.

My grandmother is a strong woman also, my mom's mom. She's had a hard, hard life. When she was twelve her mother died. She was the oldest in her family. Soon after, her brother died and then four days later her father died. She's had a lot of things happen to her. She was a single parent and had to raise four kids. They were migrant farmworkers. Although things were hard, she did the best she could, and I admire her. When she talks, you sit and listen to her. The stuff that she's gone through—Oh my God! I ask myself, would I be strong enough to handle those things? My grandmother is very, very smart. She's always watching the news and she's trying to understand. She's very political and very aware. She takes voting and politics very seriously. I admire her for that because I think a lot of educated people don't.[2]

Alicia Z. Maciel's reply:

Once again, I go back to the definition of what is a feminist? My grandmother Otilia, who is my father's mother, and even my grandmother Sara, who's my mother's mother, they both had to survive. I'll use Otilia as an example. Her husband died when she was twenty-five years old, basically my age. She had four kids to raise. She worked by selling *tamales* for a living. So I also consider her an entrepreneur. In that respect, she's very much a feminist. She didn't go to the first man who offered her, "Come, I'll take care of you and the kids." No way. She said, "No, I can do it on my own," and she did. She never remarried, and she was widowed at twenty-five. I consider that feminist.

My grandmother Sara also. She's never ever depended on anybody to take care of her. She has a plot of land in Mexico, and she either does it herself or hires someone to farm the land. She lives off of the wages that come from the land, and that's a feminist to me. She's not waiting for someone to come take care of her. So, in that respect, they have been tremendous role models for me, even though sometimes they might not understand my choices in life or what I'm doing at Harvard Business School. It's all about the same concept of being self-sufficient, taking care of yourself, and fending for yourself instead of being dependent on people and at somebody's mercy.[3]

Valerie reply:

I have a lot of strong women in my family, but they wouldn't call themselves feminists. They would say, "Well, I'm just standing up for what is right," or "Sexual discrimination isn't fair." I asked my mom whether she was a feminist because I did some readings in college about the concept. She's like, "Oh no!" Like feminist was such a bad word. I'm like, "Well, don't you think women should receive equal pay?" She's like, "Oh yeah! Are you kidding!" So I said, "Then you can be a feminist." So now we talk about issues not in terms of feminism but talking about what real women experience. For example, a woman has a right to be independent if she chooses and women should have the power of choice. So I don't use the word feminist very often.

I also think my father's mother, my nana, is a feminist. She is very independent, because she left my grandpa, and she's always worked, and she hasn't depended on men.[4]

As illustrated above, respondents did not speak of feminism per se. Instead, they spoke eloquently and at great length about the different women in their lives as illustrations of women's strength, courage, independence, intelligence, and, most importantly, ability to survive. They had learned their feminisms through women's (and some men's) lived experience.

Speaking Feminisms through Lived Experience:
The Definitional Wars

"Do you consider yourself a feminist?"

"I do. I'm a radical feminist."

—Camila Fuentes, twenty-six-year-old respondent,
Cambridge, Massachusetts

The majority of respondents (51 percent) readily labeled themselves feminist. There were also a sizable number of respondents (33 percent) who ascribed to the label but with reservations, and only a minority did not identify themselves as feminists at all (17 percent). Regardless of their orientation toward feminism, however, all had very definite notions of how their lives were affected by the fact that they were women, marked by their Color, judged by their sexuality, and influenced by their class background.

Many respondents had problems answering the question of whether they considered themselves feminists and inevitably answered, "It depends what you mean by feminist." When I replied that it was up to them to define it, a long discussion often ensued about the war of definitions, rather than the essential goals of feminism. Most respondents felt that feminism, as currently defined, applied to middle-class, educated, white women and was not pertinent to the complexity of their lives. As Rosario stated, "I guess the term 'feminist' confuses me so much because you have such different perceptions of what a feminist is. I guess I am, in the sense that I am pursuing a doctorate in education, I'm out working, I do have a family."[5] On the other hand, although she and her husband "talk about everything and we make all decisions together," she still saw "him as the head of the household and ultimately he has the final say." Rosario did not "have a problem with that, because I know that we are both equals." Rosario knew that on the surface there was an apparent contradiction and that some might construe her adaptation as adhering to an ideology of "machismo," but she felt that although her husband was of Mexican descent, "he isn't that type of person because his family doesn't have that background."

Many respondents made a distinction between their subjective definitions of feminism and others' assessments of their behavior. Many times respondents asserted, "I'm not a feminist," immediately followed by "but others think I am." Conchita explained that she "supported women's rights."[6] At the same time, she "supported the old ways. I like having a gentleman around. I like chivalry." She concluded that because of these contradictions, "I don't really think I am a feminist." However, Conchita was quick to point out that if "you ask my roommate, he'll tell you I am a feminist. He's a little bit chauvinistic but he does it supposedly jokingly. Like he'll tell me to do something for him and I'll tell him no! You've got two legs; do it yourself." Conchita's assertiveness was "part of the reason why he thinks I am a feminist." Her roommate was not the only one who thought Conchita was a feminist. "Other people think that I am because of the way that I support women's issues."

The concern over definitions of feminism often led to the issue of whether respondents had any feminists in their families. Respondents often gave examples of what they considered to be *feminist behavior* but with the caveat that many of the women they were describing would not call themselves feminists and perhaps even other feminists would not define them as such. They explained how these strong women fought for equal treatment in the family and in the workplace; they spoke of women's heroic efforts to raise large families without the support of a husband or men in the family and of working, often several jobs, to support their families. After listing the reasons they considered these women strong, respondents often said, "I guess they are feminists, but they wouldn't call themselves one."

Regardless of their identification, most respondents expressed reservations about a "white" definition of feminism, which, from their perspective, entailed either distancing themselves from men (several referred to "man hating") or having to forsake the gendered etiquette that many enjoyed, such as having men open doors for them or paying for them on dates. In other words, respondents' reservations about labeling themselves feminists stemmed in part from wanting what they called the "benefits of being a woman." The value they placed on chivalrous behavior in no way diminished their advocacy of equality and economic independence, nor their intolerance of physical abuse. The core of these young women's feminisms lay in what they variously called "independence," "the right to decide," and having "control." At issue was not so much the assignment of gendered tasks, like cooking or cleaning, but the right to decide whether they wanted such assignments, rejecting the *expectation* that the tasks were their responsibility simply because they were women. This was key for most of my respondents. No doubt there were also respondents who did not want to do these gendered tasks under *any circumstances,* but these were the exception rather than the rule.

The concern over how to define feminism and whether they themselves fit existing definitions was best summarized by Alicia Z. Maciel. I asked whether she considered herself a feminist.

> I think, in many ways, but it depends how you define a feminist. I'm someone who believes in being very independent and does not need a man to take care of her. Financially, I think, is one way in which I don't need a man. But emotionally I love to have my husband there for me, and I fully take advantage of that gift. I can be a little girl around him. In that respect, people would say, "Oh, my God, she's not a feminist! She needs all this love and attention." And I do. But, at the same time, if I don't have a boyfriend or husband, I'm not going to fall apart, and I'll enjoy life by myself. So I can go either way. I like to be very feminine in the way I dress. In other ways, I'm a feminist in that I really, really stand up for women's rights and that I believe that I can survive on my own and fend for myself and that the man doesn't have to be the one to earn more money. I feel very comfortable saying, "Well, you can stay home with the kids. I'll go to work."

Mapping a Feminist Consciousness: Women's Struggles and Triumphs as Feminist Lessons

A favorite activity among many of my respondents was to listen to women in their families tell them stories about their lives. Mothers related how they met their husbands, how grandmothers traveled alone great distances to provide a better life for their families, and how women sometimes let passions overrule their better sense. There were also stories about women's *triunfos* (triumphs) over adversity. There were many other themes, but the central purpose of the storytelling was to teach respondents how to avoid repeating other women's mistakes and to relish women's resilience.

Through these stories of success and struggle my respondents gained a deep understanding that talent, drive, and discipline alone were not sufficient to gain independence and have a "life of one's own." Respondents heard stories of women who tried to go to school, have a profession, and live alone but had few opportunities to do so. The historical time was not propitious for women's independence. At the same time, many had come to terms with their lives and instead of living in regret, they tried to build families and provide their daughters a different life than their own. Sofia's mother illustrated this lesson well.[7] Sofia's mother fought hard until her late twenties to build an independent life that did not include marriage and children. She began by rebelling against her father's requirement that she work in his store and went back to *la secundaria* (high school) at the age of seventeen. She was a reentry student when there was no such concept in Mexico. She had dreams of pursuing an education and having a career. According to Sofia, her mother "had things that she wanted for herself, but because of circumstances in her life, she wasn't able to really fully accomplish what she probably could have if she had had other opportunities." Nonetheless, Sofia's mother persisted as long as she could, including delaying marriage until she was twenty-nine. Instead of marrying early, which was the norm in her community in Mexico, Sofia's mother finished high school and "did two years of secretarial school in Mexico. She worked at a county office. She tried to do her thing; she didn't want to get married." The main motivation for resisting marriage was seeing "her mom with fourteen kids. Her older sister had nine. The one sister right below her had eight. I don't think she wanted that for herself. She always challenged what she saw around her, but at the same time, like I said, in some ways you could see her also as a traditional mom."

Respondents often related stories that verged on the mythical about the accomplishments of strong women in their families. These stories, however exaggerated, inspired my respondents in multiple ways. For Conchita it was her paternal grandmother, whom she barely knew, that inspired her. Conchita's father told her "stories about how she stopped a runaway carriage by walking on the bar that they put between the horses; she walked the bar and held the reins and pulled the horse back. Stories like that kind of make me feel maybe she was a little bit of a feminist."

Many of my respondents mentioned watching the women in their lives, taking note of the characteristics worth emulating. Unlike the notion of "role models," however, respondents saw both women's strengths and weaknesses and actively chose which characteristics to cultivate. Magdalena felt that different aspects of herself were related to the three significant women in her life—her mother, her grandmother, and her aunt.[8]

From her mother Magdalena felt she "got my strength, my willpower to do things with or without help." In contrast, from her grandmother she got "the homemaker," and "I get the outgoing part from my aunt who has always been really *loca* [crazy]. So I always think I got the best of the three women in my life if you put them together."

Respondents told countless other stories about women around them who showed them what it was like to live as a woman of Color in this society. My respondents used these women's lived experiences to define their feminisms.

Feminism in the Body: Sensuality and Pleasure

My mom taught me about the value of laughter when you're in pain.
—Sonya K. Smith, twenty-four-year-old respondent,
Ann Arbor, Michigan

Although many of my respondents undoubtedly experienced harsh times, they also spoke about their families' sensuality around food, music, relationships, celebrations, and, above all, humor. Irma Martínez's father, before he died prematurely at the age of sixty-four, enjoyed music and other pleasures like eating well.[9] This was a lesson she learned from him and one she treasured. Before his untimely death, Irma's father had a series of complications related to his diabetes that hospitalized him several times. During one of his hospital stays, he advised her on a more healthy and joyous lifestyle. He told her, "*Hija cuídate. No te mal pases, no te desveles.*" (My daughter, take care of yourself. Don't skip any meals and get your sleep.) Irma's father had a special love for folkloric music and religiously listened to the radio. Whenever a special song played, he asked his wife, "*Oye vieja, quién canta esa canción?*" (Hey, old lady, who is singing that song?) And she would say, "*Oh, yo no se.*" (I don't know). "*Ay tú! No sabes nada!*" (You don't know anything!), he would say playfully. Irma recalled that her father "knew every song and songwriter and what date the record was released and what he was doing when it came out. Every Sunday morning he loved playing one of is records; a trio or some kind of music." Irma also had inherited her father's love of food. "He loved to eat. I love eating. I think that's something that is not very [U.S.] American. I love having a nice meal and he did too."

Another aspect of many women's sensuality was the pride they took in their looks. Christine Granados's mother was famous in her family for maintaining her appearance.[10] Christine stated, "My mother was *la reina* [the queen] of the house. She enjoyed being the center of attention because of what she wore or the way she looked. She loved compliments." At fifty-seven she was still a "looker" and very "beautiful."

Although Christine's mother was very liberal in all other respects and very egalitarian in how she treated her daughters and her sons, personal appearance was the only area where there was a pronounced gender difference. Christine's mother had emphasized to her daughters to "wear lipstick, eyeshadow, makeup," and directly told them if she thought they "looked frumpy." Christine concluded with a laugh, "My mother would die if she saw what I was wearing now. She would be appalled if my purse didn't match my shoes." Christine did not necessarily agree with her mother's opinions but nonetheless was influenced by her views as she recognized that she had "a lot of her in me. I notice if a woman's shoes are not impeccable. If the heel is worn then I know that she doesn't care about the way she looks. I have that in my head."

Humor was also central in many of my respondents' families, as several commented that they had inherited their "outrageous senses of humor" from various family members, including their mothers. Many times seeing the comical aspects of a situation served the purpose of fending off racist and sexist attacks, safeguarding them against pain. Sonya K. Smith, whose father was white and whose mother was of Mexican descent, did not resemble her mother.[11] So much so, that when Sonya was young she thought she was "adopted because everybody said, You don't look like your mom." Her mother knew that Sonya would confront these attitudes the rest of her life, so she taught Sonya to be "tough" and to "be true" to herself, to always listen to her "gut" and not rely on others' judgments of her. Sonya's mother gave her the fortitude to follow her dreams and not be curtailed by others' views of her mixed heritage by teaching her "the value of laughter when you're in pain." For example, when Sonya and her mother went to grocery stores or malls, they would "be tagged and followed by security guards." They worked out a routine, which they "started by cracking jokes really loud. 'Oh yes, my little Mexican maid and I'm the rich girl,'" and Sonya knew to tell the guards, "Oh, she's my nanny. She's not my mom." According to Sonya, they were "just kind of saying 'Fuck you!' to everybody around us who is watching us." Similarly, when Sonya's mother visited her in the Midwest where Sonya was attending graduate school, she remembered, "We were riding the city bus because I didn't have a car and my mom would outright tell people who were staring at us, 'Haven't you ever seen a Mexican before?' So she taught me to be feisty and think of creative coping strategies. Humor definitely was a must."

Underground Feminisms, or
"The Mouse Will Play while the Cat Is Away"

Several women were unable to assert their sensuality in the presence of the men in their families, either because they wanted to avoid the men's negative judgments or because the men prohibited them from experiencing pleasure through such activities as listening to music and *platicando* (chatting) with other women. Respondents told stories of the women in their families circumventing male authority by asserting their preferences while men were away. Misty's grandmother held a certain amount of authority in the family, because although Misty's grandfather "made the money, as soon as he got the paycheck he brought it home to my grandmother. And she divided it up, the first cut went directly to the church and the rest went to feed the kids."[12] Nonetheless, Misty's grandfather "was very controlling. As soon as he would leave the house, I remember she'd put on the Mexican records. [*Laughing.*] That was her joy. She knew when he would be coming home, and she turn them off." After Misty's grandfather died, her grandmother "lived on her own, learned how to drive a car, and visited people." As it did for Misty's grandmother, sometimes ultimate freedom for many women came after their spouses died.

Victoria lived in a female-dominated household until her father came home and changed the atmosphere dramatically.[13] Even though Victoria had been raised by both parents and they had been married for twenty-four years, she "never really had a lot of direct contact with my dad" because of his emotional distance. Everybody in Victoria's family was "very afraid of my father. We would hear the car drive up, we'd hear his keys, and we would say oh God! Everything changed whenever my dad came home; we would always go to our rooms and be really quiet."

Many respondents had witnessed women's struggles to create a space of their own. Sometimes it happened at the death of a spouse, as it did for

Misty's grandmother. Other times it happened after women left abusive relationships and they blossomed, or after women had raised their children and they had more time and space. After all the children left for college, Camila Fuentes's mother began by making her husband "do his own laundry" and telling him "*ya no voy a andar detrás de tí limpiando!*" (I'm not going to be behind you cleaning up!)[14] Then she took over her children's bedrooms after they moved out and used each one for her "different pleasures"—one bedroom became her "makeup room," and the other bedroom became her "reading room."

Making Women into Feminists

I definitely think I'm a feminist. My mom raised me to be one.
—Gloria, twenty-seven-year-old respondent,
Albuquerque, New Mexico

Many of my respondents learned about feminism by observing women's lives. But they also received very direct messages about two core issues: to refuse abuse from men and to become economically self-sufficient at all costs, mainly by obtaining an education. In many women's minds, these two issues were interrelated. They could not escape abuse unless they could stand on their own feet economically. Some were told directly by their mothers that they were "making them into feminists" without necessarily using the word but by describing what my respondents later labeled feminist. Gloria's mother told her not to get married and to generally avoid men at all costs. "My mother always told me that boys only wanted one thing from you and that men in general were evil. 'You don't want to get married. You want to have an education, you want to be able to support yourself, and if you can do that, why do you need a husband? You'd only be somebody's *criada* [servant].'"

Gloria's mother applied the same standard to her own marriage and told Gloria, "The only reason I got married was because I wanted children and I didn't have an education and I wanted to leave Mexico and your dad came along." He was a "U.S. citizen and she wanted to leave. She was older; she got married when she was twenty-eight, which is very old for Mexican standards. My dad was nearly thirty-nine. They're eleven years apart." Furthermore, according to Gloria,

> My mom always raised us with the notion that you're equal or better than men. You don't need a man in your life for anything and you shouldn't count on a man. My mom always told us you should have your own money. You should get a degree so that if you want to get married it's your choice. But if the guy's a jerk, you can leave him. So she always kind of instilled that attitude in me.

Gloria understood the difference between her mother's admonishments about men in general and her assessments of her own marriage. Gloria felt that "my parents have a good relationship, but my mom's just a big talker."

Similarly, Marissa's mother told her to "enjoy yourself," to "take advantage of the freedom of being single," and to "travel as much as she could before getting attached to a man." Marissa's mother was especially adamant because of her own experience of getting pregnant before finishing high school. She went on to attend college, and graduated from one of the top law schools in the country while she was raising Marissa. Her mother also defended Marissa against her relatives' query, "When is Marissa getting married?" Her mother inevitably replied, "Hopefully not anytime soon!"

Women's Contradictions: "Live as I Say, Not as I Do"

> My mom is probably the closest thing to a feminist, even though she didn't want to stand up to my dad. She told us, "Don't get married when you're young. Live your life; do what you want to do; don't be dependent on a man"—even though she never took her own advice.
>
> —Victoria, twenty-four-year-old respondent, Santa Cruz, California

Many respondents noted the contradictions between their mothers' admonishments against men and the examples from their mothers' own lives. In Carolina's extended family, most could be considered "feminists," if the term is defined as someone who believes in "the equality between the sexes, women having equal rights, and women having as equal an access to opportunity as men."[15] Both men and women in Carolina's family held these beliefs. However, Carolina thought, "At the same time there's a big difference between my mother and her younger sisters. My mom is the oldest of eight kids. Most of her five sisters are ten years or more younger than her (with the youngest being my age!). I think this contributes to the generation gap." Her parents got married in 1968 when Carolina's mother was twenty, and even though Carolina thought that her father was "very Americanized, born in the United States and his parents were also born in the United States, he's still very old school." Carolina's "father would not even dream of washing a dish or doing laundry." Carolina's mother justified not sharing household chores with her husband by claiming that his job driving a truck and moving things into storage was very "hard physical labor." According to Carolina "letting my dad get away with doing nothing in the house was the fact that she found taking care of a husband and one baby quite easy compared with taking care of her father and her brood of younger brothers and sisters!" Carolina's grandmother "was mentally ill and in and out of mental hospitals. My mother had to do everything in the house—cook, clean, all of it. She says she missed so much school because there was always something to do, another crisis to manage."

Regardless of her mother's contradictions, Carolina thought, "My mother is my feminist conscience voice because she has been very vocal about things." Carolina's parents had been married for thirty years and their patterns of behavior were so well set that, according to Carolina, "How can you teach an old dog new tricks?" During weekends, her mother caught up on household chores, while Carolina's father had "lazy-hazy Sunday, watching football all day." Most recently, however, Carolina's mother had "started making him fold his laundry, so he's there folding his underwear."

Collaborative Feminisms:
The Centrality of Women in Respondents' Lives

I love my sister more than my husband.

—Cristina, twenty-year-old respondent, McAllen, Texas

My respondents inhabited a world filled with women—mothers, sisters, aunts, grandmothers, and women friends. Most of their primary relationships (aside from the lovers of heterosexual women) were with women. Most respondents were not completely conscious of this fact because men (fathers, brothers, lovers, male relatives) were a constant meta-presence (although most in "virtual" form) in their lives. That is, what men thought and did affected respondents in a constant way, but the people they talked to, they spent time with, and they depended on, and who returned much of what they gave, were women. It was from this female-dominated context that my respondents drew their map of feminisms "in the flesh" (Moraga and Anzaldúa 1981, xix).

Many of my respondents demonstrated their connection to women in their lives by encouraging them to go back to school or change jobs that were better suited for them. Other times they helped women in their families to leave relationships, sometimes with their fathers or stepfathers. Sisters often helped each other, the oldest usually counseling the youngest about such things as going into higher education or handling their parents when they had conflicts. Whatever the issue, there was an exchange of roles in which the daughter played the role of supportive friend nudging the mother to take action on her own behalf, or the sister acted as a mentor, teacher, or mother to the other. Aunts and grandmothers also took part in this woman-circle that facilitated much of my respondents' success and happiness.

Cristina considered herself a feminist largely because of the influence her older sister Anna had had throughout her life.[16] Cristina felt that Anna had taught her "everything. She's been in charge, she just, I'm getting emotional." Cristina began crying, overwhelmed by how much she loved her older sister and how much she had learned from her.

> [*Crying.*] She's just everything. She's totally supportive. [*Whispering and crying.*] Without my sister, I don't think I would be alive. She motivates me to strive as much as I can. I hardly had a mother, she was sick [her mother was diagnosed as schizophrenic]. But Anna's been everything—my mom, my best friend, everything. I love her more than my husband.

Anna had been especially helpful when Cristina got married at the age of fourteen and had a child at fifteen. Cristina was expecting her second child and was a junior in college majoring in occupational therapy. Throughout her difficulties, Anna had always supported and encouraged Cristina to continue in school. Anna was only six years older than Cristina and was in her last year of medical school. Cristina took inspiration from Anna's accomplishments and planned to pursue a career in the medical field after finishing her degree and when her kids were older. Cristina's dream of "eventually pursuing a medical degree" came directly from Anna's belief that Cristina "could do it and I see her and she is so happy. I've always wanted to be like my big sister. She's great. She's really motivated me."

Besides pursuing education, often women also helped each other leave destructive relationships. Maritza C. Resendez's mother had taught her daughters not to put up with abusive men.[17] "I see how some of my mom's sisters put up with their husbands. My mom's always been there for them. One time she even hit my uncle on the back with a broom because he was trying to hit her sister. She wasn't going to accept that." Maritza's mother told her brother-in-law, "You don't hurt my family in front of me." Maritza felt that her mother had "always been very protective of her family and the people she loves and real strong about that. I can't be like her, but I learn from her, and I try to be like her. They're good survival skills."

Several other respondents spoke of their mothers and grandmothers taking the metaphorical "broom" to some man's back to defend a woman. Sandra Saenz's mother physically fought with her husband to let Sandra continue with her education.[18] Kim Rivera-Figueroa's grandmother, at the age of fifteen, threw her own father out of their home because he was an abuser.[19] All these women were creating a circle of solidarity against abuse, neglect, and humiliation. They never called it feminist, they simply were defending women out of a sense of empathy and identification with their plight.

The Role of Men in Respondents' Lives

Feminist Men

> Mi padre el filósofo
> El que nunca fue a la escuela
>   pero sabe mucho
> Al que le hicieron daño y perdonó
> El que dañó y se perdonó a sí mismo
> El que concebió hijos y se alegró
>
> [My father the philosopher
> The one who never attended school
>   but has wisdom
> The one who was harmed and forgave

The one who caused harm and forgave himself
The one who conceived children and rejoiced.]
—Hurtado 1986

A main impetus behind feminist organizing and theorizing is to mitigate the deleterious effects of patriarchy on women's lives. Many Chicana feminists have analyzed the specific workings of patriarchy, which my respondents experienced in a myriad of ways: from sexual abuse by fathers, to abandonment by fathers, to sexual harassment by male professors. Also present in my data, and much less discussed in feminist writings, are the positive effects men can have in women developing a feminist consciousness. My respondents spoke with passion about their fathers, lovers, brothers, uncles, male colleagues, and male professors who helped them become independent women and embrace their full potential—men who were important in "making them feminists."

Many of my respondents described relationships that they considered healthy egalitarian relationships with men. Even in these relationships, however, respondents acknowledged that these men were still capable of sexist behavior. Many respondents who were married or engaged described their relationships as very egalitarian. Gloria, who was engaged to be married, recounted that she had never considered changing her name, but "my fiancé suggested that we both hyphenate our name. It never occurred to me that he would do that, and it took a while for me to come around to it. But I think it's a good thing, so we're both hyphenating our name." Regardless of his non-sexist behavior that included Gloria's fiancé's willingness to "help around the house," according to Gloria, "There's still some points of contention where I think he's slacking on some things. But I think we have a very equal relationship and he knows what I expect." Gloria had explicitly negotiated with her fiancé the circumstances under which she would have children.

> He knows that I'm a very demanding person and if we have children it's because we both want them. If there is a chance he's not going to be around, I won't have children. I refuse to do the single mom thing. I'd end up killing the child and probably myself. [*Laughter.*] I'm not patient. I also don't think that all women should have children. I think it should be your choice. I don't

think that just because I was born with a uterus, I have to bear a child. [*Laughter.*]

Victoria and Rafael came from very traditional families, but they made a decision to make their marriage "fifty-fifty." Victoria and her husband both attended college, and they were very happy about how they divided household chores and decision making. "When I hurt my back, Rafael did all the housework, and it wasn't an issue. He picked up my half of it, 'cause we have it split down the middle. So I am very lucky in that way. Any decision we make, we make as a team." Victoria also believed that she would not have married Rafael "if our relationship had been otherwise."

Several respondents were married to men who were not as educated as they were, but for the majority of them, this disparity was not an issue. In fact, many of the spouses were extremely supportive and proud of my respondents' accomplishments. Kim Rivera-Figueroa's husband was the director of a boys' and girls' club at the Hellot River Reservation and "loved kids. That's part of his job." He had been very willing to postpone having a family until Kim graduated, which was finally happening in June. "We are going to have our family finally; so he'll be happy. His family has been praying for a grandchild since we got married. So they're happy." Overall, Kim felt that her husband "loves that I'm going to school, because I love school a lot. He supports everything I do."

At times, my respondents' partners were the ones to nudge them to accomplish as much as possible, even when respondents were reluctant to take risks themselves. After Maria Villa had her baby she wanted to stay home, but her husband said "'No.' And He made me go take those entrance exams" and "he kind of gave me that little push."[20] When Maria found herself procrastinating, her husband told her, "You gotta go study. Go! Go study." Overall, Maria felt that her husband was "really committed to both of us finishing school." Whereas Kim Rivera-Figueroa's husband had less education than she did, Maria Villa's husband was also attending the university.

There were only a few respondents whose partners were ambivalent about my respondents' educational achievements and their feminist views. When I asked Cristina whether her being a feminist caused difficulties in her marriage, she replied, "Yeah. Yeah, that's why we had all our problems in the beginning [of her six-year marriage]." The values with which Cristina had been raised clashed with the values Mario's U.S.-born parents had instilled in him. According to Cristina, Mario came "from a family where his mom thinks that you should be barefoot and pregnant. And if your husband beats you, or hits you, or whatever, then you have to take it." Mario apparently accepted these views because his father "was very abusive towards his mother and it was terrible. She was like a maid to them. She still acts like it. She wanted me to be that way and I was never treated that way in my family." Cristina said, "Mother never really told me, Oh you have to make *tortillas de harina* [flour tortillas]. You have to wash. And when I got married my mother-in-law wanted me to do everything for Mario. She wanted me to be on my hands and knees for him and I couldn't, I wouldn't. I wouldn't do it." Cristina's lack of compliance led to her mother-in-law accusing her of being "the laziest person in the world. I was like, That's not fair. I go to school. I work. I take care of Rina. Then I have to come home and cook, clean, and wash? I said, That's not fair! So, yeah, we had a lot of problems." Mario slowly became more sensitive to Cristina's needs, a change largely prompted by the fact that Cristina separated from him for a short period of time. Most recently, when Cristina did not feel like cooking, "He takes us out. He helps me out with Rina. He's a lot more patient. He's starting to realize that if he wants our marriage to work, he's going to have to give in some of the time."

Fathering Feminists

Fathers were also important in making their daughters feminists. Ironically, they created feminists by raising their daughters like boys rather than girls. That is, they approved, encouraged, or simply did not obstruct their daughters' gender transgressions. Some of the respondents talked about being both their father's son and daughter, either because there were no boys in the family or their father related better to daughters than sons. Lucinda considered herself a tomboy who had always been involved in sports.[21] Even though she had a younger brother, "Cutting the lawn became my responsibility because it was switching the gender roles between my brother and I because I was older. I was the one doing the chores that normally my brother should probably be doing." Although Lucinda's father wanted his son to do these chores, he neither made him do them nor prevented Lucinda from taking on these "manly man" tasks.

Several respondents thought they had closer relationships with their fathers than with their mothers and spoke about the companionship and mentorship that their fathers provided. Bianca's father taught her "to be hardworking, to save, and to be political."[22] She took great pride in her civic participation through "voting and being a good citizen." Her father told her,

> "You need to access information in any way that you can." My dad is very knowledgeable about things. He loves to travel. I've learned to be a worldly person. But more importantly, from my dad I learned to debate and to analyze things. As far as I can remember, we watched *60 Minutes* and *20/20* together. He'd talk and talk and I'd talk and we'd conversate [*sic*] back and forth.

Bianca felt that the greatest lesson she learned from her dad was to "ask questions, speak up." Bianca's father belonged to the San Francisco Union for Lithographers and took Bianca to union meetings since "I was six. There were two hundred men smoking and drinking and I'd be the only girl there." These experiences led Bianca to feel that no matter what "room I'm in, I'll stand up and ask questions, and I'll tell them what I feel. I'll write letters to the editor and I'm not afraid to do it. I learned that from my dad, not from my mom."

Fathers also pushed education hard on their daughters. Several of them told their daughters to "forgo boys" until they finished their degrees. They were especially wary of their daughters marrying early. Misty's father raised her not to "question that you go to college. My dad provided a huge push. 'Forget all the men, all your fun. You need to get your degree and then you can worry about that.'"

Jennifer Trujillo's father, a high school principal, was very involved in her education.[23] Their relationship was not smooth: "We are both so stubborn but he would sit up at night with me and help me write my college essays or even in fourth grade, my speech contest. He's the one who taught me how to write and I think I am a fairly good writer now." Jennifer's father was also very invested in "toughening" her up, so she could handle a difficult profession. Jennifer went to a very prestigious college, where she was a pre-medicine major. According to Jennifer, her father "would yell at me and if I cried, he would be like, 'Don't cry. I was just telling you what to do!'" He taught her, "Don't act like a girlie-girl and start crying. You handle the situation and you deal with it." Jennifer was "thankful that he was hard on me, even though at the time I didn't appreciate it. But it's made me a stronger person." In addition to teaching Jennifer academic skills, her father and her mother also instilled in her the desire "to give back to the community."

Several respondents' grandfathers had also contributed to their feminism. Irma Martínez commented, "My grandfather was a feminist." Irma came to this conclusion after she was trying to figure out how the women in her family mostly her aunts had survived such tough times and realized that "Ultimately my grandfather is the person who helped all this happen." Irma's family's accomplishments began with her grandfather's facilitating her mother's immigration to the United States while leaving her two older children behind. According to Irma, her grandfather told her mother,

> "*Hija, si quieres irte para allá, tus hijos se quedan con nosotros y van a estar bien cuidados.*" [My daughter, if you want to go over there, your children can stay with us and they will be well taken care of.] It wasn't like this horrible thing she was doing. He never made her feel guilty about leaving them. My mother had chosen to come to the States to help provide for her children after she'd realized that their father would not be taking responsibility for them. She also knew there was no work she could do in Mexico that would help her provide for them. He allowed her to do what she thought was right and she's done the same thing with us. The whole thing about studying and doing well in school.

Irma's mother continued her own father's tradition. When it was Irma's turn to leave East Los Angeles for Princeton University,

> She never gave me a fight like some other moms who are like, You have to live here at home. I know where it comes from but it is so narrow-minded. She just wasn't like that. So I think she is a feminist. Maybe even my grandfather was a feminist. Maybe that's what allowed her to be a little more daring even though she's very, I call her *santita* [saintly], very quiet.

Lucha's Womenworld

Although Lucha did not feel "comfortable with the label" feminist, hers had been an existence in a predominantly female environment. Unlike my other respondents, Lucha did not have a father, brother, or uncle to help her understand life's struggles. She had only her sister to assist her in her womanly transitions, from understanding menstruation to flirting with her first boyfriend. Lucha's world was one of women—her sister, her friends, and female lovers. She ventured out of this womenworld when she took on male lovers and even a fiancé, but ultimately she always returned to the only safety she had ever known—the womencircle that ultimately had been her salvation.

9

■ ■ ■ ■ ■ ■ ■ ■ ■

Political Understandings

Lydia Camarillo, chief executive officer of the Democratic National
Convention Committee, got her first lesson in political activism as a
child when her mother walked into an El Paso, Texas housing authority
and slammed a rat down on an official's desk. . . . The family was living
in a barrio basement apartment. There was no indoor plumbing, water
would cover the floor with each rain, and rats came in through cracks in
the walls. Rat in hand, Camarillo's mother demanded safety for her
children and won the family a better apartment in a housing project.
—Leyveld 2000

MY SAMPLE OF RESPONDENTS represents the next generation of
leaders for Chicano and Latino communities in this country. A central
question is whether their climb up the ladder of success will be accompanied by a diminished identification with the political struggles of their ethnic and racial communities. As my respondents obtain degrees, get hired
in prestigious jobs, and no longer struggle economically, will they stop relating to their parents' struggles or, like Lydia Camarillo, will they use their
new found success and professional privileges to help others like them advance as well? Furthermore, does their consciousness around gender and
its intersection with other derogated social categories like race, class, ethnicity, and sexuality result in a political understanding of how these categories affect them in the world? Will they still worry about, for example,

rat-infested apartments such as many of them, like Camarillo, experienced and that many in their neighborhoods still live in? My respondents' answers to these questions were of paramount importance for an understanding of the future of feminism among young Latinas and also for an understanding of the social change that may be fostered by this burgeoning, educated elite, which represents the future hope of their different communities.

Guarding the Body: Views in Favor of Abortion

I'm pro-choice—that's basically the simple answer—I'm pro-choice.
—Sachel, twenty-two-year-old respondent,
Albuquerque, New Mexico

Feminists fought hard to give women control over their bodies through safe and reliable contraception, a goal that was central to women's liberation. The right to choose to bear children was one of the hardest-won feminist political battles, and one that is revisited in almost every election. "Guarding the [female] body" remains a unifying battle cry of the white feminist movement. Women's right to control their biological reproduction gave them the freedom to plan for an education, have access to public work, and choose or reject marriage and was philosophically linked by white feminists to women's individual rights as human beings.

A substantial majority (78 percent) of my respondents agreed with the white feminist stance that women, and not the state, should decide whether they procreate or not. Respondents saw many women's futures crippled by unwanted pregnancies and felt that such an intimate decision should not be made by a government composed of mostly men. Canela called herself a feminist precisely because she was "absolutely totally pro-choice, completely without a doubt."[1] Canela declared,

> People making decisions about these issues are so out of touch with what's going on with the rest of the world. Most of them have privileged lives. A white male in this country has no clue what it is to be dominated, to have someone tell them what they can or cannot do, to not have a choice about their bodies and what they can do with it!

The right to choose to have an abortion had personal meaning to Canela.

[When I was in the] eighth grade I was raped by a friend of my brother's and I thought, what if I had gotten pregnant? How different would my life be right now? And for someone to be able to say what I can or cannot do with my body and to legislate that, it seems so unnatural. When it comes to such an important decision, you don't decide on paper what's right for one person versus another.

Canela's views resonated with many respondents who supported a woman's right to choose, and also echoed white mainstream feminist writings on individual rights.

A few respondents, like Liza Flores Owens, had already faced the very difficult decision of whether to have an abortion or not.[2] Although they were pro-choice, they had followed through with their pregnancies. According to Liza, "I'm pro-choice, but I could never have an abortion. When I got pregnant with her [*pointing to her daughter playing in the room*] that was a choice that I had to make. I had made an appointment to have an abortion and I couldn't do it. But I'm pro-choice."

On the other hand, there were respondents who would not hesitate in exercising their right to an abortion if they became pregnant under undesirable circumstances. Josefa was a single parent and "loved her daughter dearly" but readily admitted that she would have an abortion even though her "life right now is fine and I love my daughter, but I couldn't afford another child, especially alone."[3]

Anna Reyes was a medical student who squarely declared that "it's the woman's choice" to terminate a pregnancy.[4] At the same time, she stated that abortion "is just a very serious decision to make in your life and it's not any easy decision." Although Anna was very open-minded about letting women make their own decision, she applied a different standard to herself.

I think I would've had an abortion if I had gotten pregnant when I was younger, but I am not so sure anymore because I am older. I want to have a child and I think I could raise a child well. I'm already twenty-six. People my age are having kids. That's the right age to have children, and my biological clock is ticking.

Many respondents, like Anna, mentioned their readiness to assume parenthood if they became unexpectedly pregnant. They wanted to assume *personal responsibility* for their behavior, because they saw themselves as economically self-sufficient especially in comparison to their own parents' resources and number of children. In other words, they did not see dealing with an unwanted pregnancy as an issue of individual rights over their bodies but rather one of having agency and taking full responsibility for their actions. Respondents made further distinctions between themselves and other less privileged women, refusing to apply the same standard of personal responsibility to them.

A few respondents had abortions, and they conveyed powerfully what a complex decision it was for them. Aixa, a feminist and strong pro-choice advocate, stated,

I'm totally for the right to choose. However, it's a hard subject for me because I had an abortion. I thank God every day that I was able to have a medical one and not a surgical one, which is totally different. In a lot of ways it freaked me out that I could put down the credit card and pay for an abortion. When I realized the privilege that I have, that was very sobering. I know how fragile that right is in this country; it can be taken away with the next piece of legislation. There are women out there who when they hear they are pregnant just want to die or kill themselves. Because when I heard that I was pregnant, I was like, oh fuck! But I knew what I was going to do. It wasn't an option to keep the pregnancy.[5]

Aixa had always had a very open relationship with her parents. In fact, she had told them that she was bisexual when she was in high school. Still, she could not bring herself to tell her mother (her father had passed away not too long ago) that she had had an abortion.

I still haven't told my mom. My sister knows. And I know that I could tell my mom, but, I don't know, it's hard to, because I am so disappointed in myself that I was that stupid. In college I led safe sex education workshops.

> How could I have been so stupid! I still berate myself, and so I don't know
> if I want my mom to feel that way about me.

Aixa did not have any regrets about her choice and, in fact, after her abortion became even more supportive of women's right to choose. But she still had profound feelings about her difficult choice, which made her more open to the possibility of eventually having children.

> I believe that if I chose to have a child, the spirit of that child [that she never
> had] would come back to me. Like it was meant to be mine, it was meant to
> be mine. So she or he will come back. But now I want to give it a chance to
> come back where I never did before. And it's really weird. It's a very emotional thing. [*Tearing up.*] There is something now that I feel connects me
> to this child that should've been mine, even if it was an accident. Like there
> is a reason that it still happened.

Several married respondents had also faced the issue whether to have an abortion. Although Maria Villa declared, "I am pro-choice. I think everybody has the right to choose what they want to do," she and her husband had faced this difficult dilemma "a couple of times when I thought I was pregnant and it was right in the middle of our educations. We have Elisa. She's doing great. She's in school. She's older now. She's a great independent kid. We don't need another baby."[6] Maria's husband readily recognized that they could not afford another child and told her, "'Well, you'll probably have to have an abortion' and I had more of a struggle with it than he did." It turned out they were not pregnant, so they did not have to confront such a difficult choice.

Another argument presented by pro-choice respondents for their views on abortion was based on their commitment to personal responsibility. They felt there was a contradiction between the position taken by individuals who were against a woman's right to choose and their reluctance to assume responsibility for unwanted children once they were born. Pro-choice respondents were pained that so many unwanted pregnancies resulted in neglected children. Mariquita became a strong pro-choice advocate during college after she worked in a therapeutic day care facility for abused children.[7] She saw "little adorable children who were completely unwanted. Their parents were like, I could care less." From her experience of working with "kids who have endured things that I can't even imagine doing to an animal," she asked herself, "Is it better for a woman not to have a baby she didn't want and save that child the pain?" Mariquita came to "firmly believe that there are some people who are not meant to parent children." If "all the pro-life people, aside from endorsing their beliefs, would go out and adopt three of those kids that are in an orphanage or three of those kids that are homeless or whatever, to me that would really back up their belief that they love children. That would make me happy."

Giving Up Choice: Views against Abortion

A smaller number of respondents (13 percent) were against abortion. Most, however, struggled with their position, recognizing that many women had economic and social restrictions that limited their ability to carry through with a pregnancy. Most of these respondents were very pained about their views but could not bring themselves to "see" the fetus as a "clump of cells." Rather, they thought that life started at the point of conception. Irasema was not atypical among these respondents in saying, "I'm very pro-life and I would never do it [have an abortion], but I go back and forth too."[8] Sometimes she felt that "it would be OK for someone else to do it. But then I'd go back and forth with that. Well, why should it be OK for anyone to do it? But then at the same time, they should be able to make their own decisions. I'm pro and con all the time." As she spoke, Irasema chuckled at her own ambivalence.

Most of these respondents resolved their uncertainty the same way Irasema did, by trying to convince individual women not to have abortions. According to Irasema, if confronted with a woman who was considering an abortion, she would "talk to them and understand why they wanted to do it. But I wouldn't police them if they wanted to go to an abortion clinic."

Several respondents who were against abortion expressed uneasiness about voting in accordance with their beliefs. Anita L. Verdugo considered herself "totally pro-life all the way."[9]

Four years ago when it came down to voting, a difficult situation arose when one of my friends told me she got pregnant at a young age and she wasn't ready to have a child. The guy was a jerk—it was a bad situation. She had contemplated having an abortion, and she was glad she at least had the option if she decided to do it and at least it was safe.

Her friend's experience taught Anita that when "the issue is your friend's or someone else's safety, then the situation changes. In that instance, I did vote pro-choice, because that was fresh in my mind. Now I don't know if I'd do that again."

Jennifer Dominguez had no ambivalence and was adamantly against abortion under almost all circumstances.[10] Jennifer was a very devout Catholic, and her views were influenced by her religious beliefs.

> I believe that everybody comes into life for a purpose. From a pro-life standpoint, when the baby is a fetus, that's a life. It's already living, breathing. I think that that is up to God, I don't think that anybody has a right to take a life away. I'm not going to go and bomb abortion clinics or anything like that, but I personally wouldn't condone it.

Jennifer stated that she would vote against a woman's right to choose although she was ambivalent about cases that involved rape and incest.

> Yes, I would vote against abortion. In all honesty such issues of rape and incest, I really don't know. I mean, part of me would say, I know it would be hard to tell your kids, when they asked who's my father? Well, I don't know. It was dark. We were in an alley and he had a mask. In a case of a rape, I really don't know; it's such a hard issue. But the way that I see it, it's a life, and I just couldn't see taking that away. It's just everything. For some reason, there was a purpose for why that happened.

Some respondents were almost absolute about their opposition to abortion. These respondents felt that carrying a pregnancy through was an issue of taking personal responsibility. Isela Moncada stated bluntly,

> My views on abortion are if you play, you pay. I'm against it when girls go out and act crazy at whatever age. They know what they are getting into. They know the consequences and then they decide, oh, I can't have this baby. I'd rather have an abortion. That I don't like. I think the only time you should be able to abort is either you were raped or if having a baby could en-

danger your health. But other than that, you don't have a right to an abortion. Those are my views.[11]

A few respondents were activists against abortion rights. Their strongly held beliefs motivated them to participate in group political action rather than expressing their individual views through voting. Some had participated in anti-abortion protests and in picketing of clinics where abortions were performed. Several of these respondents had parents adamantly opposed to abortion rights, many tending to be more religious than the rest of the sample although not all were Catholic.

Christina M. Cota was one of the most committed activists in the sample and had "worked at a pro-life clinic for about two or three years on Saturdays."[12] Women came to the clinic seeking "free pregnancy tests." She described the process followed in the clinic, which began with "administering a questionnaire and depending on what the women's concerns were, we would tailor our session and show them a video." Afterwards, Christina or another counselor "would discuss with them the information we gave them." According to Christina, one of the most effective videos depicted "different abortion techniques and a lot of people don't know what was going to happen [during an abortion]. A lot of them changed their minds after seeing the video." Christina felt that many women would seriously reconsider having abortions if they had "sonograms early on and saw the fetus." She was in direct opposition to the advice given in pro-choice clinics.

> You go to a Planned Parenthood clinic or an abortion clinic and if you are two months along, they are going to say it is just a glob of cells. But no, it is not. I think that the truth is twisted when you go to places like that. There are still a lot of people who get defensive about that, but I just think that this is a child, a unique person. There is a reason why this child is in this world and if you do not want it, then at least put it up for adoption.

Political Commitment:
Identification and Consciousness

Patricia Gurin and her colleagues (1980) make the distinction between identification and consciousness:

> Identification and consciousness both denote cognitions: the former about a person's relation to others within a stratum, the latter about a stratum's position within a society. Identification refers to the awareness of having ideas, feelings, and interests similar to others who share the same stratum characteristics. Consciousness refers to a set of political beliefs and action orientations arising out of this awareness of similarity. (30)

Identification, then, is an individual's awareness of belonging to certain groups, say, a certain ethnicity, gender, class, and so on. Consciousness is the awareness that the groups one belongs to hold a certain status (either powerful or not powerful) in society. Consciousness also requires a decision whether to take action to change this status, not just for oneself but for other members of the group as well. All my respondents identified as Mexican descendants, although they applied different ethnic labels to themselves (e.g., Hispanic, Chicana, Latina, Mexican American, and so on). Nonetheless, they were all clearly "identified" according to Gurin et al.'s definition. With the exception of two respondents, they also possessed consciousness of their "stratum's" position in society. They articulated that Mexican descendants were not treated equally and that they and their families had suffered from discrimination. They did not distance themselves from these insights by claiming that they did not apply to them, or that they held no responsibility for remedying them. On the contrary, as a group, my respondents felt very privileged to have triumphed over the challenges they faced as members of derogated groups. This was very clear to most respondents. Less clear, however, was a plan of action to fight against what they perceived as discriminatory treatment for them and those like them.

There were many ways for individuals to move from *identification* with a group to *consciousness* of that group's position in society. Although my respondents used lived experience to inform their overall consciousness, there were two particular factors that facilitated the "jolt" of recognition of previously unseen discriminatory treatment. One was their exposure to knowledge as they entered higher education; the other was political activism as enacted by women in their lives.

Education as Transformation

Education was transformative in developing my respondents' political consciousness. College gave them exposure to a variety of frameworks for examining their life experiences and attitudes and those of their families. In fact, a college education was the main path through which most gained awareness about the meaning of their own and others' group memberships. Many times, it was through readings assigned in their classes that they suddenly noticed what had remained hidden from consciousness. Alicia Granillo felt that classes at the Harvard School of Education "have really made me see different perspectives and different ways of thinking."[13] A particularly influential class for Alicia was "Education for Political and Social Change." "We did all kinds of readings. Every class, I'd walk out asking myself, 'Oh my God! Am I a feminist? Am I a lesbian? Am I heterosexual? Am I a communist? Do I believe in capitalism? Am I an atheist? Am I Catholic?' It just challenged every part of my being!" This broad questioning led Alicia to read more about feminism specifically, and she started "reading a couple of books by feminist writers, like bell hooks and Maya Angelou, and I'd like to start reading more about Latina feminism because I am very interested." In spite of her questioning, Alicia considered part of herself "still very conservative. I still want to have some sort of structure in my life once I have children. I want to provide them with some sort of institution, whether it be the Catholic Church or something like that."

Respondents consistently mentioned that during their college years their attitudes on sexuality went through considerable "transformation." Several came to recognize their lesbianism, and others who were lesbian became determined to inform families of their sexual orientation. Still others for the first time recognized gay members in their families who had remained "in the closet." When Carolina read Cherríe Moraga's book *Loving in the War Years* for a class, she recognized that her aunt was gay and had had a long-term relationship with somebody simply considered by her family as a "roommate."[14] Carolina noted with sadness in her voice that "my aunt Carol died unexpectedly of a kidney problem," and she and her "roommate" had "been together for maybe eighteen years." However, nobody in Carolina's family discussed her aunt's lesbianism and most of them, including Carolina, "had no clue." Carolina's aunt and her partner, Mona, "had a baby together. Mona gave birth to the baby." Carolina never realized that they were together as a family raising their baby; she just "figured that it was Mona's baby."

Exposure to education also allowed students to appreciate their ethnic backgrounds, when, at times, they had been taught by their parents or previous schooling to derogate being Mexican. Misty's father, who was of Mexican descent, was very ambivalent about his ethnic background. He refused to teach his children Spanish and avoided exposing them to working-class Mexicans outside their family.[15] Misty described her father's "anti-Mexican" sentiments:

> We visited my grandparents regularly, about five or six times a year. It wasn't uncommon for migrant workers from Mexico to make their way to my grandparents' (mainly because grandma was so active in church); they knew that her house was a safe place (which was sometimes difficult to identify in a relatively small Nebraska city). Dad would usually take us kids away (usually to a park or out to get ice cream) if the workers came in. Quite often we'd drive by the farm fields and he'd say, "Now this is what you don't want to be like. I'm not saying they're bad people. You educate yourself so you don't have to work in the fields."

Her father's ambivalence toward his Mexican background and Misty's exposure to Chicano studies in college radicalized her in profound ways.

> That's one reason that in my undergrad days I became pro-Mexican in reaction to my father. I found out that I could be proud of being Mexican and not be ashamed. I resented him for not teaching me more about my history and not teaching us Spanish. I was really mad at him for quite a while about that. I didn't understand why he couldn't be proud.

When Misty went to college she "was very politically active and very in-your-face." She took many ethnic studies courses and tried to talk to her father, but to no avail. Whenever she "brought up racial issues, he'd just refuse to talk and say, 'Oh, that's nice.' That was it; I couldn't get a reaction one way or the other." After years of trying, Misty had made some progress. "He's beginning to be more honest about why he didn't want to be called Mexican and why he wouldn't teach us Spanish. But he still hasn't explained that one completely, at least as far as I'm concerned."

Once respondents gained knowledge that challenged their previous views and values, many of them were anxious to *compartir* (share) their newfound insights with their families. Besides trying to educate her father about ethnic issues as discussed above, Misty also made efforts with her mother's Irish American side of the family, who lived in a small town in rural Nebraska. Whereas her mother was very open-minded and agreed with many of Misty's views, her mother's extended family was very conservative. Misty felt that "I was viewed as the radical in my family, not necessarily on feminist issues but racial and cultural issues."

In spite of her reputation as a radical, Misty thought of herself as "moderate compared to some people at the university level," but she came from "a town of four hundred," which made her family rather "sheltered." Misty stated, "I love my family. I wouldn't change them for anything." Nonetheless, she still argued with them when they made racist remarks on her visits home for the holidays. "I remember one Christmas dinner. Somebody was talking about walnuts but my family called them nigger toes." Misty challenged them on these comments as well as others and tried to educate her family by bringing home many of the books she was reading at school. She remembered in particular when she was taking "a gay/lesbian literature class one semester and I brought home the books because I had reading to do. But I purposely left them out to see their reaction." Misty's preadolescent cousins picked them up and asked her, "Did they teach you how to be gay in that class?"

> I tried to explain it. And they were just like, "Oh, that's so gross!" Their parents were sitting there the whole time uneasy, because I was trying to explain that whether you realize it or not, we have gays and lesbians in our family. I feel like I'm trying to educate them every time I go home. Although it's really important to do it in a manner that doesn't offend or sound condescending.

Sofia and her two sisters were involved in progressive political causes in college.[16] Sofia attended Williams College, her older sister attended Yale University, and her younger sister attended Brown University. When I asked Sofia how her parents would react if she brought home a woman, she replied, "Probably not too good." However, Sofia added an important caveat: "Because all three of us went to college," her parents' initial reaction would probably change. She explained,

My sister had a lot of friends in college who were gay men. They loved her, she loved them. My parents had a concern at first, but I think she was the one who challenged my parents. When you go to school you are exposed to different kinds of people with different ways of thinking. We always tried to bring back what we learned to our parents. Instead of separating and being like, "Oh, they won't understand," we confronted them a lot and challenged them and talked to them.

Transformative education was not only obtained in institutions of higher education or imparted from children to their family members; there were parents who actively educated their children about their history and the significance of women in that history. Camila Fuentes's mother had only about eight years of education, but she taught Camila about Mexican history and about "women heroes."[17] Camila attributed "developing what I can now label a feminist mind-set [to] the empowerment of reading." Her mother "would read stories about women heroes or how women played roles *en la revolución Mexicana* [in the Mexican Revolution]. In a way my mom would always talk about the power and strength of women and I think that's a very feminist way of teaching your children."

Women's Activism

I see myself as a political person in every space.
—Nicole Rodriguez, twenty-eight-year-old respondent,
Berkeley, California

There were a few women in my respondents' lives who were activists. Most of their activism was church-related, and a few participated in political organizations and electoral politics. My respondents viewed these activities as examples of efforts to bring about social change. Mariela felt that, "If I learned about speaking up, it was from my mom. She always did volunteer work."[18] Mariela had learned not only to be outspoken but also to take political stands by watching and helping her mother with her church activism. Mariela's family lived in Weslaco, Texas, not far from the U.S./Mexican border, and her mother belonged to the women's group in her Catholic parish. Her mother's activism started by responding to a call from "a lady from Progreso [a border town in Mexico across from Weslaco] who needed drivers to take disabled children to the Shriners' clinics in La Feria [another border town]." The "lady was really old," so Mariela's mother took over and organized the women in her parish. Mariela observed, "I swear, my mom and her friends are a pack. My mom and the other ladies from the church group are getting clothes, raising money for the poor people in Mexico, waking up at three o'clock in the morning to take disabled children to clinics, doing all that stuff."

Mariela also understood how unusual it was for her mother to participate in these activities and not get harassed by her husband for spending time away from home. Mariela's father's approval did not happen automatically but was the result of a hard-won fight by her mother. Mariela felt that her mother was a feminist, because she had forced her husband to recognize her right to participate in activist church activities. She told him, "You know I'm not going to cheat on you or be with somebody else. You know where I am at all times." Mariela's mother not only had to set her husband "straight from the beginning" but also had to cope with people saying, "'Oh, you're just a homemaker,' not seeing the importance of her political work because it was perceived as church-related, volunteer work."

Respondents' Political Involvement in High School

Most respondents were not involved politically with ethnic and women's political issues during high school, because organizations addressing these concerns were nonexistent. As Minerva stated, "The school I went to was all females but they were predominantly white. There weren't any organizations formed on the basis of ethnicity."[19] The only high school organizations that dealt with what remotely could be called "cultural and gender issues" were organizations like Spanish club and international club, and for women there were organizations like the cheerleading squad. Many of my respondents were involved in student government, sports, and special-interest clubs like drama club or the school newspaper. It was in college that respondents were exposed to their ethnic group's history and valorization of culture. Certainly, most were not exposed to feminist political issues until they attended college.

In some instances, during high school respondents organized their own groups or pressured their school administrations to establish clubs for them. Sachel attended a prestigious private high school in Albuquerque, New Mexico, called the Academy.[20] She and

> a group of four male Black friends, in response to a racial incident that happened on campus, formed a group called the Minority Awareness Committee. We held forums. It was mostly an educational awareness group for the school, and it was also a way to protest the dominance of the Anglo culture in the canonized curriculum.

In addition to this organization, Sachel also started support groups for younger students of Color to avoid feelings of alienation because "at Academy there was absolutely no support system for minority kids." The groups met once a week during lunch and they "talked about whatever. It could be political or not. We sat around and joked, ate good food, laughed."

Sachel developed a working relationship with her high school that continued after college graduation and admission to graduate school in American studies at the University of New Mexico. She was about to teach a class to her former high school teachers focusing on "locating the school in the Southwest and looking at Mexican history, at least to create a basic foundational context for the teachers so that they can incorporate it into the curriculum." Sachel's high school activist experience, however, was the exception rather than the rule.

Respondents' Political Involvement in Higher Education

Most respondents (71 percent) belonged to ethnic organizations during college, whereas participation in women's organizations was considerably lower (24 percent). Respondents who were not politically involved still identified strongly with their Mexican background. Their lack of political participation was related to other factors: many of them had to commute to school or hold down several jobs to finance their education, or they did not know enough about political issues to confidently join an organization. At times, they were also married with children or single parents who had extremely limited time. These respondents' educational experience was very different from that of students who went away to college or resided in dorms and apartments even if they did not move away from their home town. Lidia Tovar and Noelia were typical of the respondents who were not involved politically. They both had grown up in rural South Texas and had gotten married in their late teens. They both had school-age children and worked as secretaries for different academic departments at a local state university. They were both going to college part-time while they worked full-time. Lidia had earned enough hours to be a junior.[21] Noelia had slowed down her academic progress because she had recently become a single mother.[22] These respondents, like others, did not feel connected to student organizations and did not feel they knew enough about political issues to be actively involved on their own.

Many respondents used student organizations primarily for socializing and for cultural reinforcement. This was more usual when students went to predominantly white institutions. Ruth N. Lopez Turley joined the Stanford Society of Chicano/Latino Engineers and Scientists not because she was "involved politically," but because it was more of "a social organization where we got to have parties and dances."[23] The organization

> helped me make my transition from home to college just a little easier, 'cause I thought actually moving to the Stanford area [from Laredo, Texas] was a big deal. I was like, "Wow, hardly any Mexicans here!" Boy was I wrong. Now that I'm here at Harvard University, I'm like, "There's definitely no Mexicans here!" You have Puerto Ricans but you don't have Mexicans.

Ruth continued to attend the organization's meetings even after she changed majors, because they provided support.

There were also respondents who had a desire to be politically involved but the demands of graduate school or their professions prevented them from acting on their desires. Noemi Vazquez was in her last year of her medical residency and, although she very much wanted to participate in community activities, she simply could not manage the time because she was "on call."[24]

Geographic Distance, Political Closeness

Geographical location alone did not predetermine whether the respondents were politically involved in ethnic issues. Many respondents who had grown up in the Midwest had been involved in political activities in their communities, which continued during college. Where respondents attended college also did not determine their political involvement. Many who went to predominantly white institutions actively built organizations to meet their needs. Sofia had obtained her undergraduate degree at Williams College in Massachusetts. She had grown up in a predominantly Mexican neighborhood in Chicago and was shocked at the scarcity of students of Color at that institution.

> I started out with volunteer work in the admissions office and found out that I was the only Mexicana from the city of Chicago who had ever been enrolled at Williams. From the beginning we were told you are the bicentennial class, two-hundred years of Williams College. I started thinking, that is a tragedy that they've never had Mexicanas from Chicago.

She and three other women became the core of the organization that

> was called VISTA and it was an umbrella group because we didn't have enough people to make a Mexican group and a Puerto Rican group. But I was one of the coordinators and I was very actively involved. I went to Williams from '89 to '93, which was a time when in the larger society issues of multiculturalism and diversity were being played out. We coined the term "Latina" on that campus because they always called people "Hispanics" or "Spanish." We instituted a lot of firsts—the Annual Latino Heritage Month and the First Annual Chicano Conference. I personally worked a lot.

Sofia found it very gratifying that years later whenever she encountered Latina students from Williams College they thanked her for her activism.

> I just saw someone at an event. She came up to me and said, "Did you go to Williams?" I said, "Yes, how did you know?" She's a senior there now. She saw me in pictures of the Latino group we formed. Then I met somebody else who said, "Oh, I know you from Williams." She worked in admissions. She said Williams was known for recruiting people of Color. I was like, oh really? Now that I think about it, the first time I was there was almost ten years ago. I didn't fully realize the significance of what we did in those four

years. I left before I really got to see the fruits of what we had done. So I can't say I regret my time there.

Uneasy Alliance: Ethnic Issues and Women's Issues

Like many women in the Chicano movement (Blackwell forthcoming; Córdova 1994; NietoGomez forthcoming; A. García 1997), many of the respondents thought that bringing up women's issues in Latino organizing could be divisive and they had a difficult time seeing women's issues as separate from Latino issues. Gloria grew up in Michigan and had always been involved in her Latino community.[25] Gloria felt that political organizations first had to focus on Latino issues before they specifically addressed gender issues.

> I think we should strengthen our own community first and especially in the Midwest. I don't care what sex you are as long as you're contributing. Within our own organization, we've had men and women involved, but I thought we were too young. And we had bigger issues like bilingual education, the migrant issue; those were the issues that I thought were most important. Maybe once we took care of those big pressing issues that affected our entire community, then we could start talking about some of what I consider, lesser issues. I think once you start bringing up gender issues, it's very divisive.

Several other factors also constrained respondents' involvement in women's issues. Latino activists were not numerous, especially in institutions of higher education. As Gloria put it, in describing her own experience in the Midwest, "When there's only ten of you who are doing anything, why cause a rift by bringing up gender issues?" My respondents felt they had to concentrate their efforts on only a few political causes rather than many. Gloria had moved to Albuquerque, New Mexico, to attend graduate school and she felt that the situation in the Southwest differed from that in the Midwest.

> Maybe here in New Mexico, because there's a lot more organizations, then there can be a MANA [Mexican American National Association, a national Latina organization]. Back home there was only one organization. So if I

had a choice to do this or some white women's organization, I'm going to contribute my time for my Latino community, not a bunch of white women.

Respondents also had serious time constraints because of school demands and resolved this conflict by participating in existing white women's organizations. But many found a lack of connection with the participants and the organizations' goals. Nina D. Sánchez, one of the most politically active respondents in the sample, participated in Latino organizations and worked on behalf of gay rights but did not feel much affinity with white women's organizations.[26]

I haven't been involved in [white] women's organizations, mostly because I've popped my head so much into MEChA.[27] I think the feminist movement here in Colorado College is still very focused on white women's issues. Recently there was a play called *The Vagina Monologues*, which I was supposed to be in. I read the script and I was really disappointed. Here's this powerful play and I'm thinking it's going to really talk about women's bodies. To me it just didn't have any political relevance at all. It seemed to address issues of, oh I didn't really enjoy sex. I didn't know how to have an orgasm. Which to me is the kind of stuff that white women worry about. I was like, you know, this playwright interviewed over two hundred women. Why did she pick these things to talk about when they're supposed to be women of diverse backgrounds? I think there was one monologue that had been specifically earmarked as "a Southern Black vagina." I'm serious! It was really disappointing.

The Centrality of Women's Issues

There were a few respondents who actually felt closer to women's issues than to Latino issues in general. Gabriella Gonzalez had grown up on the East Coast, although both of her parents were from El Paso, Texas.[28] Her mother, who was white, was a lawyer, and her father, who was of Mexican descent, was a bio-physicist; they were two of the several parents with advanced degrees. Gabriella had spent two years in Mexico. "When I was in college I didn't feel much of a strong tie to my Mexican-Americanness. I felt much more connected to Mexico itself than the Mexican American community because I didn't grow up in it." When she was an undergraduate at Harvard University she attended the meetings of Latino organizations on campus, but she felt "very self-conscious going to these social events," because "people would talk their 'pocho' and had a great time."[29] The Latino students appeared to "be back in the neighborhood," whereas for Gabriella "it was very foreign to me. I really didn't belong there." Gabriella "didn't speak any Spanish and so that kind of turned me off a little bit." In addition, the Latino students in these organizations were not very welcoming often questioning whether a "non-Spanish speaking New Englander" had the right to claim "to be a Chicana."

As a result, Gabriella "started to get more into feminism than Latino issues." Gabriella "was part of two groups of active female students who" produced "two publications for women on campus at that time, *Lighthouse* and *The Rag*." Gabriella preferred *The Rag*, because it "was much more political in orientation, oppositional and really radical and that was fun. You could really see a very emotional side to feminism so that was really good for me." Gabriella's "awareness" had always "been grounded more in women's issues in general or in African-American issues of discrimination and poverty" and "not so much about my own heritage as a Mexican-American." When she was living in Mexico a "Mexican friend, male as a matter of fact, lent me his copy of 'This Bridge Called my Back' and I haven't turned back since. What an impact that book made on me! . . . The power of the word is amazing."

Frida had always "been politically involved since I was elected sixth-grade president, then ninth-grade president, and student body president in all the schools that I'd ever been to."[30] In college at California State University, San Diego, she began her involvement by joining the "student environmental action coalition. But I really didn't like it. There weren't any people of Color that I could relate to and they definitely could not relate to me or the way that I performed my activism. So I just kind of left that." Next, Frida "ended up meeting these women who had started an Association of Chicana Activists (ACHA)" and within a semester she became president of the organization. They organized conferences on Latinas and in general were "very Latina-oriented." Through ACHA Frida became deeply involved in organizing the MALCS conference on her campus and "that is what I did one whole summer.[31] That was my life."

Frida, however, found problems with the Latino organizations because the dominant view among all members was to avoid divisiveness by ignoring gender issues. Frida found herself the sole spokesperson for women, a very difficult position for her.

> Still to this day, MEChA is very dominated by men. I think that is a big problem. The fact that a lot of women are made to feel that they have to be loyal to men. Actually that is why I left ACHA. I kept having to fight battles alone because they wouldn't agree with me. They had to side with "the people," with the "Chicano movement," and if that meant moving women aside, then so be it.

Frida finally left ACHA because of the women members' views. Frida had to concede that ACHA's members' way of being "feminist" was different from her own.

> That makes me really sad because there are a lot of feminist conversations that don't happen outside of the collegiate level and within people in our age range. We are such a minute community of women who actually identify themselves as feminist Chicanas. Why is that? How can we change it? I think that was the hardest part for me. I tried to explain to them, show them something; and it never worked. They are just so set in their ways. I was not going to change anyone. I guess that's their way of being feminists and that is fine.

Frida felt "more affinity with Chicanas who understand Third World women—all women in a global sense." She found her niche within MALCS and felt a renewed energy to be politically involved with issues that concerned "Third World women."

The Pull of Indigenous Roots

Several respondents identified more closely with Native American political movements than with women's organizations or Latino organizations. Tonantzin's father was born in Mexico and her mother was of Italian descent.[32] Even though Tonantzin grew up in a predominantly white suburb of Chicago and her father refused to teach her Spanish, she had always identified as Mexican American until she found out that "my dad was Mixtec. Forget it! OK! Glory be! Look at me!" By the time Tonantzin was in college, she was claiming, "I am half Italian, half Native American." Nobody else in Tonantzin's family identified with her views; her brother did not claim his Mexican heritage at all.

Once Tonantzin "hit college, I was enthralled. I was so politically involved I let my studies go." Tonantzin joined the council of a group called NATIONS—Native Americans Together in Sharing a National Sovereignty. Tonantzin was unable to join "another group called El Pueblo Unido [The United Nation]," because Latino members disqualified Tonantzin from joining because she was a "half-breed." "I'm thinking, OK, a Puerto Rican that's African American, Spanish, and Indian. Hello! And I am a half-breed? To be Mexican by definition is to be part European and part indigenous. So I was very strongly affiliated with them, but I never actually joined."

Discovering their Native American roots motivated respondents to join indigenous causes; they also participated in Chicano activities that exalted an indigenous past. Xochiquetzal had grown up with Chicano activist parents, who had exposed her to Chicano cultural activities.[33] But as she started middle school in San Antonio, Texas, she started to feel a certain distance from many of the young Chicanas in her school because "They were into putting their hair up with hair spray and lots of makeup and into boys and not into school. I was not into that at all." As a consequence Xochiquetzal "felt less Mexican."

When Xochiquetzal went to Dartmouth College she had difficulty feeling connected with the Latino organizations on campus, because they were so different from the ones she had been exposed to by her parents in San Antonio. In the course of events, Xochiquetzal found that she was more comfortable with the Native American student organization. Her parents had exposed her to many indigenous beliefs as part of Chicano cultural practice, and she felt that the Native American student organization was much more understanding and cooperative than the Latinos on campus. Xochiquetzal discovered that "the Latino community at Dartmouth was very individualistic" and was not a "social group to hang out with."

Familial Transmission of Chicanismo

Several respondents had parents who had been active participants in the Chicano movement of the sixties and had raised their children in activist environments. Several respondents went to schools that emphasized Chicano history and cultural pride, and many had attended Chicano cultural activities since they were children. Xochiquetzal's parents had a central role in the development of a cultural arts center in San Antonio, which was dedicated to Chicano arts from an activist perspective. Xochiquetzal had spent many of her formative years in this center. Xochiquetzal "started *ballet folklórico* when I was like eight." She "was in band. I was in a lot of other things." Xochiquetzal admitted that in the beginning her political views were an extension of her parents': "it started out that way, but then the Chicano community is where I feel most comfortable."

Rebeca's parents had also been very prominent in the Chicano movement.[34] Her mother had been a high-level administrator at Stanford University, where she and her husband had been resident fellows of the Chicano dorm Casa Zapata. Rebeca's father was a famous Chicano artist and writer, also one of the founding members of the Chicano comedy troupe Culture Clash. Rebeca and her brother had grown up in the midst of Chicano political and cultural activities. Consequently, when she went to college she had a difficult time finding an organization that matched her political experience. She participated in different organizations, trying to find a niche.

My freshman year I protested for the cutting of the Spanish for Spanish Speakers Program. And then I got involved with Sigma Lambda Zeta—the Chicana/Latina sorority. But I quit because once I saw that the sorority was not as supportive as it was supposed to be, it was becoming more of a traditional "wear your letter, cutesie" thing. People weren't doing community service. And when we were doing community service, it was baby-sitting for MEChA and helping serve food, the traditional roles that a lot of women's organizations play. I stopped hanging out with MEChA because I had a different upbringing. I had grown up having knowledge of the farmworkers' struggles and going to farmworkers rallies when I was little. So it wasn't as new to me as it was to a lot of MEChA people, and I wasn't as angry about it, as I saw a lot of them be. So I just felt like a lot of energy was wasted on anger and not enough action.

She explored various organizations and concluded that she could contribute without belonging to a particular group. While she was very politically conscious as a result of her upbringing, she also felt scrutinized by other Chicanos who had not grown up in a university setting with highly educated parents. Nonetheless, she cherished her version of Chicano culture so much that she compared it to fine china.

> I think my culture is like my fine china and sometimes I feel like it's hard for me to set it out because it's broken. People might think, you know, her Spanish is bad. Sometimes I'm worried about having too many plates, and I'm seen as the "militant Chicana." Mostly what I worry about is not having enough china—not being Chicana enough and not being Latina enough to sit down and have like a whole *cena* [dinner]. But when I'm really comfortable, I'll bring out what I have, and that's cool. But very rarely do I feel that. So that's why I think it's hard for me to get involved politically with organizations.

Nonetheless, Rebeca knew that her passion was in Latino educational issues, and saw herself contributing to this agenda in the future.

Fighting for Gay Rights

Very few of the respondents mentioned working on behalf of gay rights as one of their primary political involvements, although with one exception all respondents saw homosexuality as a legitimate sexual orientation. They also supported political action on behalf of gay rights. This was the case even among several lesbian and bisexual respondents who identified strongly as "queer" and were involved in either women's issues, like securing programs for battered women, or Latino issues like promoting bilingual education. Mieka Valdez, who identified as a "queer Chicana feminist," had been very involved politically when she was an undergraduate at the University of California, Santa Cruz.[35] She belonged to several organizations, particularly the Affirmative Action Coalition. Her most powerful political experience, however, was when she joined other students to fight the passage of California's Proposition 187. By participating in these political activities, Mieka felt she was carrying on her father's tradition, who had belonged to MEChA when he was an undergraduate at the University of California, San Diego. Mieka's father had become a professor of Chicano studies in Southern California, where he was the advisor for the MEChA student organization on his campus.

In contrast, Mieka never participated in women's organizations and also did not feel an affinity with "gay and queer organizations" because they were dominated by white women; "even the gay or queer groups seem to be mostly white. You could tell on the way they advertised. All the pictures were all white women and I'm like [*ironically*], 'Yeah, I want to join them?'"

Mieka was about to graduate and planned to move to San Francisco, only an hour and a half from Santa Cruz, because "there are so many more queer women of Color groups, things like queer Latina clubs. And there's queer Latina soccer teams. There's all kinds of stuff."

Nina D. Sánchez was one of the few respondents, either heterosexual or homosexual, directly involved in the struggle for gay rights. Nina had a summer internship with "a nonprofit organization here in Colorado Springs called the Gill Foundation. And the Gill Foundation's primary mission is to promote gay and lesbian rights and HIV/AIDS awareness." Nina considered her internship "an awesome experience," especially having the "tables turned on you, to have my boss assume that I was gay or bisexual. And I wasn't offended by it, I just thought it was really interesting." Nina was "one of two straight people in the entire office," which allowed her to experience what it is like to be the minority rather than the norm. Nina also had to deal with her family's disapproval and suspicions because she chose to work on behalf of gay rights. She felt that this was a great education for her and for her family as well.

> I told my mom I was working at this office, and she's like, "Why are you working there?" And I was like, "I want to do this." I think that even if you're not gay or lesbian you need to stand up for their rights as well because that means the rights of everybody. So my mom's like, "All right! All right!"

Critical Views of Latino Student Organizations

The majority of my respondents were very supportive of Latino student organizations. However, a few had severe critiques mostly centered around gender issues within the organizations—men tended to dominate them and women were not allowed to play an equal role. Other times respondents felt that Latino students were uncritically ethnocentric and appropriated nationalist symbols simply to be "cool."

Minerva felt very strongly that Latino organizations, including Latina sororities and fraternities, were not fulfilling a socially constructive role.

> I choose not to get involved in student organizations. I don't assert who I am on the basis of the color of my skin or my ethnicity. I recognize who I am and I'm proud that I am the person that I am, but I think the danger with those kinds of organizations is that they lose sight of what the real goals of the organization should be. The Latina sororities at our school, all they do is get together and drink and party. Everybody needs to have fun, I don't have a problem with that; but if that is all you do, it doesn't look right.

Minerva also had a critique of ethnic organizations that "paraded ethnic symbols" without understanding the "history and culture" behind them. For example, people often paraded the Mexican flag during the celebration of Mexican Independence Day in Chicago, a city famous for its elaborate celebrations. Similarly, students on her campus often wore t-shirts with Che Guevara's image. In both instances, Minerva felt that many did not understand "Mexican independence" and therefore should not display the flag. Minerva concluded, "These kids don't really know who they are or the struggles that we've endured. They know a few key symbols and they can throw them out, but they don't really understand them."

Regardless of Minerva's strong critique of Latino organizations, she still had long-term plans to "make life better" in the Latino neighborhood in Chicago:

> I know that I want to teach in a Latino community—I want to give back. I love Pilsen.[36] We grew up there. I wouldn't mind living there to give back to the community. There are a lot of misguided kids. My way to get to people is through kids, because I work best with kids. Right now I'm probably

going to do my student teaching in Little Village [in the Pilsen neighborhood] at this new school called Josefa Ortiz de Domínguez because I want to give back and I want to be a role model showing that if you work hard enough, if you want something, you can get it.

Respondents' Future Political Involvement

I feel like I'm a part of this chain of actions and reactions. I can't really stop. I will definitely be politically involved for the rest of my life.

—Frida, twenty-four-year-old respondent, San Diego

One important similarity among the respondents was their commitment to having some kind of long-term connection with Latino communities through their professions and involvement in various organizations. With a couple of exceptions, respondents did not see their educational achievement as disconnecting them from their communities of origin. Regardless of my respondents' political and sexual orientation, they still wanted to participate in the political, social, and economic life of their communities. A total of 93 percent of the respondents stated that they would continue to work on behalf of Latino issues, and 92 percent stated that they would continue to work on behalf of ethnic issues in general.

Respondents' participation in political issues generally increased over the course of their educational and developmental trajectory. In high school, very few respondents had ethnic consciousness or gender consciousness, although most identified strongly with their ethnicity. As they traveled their educational paths, exposure to different intellectual and political frameworks clarified their views on their groups' social and economic standing. Most respondents came out of this journey with a deeper appreciation for their ethnic, racial, and class backgrounds. However, not as many respondents culminated with an awareness of gender bias, partially because they did not find resonance with what they perceived as "white, middle-class feminisms." They saw other kinds of disadvantages based on ethnicity, race, and class as more urgent. The issue of sexuality also was not as salient to heterosexual respondents, although most were committed to anti-homophobic positions. At the same time, fighting for gay/lesbian rights was not perceived as "their issue." This was also true for lesbian and bisexual respondents. Respondents at the end of the interview did express a deep commitment to working on behalf of Latino communities in a variety of ways. One of the most common concerns among them was to increase the number of Latinos in higher education; perhaps because education had been the salvation for many of them, respondents perceived it as the most viable solution to Latinos' lack of economic and political power. Respondents also saw young Latinos, especially because many had younger siblings, as the future they had an obligation to invest in.

Most respondents felt that their political connection to Latino communities was a lifetime commitment, one that gave purpose to their lives and direction to their professional choices. Sofia expressed this view very well.

> Yes, I will be politically involved with the Latino community. I think that is something I feel, not that I don't have a choice, because I do. That's my choice. I know that no matter how long I live, our community, my community is always going to have issues and challenges and struggles and I have to be a part of that. I couldn't just sit here and say, "Oh well, now I have my nice paying job and my nice little house. I don't need to worry about those things." I want to continue to work in education, I want to have my own school and I would want it to be based on true parent involvement. Not just parents when you need them, use them and keep them in the dark, because that's what I've seen. You really have to be willing to say, I'm not going to be the sole authority. It is not all about my power. It is about a collective power. The power of having everybody play some kind of role.

Mapping Three Political Trajectories

Aixa

Aixa's political trajectory was not uncommon. Like Aixa, many of my respondents were skeptical about ethnic organizations when they started college. Most received a high school education that emphasized what they considered an "American mainstream" curriculum. In the very exclusive high school Aixa attended in San Antonio, Texas, where the majority of residents were Mexican American, the theater productions were of such American classics as *Our Town*. But there were no plays by Mexican American authors like Luis Valdez. Consequently, when Aixa went to Brown

University, on the East Coast, she did not feel very identified with the issues addressed by the MEChA organization on campus.

> Yes, I was involved politically during college, but not at first. Part of it was having to work out with my issues around race and culture. When I got to Brown, I went to events like Latino History Month celebrations, but people were "browner than thou." It was like, how thick is your accent? Where did you grow up? There was a really narrow view of what could be legitimately brown, not even, say, "Chicano." Because in the East Coast it's so predominately Puerto Rican and Dominican, so Chicanos are a minority within a minority. And then, there is Californians versus Tejanos. There are all these little factions everywhere. I didn't feel good enough to hang out with them. I didn't speak Spanish that well. I didn't dance as well as they did. We didn't listen to the same music. I felt out of place. If you questioned their notions of what constituted a real ethnic person, you would just be hunted right out. So for a little while, I hung out with a lot of white people from my dorm. My boyfriend that I was with for a long time, when we got together it was the first semester of my freshman year. I basically hung out with all his friends.

However, Aixa became familiar with other Latino students, and she eventually joined MEChA and became part of its governing board.

> Later, when I actually became part of the governing board of MEChA, they [MEChA members] told me, "You know, we'd see you in the cafeteria and thought that you were *a vendida* [sellout] and that you forgot where you came from." And I was like, "You never invited me to come sit with you." And they were like, "Oh, you're cool now, but we would look at you and think that you were not; that you just marked Hispanic to get into school and that was it." We had these talks that were really hard to have. I called them out too. I told them, "You alienated me and that's not really the way to create a real community around here."

Aixa graduated from Brown University with a double major in English and American literature and women's studies. She returned to San Antonio and, at the time of the interview, was working as a cultural arts administrator and social justice organizer with the Esperanza Center, a center dedicated to politically progressive arts and culture. Her political awareness had been raised so much that "I can't even watch a movie anymore" without analyzing it for its political content. Her work at the center had also become the core of her existence: "Working at the center is your life. You live there because your work takes twelve, fourteen-hour days."

Aixa's involvement with ethnic, racial, queer, and women's issues influenced her career aspirations, as she planned eventually to attend a doctoral program in modern thought and literature at Stanford University or English and ethnic studies at the University of California, Berkeley. "I am also thinking about the history of consciousness program at Santa Cruz. So West Coast schools." It was through her political participation that Aixa reconnected to her Mexican-origin community, her culture, her language, and ultimately her professional passion. At the time of the interview, the meetings of the National Association for Chicana/Chicano Studies (NACCS) were about to be held in San Antonio, and Aixa was a member of the planning committee. Aixa's father was one of the few parents with an advanced college degree. He had a doctorate in education and had taught ethnic studies and worked as an administrator at a regional university. Aixa had been exposed through her father to many of the people she was meeting again while organizing NACCS. Aixa's father had passed away before she could resolve a lot of her ambivalent feelings toward him. So reconnecting to ethnic studies was another way she was finding her path back to her family.

> Part of my interest in Chicano studies is growing up with my dad and that was our social circle. It reminded me of being a little girl and my dad having his friends over. Only now do I realize what it means. "Oh, you were hanging out with Tomás. It was *that* Tomás" [a famous professor in Chicano studies]. It is weird to think about that now, and again my dad is gone and I feel a little cheated that I am going down the same path as he did; we could've talked about our academic interests; we could have been friends; and he could've given me insights.

Nina D. Sánchez

Nina D. Sánchez was one of the few respondents who became politicized during high school. She attended an exclusive Catholic preparatory school that required passing a difficult entrance exam. Both her parents took extra jobs to pay for Nina and her siblings' tuition.

> For the first two years in high school I wasn't politically involved. Toward the end of my second year is when I began to really get involved with an organization called Grupo Aztlán. It was definitely a miniature version of organizations in higher education. The school was very conservative, very Anglo-dominated, very poor curriculum, very few students of Color. Most organizations had been limited to mostly cultural activities like dances or "Let me give you some Mexican food." But at that time, that's when I first started getting involved, because I began reading books by Ana Castillo.[37] I found some of her books by accident. I'm really happy that I did, because that's when I began to really become politically aware. I would be in AP [advanced placement] English class reading books by Ana Castillo, not paying attention because that is how important it became to me. My parents were like, "Why all of a sudden do you want to start speaking Spanish again?"
>
> So, at first, it was a little confusing for them. But I started to make use of the Grupo Aztlán more as a form of political expression, especially for Latino students. At that point we weren't just Chicano students anymore. So we changed our name to be more inclusive of all Latino students. Towards the end of my senior year it had become more of a political venue for a lot of students to voice their opinions about their frustrations about the curriculum and the way the administration had been treating us.

By the time Nina enrolled in Colorado College, "political involvement" had become her "middle name." As a prospective student, Nina arranged her visit to Colorado College around the MEChA meeting so she could participate.

> So I came and I sat in here, in this very room, and I yelled at everybody because they were having the stupidest argument I've ever heard of in my life. I told them, "This is very disappointing for me as a prospective student to come to this meeting and see you people fighting about a social event. And you're not even concerned about anything else that's politically relevant." I knew my intention was to come here, because I knew once you would get into college you definitely have more freedom to do political things. In high

school we were very much repressed politically when we tried to do any-thing. So my freshman year, a lot of people remembered me from that meet-ing, and I actually became cochair [of MEChA] my freshman year, right after I got here. This year I am cochair again of MEChA and I'm also on various committees that address issues of ethnicity and diversity here on campus, in-cluding one that is a special committee set up by the president of the college.

Nina had a "grand map" for her political trajectory, which ended with her ultimate goal of being elected to the U.S. Senate.

When I was seventeen, I had just graduated from high school; I won a schol-arship to do an independent study in Caracas, Venezuela. As a result, I really became interested in international politics. They flew us out to Washington, D.C., and we met with various groups of people who were in the interna-tional field. I received information about fellowships and I decided that I re-ally love traveling and I'm really interested especially in U.S. foreign policy and how that works. So now I have a fellowship in international affairs which is called the International Institute for International Public Policies and it ex-tends through graduate school. As long as I get into one of the professional schools of international affairs, they'll subsidize my master's degree in inter-national affairs. I'll do that, and then I may go to law school. I would like to work in the international arena for a while. My regional focus is Latin Amer-ica and the Caribbean. And after that I want to spend as much time at home as possible—get the residency in my district down. I'll probably start off as a city council person in Chicago and then eventually run for district four, which is a predominately Latino district that's now represented by Con-gressman Luis Gutiérrez, whom I've formally interned with. Congress is it. If I get to the Senate even better. But I definitely want to go federal.

Nina's family was surprised by her political ambitions as well as extremely supportive and proud of her accomplishments and plans. "Nobody in my family knows where I got this. They have no idea why I became so politi-cally active, and it surprises them. But they would love it if I went to Con-gress." Nina had even thought, "When I retire from my political career, I'll be a professor." I added, "Do the Stephanopolous thing?" She replied with a laugh, "Yeah. Charge lots of money and give it all to charity."

Alicia Granillo

Alicia Granillo's educational and political trajectory was not as direct as Aixa's and Nina's. Alicia Granillo was not a full-time student in residence. Throughout her undergraduate career she worked at various jobs in retail and the restaurant industry.

> I became involved during my sophomore year in a student organization of Latinos at UNLV [University of Nevada, Las Vegas] and it was an incredible experience. We thought we were pretty radical. We were the most active ethnic organization on campus, and most of our activities were outside the campus. We did a lot of outreach with new immigrant high school students, a lot of mentoring and role modeling for them. We got involved with the Latino Chamber of Commerce. We started getting involved with low-income families and for Thanksgiving we'd collect food and take it to them. Once this little boy was run over in an accident. The whole family was undocumented and so we organized a collection for medical expenses. Our group was predominantly Mexicano, but my senior year one of the radical Chicano activists from California started MEChA. It created a split, not just because of different political ideology, but there were some gender issues as well. For a long time there had been strong female leadership in our organization. I was president of the student organization for my senior year. There were some real thorny issues brought up, but I had no idea they were related to gender until one of our faculty advisors who was a Chicana (in Spanish literature and one of my role models) said, "Probably the split in the [two] organizations has to do with gender issues." I said, "Huh, what do you mean?" She said, "Look at who's on the opposing side. It's all males. Look at who's been doing all the shaking and moving and who's been running this organization. It's all females." So I was like, "Oh shit!" And that was my first experience with gender issues within *la raza*. It was really something else. I couldn't comprehend it. I didn't have any tools or any background to help me understand this process of division.

When she was accepted at Harvard University, Alicia made herself a promise not to get politically involved, a promise she failed to keep when she joined Latinos Unidos, a graduate student organization. Furthermore, Alicia wanted broader political exposure so she joined another student organization that was an alliance of all students of Color. At the end she felt that

> we have a lot of commonalities with African Americans and often we're so divided. I think we have the same goals, just different ways of approaching them. So I'm especially interested in learning more about that culture and learning more about how they organize and how we can find a commonality so we can work together.

Alicia had a very clear vision of what she wanted to do once she finished school. "I want to rule the world, basically," she said, laughing. Her next step was to obtain a doctorate in education.

> I applied to an Ed.D. program here [Harvard University] and at Columbia. I actually still have my job back at home and I was telling my friend Camila, "I'm so confused! I don't know what to do, because I'm in debt!" Part of me wants to go back and become financially stable again; but part of me wants to keep going, go teach abroad. I'm really looking to get out of my comfort zone. But then, at the same time, I'm split. Right before I came to Harvard my sister and I went out into this area that's not very populated in Las Vegas. They're selling acres of land and we priced them. I said, "OK, when I come back I'm going to buy an acre of land and you buy another acre. Then we build a house for mom so that when she gets on our nerves, we'll just send her there!" We want our whole family to live on these two acres of land. So I'm really split, because I know that if I go on to an Ed.D. program or a Ph.D. program, then more than likely I'll be moving a lot. So I'm really, really split. But I know that I definitely want to be in a position of power and I say that nonchalantly, because I don't think that power is negative. I think it's very positive. I definitely want to be in a decision-making position where I can allocate resources. I want to have the knowledge base and to not have to rely on experts. I see in our community, so many people just relying on experts and everyone is pushing their own agenda. I want to be the expert and I want to be the one making the decisions, saying yes or no. It's really frustrating to see what's going on in our community in terms of the educational system, in terms of the political system, and how funds are being allocated. It's just incredibly frustrating.

Alicia also wanted to be involved in issues beyond the Latino community.

> I think that I need to be involved with other issues, not just Latino issues. I always tell José [her fiancé], "You have to have your private agenda and your public agenda. Your public agenda is we want world peace, and we want all to live in harmony holding hands and singing 'Kumbaya,'" but my private agenda is, "Hell yeah, I want all those Latino kids going to college!" The Latino Chamber of Commerce organized Career Day where kids shadow a professional for one day. Speakers at this event got up and said, "College may not be for all of you, but we want you to see what's out there." Sometimes they pair them up with secretaries. So I'm like, "Bullshit!" That's the kind of thing that keeps them thinking, "Oh, I'm not college material." I feel very, very strongly about that—that we settle, often times, for mediocrity within our own people. "Well, you just immigrated and you want to be able to support your family. So you can go to community college." Bullshit! Even though you have to be on loans it'll pay off on the long run! There are so few Latinas out there with an Ed.D. or Ph.D., which really makes me upset. That's definitely a driving force. When I get all passionate about that, it's like family and all that can wait because I want to be a role model for them!

These three political trajectories are merely illustrative, as there were many more. Respondents took many paths to move, if they moved at all, from identification to consciousness. Sometimes respondents started college with ambivalence toward their ethnic and racial background and with little knowledge of Spanish, as Aixa did. Others, like Nina, found their ethnic and racial identity early on and by the time they arrived at college, they had their political futures planned out. Others had always had their focus on Mexican American communities and had always felt their personal destinies tied to these communities. College merely provided the discourse to describe their actions and to expand their empathy and political concerns to other similarly situated groups, as in Alicia's case. Sometimes families directly influenced their daughters' views on political issues, especially those parents who had participated in political movements. Other times families watched with bemusement as their daughters reacquired their ethnicity and language in higher education, when it had been available to them all along. In a few instances, parents felt that the best way to insure their daughters' success was to distance them from their cultural heritage and deny them their native language. Still others watched as their parents helped others when they themselves did not have much, and this profound moral lesson imprinted on them that the more they accomplished the greater their social responsibility. Ninety-three percent of respondents agreed that they wanted to "help as they climbed."

Epilogue: Lucha's Story

Lucha's political involvement began when she was in high school around the issue of abortion rights. "I was definitely into the whole pro-choice movement. I wrote papers on abortion twice and went to abortion rallies." Lucha had a deep commitment to this issue. "I don't believe in making laws regulating whether a woman has an abortion or not. I feel that is a very personal decision and I don't think anyone is justified in telling a woman what to do with her body." But like other respondents, Lucha felt that "for myself, I don't know if I could do it." Part of Lucha's reluctance to consider abortion was her uncertainty that she could indeed have children because she had endometriosis. "It would be difficult for me to have a child. I have to have some surgery, which I don't have money to do." So "if I found myself pregnant I would think, 'Oh my God, maybe this is a sign that I can have this kid!'" Lucha concluded, "At the age that I am, I don't know what reason I could use not to have a child. I feel I could get a job, I can support myself, and I could probably support this kid. It would be hard! But it's not like I'm in high school."

Lucha continued her political involvement as an undergraduate.

My first year in college I was definitely like, "Chicana! Yeah!" But then I got into MEChA, it made me feel really ugly to be part of that group because it brought up a lot of issues. I hated my adopted mother and she made me have serious hate issues with white people. So when I got involved with MEChA, there was a lot of anti-white sentiment. I looked at it from the outside and I just thought, I don't want to be like that. I can't fill myself with all that hatred or that ugliness, because there are really good white people out there. It was just this one person. I just felt that it was too exclusive.

Lucha transferred to a private liberal arts college in the East Coast where she worked to educate people around her about Latinos in general and Mexicans in particular.

> While I was in Pennsylvania I was more into educating people about Latinos. I still felt proud to be a Latina, but I didn't feel like it was so militant or exclusive. I was only educating people about things like, OK, this is where Mexico is. Then there are some Latinos that are Mexican, and then there are some that are Puerto Ricans and then there are Cubans, and they are all different. We had international students and I ran the Spanish house. I taught beginning Spanish.

Lucha's first language was Spanish, but she felt she had not learned Spanish well until she studied abroad in Spain.

> I had learned Spanish a little bit when I was younger. Officially it was our first language and I spoke Spanglish with friends. I went to a bilingual fourth and fifth grade. But I didn't really learn it as well as I know it now until college; then I lived a year in Spain. That's how I became fluent. I was a semi–Spanish literature major, so I can write, and read, and analyze literature in Spanish. That was in between my junior and senior year. I lived in Sevilla. It was the best fun of my life!

During law school, Lucha was involved with La Raza Association, the student organization for Latino law students, helping to recruit more Latino students and organize special events. At the time that Lucha was in law school, the University of California Regents were considering and eventually passed resolutions SP-1 and SP-2, which effectively abolished affirmative action in student admissions and in hiring. Lucha fought hard with others from La Raza Association to protest the actions taken by the Regents.

Lucha's first job offer was with a large corporate law firm based in Chicago that had over fifty attorneys. Lucha was "the only one they call 'Hispanic' and two Black attorneys." Lucha was going to be "doing labor and employment law." She was apprehensive about working in the firm, because after Proposition 209 passed in California (which effectively abolished affirmative action at the state level), the firm had become less concerned with issues of diversity.[38]

Lucha was uncertain about how much change she could help institute within the law firm. Instead she thought of concentrating her efforts on mentoring younger students to survive law school. Lucha was "definitely committed" to the Latino community and did not think that succeeding in school and in the job market meant "you're turning white." She felt that such a point of view was "so ridiculous!" Lucha "totally believed that you can be who you are and support your community."

From childhood, only Fuerza consistently cared for Lucha, whereas the Chicano, Latino, Mexicano communities failed her. Her Mexican "family-oriented" relatives abandoned her. Her Mexican American adoptive father rejected her. All those cultural sources of strength that worked so well for many of my respondents did not protect, cuddle, hug, and otherwise take care of Lucha or her siblings. And yet Lucha did not reject her culture— she embraced that which nourished her, she reacquired her language, and she joined political struggles to make others' lives less painful than her own. She did all of this without embracing hate and narrow-mindedness or rejecting those who were not like her. She should have been empty and bitter but instead was brimming with compassion and hope for those less fortunate than she. Lucha made a nonbeliever believe in miracles.

Review of Part III

Implications for Feminist Theorizing

ON HER WEB SITE "Making Face, Making Soul: A Chicana Feminist Homepage," Susana L. Gallardo summarized the field of Chicana feminisms: "Chicana and Latina feminists have struggled to articulate a Chicana Feminism which acknowledges both the similarities and differences with other critical frameworks of social inequality, including issues of race, gender, class, and sexuality" (2000).[1] She then proceeds to provide in her Web site "a brief sampling of some of the more recent texts in which Chicanas move toward defining Chicana Feminisms and the project of Chicana Feminist Theory." I take what Chicana feminists have written, the sampling derived by Susana Gallardo, a young Chicana feminist, and the lived experience of my respondents to theorize the interconnections between what is written, experienced, and theorized by various Chicana feminist constituencies.

Most of the quotes from the following authors can be found on Gallardo's Web site. (I am indebted to Gallardo for her insightful choice of excerpts; the subheadings I use here are inspired by her as well.)

Mirta Vidal on the Unity of "La Raza"

> While it is true that the unity of La Raza is the basic foundation of the Chicano movement, when Chicano men talk about maintaining La Familia and the "cultural heritage" of La Raza, they are in fact talking about maintaining the age-old concept of keeping the woman barefoot, pregnant, and in the kitchen. On the basis of the subordination of women, there can be no real unity. . . . The only real unity between men and women is the unity forged in the course of struggle against their oppression. And it is by supporting, rather than opposing, the struggles of women, that Chicanos and Chicanas can genuinely unite. (1971, 31–32)

Chicanas have always questioned their gender subordination. In the 1960s, however, a cadre of activist writers articulated what had always been brewing and what a few had already written. During this era, they risked speaking out even against progressive men (and some women) in their communities who perceived any feminist cause as subverting Chicano/Mexicano culture and as potentially betraying their communities (Hurtado 1998, 141). My respondents also felt this tension. When they returned from college politicized around social inequality and inspired by feminist ideas, many had to struggle to make their families understand their newfound transformation. Misty brought books home to dismantle her family's homophobic and racist views. Sofia challenged her parents' negative views of their gay neighbors and relatives. Challenging regressive elements within Chicano culture has been a central element in Chicana feminisms.

Gloria Anzaldúa on Constructing a Mestiza Culture

> Not me sold out my people but they me. So yes, though "home" permeates every sinew and cartilage in my body, I too am afraid of going home. Though I'll defend my race and culture when they are attacked by non-mexicanos, conosco el malestar de mi cultura. I abhor some of my culture's ways, how it cripples its women, como burras, our strengths used against us, lowly burras bearing humility with dignity. The ability to serve, claim the males, is our highest virtue. I abhor how my culture makes macho caricatures of its men. No, I do not buy all the myths of the tribe into which I was born. . . .

> I will not glorify those aspects of my culture which have injured me and which have injured me in the name of protecting me.
>
> So, don't give me your tenets and your laws. Don't give me your luke-warm gods. What I want is an accounting with all three cultures—white, Mexican, Indian. I want the freedom to carve and chisel my own face, to staunch the bleeding with ashes, to fashion my own gods out of my entrails. And if going home is denied me then I will have to stand and claim my space, making a new culture—una cultura mestiza—with my own lumber, my own bricks and mortar and my own feminist architecture. (1987, 21–22)

Chicana feminists have also been willing to pay the price for rebelling against their communities. They do not "buy all the myths of the tribe"; they object when "culture" is used as an excuse to oppress them. Many of my respondents, like Gloria Anzaldúa, did the same. They questioned men's brutality: Guadalupe stood up to her father in defense of her mother; Sara fought her brothers, her father, and the medical establishment to allow her mother to die with dignity; and Maritza C. Resendez's mother took a broom to her brother-in-law to stop her sister's abuse. Many of my respondents did not comply with the cultural templates (Zavella forthcoming) provided by their communities. Yet they still sought connection within their communities, feeling that "'home' permeates every sinew and cartilage in [their] body" and were willing to "defend [their] race and culture when they are attacked by non-mexicanos." At the same time, their loyalty did not deter them from critiquing the worst elements of Chicano/Mexicano culture.

Ana NietoGomez on Race and Class

> The Chicana's socio-economic class as a non-Anglo Spanish-speaking, low-income Chicana woman determines her need and therefore her polit-ical position. The low-income Anglo woman does not have to deal with racism nor is she punished because she speaks another language. The mid-dle-class Anglo woman only shares with the Chicana the fact that they are both women. But they are women of different ethnic, cultural, and class status. All these factors determine the different socio-economic needs and therefore determine the different political positions of these women. (1974, 39)

Chicana feminisms were not alone in emphasizing lived experience as the nexus for feminist theorizing. All feminist paradigms adhere to this fundamental assumption. However, hegemonic white feminisms have focused on the lived experience of white, mostly middle- and upper-class women. Other women's lived experience has not been as central to the development of their theorizing. The reason this matters is that the social construction of womenhood's is influenced by race, class, sexuality, and ethnicity. Different groups of women serve white patriarchy differently which in turn influences their identity as women. The majority of my respondents came from a working-class background; many were subject to racism because of their skin color; others had experienced discrimination because of their lack of English skills; and almost all had experienced restrictions because they were women. My respondents' views on feminism reflected the fact that they were multiply positioned by their "socio-economic class" as "non-Anglo Spanish-speaking, low-income Chicana" women.

Cherríe Moraga on Chicana Feminism as "Theory in the Flesh"

A theory in the flesh means one where the physical realities of our lives—our skin color, the land or concrete we grew up on, our sexual longings—all fuse to create a politic born out of necessity. Here, we attempt to bridge the contradictions in our experience:

We are the colored in a white feminist movement.

We are the feminists among the people of our culture.

We are often the lesbians among the straight.

We do this bridging by naming our selves and by telling our stories in our own words. (Moraga and Anzaldúa 1981, 23)

Chicana feminists believe in a "theory in the flesh" that takes into account lived experience in all its complexity. My respondents were aware that their sexualities were racialized because of "skin color," and they were keenly aware that they did not meet hegemonic racialized standards of femininity. They were reminded of this by the media, by their interactions with whites, and by the beauty assessments of members of their own communities. They had to negotiate this failure while simultaneously rescuing a sense of self strong enough to succeed in the toughest academic environments in

the country. Chicanas' "theory in the flesh" does not deny the role of sexuality in the oppression of Chicanas. A number of my respondents claimed
their lesbianism and bisexuality and confronted their families' prejudices.
They did not deny the desires of "the flesh" and subsume them to issues
of race, class, and ethnicity. Instead, they proclaimed feminisms that would
take all oppressions into account.

Gloria Anzaldúa on Haciendo Teorías

> What is considered theory in the dominant academic community is not nec-
> essarily what counts as theory for women-of-color. Theory produces effects
> that change people and the way they perceive the world. Thus we need
> teorías that will enable us to interpret what happens in the world, that will
> explain how and why we relate to certain people in specific ways. . . . Nece-
> sitamos teorías that will rewrite history using race, class, gender and ethnic-
> ity as categories of analysis, theories that cross borders, that blur bound-
> aries—new kinds of theories with new theorizing methods. We need theo-
> ries that will point out ways to maneuver between our particular experiences
> and the necessity of forming our own categories and theoretical models for
> the patterns we uncover. We need theories that examine the implications of
> situations and look at what's behind them. And we need to find practical ap-
> plication for those theories. We need to de-academize theory and to connect
> the community to the academy. "High" theory does not translate well when
> one's intention is to communicate to masses of people made up of different
> audiences. We need to give up the notion that there is a "correct" way to
> write theory. (1990, xxv)

My respondents "theorized" (in Anzaldúa's definition of theorizing)
about their lives from their own experiences and by extracting feminist
lessons from the lives of the women and men around them. They were indeed trying to adhere to "feminisms" in the flesh (Moraga 1981). Conchita recounted how her great-grandmother stopped a runaway carriage
by jumping on it and pulling the horses into submission. Marissa expressed
deep admiration for her grandmother's struggle to raise four children
working as a migrant farmworker. Marissa's own mother became pregnant
as a teenager, finished high school in a small town in Texas, and eventually
finished college and obtained a law degree at the University of Michigan,

the same university Marissa received her college degree from. Many of my respondents used women's lives as the "data" from which to create "*teorías* [to] enable [them] to interpret what happens in the world."

Cherríe Moraga on the Danger of "Ranking the Oppressions"

> In this country, lesbianism is a poverty—as is being brown, as is being a woman, as is being just plain poor. The danger lies in ranking the oppressions. The danger lies in failing to acknowledge the specificity of the oppression. The danger lies in attempting to deal with oppression purely from a theoretical base. Without an emotional, heartfelt grappling with the source of our own oppression, without naming the enemy within ourselves and outside of us, no authentic, non-hierarchical connection among oppressed groups can take place. (1983, 52–53)

Chicana feminisms adhere to a *relational* analysis of power (Hurtado 1996a) that takes all claims of oppression seriously in order to dismantle the existing status quo. My respondents resonated with this analysis as they fought on multiple fronts against inequality. Nina D. Sánchez as a heterosexual woman participated as an intern in an organization fighting for gay/lesbian rights. Alicia Granillo attended the meetings of the DuBois Society while at Harvard University to expand her political consciousness. Frida had been politically involved since she was in elementary school and affiliated herself with women of Color and Third World feminisms. Many of my respondents were reluctant to rank "the oppressions" and instead worked to further the goal of an "authentic, non-hierarchical connection among oppressed groups."

Gloria Anzaldúa on Chicana Feminisms as "Borderlands"

> The actual physical borderland that I'm dealing with in this book is the Texas-U.S. Southwest/Mexican border. The psychological borderlands, the sexual borderlands and the spiritual borderlands are not particular to the Southwest. In fact, the Borderlands are physically present wherever two or more cultures edge each other, where people of different races occupy the same territory, where under, lower, middle and upper classes touch, where the space between two individuals shrinks with intimacy. (1987, vi)

Many of my respondents were invested in crossing borders to expand their sense of who they were and to cultivate their critical consciousness about oppression. The borderlands as metaphor was further reinforced for many of my respondents by regular travel to Mexico, Puerto Rico, and Colombia. As bilingual, multicultural subjects, they were socialized into multi-layered social meanings that gave them insight into the constructed nature of all social categories. They understood this well when they traveled to Mexico and all of a sudden received male attention whereas they were not considered physically attractive in the United States. Others worked with people of different racial and ethnic backgrounds, and their own ethnicity and race were read differently according to context. And still others saw the advantages and disadvantages of all the cultural and social systems they were exposed to. My respondents were "hurdle jumpers" (Cuádraz 1989), border crossers (Anzaldúa 1987), and "internal exiles" (Judy Baca, quoted in Anzaldúa 1990, 25–26) who used *las fronteras* (the borderlands) to further their understanding of their feminisms.

Gloria Anzaldúa on the Tasks Ahead

> Some of the tasks ahead of us then: to go beyond explaining why women-of-color aren't writing more theory, why our work isn't being published or distributed, and, instead, to strategize about ways to get our work out; to change the focus from the topic of white women's exclusionary practices to address the quality of what has been included and the nature of this inclusion. If we have been gagged and disempowered by theories, we can also be loosened and empowered by theories. (1990, xxv–xxvi)

Chicana feminisms suggest organizing tools for political action and are committed to the joys of struggle rather than the pain of oppression. An integral part of Chicana feminist theorizing is the reluctance to claim victimhood. As Anzaldúa outlines, "Some of the tasks ahead of us" are "to go beyond explaining why women-of-color aren't writing more theory . . . and, instead, to strategize about ways to get our work out." Chicana feminists have stressed women's agency and in general have focused on survival rather than defeat (Mora and Del Castillo 1980). In fact, one area where Chicana feminisms lack clarity is in delineating the human cost of oppression based on multiple group memberships. Many times the oppression is acknowledged, but documentation then proceeds to highlight resistance (Anzaldúa 1987, 21). The advantage to this approach, however, is that through the documentation of survival, strategies for resistance and for coalition building become apparent. There were multiple examples in my respondents' narratives of their efforts to go beyond their acknowledged disadvantages. In fact it was difficult to get them to express their pain and describe their difficult experiences in life without immediately moving to a narrative of success and reassessment of how many privileges they had in comparison to others in their communities. Many expressed exasperation with hegemonic white feminist paradigms that emphasized "victimhood" and were eager to create alternatives to existing oppressions. In particular, Rebeca did not want to dwell on past injuries as many members of MEChA, in her estimation, did. Instead she wanted to develop creative strategies to recruit Latinos, especially women, into higher education. Sofia wanted to create her own school where Latino parents could be truly empowered to direct their children's education. Belinda Martínez had dreams of owning a publishing firm for Latino writers, and Alicia Z. Maciel wanted to become a motivational speaker to inspire young Latinos to become entrepreneurs and increase the community's economic power.

Chela Sandoval on Differential Consciousness

> Differential consciousness represents the strategy of another form of oppositional ideology that functions on an altogether different register. Its power can be thought of as mobile—not nomadic but rather cinematographic: a kinetic motion that maneuvers, poetically transfigures, and orchestrates while demanding alienation, perversion, and reformation in both spectators and practitioners. Differential consciousness is the expression of the new subject position called for by Althusser—it permits functioning within yet beyond the demands of dominant ideology. This differential form of oppositional consciousness has been enacted in the practice of U.S. third world feminism since the 1960s. (1991, 3)

Chicana feminisms adhere to an eclectic paradigm for political mobilization. The primary sources for theorizing about social change are everyday interactions with representatives of repressive institutions designed to control and oppress communities of Color, such as the police, school officials, employers, and welfare workers (Hurtado 1989). Instead of proposing a grand theory of social change or adhering to dominant academic paradigms like "socialist feminism" or "Marxism," Chicanas propose strategies that are context-dependent and largely the result of "street smarts." They apply lessons from their daily lives and the daily lives of the women around them. The situationally based resistance is usually documented by Chicana feminists through *cuentos* (stories), myths (e.g., La Llorona), *chistes* (jokes), or concrete actions that verge on performance art. Chicana feminisms advocate the creation of flexible, almost poetic discourses that allow the uncovering and documentation of the consciousness exhibited by many of my respondents, "a differential consciousness."

My respondents' differential consciousness, that is, the "strategy" to function "within yet beyond the demands of dominant ideology," was evident in their ability to maneuver through systems of higher education. Many of my respondents were extremely successful in the most demanding graduate programs and professional schools in the country. Yet in those contexts, instead of assimilating to the dominant ideologies, they "poetically transfigured" the "master's tools" (Lorde 1984) to create social change. Their differential consciousness allowed them to act in "opposition" to what they were being taught. Sofia created a recruitment program at Williams College to increase the number of Latina students; Christine Granados left the editorship of a successful national magazine to follow her dream of becoming a creative writer; Anna Reyes rejected a prestigious medical residency at the Mayo Clinic, because it served a mostly white population, for a medical residency in her hometown of McAllen, Texas, that serves a predominantly Chicano population (Granados 2001, 102).[2] All these respondents felt that being feminists meant *choosing* to do "heart work" (Granados 2001, 103) rather than merely working for a living.

Rosa Linda Fregoso on Cinema and Social Location

I first re-claim a nationalist intellectual legacy that has a long history in the U.S. Southwest. I trace my genealogy to the nineteenth century when the population of Mexican origin first confronted Anglo-white immigrants who would later conquer the U.S. Southwestern territories. This indigenous intellectual legacy of symbolic cultural forms and practices includes written essays, folk songs, music, and poetry. I have come to understand these social symbolic acts in their mutual determinations and interrelations with historical forces, as cultural forms mixed with and within relations of power. In its nationalistic tendency to ignore questions of gender and sexuality, my legacy reaches its impasse.

Second, I draw from feminism's critical discourse on film, in particular its insights on the role of cinema in the construction of gendered subjectivities, that is, the relationship of human gender to representation. I retreat from feminist film discourse when it lodges itself in a male/female binary, thus eliding racial, class, and sexual subjectivities: the crucial differences among women, rather than simply between men and women. Third, from poststructuralism I have learned about subject formation and difference. Its shortcomings include the lack of rigor in theorizing about the subject positions of non-Western subjects. More often, in Euro-American incantations of poststructuralism, "difference" is a new word for the good ol' American concept of pluralism. As a critique of Eurocentrism, the critical discourse on postcoloniality has been helpful. But it too has certain drawbacks, especially when its nationalism is informed by earlier geopolitical configurations of the nation-state. Postcolonial intellectual angst, say, its sentiment of "transcendental homelessness" (to quote Saidiya Hartman) is particularly useless for "subalterns" like myself who feel pretty much at home in the "belly of the beast" (the U.S. of A.). (1993, xxi–xxii)

Chicana feminisms claim disruption as method (Arredondo et al. forthcoming; Hurtado 1998, 135). They do not absolutely align themselves with any one particular intellectual field, but instead they dovetail in and out of various intellectual frameworks to glean the most important contributions and from that position construct their own paradigms. At the same time that they participate in these frameworks they also stand back and speak out against what does not fit in their own historical and social experience. Fregoso claims "a nationalist intellectual legacy," "feminism's critical discourse," and "poststructuralism," but at the same time she deconstructs all their shortcomings and "re-claims" her own "hybridized eyes" with which she "re-view[s] and re-read[s] Chicano films. For as these cultural forms are hybrid productions, so too is my cultural studies approach a mestizaje, a bricolage" (Fregoso 1993, 21–22).

Similarly, my respondents' cultural, linguistic, racial, economic, and social "bricolage" is a direct result of their U.S.-based "American" experience. Chicana feminists, just like my respondents, did not consider themselves "foreigners" but clearly situated themselves as U.S.-based hybrid "Americans." Many of them traveled across "the border" and loved their "Mexicanness" and "Latinoness." They felt a connection and several felt "at home" outside the United States. *At the same time*, they claimed their U.S.-based "Americanism" and, like Rosa Linda Fregoso, "pretty much" felt "at home in the belly of the beast."

Ana Castillo on Xicanisma

> As a poet, writer, and educator, my own educational process led me to accommodate Paulo Freire's philosophy to my status as a mestiza in the United States. . . .
>
> By the beginning of the new decade [1970s], however, many Chicana/Latina activists, disenchanted, if not simply worn down, by male dominated Chicano/Latino politics, began to develop our own theories of oppression. Compounding our social dilemmas related to class and race were gender and sexuality. For the brown woman the term feminism was and continues to be inseparably linked with white women of middle- and upper-class background. (This is also the case, by and large, in México.) Feminism, therefore, is perhaps not a term embraced by most women who might be inclined to define themselves as Chicanas and who, in practice, have goals and beliefs found in feminist politics. Therefore, I use the term conscientización as it has been applied among Spanish-speaking women activists. (1995, 10–11)

Although they claim their U.S.-based "Americanism," Chicana feminisms have not felt an affinity with white hegemonic feminisms (Sandoval 2000; Hurtado 1996b). Instead, their alliance has been primarily with African American feminisms and Third World feminisms. Even Mexican-based hegemonic feminisms, because they originated from the same class as U.S. hegemonic feminisms, did not speak to Chicanas' experiences in the United States. Those feminisms that were integrally involved with race and class issues were the ones that best articulated Chicanas' views on gender. Chicana theorists adhere to a feminist paradigm that places women's lived experiences at the center of their analysis. From these *sitios* (spaces) it was impossible for them to ignore their working-class status, sexuality, race, and ethnicity when examining their condition as women. Together with African American feminists and other feminists of Color, Chicana feminists have been at the forefront of advocating the examination of all their stigmatized group memberships *simultaneously*, a position that took the active advocacy and downright political activity on the part of women of Color to convince many white feminists that gender did not take primacy in women's oppression. It is an activist feminism intimately tied to social change. Almost all my respondents saw themselves involved politically for the rest of their lives (93 percent). The spheres of involvement, however, varied dramatically—from education to health issues, electoral politics, environmental issues, and Native American rights. Theirs was a "bricolage" of causes clearly situated in their U.S. backyards but with international connections to other oppressed people in the world.

Gloria Anzaldúa on an Inclusive Feminist Vision of Humanity's Possibilities

> [I]n our daily lives, we women of color strip off the máscaras others have imposed on us, see through the disguises we hide behind and drop our personas so that we may become subjects in our own discourses. We rip out the stitches, expose the multi-layered "inner faces," attempting to confront and oust the internalized oppression embedded in them, and remake anew both inner and outer faces. . . . We begin to acquire the agency of making our own caras. "Making faces" is my metaphor for constructing one's identity. "[U]sted es el modeador de su carne tanto como el de su alma." You are the shaper of your flesh as well as of your soul. (1990, xvi)

Chicanas do not deny the fact that they have been oppressed and that oppression can have devastating effects by making them internalize what others have constructed about them, but they nonetheless assume agency. Agency is constructed by the collectivity, not simply by individuals who "pull themselves up by their own bootstraps." Chicanas have collective bootstraps, which they have constructed by appropriating the space and discourse to reconstruct and invent who they are. My respondents were aided in this process of reconstruction and invention by their close relationships with women—mostly friends but also mothers, aunts, and sisters.

They also removed their *máscaras* through creative production and cultural practice. Mieka Valdez felt renewed and reconstituted through her radio program and her photography, Irma Martínez through dancing in a *ballet folklórico,* and Rebeca through writing poetry and compiling an anthology that included writings by Chicana/Latina students at Harvard (Burciaga and Tavares 1999). These young women rejected what others had written on them by finding spaces where they could explore who they really were without wearing any *máscaras.* It was in those spaces that they were "making faces, making soul" (Anzaldúa 1990).

Conclusion

It is important to recognize that there are many feminisms and that their definitions are currently in flux. Griffin (1989) and others argue that the definitions of feminism, feminist identity, and feminist consciousness should remain flexible to maximize the inclusion of a diversity of women's experiences. I would also argue that the inclusion of the cultural, artistic, and scholarly productions of women of Color is essential in informing these evolving definitions. As Ana Castillo advocates, it is important to take feminisms out of the "suffocating atmosphere of conference rooms, the acrobatics of academic terms and concepts and carry it out to our work place, social gatherings, kitchens, bedrooms, and society in general" (1995, 10–11).

Chicanas' definitions of their feminisms come from a multiplicity of perspectives. Some of these theorists are community activists, others are writers, academics, and poets, and most are a combination of these. Yet these different perspectives all claim hybridity as the *sitio* from which they theorize, fully embracing the racialized nature of their existence in the United States. They also explicitly state that hegemonic white definitions are inadequate for their struggles. They speak in opposition to "white women and men" (Anzaldúa 1987, 1990), to the narrowness of heterosexism (Moraga 1981, 1983), to the regressive elements in Chicano culture (NietoGomez 1974), to the brutality of all men, and to poverty. A cacophony of voices speak through these definitions and leave no oppressive stone unturned. They scrutinize everything and everybody to uncover the hidden and overt technologies of oppression. It is this multiplicity of definitions, as partially reviewed in this section, that best fits my respondents' views on their color, feminism, and politics.

10

■　■　■　■　■　■　■　■　■

Conclusions and Ruminations

WHEN I BEGAN THIS BOOK I started out with the very naïve notion that I wanted to explore whether writings by Chicana feminists in any way reflected the lives of the young women we were supposed to be theorizing about. Whereas the literature on theorizing Chicana feminisms was voluminous, there were only a few studies that directly dealt with the feminist views and ideologies of Chicanas (most notably, the work of Beatriz Pesquera and Denise Segura).[1] I wanted to ask young women of Mexican descent what they were experiencing and whether the writers just barely a generation before them had "gotten it right." I knew that many of my potential respondents would have only minimal knowledge of this literature, but I also assumed that theoretical concepts and analyses would have seeped into their education through the exposure of many of their professors to this body of knowledge. Many of us who write about Chicana feminisms were, in fact, the same age as the mothers of my respondents. These young women were our intellectual daughters, and I wanted to see how adequately we had mothered.

Most social science researchers rarely experience the jolt of discovery encountered in other fields such as, for example, finding a new enzyme, stumbling upon a new planet, or developing a new medicine for a previously incurable disease. Social scientists mostly document what is already known or add small twists to what has become common knowledge. Sometimes, if we are lucky, we actually give an interpretation that is novel but rarely newly discovered. In conducting these interviews and analyzing them within the framework established by Chicana feminists, I felt a jolt of recognition: everything that was theorized about actually had "a lived meaning." As my respondents spoke, my mind crackled with connections between what they were telling me and what Chicana feminist writers (and a few other white feminist writers) had proposed. I never thought they would be so right.

In contrast to the richness of feminist theorizing, social science theory proved inadequate for helping to explain my respondents' achievements. I knew that if I had written the social histories of each of my 101 respondents and asked trained social scientists to predict these young women's chances in life, few could have imagined their achievements. How could we have been so blind to the potential of human beings that our theories are so grossly inadequate in explaining their success? The answer is quite simple, as most elegant theorems are. Feminists in general, and Chicana feminists in particular, did what social scientists often failed to do: we took women's experiences seriously. We tried to understand women's social existence from their point of view. Simply but profoundly, we allowed women to speak. In doing so, we discovered previously unmined knowledge that will send us back to the theoretical drawing board to reconstruct our social science theories and to take seriously feminist theoretical developments.

Disjunctures and Continuities

I Want to Be Known as a Hurdle-Jumper, Not as a High-Achiever

> *You see, high-achiever connotes an easy path,*
> *I am here to say it wasn't.*
> *And it still isn't.*
>
> *High-achiever connotes you've arrived somewhere*
> *And I am here to say I'm still going.*
> *. . .*
> *I am a Hurdle-jumper because I don't come from*
> *A Class of "Achievers"*
> *I come from a Class of*
> *Mexican jumpin' beans.*

*For your information,
that makes me a Hurdle-jumper.* —Cuádraz 1989

My respondents' lives were marked by constant disjunctures—disjunctures that were taken as opportunities to clarify who they were, what they thought, and how they behaved. Clashing social realities (and sometimes even physical realities as they moved to predominantly white communities) were constant in their lives. There was a breach between how they grew up, the values they were taught, the institutions they were functioning in, and the standards of performance imposed on them, among many other things. Many were born to young women (as young as fourteen), to immigrant parents or in another country, to single mothers, to poverty, to working-class status, to mixed marriages—all of which cause disruption in this society. Only a few lived in the protected wombs of the suburbs from which they emerged at the age of eighteen when they went off to college. Their entire lives were characterized by contradictory, belligerent, incoherent, inconsistent, and chaotic social realities. My respondents, unlike others born in similar life circumstances, survived the chaos of their lives and even thrived. By the time I interviewed them, they were successful "hurdle jumpers" who were almost balletic in their adroitness in navigating obstacles. How did they do this, and how can these young lives inform our feminist theorizing?

Mestiza Consciousness:
The Development of Multiple Subjectivities

Gloria Anzaldúa speaks of a *mestiza* consciousness that both embraces and rejects simultaneously so as not to exclude what it critically assesses. A *mestiza* consciousness can perceive multiple realities at once:

[I]t is not enough to stand on the opposite river bank, shouting questions, challenging patriarchal, white conventions. A counterstance locks one into a duel of oppressor and oppressed; locked in mortal combat, like the cop and the criminal, both are reduced to a common denominator of violence. The counterstance refutes the dominant culture's views and beliefs, and, for this, it is proudly defiant. . . . But it is not a way of life. At some point, on our way to a new consciousness, we will have to leave the opposite bank, the

> split between the two mortal combatants somehow healed so that we are on both shores at once and, at once, see through serpent and eagle eyes. . . . The possibilities are numerous once we decide to act and not react. (1987, 78–79)

Other Chicana feminists have called this *facultad* (ability) an "oppositional consciousness" (Sandoval 1991), "multiple realities" (Alarcón 1990), or a state of "conscientización" (Castillo 1994a, 171). My respondents embodied this *facultad*, born out of their daily existence. They developed what I call *multiple subjectivities* that allowed them to *see* the *partial truths* in what on the surface appeared to be contradictory social realities, including racism, gender and class discrimination, and cultural differences. They had to function in a social context of psychological limbo in almost every aspect of their lives.

Coping with many social realities forced my respondents to articulate their *positionality* (Collins 1991). That is, because of the almost daily clash with different belief systems, different languages (let alone different speech styles within languages), different cultural practices, and different moral values, my respondents had to think and articulate coherent (or at least semicoherent) views of themselves. That is, they had to make *explicit* where they stood on many issues, and *why* they felt the way they did. Very few of their positions or values could a priori be taken for granted, because at one point or another in their young lives, they had to *explain* to somebody how they felt, what they believed in, and why they lived the way they did. In other words, they did more translating than "the Gawdamn U.N." (Rushin 1981, xxi).[2] When Tomasa was admitted to the private, elite University of Chicago, where most students were very well-off, she had to come to terms with her parents' poverty, lack of education, and low-status jobs. She did not take her privilege for granted as many upper-middle-class eighteen-year-olds do. Instead she had to do the necessary cognitive work to rescue a stigmatized view of her parents and to resist becoming alienated from them. She reconfigured her view of them in order to see their strength, dedication, devotion, religiosity, and courage within what appeared to be a negative and undesirable status in life. Tomasa had to *see* what society thought of dark, uneducated, poor people while simultaneously *seeing* their strength, beauty, intelligence, and dedication—all of this while still excelling academically.

But it was not only the outside world my respondents had to negotiate; they also came to function as *bridges* between their academic, social, and professional worlds and the world of their families. Belinda Martínez did not feel that premarital sex with her boyfriend, whom she planned to marry someday, was morally wrong. And certainly these views were congruent with those of her peers at the University of California, Los Angeles, where she was an undergraduate. She knew that her parents, especially her mother, would disagree, but she did not want to lie to them. Disclosing the truth to her mother led to ostracism and a month of silence. Instead of distancing herself from her mother or complying with her parents' views, Belinda wrote them a long letter explaining her behavior in terms that her parents could understand. She addressed her parents' fears that she was trivializing sex by reassuring them that she and her boyfriend had a significant and loving relationship. She also reassured them that he was not taking advantage of her, but that sex was the beginning of a greater commitment that would ultimately end in marriage. Belinda did not tell her parents they were wrong or try to tell them to change, or change her views on premarital sex. She was "see[ing] both through serpent and eagle eyes" (Anzaldúa 1987, 78–79) and helping her parents *see* her point of view by *seeing* theirs. All of this was done by Belinda at the age of twenty while attending one of the most competitive undergraduate schools in the country and preparing to apply to law school. At the time of the interview, Belinda had graduated from UCLA, was in her second year of law school at Columbia University, and had married her boyfriend, who was attending law school at Harvard. All of this requires focus on multiple levels. The cognitive and moral multitasking my respondents were capable of was awe-inspiring.

There were many examples of my respondents' *facultad* to simultaneously view multiple social perspectives. Like viewers of an Escher lithograph in which, depending on one's focus, one will see either fields of wheat or flying geese, many of my respondents had the ability to Escherize their social realities as a manifestation of their *mestiza* consciousness.

Personal Responsibility Transformed to Personal Independence and Political Commitment

Letting Go

> *Nobody's going to save you.*
> *No one's going to cut you down*
> *cut the thorns around you.*
> *No one's going to storm*
> *the castle walls nor*
> *kiss awake your birth,*
> *climb down your hair,*
> *nor mount you*
> *onto the white steed.*
>
> *There is no one who will feed the yearning.*
> *Face it. You will have*
> *to do, do it yourself.*   —Anzaldúa 1987

A lot of what I am, I get from my mother—buying her own home, going to school after she divorced my dad, all that I see as feminist actions. No one is going to do it for her, and she has to do it for herself. She has relied on men before and they don't come through. If I want to accomplish things, I have to do them for myself.

    —Hilda, twenty-seven-year-old respondent, Tempe, Arizona

A recurrent theme in many respondents' life narratives was a commitment to independence, especially economic independence. Many women considered having their own money the key to freedom. A constant refrain was "that way you don't have to stay with your husband if you don't want to." As part of this economic struggle, women in my respondents' lives sold *tamales* and *queso* (cheese) in the plaza in Mexico, raised cattle, and sold sodas and candies at their workplace for extra cash.

My respondents were socialized primarily by their mothers to have a deep commitment to *personal responsibility* (see chapter 3). The sense of personal responsibility was the grid from which many of my respondents constructed their lives. Most assumed, as Gloria Anzaldúa warned in her poem, "Nobody's going to save you. . . . There is no one who will feed the yearning. Face it. You will have to do, do it yourself." The personal responsibility, so deeply ingrained in most of my respondents, in turn shaped their *personal independence*. Many respondents took great pride in being self-sufficient and in having worked since they were quite young. At the same time, they always sought emotional connection to others. Seeking a loving relationship with a partner was an integral part of their "relatedness." Whereas the Western notion of "self-sufficiency" translates inevitably to "individualism," for many respondents, self-sufficiency translated into greater freedom to choose whom they wanted to be with. Instead of selecting lovers out of economic and social need, many respondents expressed confidence in their own personal survival skills if the relationship failed, instilling in them the ability to risk interdependence with others.

The Chicana feminist sociologist Maxine Baca Zinn theorized this *interconnected independence* twenty-five years ago, proposing that Chicanas' familial commitment could potentially be transformed to *political familism*. According to Baca Zinn, the "fusing of cultural and political resistance may be referred to as political familism" (1975, 16). My respondents' self-sufficiency, which led to their independence, also spurred them to choose political commitment as an extension of their early socialization into *personal responsibility*. As their mothers had taught them to clean the house until it was "spic and span," they inspected the social conditions around them and readily saw the debris left behind by social injustice. They had been highly trained to notice imperfections, contradictions, and inequality. Their *mestiza consciousness* was applied not just to their personal experience but also to the economic and social injustices in the world. Instead of assuming that they were victims—although they readily saw their structural disadvantages—they assumed *personal responsibility* for improving social conditions. Most respondents were buzzing with ideas and plans about what needed to be changed in society. Many had successfully circumvented numerous obstacles to obtain very high levels of achievement.

Physicality and Feminism

The conversation of women of Color can be bawdy, rowdy, and irreverent, and, in expressing opinions freely, women of Color exercise a form of power.
—Hurtado 1996a

In the movie *Stand and Deliver* the inspirational teacher Jaime Escalante told his students that in order to succeed in calculus they had to have *ganas* (desire). As hokey and, to a certain extent, unrealistic as this advice was for students who faced enormous structural barriers such as poverty, poor schooling, and violence, there was also an underlying truth to his advice. My respondents not only had *ganas* but something even deeper, *ánimo*—roughly translated as animus—the soul to fight back through love, humor, optimism, and an unmovable belief in the future. This animus came from their families and primarily from their mothers, who were crucial in teaching them to use humor to turn offenses into life lessons. My respondents listened to stories that were poignant, humorous, and painful, which taught them about morality, life, ethics, and resistance. My respondents, as a group, were some of the happiest, most optimistic and joyful group of people I have ever met. Our interviews were often filled with laughter, sardonic humor, poignant vignettes of fighting and talking back to representatives of power structures, and open reflections of their own role in many of their contradictions.

The animus was *embodied* so that it was not unusual during the course of our interview for many respondents to belly laugh, lean over and slap me on the knee, and even spontaneously hold each other's hand as they told painful stories. They also readily hugged me—tight and deep—in a form of *despedida* (farewell) after the interview was over. My respondents were women who had "lived in their bodies" and who were not afraid to exert them in physical space. Listening to their life histories, I realized that they had learned their physicality from the household and other labor they had performed from an early age. Their experiences with physical labor made them appreciate even more the moments of respite and the positive aspects of enjoying the body as well. Respondents commented often that they were taught to "work hard" but also to "party hard." Many respondents expressed appreciation for good food, dance, and joyous laughter. Their *ánimo* came from their physical being.

Physical Labor

This was one of the supreme ironies of slavery: in order to approach its strategic goal—to extract the greatest possible surplus from the labor of slaves—the black woman had to be released from the chains of the myth of

femininity. . . . In order to function as slave, the black woman had to be annulled as woman.
　　　　　　　　　　　　　　　　　　　　　—Davis 1971, 7

Women of Color [are perceived] primarily as workers.
　　　　　　　　　　　　　　　　　　　　　—Hurtado 1996a

Many of my respondents, as well as the women in their lives, had a long history of participation in the labor force, mostly doing physical, unskilled labor. Undoubtedly, the low-paying jobs respondents were confined to and their early age of employment were a burden, but there was also liberation in knowing how to work. In other words, many of my respondents emphasized physicality as part of their independence. This was also true of my respondents' mothers and other female relatives. My respondents prided themselves in their abilities to do physical work like changing the oil in their cars and doing "male chores" like mowing the lawn.

Many respondents saw all work, whether it was physical or not, as worthwhile, because it led to economic independence no matter how limited. For example, when Guadalupe worked as a maid in a hotel at the age of twelve, she did not perceive this as hard labor but actually as a step up from working in the farm fields. Guadalupe would "turn on the air conditioning" and "play her tunes" on the radio and do her work leisurely. For a teenager, this was blissful privacy and control over her work environment. Guadalupe especially felt this way because her family of seven lived in a one-bedroom mobile home. The temporary "space of her own" allowed her to reflect and daydream about her life. Furthermore, she got to keep "her money" to spend as she liked. This was the beginning of her sense of independence, which led to better-paying jobs and ultimately helped her cope with being a single parent.

Many respondents compared the harshness of the beginning of their work life to the ease of student life. While in college Guadalupe was in awe of the fact that she made more money working part-time than her parents did full-time and she lived in a nicer apartment with her daughter than her parents' one-bedroom mobile home. All this before she was twenty-two. Every hurdle was minimized by Guadalupe's early experience of working as a maid in a local hotel.

Many respondents' experiences in the labor force translated into self-efficacy. They felt they could do anything when it came to other areas of their lives. This self-efficacy was undergirded by an inordinate amount of self-discipline, learned early on in life, and by social comparison with more affluent people around them, especially when they entered higher education. Many respondents noted the wasted time and energy that better-off students spent on "whining" about the smallest of obstacles. Although many respondents were keenly aware of their lack of resources, especially when attending wealthy schools, they also felt more resourceful because they had always had less. Rather than expressing only disempowerment, respondents often poked fun at wealthy students' "burdens." They looked forward to becoming professionals and had dreams of having multiple professions during the course of their lifetimes.

Physicality also liberated many of my respondents from strict bifurcation of tasks by gender. To a certain extent, they were "degenderized subjects" in terms of their physical assertion in the world. They had few expectations that men would do for them such tasks as moving furniture, painting their rooms, or physically protecting them. They could do these things for themselves. Victoria was not unusual in asserting that "hanging out" with her father "on the ranch," where she helped him "put up fences" and do other "physical labor," made her more competent than her husband to "take care of things around the house." Many respondents spoke about taking public transportation, working long hours, living alone, traveling, taking care of children, cleaning house, repairing broken-down cars—all of which were perceived as a normal part of their existence rather than something they should complain about.

Many times respondents, regardless of their size and strength, seemed oblivious to their physical limitations, thinking they "embodied" a larger physical space than their actual size. Alejandra Dominguez discovered her distorted perceptions of her own physical strength when she tried to push her father's truck out of her garage without help. She managed to get it out the garage door but could not control it and ended up crashing it into the wall of the garage. Her father asked her, "What were you thinking?" Alejandra laughingly replied, "I thought I was that strong!"

Sensuality and Pleasure

Laughter [is] a patently oppositional tool of the popular masses. . . . the culture of laughter in its many forms and manifestations has traditionally opposed the authoritarianism and protective seriousness of the ruling class. Through the ages laughter has for the oppressed functioned as a rehearsal of freedom.   —Broyles-González 1994, 30

Chicana feminists, by writing about sexual pleasure, have debunked the notion that Mexicana/Chicana women do not fully participate in their own sexuality (Zavella forthcoming; Moraga 1983; Castillo 1986). Certainly poets and creative writers exposed the sensuousness and sexuality of Chicano/Mexicano culture. Although my interviews did not focus explicitly on sex, related topics like virginity, menstruation, and mating decisions slipped into discussions of physical pleasure and passion. I was surprised, given the silence around these issues in many of my respondents' families, how freely they discussed "the pleasures of the flesh." Many of my respondents had come to terms with their physical beings: their physical appearance, the use of their bodies in labor and so forth. They fully enjoyed physical activities like dancing, cooking, eating, and shopping. Only one respondent explicitly talked about having had an eating disorder when she was in early adolescence. Many respondents mentioned their concern around weight but often threw their heads back in laughter at their own assessments. Many respondents talked about "taking care of themselves" and "working out" on a regular basis to cultivate their looks. Many saw "using makeup" as antithetical to calling themselves feminists, so they rejected the designation rather than abandon their *costumbres* (practices). They also liked to "dress up" and go dancing and enjoyed others' admiration of the way they looked. Many respondents repeatedly mentioned that "looking nice" and doing all these "feminine" things distinguished them from white women. These practices around their appearance bonded them with other women of Color, especially African American women, whom they considered to have a similar aesthetic. However, many thought of themselves primarily as "intellectuals" and fluctuated in appearance if they had a deadline or a job to be done. There was no doubt that many of my respondents "lived in their bodies" and enjoyed every minute of it.

Their sensuality extended to their use of humor and freedom with laughter. With only a couple of exceptions, respondents peppered their stories with funny anecdotes and turns of phrase, told jokes, used *dichos* (proverbs), and code-switched between English and Spanish to tell a bilingual joke or to create dramatic effects in their narrative. Their laughter and joy were contagious and their freedom of expression liberating. Many respondents felt that the ability to express themselves emotionally and with a lack of somberness distinguished them from white feminists, whom they perceived as "too serious" and ascetic. Although respondents spoke about grim topics, they did so with gusto, passion, and in very loud voices. Many times during our interviews, when the conversation turned too serious, they rescued the mood by making fun of themselves, giggling at their own *peripecias* (incidents), or finding something ludicrous in the narrative. For example, when we discussed menstruation, many respondents called sanitary napkins *pañales* (diapers); others mentioned the crinkling noise the *pañal* made as they walked. Still others recalled their naïveté when first using sanitary products, not removing the encasing before they inserted a tampon or using a sanitary napkin upside down so that the "sticky part" made a respondent "go bald." Others related their exploits in hiding their *pañales* during elementary school, by using a "little old lady's handbag" in the fifth grade. Usually by this time the focus group was crying with laughter as each respondent tried to top the other's *peripecias* around the trials and tribulations of menstruation. Instead of focusing on their confusion, fear, and shame around menstruation—all tragic consequences of silence on all things sexual—they highlighted the absurdity and ridiculousness of the situation. This strategy was used repeatedly by respondents with every topic covered in the interview. In other words, our interviews were "bawdy, rowdy, and irreverent" (Hurtado 1996a, 17).

Negotiating Beauty

Memory as history, as social construction, as politics, culture, race—all are inscribed upon the body. Inscriptions upon the body are memory and history. The body is historically and socially constructed. It is written upon the environment, by clothes, diet, exercise, illnesses, accidents. It is written upon the kind of sex that is practiced upon the body and that the body practices.

—Pérez 1999, 108

When you're small and you start having crushes on boys, they never liked the smart girls. I was always the smart girl so nobody found me interesting.

—Tomasa, twenty-year-old respondent, Chicago

Many of my respondents were politicized early in life as they negotiated the color line (see chapter 7). Negotiations about physical beauty were inextricable from the battles around color. About a third of the respondents (32 percent) assumed that they were not physically beautiful because they did not meet white, hegemonic standards of beauty. Lucha did not consider herself beautiful because she "loved fashion magazines but when I look at them, I see all these beautiful women who are white. So I say to myself, 'OK, here is me, and that is what is supposed to be beautiful. OK, so I'm not beautiful, but I have a good personality [*laughing*].'"

Many of them also did not have the economic resources to modify themselves to meet these standards. Orthodontics, expensive clothes, private dancing lessons, or participation in sports were too expensive and, for those who had to work after school, too time-consuming. Working-class parents could not provide an economic cushion and, as a precaution, prepared their daughters to take care of themselves. They confronted early on their lack of feminine "frailty," partly contributing to their notion that they were not "very physically attractive."

The arbitrariness of beauty standards often allowed respondents to develop other dimensions of worthiness, like a sense of humor, an attractive personality, and, most of all, intelligence. As Lucha laughingly said, "My sister is definitely the type to say, 'I'm not beautiful but I'm number one in my class!'" While respondents were relentless in their self-judgments, outlining the unacceptable aspects of their physical selves, at the same time they embraced their intelligence as a badge of honor and superiority. Tomasa recalled that as a child she "was small and skinny—even bony," but she had always been told that "'she's the smart one.' It was not like, 'She's the pretty one,' but rather, 'She's the smart one.'"

Perhaps because respondents had a tough time negotiating hegemonic standards of beauty in their romantic relationships, they desired very gender-specific treatment. Repeatedly, regardless of their commitment to economic and physical independence, respondents such as Valerie spoke of wanting to "be treated like a lady. I love it when my husband opens the door. To me, that's treating me like a lady." Valerie still wanted the same "pay rate" as men and wanted her "opinion respected," but she "loved chivalry. I think it's really nice."

Transgressive Worshiping:
Appropriation of Cultural and Religious Rituals
through Artistic Production

La Cultura Cura [Culture Cures]
> —Popular slogan during the Chicano movement of the 1960s

Art is about healing. When people participate in art, when they make it, when they view it, it is the same as making yourself well.
> —Amalia Mesa-Bains, Chicana artist, interviewed in Portillo 1990

I felt a void when I didn't go to church. . . . I told a bunch of my friends, "Come on, let's go to my church for the Virgen de Guadalupe celebration. Let's listen to the *mariachi* sing the *mañanitas*."[3] It was the whole thing of religion and culture again. I have the Virgen de Guadalupe's picture in each of the rooms in my house. [*Laughter.*] I don't know why, it looks nice there, and I feel comfortable—I'd be lost without it.
> —Irasema, twenty-six-year-old respondent, Tempe, Arizona

"Silence equals death," many social groups have proclaimed. Chicana feminisms have joined this rallying cry and renounced the silence surrounding Chicanas/os' history and culture. They focus on restoring "social memory" to build a positive collective identity as one path to individual health. The colonization of Mexican territory known now as the "American Southwest" devastated Mexicano/Chicano communities. Many of the efforts of the Chicano movement and of Chicana feminisms were to uncover the "hidden" and elided history of Mexican descendants (and of other people of Color) in this country. Memorialization included revisioning official history and reconstructing everyday Chicano/Mexicano cultural practices. Chicana feminist writers and artists have been at the forefront of the appropriation of religious and cultural rituals for the restitution of self that leads to individual "empowerment" as well as to political mobilization.

The rituals celebrated in Mexicano/Chicano communities set the stage for later appropriation for feminist interventions. Chicana feminist writings refuted assimilation theory's assumption (oddly enough also present in white feminist theorizing) that Chicanas become more "liberated" the closer they resemble white middle-class feminists. *Chicana liberation* was constructed in the context of Mexicano/Chicano culture—albeit modi-

Fig. 3. Yolanda M. López, *Our Lady of
Guadalupe: Margaret F. Stewart*, 1978.
Reprinted by permission.

fied, reconstructed, examined, analyzed, criticized, and ultimately recycled
through a feminist lens. Chicana and Latina feminists documented "a history of their own" through music, paintings, performances, and writings,
thus providing social frameworks for memory. A powerful example was the
appropriation of the iconic figure of "Mexicanness" represented by the national saint of Mexico, La Virgen de Guadalupe. Yolanda M. López
painted her in a series depicting the different facets of Chicanas' working-
class subject positions—from factory worker to the quintessential *abuelita*
(grandmother), to liberated athlete running with her skirt in the air (see
figs. 3, 4, and 5).

In 1975 Ester Hernández was the first *artista* (artist) to appropriate and
liberate La Virgen by representing her as a karate fighter, a tradition she
continued with *La Ofrenda* (see fig. 6).

Fig. 4. Yolanda M. López, *Our Lady of Guadalupe: Victoria F. Franco,* 1978. Reprinted by permission.

Ana Castillo (1996) edited a book of essays by Chicana feminist writers highlighting what La Virgen means to them. Carla Trujillo made La Virgen her lover in her essay, "La Virgen de Guadalupe and Her Reconstruction in Chicana Lesbian Desire." Sandra Cisneros appropriates La Virgen to refute the image of *la madre sufrida* (the suffering mother) and replaces it with La Virgen as "sex goddess":

> When I look at *la Virgen de Guadalupe* now, she is not the Lupe of my childhood, no longer the one in my grandparents' house in Tepeyac, nor is she the one of the Roman Catholic Church, the one I bolted the door against in my teens and twenties. Like every woman who matters to me, I have had to search for her in the rubble of history. And I have found her. She is Guadalupe the sex goddess, a goddess who makes me feel good

about my sexual power, my sexual energy, who reminds me I must, as Clarissa Pinkola Estés so aptly put it, "[speak] from the vulva . . . speak the most basic, honest truth," and write from my *panocha* [cunt]. (1996, 49)

Needless to say, these appropriations have not resulted in universal approval, but they have forced people to rethink Mexicano/Chicano culture, not by rejecting it or accepting it but by critically reassessing it through the prism provided by Chicana feminist production. In fact, as I was finishing this chapter, a national controversy erupted around the portrayal of La Virgen de Guadalupe by the Latina/Chicana artist Alma Lopez exhibited at the Museum of International Folk Art in Santa Fe, New Mexico (fig.7). Various newspapers described the Virgin as a "bare-midriff Mary" (Benke

Fig. 5. Yolanda M. López, *Portrait of the Artist as the Virgin of Guadalupe,* 1978. Reprinted by permission.

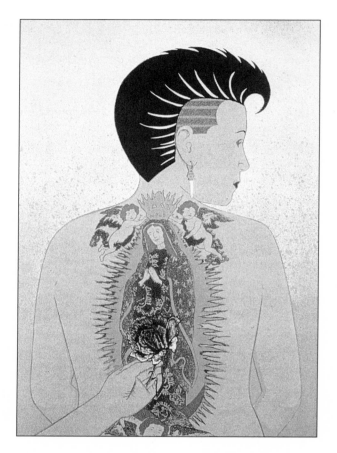

Fig. 6. Ester Hernández, *La Ofrenda* (The Offering),
Reprinted by permission.

2001b), "bikini Virgin" (Benke 2001a), and, less inflammatory, "a com-
puterized photo collage of Our Lady of Guadalupe wearing a two-piece
swimsuit of bright roses" that also featured "a barebreasted angel holding
the virgin aloft" (Janofsky 2001).[4] To nonbelievers, the image "seems
rather innocuous," but for many Mexicano/Chicano believers, especially
in the predominantly Catholic state of New Mexico, it "has caused such an
uproar that museum officials say they have been threatened with physical
harm and state law makers have suggested that the museum should lose
some of its funding" (ibid.).

Where many saw offense and blasphemy, the artist, Alma Lopez, claimed that as a Catholic, she was showing La Virgen "as a strong woman 'and not as the young, passive' more traditional image with head bowed and hands clasped" (ibid.). In addition, Lopez defended "the angel by saying the bare breasts represented beauty and nurturing" (ibid.). Lopez's depiction of La Virgen was inspired by another feminist, Sandra Cisneros, who "in one of her stories wonders what Our Lady of Guadalupe wears underneath the mantle" (Gonzales and Rodriguez 2001). Lopez, together with the model for the image, concluded that it must be "roses" (ibid.). Alma Lopez is part of a group of artists called Cyber Arte, which "features computer-inspired work by contemporary Hispana/Chicana/Latina artists, all of whom intentionally combine elements traditionally defined as "folk" with current computer technology to create a new aesthetic. Artists include Elena Baca, Marion Martinez, and Teresa Archuleta Sagel" (Lopez 2001). Instead of rejecting their culture or damning it as "close-minded"

Fig. 7. Alma López, *Our Lady,* 1999.
Reprinted by permission.

and "machista" as many do, especially in assimilationist popular magazines,[5] Chicana feminists engage head-on with the controversy. This was
dramatically demonstrated when, in reaction to the attack on Alma
Lopez's representation of La Virgen, the Chicana feminist Patrisia Gonzales wrote a syndicated column with an interview with Raquel Salinas, the
model who posed for the image. Her participation as a model was also a
feminist intervention to help her heal from a rape suffered at the age of
eighteen, after which many close to her "made her feel shame and told her
it was God's punishment. Guilt-ridden, she was made to believe it was she
who had precipitated her own rape" (Gonzales and Rodriguez 2001). The
lack of support was one of the factors that led Salinas to drinking and
"caused her to cover herself up—to hide her body, her curves . . . her femininity" (ibid.). According to Patrisia Gonzales, Salinas

> led a double life. Fiercely proud of her heritage, she became politically active
> at a young age. She witnessed the raw brutality of police officers against pro-
> testers at the East L.A. Chicano Moratorium in 1970. "When I saw that bru-
> tality, I committed my life toward fighting injustice." Yet, through all the po-
> litical movements she participated in, she was always silent about her rape.
> (Ibid.)

Salinas began her healing when a woman friend told her, "It wasn't your
fault. You didn't ask to be raped" (ibid.). Salinas began modeling for art
classes at the University of California, Los Angeles, to rid herself of her
"guilt around her body." The image created by Lopez was a culmination
of sorts for Salinas, who now "adheres to an indigenous spirituality that
views Our Lady of Guadalupe as Tonantzin—her common name in Nahu-
atl—meaning 'Our Most Venerable Mother'" (ibid.).

Furthermore, Patrisia Gonzales's column was a layered feminist intervention, because only a month before she covered the Lopez and Salinas
controversy, she wrote a moving account about her own traumatic rape at
the age of twenty-five (Gonzales 2001a). She received hundreds of emails
and letters from women who had undergone the same violence. Roberto
Rodriguez, her husband and coauthor in many columns and several books,
wrote a reaction to Patrisia's account explaining his feelings about the vi-
olation of his wife and witnessing her continuing pain (2001). It is a pain
that he then connects to his own experience of being brutally beaten by

the Los Angeles police and over which he sued and won a substantial economic settlement. At the same time, he discussed how much more of a vi-
olation Patrisia suffered in comparison to his trauma, although he still pe-
riodically experienced post-traumatic stress syndrome (PTSD) as a result
of the police beating.

Most recently, Patrisia wrote another column expressing her allegiance
to La Virgen from a feminist and Buddhist perspective. Although she was
asked by her "Buddhist teachers" to "relinquish" La Virgen, Patrisia chose
"*La Lupita*, [to return] to my home." Patrisia's husband related that as
part of her healing process, Patrisia "maintains an altar, which has helped
to reconstruct her violated spirit" (Rodriguez 2001). According to
Roberto, "On it are things sacred, including an eagle feather and pho-
tographs of ancestors. There I see many things connected to the earth, especially those with which to heal herself and to help others heal. This is
what makes our house a home" (ibid.).

Alma Lopez, Patrisia Gonzales, and Raquel Salinas, with sympathetic
compañeros like Roberto Rodriguez, critically embrace Chicano/Mexi-
cano culture, engaging different constituencies to reconfigure regressive
elements in Chicano communities and, through mutual struggle, creating
circles of dialogue. Art, creative writing, essays, and interviews are all
geared toward the goal of raising the level of understanding of the position
of all Chicanos. Patrisia notes with pride, "We wrote about the recent 'Our
Lady' controversy and the tale of Salinas, who posed for the image to heal
herself as a rape survivor. One reader responded that her 83-year-old
grandmother, given the context, found a new meaning in the art: 'Now I
understand. The artwork should stay in the museum.'"

Chicana feminisms make conscious that which is taken for granted because it has become naturalized through cultural practice. In social psychological terms, they make us aware of the profiles that, as background,
are essential to our perception of the white vase (see fig. 8). The "taken for
granted silences" of Chicanas as well as other women were essential to
maintaining their invisibility. By making the background as salient as the
foreground, Chicana feminists attempted to raise awareness to a new level.
Furthermore, by making dialogue and disruption essential parts of their
intervention, they invite others to further their deconstruction
(Arredondo et al. forthcoming). In the Alma Lopez controversy, Roberto
Rodriguez's engagement with his feminist wife's commentary creates ever

Fig. 8. Perceptual Figure I

Fig. 9. Perceptual Figure II

widening ripples of analysis that culminated with the *conscientización*—to use Ana Castillo's term—of a devout, Catholic, eighty-three-year-old *abuelita*, who finally understands why Alma Lopez's representation of La Virgen is not blasphemous (Gonzalez 2001b). Figure 9 is the social psychological representation of this ongoing process of deconstruction of hierarchies within each white vase, with the ultimate goal of creating a just society.

The Acquisition and Transmission of History through Cultural Ritual

Chicana feminist interventions were produced within the historical and cultural framework of Chicanas' heritage and created feminisms from within their communities. Chicanas took their own experience and ancestry to create a *critical positionality* from which to reconstruct gender relations and to assess the dominant group's treatment of Chicanas and Chicanos. The meanings Chicano cultural ritual were turned on their heads for more radical purposes. Take the *quinceañera* (fifteenth birthday celebration), which has traditionally signaled a young woman's availability for marriage (see chapter 2). Chicana feminists converted it into a *cincuentañera* celebration (a fiftieth birthday celebration), celebrating *el cambio de vida* (the change of life—menopause) and highlighting a woman's accomplishments, which may or may not include marriage and children. Norma Cantú, a Chicana feminist writer and professor, writes about her own and other Chicana feminist intellectuals' *cincuentañeras* (N. Cantú 2002). *Cincuentañeras* usually have all the accouterments of a *quinceañera*, a dance, a formal dress, *madrinas* (sponsors), the participation of parents, but instead of signifying a "young lady's entrance into society," the ritual signifies the celebration of a mature woman—an intellectual—coming of age and celebrating with her family, friends, and community through rituals originating in her own culture. Although *cincuentañeras* follow the basic traditions of a *quinceañera*, they also modify it to serve feminist purposes. The traditional *quinceañera* figurine on top of the birthday cake (akin to the bride and groom on a wedding cake) was replaced in Judge Hilda Tagle's *cincuentañera* cake by replicas of her publications and books. The court of young *damas* in Professor Norma Cantú's *cincuentañera* was replaced by a court of Chicana professionals in their forties and fifties. *Madrinas* sponsoring such things as the missal and rosary were replaced in Dr. Laura Rendón's *cincuentañera* by *madrinas* of "sensuality" and of "spiritual growth." Each *cincuentañera* substitutes the traditional rituals with her own feminist interventions.

The *cincuentañera* serves as a "teachable moment" in celebrating *within* and *requiring* the participation of community members who may not have obtained higher education. It brings intellectuals and professionals into Mexicano/Chicano communities where they might no longer live to reconnect with their roots. If Chicana feminists had failed to retain and participate in Chicano/Mexicano culture, their feminist expression, when and if they reached gender consciousness, would be dominated by white, middle-class, and academic frameworks. For Chicana feminists unfamiliar with *quinceañeras*, the *cincuentañera* celebration can be a reacquisition of cultural traditions that had been lost in their families or that never existed. It potentially expands feminists' cultural horizons. There is a multiplicity of reappropriated rituals (not just *quinceañeras* and *cincuentañeras*), allowing a diversity of avenues for feminist interventions. Chicana feminists opened the door to a variety of activities designed to re-create, invent, and renew their culture with a feminist twist. The heterogeneity of appropriation is especially important because of the diversity of the Mexican and Latino population, much of it varying by geographical region.

The practice of Catholicism was also reconstituted. Although many respondents were very skeptical of the church's authority, many still attended Catholic mass because they loved the rituals, the music, the use of Spanish, and the sense of community created during mass. Many attended only "Spanish mass" or went only to their "home church"; otherwise the rituals failed to fulfill their need for community and for the celebration of Chicano/Mexicano culture. Furthermore, the Catholic practice of constructing home altars for favorite saints and celebrating El Día de Los Muertos was appropriated by Chicana feminist artists like Amalia Mesa-Bains to pay homage to notable women like Frida Kahlo and Dolores del Río (see fig. 10).

Chicana feminists who are not artists also construct altars, not to venerate the Catholic Church but rather to feature their own personal experiences. For example, Professor Sandra Pacheco gave a guest lecture in my "Chicana Feminisms" class that focused on her experiences as a woman of Color going through the academy. As part of her guest appearance she

Fig. 10. Amalia Mesa-Bains, An *Ofrenda for Dolores del Río,* Reprinted by permission.

constructed an altar to illustrate her journey (see fig. 11). She had obtained her doctorate in experimental psychology and felt that in order to survive the doctoral program, she was required to deny her ethnicity as a Mexican-descent woman. As she approached graduation, she realized that what she wanted most at her hooding ceremony was to hear *mariachi* music. Pacheco refused to attend the graduation ceremony and instead participated in the Chicano/Latino celebration and had a Chicana professor do the official hooding that welcomed her into the academy. Her altar represented all these conflicts as well as her process of self-healing. She reclaimed her roots through the strong women in her life, primarily her maternal grandmother. She also placed on her altar several pictures of Chicana academics who had not denied their background as they obtained their degrees and succeeded in the academy. She equated her intellectual and emotional journey to a spiritual quest that was aided by many different

Fig. 11. Altar building by Professor Sandra Pacheco, April 25, 2000.
Photograph by Dawn Scavo. Reprinted by permission.

religious beliefs, not just Catholicism. So she included religious iconogra-
phy in her altar but secularized it by appropriating saints like La Virgen de
Guadalupe and San Martín de Porras because of their personal significance
to her rather than because of the saints' religious significance (see fig. 12).[6]
Pacheco also included statues of Aztec goddesses and Buddhist prayer
flags. She constructed her altar in the Psychology Department's conference room, where the faculty held its "scientific colloquium series." By appropriating this space, Pacheco expressed her identity in a visible, tangible
way and asserted that being a woman, a Chicana, and of working-class origins did not stop her from being an intellectual and a scientist. To cleanse
herself of all the negative assertions that are written about women, when
she finished constructing her altar she read aloud various quotations from
male psychologists about "women's essential nature." After she finished
reading, she burned each piece of paper, urging students to construct their
own identities and not let others dictate their paths in life.

Creating a Space of One's Own:
Cultural and Artistic Production

Several respondents used creative space as a way to build a feminist consciousness. For many, creative works were a good alternative or supplemental activity to direct political involvement, which many times was fraught with tensions and contradictions. Mieka Valdez, who never found a political student organization that completely satisfied her, hosted a radio show with a friend while they were undergraduates as a way to create a "space for women of Color." Mieka felt that by "being a DJ with my friend Susan, who's Vietnamese," and "having a show that was for women of Color," she created a "very powerful space for us to play."

Most respondents who participated in cultural projects were unable to articulate their significance; they had no intellectual framework for theorizing their everyday experience. For example, many respondents participated in Mexican *folklórico* groups (also called *ballet folklóricos*). Some groups had formed in high school or in local parishes to learn the different regional folkloric dances from Mexico. Other respondents were in

Fig. 12. Professor Sandra Pacheco's identity altar, April 25, 2000.
Photograph by Aída Hurtado. Reprinted by permission.

folklórico groups in college. Participation in *ballet folklóricos* exposed respondents to Mexican music, reinforced the use of Spanish, taught them Mexican history, and exposed them to a Mexican aesthetic through dance and costume. Respondents participated because "it felt good," because they "liked to dance," and because it connected them to "their communities," especially when they were attending predominantly white institutions. Playing in *mariachi* bands, although not as widespread, was another cultural practice of great significance to several respondents. The reasons respondents participated in *mariachi* bands were similar to their reasons for participating in *ballet folklóricos*.

Participation in these cultural activities helped respondents create a "space of their own." Many of the *folklórico* groups were female-dominated, giving women an opportunity to practice their leadership skills. To be sure, there were dances and songs that were very empowering for women in their traditional form. However, respondents used their exposure in college to gender and racial issues to critically analyze the sexism (and sometimes racism and classism) in some of the traditional Mexican dances and in the lyrics of Mexican songs. Often they modified them to correct these biases without destroying their essence. Although *mariachi* bands were more likely to be integrated by gender, sometimes there were "all-girl" bands. Participants discussed and critiqued the lyrics in many Mexican folk songs and reconstituted them to correct their sexism, a practice that the anthropologist Olga Nájera-Ramírez described as a feminist intervention among female Mexican professional performers:

> by participating actively in what was predominantly a male genre, women have been able to employ the *ranchera* for their own purposes, sometimes highlighting their subordination, sometimes talking back to that subordination, but always calling attention to their concerns, desires, experiences, and needs. . . . through the manipulation of text, costume, and performance style, women may use the *ranchera* to challenge, transgress, and even ameliorate gender constraints prevalent in Mexican society. (forthcoming)

Another way respondents gained feminist consciousness was exposure to Chicana feminist cultural production, which was mostly discovered by accident. Chicana feminist creative writers were especially important. A substantial number of respondents had attended readings by Chicana authors, who spoke to them in very profound ways. The discovery of Chicana art production led some respondents to closely follow the writers and attend their readings in several cities. Feeling empowered by the works of Chicana feminists, many respondents began to write as well. Rebeca produced a collection of literary works that included Latinas at Harvard University reflecting on their experiences at that institution (Burciaga and Tavares 1999). Mieka Valdez's exposure to Chicana feminist writings and art production inspired her to move to San Francisco after graduating from college to continue working on her photography.

At the end of many of my interviews, respondents expressed a hunger for art, poetry, and performance that reflected their own lived experience. They often asked me for book references and jotted down names of videos or films featuring Chicana artists. It was obvious that regardless of the underground nature of Chicanas' cultural production, many of my respondents found resonance with their work.

Theorizing Patriarchy

There is no doubt that patriarchy was enforced on my respondents from birth. Like Cleófilas Enriqueta DeLeón Hernández,[7] my respondents were born with a well-defined map of women's lives: marriage, children, and work. In rare instances, mothers, themselves victims of this same map, openly advised their daughters to pursue all those dreams that had been denied them and to reject the set route: "don't have children," "don't get married," "have a career," "travel and be free." More commonly, the opposite was the case. But then life happened. From birth my respondents did not fit this map. Many fathers, if present, did not want to inflict on their girl children the same misery many of them had seen their own mothers suffer. So they worked extra hard to give them an opportunity for education. When at a loss as to how to provide this freedom, they simply stayed out of their way as mothers and other womenfolk took over the emancipation of their daughters. Yet, ideologically, many of these emancipators proclaimed their allegiance to the roadmap that they themselves had subverted their entire lives. So it was a patriarchy that had fault lines through which many of my respondents escaped.

Because the enforcement of patriarchy was uneven, many of my respondents did not see all men—the beneficiaries—as the same. They had witnessed the pain of their fathers as they died after years of excelling in dead-end jobs and ending up depressed during the last years of their lives, as Irma Martínez had. They had also heard their fathers' confessions of humiliations as their racist bosses passed them up for promotions simply because they "were Mexican," as Alejandra Dominguez had at the age of twelve. They had seen their brothers, who only five years earlier played on the swings, condemned to life imprisonment, as Sobeida's was. They had uncles whom they adored as fathers being mistreated because they were gay, as Agustina had. Some also had husbands and lovers who stayed at home with the children while they pursued their dreams of higher education, as Sara had, or who supported them in myriad other ways. They had also endured rape, incest, physical and psychological battering, and neglect—as Victoria, Carina García Guzmán, Mariposa, and Lucha had. They had experienced both love and brutality from men, and my respondents refused to see all men as the same. They wanted feminisms that allowed them to both accept and reject, to embrace and critique, to love and loathe, to "see through serpent and eagle eyes" (Anzaldúa 1987, 78–79) so they could avoid discarding those they still considered human in spite of all their shortcomings. Their views of patriarchy were accordingly complex.

Enforcing Patriarchy

The construction of Chicanas' sexuality is at the core of the gender dynamics that results in sexism in Chicano families and communities.

—Hurtado 1996a, 49

Chicana feminists agree with other feminists that patriarchy is enforced on women through socioeconomic structures and through everyday social interaction. Chapter 2 documented the social restrictions imposed on most of my respondents as well as the ideological adherence to virginity, practices that legitimated their fathers as the ultimate gatekeepers of their virtue. Mothers were *virtual fathers* in single-headed households, often enforcing patriarchal messages even when the patriarch was not present.

Patriarchy was enforced in my respondents' households in subtle and not so subtle ways. One of the most direct was the restriction of respondents' interactions with boys of their own age. Parents often enforced sexual chastity by never specifying rules around dating and postponing their permission each time the daughter reached the agreed upon age—"*No, cuando cumplas quince*" (No, when you turn fifteen), "*No, cuando cumplas veintiuno*" (No, when you turn twenty-one), and so on. A less direct way was to give boyfriends the "cold shoulder," creating anxiety in respondents about appropriate behavior. Many respondents reported restraining themselves to avoid angering their parents.

When respondents were allowed to date, many were accompanied by younger siblings, thus continuing the cultural practice of "chaperoning" common in the 1940s, according to the Chicana historian Vicki Ruiz (1998, 51). Parents relaxed rules with subsequent children, often reversing themselves by finally allowing boyfriends into their homes (but only with others present, insuring that "no touching" occurred). Fathers frequently gave boyfriends the "silent treatment," demarcating their authority as head of the household even though they had bent the rules. Many respondents accepted these restrictions, although they did not like them, because they saw the enforcement of patriarchy stemming from love rather than power and thus excused the enforcers. As part of their acceptance of patriarchy, many respondents overlooked the fact than they faced many more restrictions than their brothers did. The enforcement of patriarchy "Chicano style" set the stage both for my respondents' compliance and for their rebellion, sowing the seeds for their nascent "*mestiza* consciousness."

Rejecting Patriarchy: Disruption as Method

how do you tame a wild tongue, train it to be quiet, how do you bridle and saddle it? How do you make it lie down?   —Anzaldúa 1987, 53

Chicana feminisms were born out of acts of disruption, especially in the Chicano movement. Chicana feminists created spaces of resistance to patriarchy in general and patriarchy in their own ethnic and racial groups (A. García 1989, 219). Disruption, that is, head-on confrontation, is one of the most powerful methods used by Chicana feminists to include their issues on the political agenda. Many Chicana feminists disrupted all the movements they participated in: if working within the Chicano movement, they would argue for women's issues (Segura and Pesquera 1992, 78); if working with white feminists, they would argue for including ethnicity and race (Sandoval 1991); if working with Chicana women's organizations, they would argue for including lesbian and gay issues (Pesquera and Segura 1993, 107).

The head-on engagement, however, had to be context-specific. It was understood that one cannot engage a white male professor as one would engage a Mexican immigrant male farmworker who only attended third grade and did not speak English. The material conditions of both men, although benefiting from patriarchy, required a feminist disruption to be calibrated accordingly. There were many examples of respondents using disruption as method without necessarily being fully conscious of it or articulating it. Gloria, for example, drew the proverbial line in the sand with her mother, who did not miss an occasion to belittle her. Gloria, with the help of a therapist, told her mother to stop or else refused to continue the conversation. Under no circumstance, however, did Gloria distance herself from her mother or permanently stop talking to her. Instead, "it was a head-on confrontation" (Hurtado 1998, 135) with her mother within the context of connection. Similarly, Carolina prided herself on "being a big time feminist" but when it came to her father, she tolerated "racist remarks" that reminded her of "Archie Bunker." She still argued with him at times, but at other times she would "let it slide." Most of all, she felt extremely connected to her father and called herself a "daddy's girl."

Carolina's way of dealing with her father's racism also illustrates a *mestiza* consciousness at work. Carolina saw several levels of "truth" simultaneously and connected to those that were most congruent with her points of view. My respondents can be understood as postmodern subjects who perceived social reality as fragmented and subject to multiple interpretations. They positioned themselves on particular planes after considering various points of view. Carolina, for example, did not outwardly reject or accept her father's racist views; she understood that he was not ready to change his attitudes. Instead of rejecting him, she focused on his positive aspects: he had worked hard his entire life for his family; he loved his wife and showed it in front of his daughters; and he adored his daughters and never hampered their educational achievement. She could preserve her connection and at the *same time* be critical of him. Carolina also felt that there might come a time when he would be ready to change—at which point she would readily challenge him. Until that happened, she was unwilling to reject him.

My respondents applied refined disruption in their social relationships and in their interactions with institutions as well. A central disruption was their questioning of the Catholic Church. Most respondents considered themselves "spiritual" rather than "religious," even though a substantial number were raised Catholic and had attended Catholic school. They specifically questioned women's role in the Catholic Church's hierarchy, the prohibition against women's ordination, having to confess to "a man in a box," and the church's position against homosexuality. In general, many respondents saw the Catholic Church as manifesting a great degree of hypocrisy.

It was not unusual for respondents to have learned their critical views from their mothers. However, many of these same mothers still raised their families as "culturally Catholic." For example, Gloria's mother cautioned her against believing everything in the Bible, because it was "written by a bunch of men." Alicia Granillo's mother saw many churchgoers' hypocrisy, those who "pounded their chest" while attending mass but did not help their communities.

Many respondents' willingness to critique the Catholic religion, which controlled so many of their cultural beliefs and practices (although not necessarily their religious practices), increased the significance of their disruption as they also reassessed the inherent sexism of not only the church but Chicano/Mexicano culture as well.

The Deconstruction of Binaries

Social science has assumed . . . that there is a general movement in acculturating groups toward family egalitarianism. . . . Overall shifts occur from extended kinship units with rigid sex role divisions to nuclear, autonomous, egalitarian family units. . . . This modernization is said to give rise to a new "modern" orientation among women and to bring about a trend toward greater equality between the sexes. —Baca Zinn 1975, 13–14

Much of the social science literature asserts that patriarchy is more severely enforced in ethnic and racial communities than in white communities. The solution, therefore, is to strive to become more like whites. My respondents expressed deep discomfort with simply dichotomizing gender relations along racial and ethnic lines. In fact, many of them rejected white, middle-class feminisms precisely because, from their point of view, these feminisms entailed adopting a "white cultural" template. They expressed reluctance to distance themselves from men at the same time that they recognized male privilege and challenged it on a daily basis.

Many of my respondents felt that adopting the label "feminist" was not necessary to fight for gender equality *within* their own lived experience. They did not accept the linear assumptions of assimilation theory that liberation and education were possible only if one "became white." Several respondents explicitly claimed a Chicana feminist perspective as the framework that allowed them to salvage their cultural identity at the same time that they rejected patriarchal domination. When I asked Mieka Valdez whether she thought she was a feminist, she replied, "not just a feminist, a Chicana feminist," because otherwise she could not claim the feminist label. Similarly, whereas Frida did not find resonance with Chicano organizations like MEChA or with white environmental organizations, she found her political niche with the feminist organization Mujeres Activas en Letras y Cambio Social (MALCS), which "addressed Chicana gender issues" directly in solidarity with other Third World women.[8]

Respondents of mixed heritage were particularly adroit at deconstructing binaries because their vantage point was informed by their familial experience with their Mexican and "white" families. They saw sexist, racist, and homophobic attitudes and behaviors from members of both sides of their families.

Attitudes toward sex and virginity were also not linear as predicted by assimilation theory: more educated or white parents did not necessarily have the most liberal or egalitarian views. Sonya K. Smith did not speak to her white, educated father about sexual matters, fearing that it would "make him uncomfortable." Mieka Valdez had as much difficulty disclosing her lesbianism to her white, educated mother as she did to her Chicano, educated father. Nicole Rodriguez had an easier time speaking to her educated Chicano father about menstruation and romantic relationships, including sex, than to her educated Armenian mother. On the opposite side of the educational divide, Alicia Granillo's mother, who had only attended second grade, did not speak English, and was a dishwasher at a casino in Las Vegas, had the most radical views against marriage and childbearing and was adamantly pro-choice. Similarly, Gloria's mother, who had only nine years of education and was a classroom assistant at an elementary school, told her not to get married and to become economically self-sufficient by obtaining an education. Christine Granados's mother, who considers herself "Mexican American" and had graduated from high school but not attended college, urged her to get on the pill and to have an abortion if she became pregnant. Views on sexual orientation were also not necessarily reflective of the respondents' degree of "assimilation." Jessica Delgado's "Spanish American" family from New Mexico, including her *abuelita* (grandmother), fully accepted her romantic partners as if they were "married." Gabriella Gonzalez's "Mexican American" educated father told her, "I'd much rather my daughters be lesbians than promiscuous." The enforcement, compliance, and resistance to patriarchy were much more complex than the "social science" assumption "that there is a general movement in" acculturation among women to "bring about a trend toward greater equality between the sexes."

Applying Feminist Lessons to Men

> My brother is fifteen now, and I know he's a guy but I talk to him. "You know, *mijo* [my son], if you're gonna do anything, use protection." It would break my heart if he lost his virginity before marriage. It would also break my heart to see him get a girl pregnant; he has so much potential. If this happened then he'd have to quit school and probably start working.
>
> —Magdalena, twenty-one-year-old respondent, Chicago

My respondents applied many of the feminist lessons learned from their mothers and others to the men in their lives, especially to younger siblings. As they grew older, respondents internalized the logic behind their mothers' (and to a certain extent their fathers') strictness. Although there was variation among parents' level of acceptance of their sons' sexual transgressions, they did not reprimand or restrict them as they did their daughters. Many parents expressed the view that the consequences for the boys were not the same as for the girls, which, practically speaking, was quite true. Many respondents had internalized their parents' warnings about the negative consequences of premarital sex and did not want their siblings, including their brothers, to engage in sex prematurely. For example, Magdalena worried about her younger brother having sex before marriage, because she felt that it was not morally desirable and because "if he got a girl pregnant," he would "ruin his life." These were exactly the words spoken to Magdalena by her mother, grandmother, and aunt.

Respondents worried about unplanned pregnancies for their brothers, and more generally were very invested in seeing them succeed educationally. Nina D. Sánchez was pushing hard for her ten-year-old brother to go to college and to attend the same academically rigorous high school that she had attended. Nina laughed at herself as she realized that "he's still young" but stated resolutely, "he will go." Nina's parents made great sacrifices to send all their children to private Catholic schools. Nina was grateful for her parents' dedication, strongly believing in the freedom afforded by education. She wanted the same educational opportunities for all her siblings, including the boys.

Interstitial Feminisms:
The Continuation of the Motherline

El Colorete

She loved red lipstick. It shocked people. They looked at her the way they look at bag ladies—with disgust and fear. She always thought to herself "bag ladies are us in a braver state." But why did she like red lipstick? She remembered her *abuelita* Chencha, she too scared people. She didn't give a damn what they thought about her. She had fire in her eyes—scary when women are that free. Every afternoon her grandmother, who lived in Laredo, dressed in her finest, got her shopping bag, put on red lipstick, and went downtown to the matinees or to have coffee and read the paper. It was her daily ritual, her reclaiming of self after she worked all day tending to everybody else's needs. If you were really lucky, she would take one or two of the grandchildren on her daily expeditions. . . . Red lipstick marked the presence of her grandmother as a full human being. She had kept the tradition. Funny, the other day her five-year-old niece had come in with a full-red mouth she acquired by stealing her mother's red lipstick.

—Hurtado n.d.

I was in Michigan when my mother called me and told me, "I need you." That's when I knew it was serious, because my mother never—she was a very strong woman, did her own thing—never said that she needed me. . . . After that, we went back home from the hospital. That's when I started changing

her bed sheets and taking care of my mom who became paraplegic while suffering from cancer.

—Sara, twenty-nine-year-old respondent, Ann Arbor, Michigan

A dominant theme in Chicana feminist writings has been the adherence to a postmodern paradigm that dismantles the myth of the "coherent sub-ject." The multiplicities of experiences as well as the cross-national nature of many Chicanas' lives challenge our theories of how they construct their self-concepts. Emma Pérez, who was influenced by the field of cultural studies, states that to understand Chicanas, we should conceptualize them as "diasporic subjects":

> As Stuart Hall posits, "diaspora identities are those which are constantly producing and reproducing themselves anew, through transformation and difference." Although seemingly adaptive, diaspora's transformative mobil-ity is in actuality its most creative oppositional function. Unlike adaptive im-migrants, transformative diasporic subjects travel and "live inside with a dif-ference." In the difference is the diasporic subject's mobility through and about, weaving interstitially, to create, always create, something else, whether music, food, clothes, style, or language. The diasporic ushers in an adaptability as only one of many ways to keep moving, to keep weaving through power, to grasp and re-create culture, to re-create oneself through and with diasporic communities. The diasporic subject . . . is not only Mex-ican or American, or Mexican American, or even Chicano/a, but more, much more, is always re-creating the unimagined, the unknown, where mo-bile third space identities thrive, and where the decolonial imaginary gleans the diasporic's subjecthood. (Pérez 1999, 79)

My respondents' views on feminism were influenced by the many strong women in their lives—grandmothers, aunts, sisters, cousins, and friends. Central to their socialization, however, were their mothers, most of whom were working-class with very little formal education, women Pérez con-siders "diasporic subjects," who as active agents take their lived experience, "weaving interstitially, to create, always create, something else, whether music, food, clothes, style, or language. . . . weaving through power, to grasp and re-create culture, to re-create oneself through and with diasporic communities." Social science literatures have generally emphasized only one aspect of Chicanas' identities *at a time*, ignoring the complexity of these women's historical, cultural, and linguistic trajectories. Take the identity "immigrant." All the attitudes and behaviors around sex and gender roles are likely attributed to the fact that these women come from Mexico and are the first generation in the United States. The totalizing inherent in the "immigrant identity" obfuscates the complex negotiations articulated by many of my respondents' mothers, who, as diasporic subjects, weaved together their lived experiences on both sides of the border with their dreams to provide their daughters with the best advice at a particular point in time. When proven wrong, many mothers changed accordingly. Sara's mother apologized on her deathbed as she succumbed to cancer for doubting her daughter's choice to leave California for Michigan to attend graduate school. Sara, once considered *malhablada* (foulmouthed) by her entire family, including her mother, earned praise for her outspokenness. Sara's *lengua* (tongue) garnered her mother the morphine that made her last days with cancer bearable. Her mother redeemed Sara's choices even though they were not the ones she had advised her to take.

Chicana feminists have outlined the "interstitial" nature of Chicanas' existence (Anzaldúa 1987; Hurtado forthcoming; Saldívar-Hull 2000; Pérez 1999) as they live "betwixt and between successive lodgments in jural political systems" (Lugones 1992, 6–7). They have inhabited the limen, glimpsing at its liberatory potential through their multiple subjectivities. As "limen creatures" (Hurtado 1996a, 85), Chicanas have negotiated multiple judicial, cultural, and political systems and from that "in-between" space created resistance. Emma Pérez (1999) named these resistance moves "interstitial feminisms" that could potentially build a "decolonial imaginary," challenging existing structural arrangements.

> I also argue that for historians, revitalizing Foucault's archaeology, the precursor to his genealogical method, can help us examine where in discourse the gaps, the interstitial moments of history, reappear to be seen or heard as that third space. Thus, Chéla Sandoval's notion of differential consciousness is also useful to my uncovering of women's history. Sandoval theorizes that differential consciousness allows for mobility of identities between and among varying power bases—for example, the move from liberal to socialist to feminist ideologies as forms of tactical intervention, or practice. I argue that the differential mode of consciousness to which Sandoval refers is pre-

cisely third space feminist practice, and that practice can occur, only within the decolonial imaginary. . . . Like differential consciousness, the decolonial imaginary in Chicana/o history is a theoretical tool for uncovering the hidden voices of Chicanas that have been relegated to silences, to passivity, to that third space where agency is enacted through third space feminism. (Pérez 1999, xvi)

An essential part of "interstitial feminism" is the rejection of the binary of "victim" and "oppressor" for a more contextual analysis of power.

The oppressed as colonial other becomes the liminal identity, partially seen yet unspoken, vibrant and in motion, overshadowed by the construction of coloniality, where the decolonial imaginary moves and lives. One is not simply oppressed or victimized; nor is one only oppressor or victimizer. Rather, one negotiates within the imaginary to a decolonizing otherness where all identities are at work in one way or another. (Pérez 1999, 7)

My respondents' mothers served as both facilitators of and obstacles to their daughters' emancipation. But it was a negotiated struggle that was done with the overriding goal of remaining connected in spite of the disagreements. Mothers and daughters were both enacting interstitial feminisms and not assuming absolutely the role of victim or victimizer. And while they existed in and were sanctioned by patriarchy, respondents and their mothers were certainly not "merely a backdrop to men's social and political activities, they [were] in fact intervening interstitially while sexing the colonial imaginary" (Pérez 1999, 7), because "diasporic experiences are always gendered" (79). All my respondents and their mothers were practicing, at some level or another, interstitial feminisms, trying to escape "the colonial imaginary" so as not "to remain the colonial object who cannot be subject until decolonized. The decolonial imaginary challenges power relations to decolonize notions of otherness to move into a liberatory terrain" (110).

What Remains to Be Done

There are still many thorny theoretical questions about Chicanas' feminisms. Why, for example, are respondents reluctant to embrace the label "feminist" even though they have internalized "feminist" ways of being? Feminism has always been a political movement rather than only an academic discipline or paradigmatic orientation. Feminists' struggles for a presence in university departments aimed to both change the structural advantages of patriarchy and produce feminist scholarship. Within the next ten years my respondents will become the educated elite. They will be policy makers, college presidents, corporate lawyers, public defenders, medical doctors, university professors, and so on. Living "feminist lives" versus respondents labeling themselves feminist will have enormous implications for feminist organizing to create social change.

How do current feminisms contribute to my respondents' reluctance to call themselves feminists? One answer to this question lies in an image problem. The portrayal of feminists mostly by popular media as "man-hating" and as "separatists" has damaged the recruitment to the feminist movement of younger women of all races and ethnicities (Frith 2001). Hate does not attract healthy, productive people—whether the hate is real or a media creation. My respondents, like many other young women, are too compassionate to embrace a movement perceived as excluding and "othering" even when the objectification is of those with power. This perception of a "man-hating feminist movement" is largely an image problem exaggerated in the popular media to weaken an otherwise vibrant movement. A recent example is a *Time* magazine article declaring feminism dead. To emphasize the point, the cover featured the disembodied heads of Susan B. Anthony, Betty Friedan, Gloria Steinem, and the television character Ally McBeal, signifying how "feminism has devolved into the silly" (Bellafante 1998, 58). Not only has the demise of feminism been announced in the popular media, but scholarly analyses also debate whether younger women are committed to the ideals set forth in the second wave of the movement (Frith 2001).

A second answer to the problematic posed above is the serious political differences among feminists. All feminists are responsible for not working effectively across differences in race, class, ethnicity, and sexuality. As a result of the debates among the adults, new generations of women do not know how to best align themselves and are choosing to avoid the fray. Unfortunately, the latest feminist writings confirm these criticisms and do not afford young women concrete alternatives. Perhaps it is time for older feminists to step aside and let the young ones take over this problematic.

A third issue that contributes to a lack of feminist identification among the young is feminism's relationship to class privilege. Most of my respondents come from working-class backgrounds and failed to see feminist writings' connection to poverty. Chicana feminist writings came closer to my respondents' views on class struggles. However, there was a small minority of respondents who thought of themselves as middle-class and aspired to corporate careers. They asked whether any kind of feminism applied to them. Feminism, as a disciplinary field and as a political movement, promotes a "feminist agenda" that avoids class issues. For example, some feminists lauded Elizabeth Dole's presidential bid because she was the "first" woman to run for president from a major political party. Yet these supporters ignored Dole's problematic positions on a variety of issues affecting poor women in general, poor women of Color specifically, and poor men as well. Why, then, was support for Dole a "feminist" political move?

These contradictions and muddy issues did not escape my respondents—we taught them well. They applied the same analytical apparatus used to deconstruct patriarchy and the privileges of class, race, and heterosexuality to spotlight our own contradictions and blind spots. They were indeed our intellectual daughters.

Epilogue

I have a fantasy. I envision all my respondents spending a weekend together in a magical place like Santa Fe, New Mexico, time spent reading each other's stories, affirming their extraordinary gifts, and celebrating their accomplishments. I fantasize about respondents sharing each other's poems and stories through listening circles, where they can disclose to each other as they did to me. I wish we could stand side by side in one big circle of 102 women—all Chicanas—holding hands under the turquoise sky and laughing about how we have survived.

I'm not sure whether this *deseo* (desire) will ever come true, but in my mind's eye, and I hope in the minds of the readers of this book, this is the image that lingers after they have turned the last page.

Appendix*

Respondents Who Chose to Use Their Names (N=48)

Alvarez, Patricia, quoted in chapters 3, 5, 7

Castillo, Cynthia C., not quoted

Cota, Christina M., quoted in chapter 9

Delgado, Jessica, quoted in chapters 1, 2, 3, 6, 7, 10

Dominguez, Alejandra, quoted in chapters 3, part II intro, 10

Dominguez, Jennifer, quoted in chapters 1, 9

Duarte, Cynthia, quoted in chapter 7

Flores Owens, Liza, quoted in chapter 9

García Guzmán, Carina, quoted in chapters 2, 5, 6, 7, 10

Garza, Norma I., quoted in chapters 3, 7

Gonzalez, Gabriella, quoted in chapters 1, 9, 10

Gordo, Blanca, quoted in chapters 3, 4

Granados, Christine, quoted in chapters 6, 8, review of part III

Gutiérrez, Annette, not quoted

Hernández, Maria A., not quoted

Hernández-Martínez, Gisela, not quoted

Lazo, Rosa, quoted in chapter 5

López, Dorian, quoted in chapters 1, 2, 6

* Not all respondents were quoted in the book, although all interviews were analyzed and used in the writing of this book.

Lopez Turley, Ruth N., quoted in chapters 2, 9
Maciel, Alicia Z., quoted in chapter 8, review of part III
Martínez, Irma, quoted in chapters 4, 5, 8, review of part III, 10
Matthews, Ana, not quoted
Mendez, Maria L., not quoted
Moncada, Isela, quoted in chapter 9
Perales, Nina A., quoted in chapters 3, 4
Peralta, Carla, not quoted
Perez, Ramona, quoted in chapter 1
Resendez, Maritza C., quoted in chapters 5, 8, review of part III
Reyes, Anna, quoted in chapters 7, 8, 9, review of part III
Reyes-Torres, Belen, not quoted
Reynoso, Christina J., quoted in chapters 2, 3
Rivera-Figueroa, Kim, quoted in chapter 8
Rodriguez, Nicole, quoted in chapters 1, 2, 5, 9, 10
Rodriguez, Claudia, quoted in chapters in 5, 7
Rodriguez, Zulma, quoted in part II intro, 5
Sandoval, Nicolassa I., quoted in chapters 1, 3, 6
Santos, Maria del Rosario, quoted in chapters 5, 6, 7
Santana, Christina, quoted in chapter 2
Sanchez, Nina D., quoted in chapter 9, review of part III, 10
Sedano, Leticia, quoted in chapters 2, 7
Smith, Sonya K., quoted in chapters 1, 2, 6, 8, 10
Solis, Jocelyn, quoted in chapters 2, 6
Tovar, L. Lidia, quoted in chapter 9
Trujillo, Jennifer, quoted in chapters 6, 7, 8
Valdez, Mieka, quoted in chapters 1, 2, 3, 5, 9, review of part III, 10
Vazquez, Noemi, quoted in chapters 5, 10
Verdugo, Anita L., quoted in chapter 9

Respondents Who Chose to Use Pseudonyms
(N=53)

Agustina, quoted in chapters 3, 5, 6, 10
Aixa, quoted in chapters 5, 9, 10
Bianca, quoted in chapters 1, 2, 4, 6, 8
Canela, quoted in chapter 9

Carolina, quoted in chapters 3, 5, 8, 9, 10

Conchita, quoted in chapters 3, 8, review of part III

Consuelo, not quoted

Cristina, quoted in chapters 2, introduction to part II, 6, 8

Desireé, quoted in chapters 2, 7

Fabiola, not quoted

Felisa, not quoted

Frida, quoted in chapters 2, 6, 9, review of part III, 10

Fuentes, Camila, quoted in chapters 7, 8, 9

Generosa, quoted in chapter 3

Granillo, Alicia quoted in chapters 3, 5, 6, 7, 8, 9, review of part III, 10

Guadalupe, quoted in chapters 3, 5, review of part III, 10

Gloria, quoted in chapters 2, 4, 5, 6, 7, 8, 9, 10

Hilda, quoted in chapters 1, 3, 4, 10

Irasema, quoted in chapters 9, 10

Josefa, quoted in chapter 9

Julissa, quoted in chapters 2, 3

Lucha, quoted in chapters 2, 3, 4, 5, 6, 7, 8, 9, 10

Lucinda, quoted in chapters 6, 7, 8

Magdalena, quoted in chapters 2, 3, 8, 10

Marie, quoted in chapter 2

Mariela, quoted in chapters 3, 9

Mariposa, quoted in chapters 1, 2, 10

Mariquita, quoted in chapter 9

Marissa, quoted in chapters 8, review of part III

Martinez, Belinda, quoted in chapters 2, 7, review of part III, 10

Minerva, quoted in chapter 9

Misty, quoted in chapters 1, 5, 7, 8, 9, review of part III

Natalie, not quoted

Nayelli, quoted in chapters 2, 3

Noelia, quoted in chapter 9

Patty, quoted in chapters 2, part II intro, 10

Rebeca, quoted in chapter 9, 10

Rita, quoted in chapters 2, 5, 6

Rosario, quoted in chapters 6, 8

Sachel, quoted in chapter 9

Sandra, quoted in chapter 3

Saenz, Sandra, quoted in chapters 4, 8
Sara, quoted in chapters 2, 3, part II intro, review of part III, 10
Sofia, quoted in chapters 8, 9, review of part III
Soledad, quoted in chapters 2, 3
Sobeida, quoted in chapters 3, 6, 10
Sylvia, not quoted
Tomasa, quoted in chapters 3, 4, 5, 6, 7, 10
Tonantzin, quoted in chapters 1, 3, 5, 8, 9
Valerie, quoted in chapters 4, 6, 8, 10
Victoria, quoted in chapters 2, 3, 8, 10
Villa, Maria, quoted in chapters 6, 8, 9
Xochiquetzal, quoted in chapter 9

Notes

Notes to Chapter 1

1. La Virgen de Guadalupe is the patron saint of Mexico and for many the Catholic version of the Aztec goddess Tonantzin. La Virgen de Guadalupe also has special significance because she is Indian, and for Chicana feminists symbolizes the redemption of *mestizaje* (the mixture of European, Indian, and African "races"). For an extensive feminist analysis of La Virgen de Guadalupe, see the edited book by Ana Castillo, *Goddess of the Americas/ La Diosa de las Américas: Writings on the Virgin of Guadalupe* (1996).

2. Chicana feminists appropriated La Virgen de Guadalupe as a symbol of Chicanas' racial hybridity and recognition of women's sacrifices on behalf of their families as essential to the group's economic and cultural survival. (See chapter 10 for a discussion of this appropriation by Chicana artists and writers.) Sor Juana Inés de la Cruz, a seventeenth-century Mexican nun, was a scholar, poet, playwright, and intellectual who in her work addressed the unfair condition of women. La Llorona is a figure in a legend that first appeared in sixteenth-century colonial Mexico and has persisted to the present in Mexico as well as in Chicano communities in the United States. According to the legend, La Llorona (or weeping woman) wanders the streets at night wailing over the loss of her children, whom she killed by drowning after her husband betrayed her with another woman (Limón 1991, 414–15). Frida Kahlo was a committed Marxist and political activist (Herrera 1983).

3. I required potential respondents to be between the ages of twenty and thirty, to have at least one parent of Mexican descent, and to have had some kind of education beyond high school. Several respondents came long distances and had made elaborate arrangements to be interviewed. When I found out that the age requirement was slightly off, I still interviewed them and included them in the sample. I did not have any problems with the other two requisites.

4. One respondent was born in Spain because her parents, both U.S. born, were abroad as part of her father's military assignment.

Notes to Chapter 2

1. Rita was twenty-seven, living with her parents in Watsonville, a rural town in Northern California, and working as a teacher in the predominantly Latino Alianza Elementary School. Rita first attended Cabrillo Community College and then transferred to the University of California, Santa Cruz, where she obtained her bachelor's degree in American studies with an emphasis on ethnic studies. She lived at home until she graduated and moved to Santa Barbara to obtain her master's in education from the University of California. When she finished, she returned home and began her job.

2. Victoria was twenty-four. She had attended the University of California, Santa Cruz, for three years but had health problems and discontinued her studies. At the time of the interview she was working as a community organizer for Neighborhood Services in Watsonville, California. She was also considering going back to school and finishing her bachelor's degree.

3. Gloria was twenty-seven and had received her bachelor's degree in Spanish and political science at Western Michigan University. She moved to Albuquerque to attend the University of New Mexico, where she was working on her master's in sociology.

4. Soledad was twenty-seven and a graduate student in the doctoral program in education at the University of Michigan.

5. Sara was twenty-nine and in her third year of the doctoral program in sociology at the University of Michigan. She first attended Hartnell Community College and then obtained her bachelor's degree in child development and social sciences at San Jose State University and her master's degree in sociology at the University of Michigan.

6. Mariposa was thirty and a doctoral candidate in sociology at the University of Michigan, Ann Arbor. She completed her undergraduate degree at the University of Minnesota in sociology and criminology.

7. Patty was twenty-three and had received her bachelor's degree in psychology and sociology at the University of California, Santa Cruz. She was taking a year off before she attended graduate school, working as an office clerk at Safeway, a grocery store chain in Oakland, California. By the time I was writing this chapter, she had recently graduated from Columbia University with a master's degree in education and was working with the Mexican American Legal Defense Fund and Education (MALDEF), an organization akin to the NAACP.

8. Ruth N. López Turley was twenty-four and a doctoral student in sociology at Harvard University. She obtained her undergraduate degree at Stanford University in sociology and Spanish.

9. Mirandé defines machismo as a "term that has numerous and diverse connotations in México and in the United States and is often associated with exaggerated masculinity, male chauvinism, or an extreme male supremacist ideology" (1997, 149).

10. These rituals, however, are not consumed or performed uncritically and have been appropriated by Chicana feminists to raise consciousness around gender issues in their communities. (See chapter 10 for an extensive discussion of Chicana feminist interventions utilizing Chicano cultural practices.)

11. Belinda Martínez was twenty-four and a second-year law student at Columbia University. She received her bachelor's degree in Chicano studies at the University of California, Los Angeles.

12. Nayelli was twenty-one and a senior majoring in psychology at the University of California, Santa Cruz. She was born and grew up in Los Angeles. At the time I was writing this chapter, Nayelli had graduated from college and was in her first year of a master's program in education at Columbia University.

13. Norma Cantú (1999) writes that as part of the *quinceañera* celebration there is a "*Corte de Honor* [Court of Honor], as the *damas* and *chamberláns* are called collectively" (78). There are as many as fourteen *damas* coupled with fourteen *chamberláns* (the *quinceañera* is the fifteenth person), and they are required to perform "ritualized actions both during the mass and during the dance and reception" (ibid.).

14. This is consistent with the available research that indicates that *quinceañeras* are celebrated in cities all over the United States, such as Austin (Lankford 1994), Chicago (Dávalos 1996), Detroit (Summers 1995), Laredo (N. Cantú 1999), Miami (Martínez-Chavez 1989), New York City (Martínez-Chavez 1989), and Phoenix (Orlean 1990). Mexicanos and Chicanos from all social classes celebrate *quinceañeras*. Of course, as in my sample of respondents, the celebrations are tailored according to the economic resources available and the preferences of the families.

15. Jocelyn Solis was twenty-eight and lived with her parents in Queens, New York. She was a doctoral student in psychology at the City University of New York. She received her bachelor's degree in psychology and romance languages at New York University. She studied in France during her junior year in college. That was the only time she had lived away from her parents.

16. Dorian López was twenty and an undergraduate in architecture and construction at Farmingdale University.

17. Although most respondents felt this way, a few stated that their parents took over the celebration and they had little or no input. For example, Magdalena chose to have a *quinceañera* instead of a family trip to Hawaii, a choice she regretted because her parents took over the celebration and only played *rancheras* (traditional Mexican songs) at the dance, not allowing more contemporary music to be played by the disc jockey hired for the occasion.

18. Desireé was twenty-five and had received her bachelor's degree from the University of California, Santa Cruz, in history. She worked as an administrator for the California Policy Project at the University of California, Berkeley. She eventually completed a professional master's program at the University of California, Berkeley.

19. Zavella (forthcoming) also finds a great deal of silence about sexuality with her Mexican-descent respondents.

20. *Tamales* are a Mexican dish. Dough is spread on the leaf of a corn husk and a filling is put in the middle and then wrapped tightly, arranged in a pot, and steamed until the dough is cooked. Making *tamales* is usually an all-day event and, therefore, they are made only on very special occasions.

21. Christina J. Reynoso was twenty-three. She graduated from the University of California, Santa Cruz, with a bachelor's degree in history. At the time of the interview, she was working as a community organizer for Neighborhood Services in Watsonville, California.

22. Christina Santana was twenty-one and a senior at the University of California, Santa Cruz, majoring in sociology. She was born in Tulare, California, and raised in Farmersville, California.

23. Marie was twenty-eight and a doctoral student in the sociology program at the University of Michigan. She received her bachelor's degree from California State University, Bakersfield.

24. Cristina was twenty and a junior majoring in occupational therapy at the University of Texas, Pan American.

25. Caller ID is a telephone service that identifies the caller's number and name on a small screen.

26. Bianca was twenty-six and was engaged to be married to the father of her three-year-old son. She was a doctoral student in the political science program at the University of New Mexico. She had attended the University of California, Davis, and had received her bachelor's degree in Chicano studies and political science and a master's degree in political science at the University of New Mexico.

27. Sonya K. Smith was twenty-four and a doctoral student in the American culture (Chicano studies/Asian American history) program at the University of Michigan. She received her bachelor's degree from Stanford University in American Studies with a specialization in race and ethnicity.

28. Carina García Guzmán was twenty-three and a senior at Colorado College majoring in Hispanic studies and Spanish literature.

29. In the "dollar dance," wedding guests pin money on the bride and groom and take turns dancing with them.

30. Two of the three bisexual respondents had had long-term relationships with other women but had heterosexual relationships thereafter. In one instance, the respondent was currently married with a child. In the second instance, the respondent still had a very close friendship with her former lover but had a boyfriend and was very interested in getting married and having children.

31. Jessica Delgado had received her bachelor's degree from the University of California, Santa Cruz, in politics and was in her third year of law school at the University of California, Berkeley's Boalt Law School. She was a member of the editorial board of the school's law review journal and was one of the very few students of Color in such a prestigious position.

32. Jessica's father lived in Florida but was originally from Colombia, and his family lived mostly in Cartagena. Jessica had met her father's family but did not have a long-standing relationship with them.

33. Frida was twenty-four and a senior at California State University, San Diego. She was majoring in social science with an emphasis in anthropology and women's studies.

34. Mieka Valdez was twenty-two and a senior majoring in American studies at the University of California, Santa Cruz.

35. The fathers were generally not involved in these newer, open discussions about sexuality.

36. Leticia Sedano was twenty-one and an undergraduate in American studies at the University of California, Santa Cruz.

37. Julissa was twenty-eight. She had received her bachelor's degree in sociology and Chicano studies at the University of California, Davis, and her master's degree in education at University of California, Santa Cruz. She was a doctoral student in the education graduate program at the University of California, Berkeley.

38. Nicole Rodriguez was twenty-five and in her last year of law school at the University of California, Berkeley, Boalt Law School. She received her bachelor's degree from Yale University and majored in American studies and studies in the environment.

Notes to Chapter 3

1. Of the remaining respondents, one lived with foster families and two were raised by their grandparents.

2. Nicolasa I. Sandoval was twenty-eight, born in Sacramento, California, and raised mostly in Southern California. Nicolasa received her bachelor's degree in public relations with an outside concentration in art history at Pepperdine University. She received her master's degree in museum studies at George Washington University and worked as an administrative assistant in a prominent museum on the East Coast. Nicolasa was the oldest of seven children. Her mother was a Chumash Indian from California. Her father was from the state of Jalisco. Nicolasa's parents divorced when she was eight; her mother raised four daughters and her father raised two daughters and a son.

3. The difference in socialization regarding "personal responsibility" for brothers in the family contradicts the research conducted by Mirandé (1997), who argues that *machismo* entails the expectation that men take care of their families and are the household's main breadwinner. However, most fathers in this sample *did*

act upon the discourse of personal responsibility by working, often times several jobs, to support their families and help their daughters pursue higher education.

4. Julissa was born and raised in San Jose, California. She had three siblings. Both of her parents were born in Jiquilpan, Michoacan, Mexico, and they were married. For more biographical information on Julissa, see chapter 2.

5. Nayelli was born and raised in Los Angeles. Her parents were born in Guanajuato, Mexico. She had two siblings and her parents were married. For more biographical information, see chapter 2.

6. Sara was born and raised in King City, California. Her mother was from Watsonville, California, and her father was from Mexico. She had two older brothers, and her parents were married until her mother's death a year before I interviewed Sara. For more biographical information, see chapter 2.

7. In several instances I picked a pseudonym for respondents based on my experience with them. In this case, Generosa, whose name means "generous" in Spanish, came to my hotel room in Ann Arbor, Michigan, never having met me before. She had responded to my email message asking her to participate in my study (I obtained her name through a colleague). She arrived at my hotel room with a small shopping bag from the local university bookstore. As we sat down to wait for another respondent, she handed me the shopping bag. In it was a mug from the University of Michigan (my graduate alma mater). Generosa had bought it for me, because she figured it was tough to conduct fieldwork away from home, staying in hotel rooms. She gave me the mug as she told me, "At least you won't have to drink coffee in the morning out of a styrofoam cup." I was deeply touched. Her generosity of spirit and kindness overwhelmed me. This is perhaps one of the kindest acts I have experienced in my life and I will treasure it forever. Generosa was thirty-one and received her bachelor's degree in sociology at California State University, Los Angeles. She was a doctoral student in the sociology program at the University of Michigan.

8. I had another respondent in a similar situation. While she was attending Stanford University, her twenty-year-old brother was going through a trial for a drive-by shooting in Los Angeles. She wrote letters, helped lawyers prepare motions, and translated the court proceedings for her parents. At the time I was writing this chapter, her brother was serving a long prison sentence, and she was beginning her first year in the doctoral program in psychology at the University of Colorado, Boulder.

9. Alejandra Dominguez was twenty-one and an undergraduate majoring in Spanish and Latin American Studies at the University of Illinois, Chicago. She was born in Los Angeles and had a brother and a sister. Her parents were married and were from Uriangato, Guanajuato, Mexico.

10. Soledad was born and raised in Chicago. Her parents were born in Guadalajara, Jalisco, Mexico. She had a brother and a sister and her parents were married. For more biographical information, see chapter 2.

11. Jessica Delgado was born in Los Angeles. Her mother was born in Santa Fe, New Mexico, and her father in Cartagena, Colombia. She had a younger brother and her parents were divorced when she was twelve. For more biographical information, see chapter 2.

12. Christina J. Reynoso was born and raised in Oakland, California. Her parents were from San Gaspar de los Reyes, Jalisco, Mexico. She had two younger brothers. Her parents were married. For more biographical information, see chapter 2.

13. Mary Romero, personal communication, 16 February 1998.

14. Many respondents mentioned that special programs were essential to their educational success. Among them were undergraduate recruitment programs like Upward Bound, programs designed to increase the transfer rates from community colleges to four-year universities, and research opportunities provided by summer internship programs. Almost all respondents had received financial aid targeted at poor students and Latinos. All respondents felt that their family support and their talent alone were not sufficient to succeed educationally.

15. Agustina was twenty-one and a senior at the University of Chicago majoring in languages and literature. She was in the process of applying to six law schools, including Harvard University. She was born in Chicago and both of her parents came from Mexico. Her mother came from Salinas, Nuevo Leon, and her father from Tampico, Tamaulipas. Her parents were divorced. She had three brothers and one sister.

16. Alicia Granillo was twenty-six and a graduate student in the master's program in education at Harvard University. She received her bachelor's in business at the University of Nevada, Las Vegas. Her family emigrated from Durango, Mexico, in 1970. Her mother came with four children and within a year after her arrival in the U.S. became pregnant with Alicia, who was born in Los Angeles. Alicia's parents were separated. She was raised in Los Angeles; at the age of fourteen, she moved to Las Vegas and lived with her aunt until her mother relocated from Los Angeles to Las Vegas.

17. Mariela was twenty-one and a senior at the University of Texas, Pan American, majoring in history with a minor in philosophy and a certification in education. She was born in Weslaco, Texas; her mother came from Guanajuato, Mexico, and her father came from Mexico City. She had three sisters and two brothers. Her parents were married.

18. Carolina was twenty-nine and had received her bachelor's degree in psychology from the University of California, Santa Cruz. She was a doctoral student at the University of California, Berkeley. At the time of the interview, she was writing her dissertation and living in Cambridge, Massachusetts, with her fiancé, who had a postdoctoral fellowship at Harvard University. She was born and raised in Los Angeles. Her father was born in Albuquerque, New Mexico, and her mother was born in East Los Angeles. Carolina had a younger sister and her parents were married.

19. Tomasa was twenty and an undergraduate at the University of Chicago majoring in public policy. She was born and raised in Chicago and her parents were from the outskirts of Mexico City. She had two siblings and her parents were married.

20. Norma I. Garza was twenty-two and an undergraduate at the University of Texas, Pan American, majoring in political science. She hoped to eventually attend law school. She was born in Fort Hood, Texas, and raised in Alamo, Texas. Her mother was from Aransas, Texas, and her father was from Alamo, Texas. She had two sisters. At the time of the interview, her parents were in the middle of a divorce.

21. Victoria was born in Oakland and raised in the Bay Area until she was eleven, when her family moved to Patterson, California. Her parents were born in San Gaspar de los Reyes, Mexico. Victoria had two younger sisters and her parents were married. For more biographical information, see chapter 2.

22. Mieka Valdez was born in Escondido, California, and raised in San Marcos, California. Her mother, who was white, was from Arcadia, California, and her father, who was of Mexican descent, was from Lemon Grove, California. She had an older brother and her parents were divorced when Mieka was three years old. For more information, see chapter 2.

23. Hilda was twenty-seven and had received her bachelor's degree from Colorado State University. She was in her second year of a master's degree at Arizona State University. Her mother was half white and half Mexican and her father was of Mexican descent; both grew up in Texas. Hilda and her brother were born and raised in Texas.

24. Guadalupe was twenty-four and a senior at the University of California, Santa Cruz, majoring in sociology. At the time of the interview, she was working at the Women's Crisis Support in Santa Clara. Guadalupe was born in Mexico and raised in Morgan Hill, California. Her parents, who were still married, were born in Mexico and had eight children.

25. Magdalena was twenty-one and a senior majoring in psychology with a minor in French at the University of Chicago. At the time of the interview she was in the process of applying to doctoral programs in clinical psychology and she was particularly interested in attending the University of Texas, Austin. She was born in Elk Grove, Illinois, and was raised by her grandparents, who were from Mexico. Her mother and father were also born in Mexico. She had two half-brothers from her mother's second marriage. Her parents were divorced, and both parents were remarried. Magdalena was raised primarily by her maternal grandparents, who had also recently divorced. Magdalena had contact with her mother but had very inconsistent contact with her father.

26. Nina A. Perales was twenty-one and a junior majoring in policy studies and psychology at the University of Chicago. She was born and raised in Austin, Texas, and both her parents had been born in Texas. Nina was the youngest of four sisters. Her parents were married.

27. Sandra was twenty-two and had received her bachelor's degree in psychology at the University of California, Santa Cruz. She was a graduate student in the master's program in education at Columbia University. Sandra was born in Mexico and raised in the United States after the age of seven. Her parents were born in Guanajuato, Mexico, and they were married. Sandra had seven brothers and three sisters.

28. Blanca Gordo was twenty-six and had received her bachelor's degree in sociology and Chicana/o studies at the University of California, Los Angeles. She was a doctoral student in urban planning at the University of California, Berkeley. Blanca was born in Zacatecas, Mexico, and raised in Pasadena, California. Her father was born in Calera, Zacatecas, and her mother was born in Los Aguajes, Zacatecas. Her mother died of cancer when Blanca was an undergraduate. Until her mother's death, her parents had been married. She had five siblings.

29. Patricia Alvarez was twenty-four and had graduated from Illinois Institute of Technology majoring in psychology. At the time of the interview she was working at Reuters (a financial news wire service) as a news assistant. Patricia was born and raised in Chicago. Her parents were from Zacatecas, Mexico. She had one sister and two brothers. Her parents were married.

30. *Mija* is the contraction of *mi hija* (my daughter).

31. Magdalena's mother and aunt had gotten pregnant in their teens.

Notes to Part II

1. *Canícula* is what people in South Texas and Mexico refer to as the particularly intense part of the summer that falls between July 14 and August 24—a "miniseason" between "summer and fall" when "most cotton is picked in South Texas," and it is so hot that "not even dogs venture out" (Cantú 1995, xi–xii).

2. My assessments of these respondents' individual identities may or may not overlap with their own assessments. *Personal assessments* are made by clinical and personality psychologists because they are trained to deal with "individual differences." As a social psychologist, I examine social identities, which have overarching similarities when individuals belong to the same social groups.

3. I will address race (which is one of the master statuses) in chapter 7, because respondents' views about race were entwined with their views on politics.

Notes to Chapter 4

1. A few respondents (7 percent) were Protestant (Pentecostal, Presbyterian, Nazarene, etc.). Almost a quarter of my respondents did not have a religious affiliation (24 percent). However, almost all respondents, regardless of the religion they grew up with, were well aware of Catholic rituals used in Chicano communities as cultural practice.

2. Bianca was brought up Catholic but her parents never attended church consistently. For more biographical information, see chapters 1 and 2.

3. Tomasa considered herself Catholic, as did her parents. For more biographical information, see chapter 3.

4. Irma Martínez was twenty-eight and had received her bachelor's degree in romance languages and literatures at Princeton University. At the time of the interview she was working for Bill Richardson, the secretary of energy under the Clinton administration. She worked as a Special Assistant, Office of Scheduling and Advance. Irma was raised Catholic.

5. Lupita is the diminutive of the name Guadalupe.

6. Tomasa's mother worked as a janitor for a bank in Chicago.

7. Valerie was twenty-nine and had received her bachelor's degree in social sciences with a minor in sociology at the University of California, Irvine. Valerie had just finished her doctorate in education at the University of California, Los Angeles. Valerie's parents were not consistent about attending mass, although they identified as Catholic.

8. "Cholo" is a slang word used in Chicano communities to refer to individuals who may identify with gangs. Cholos are characterized by their baggy clothes and distinctive speech style, referred to as Caló.

9. In Roman Catholic practice, the Host is a consecrated wafer that is pure white in color, unleavened, and baked in small disks. During the mass, individuals who have taken confession walk up to the altar and the priest dispenses the Host, which they eat; the Host symbolizes the body of Christ and forgiveness for their sins (http://encyclopedia.com).

10. Hilda considered herself Catholic. Her parents were divorced and her mother was Catholic. For more biographical information, see chapter 3.

11. Blanca Gordo's father was Catholic. For more biographical information, see chapter 3.

12. For biographical information on Nina Perales, see chapter 3.

13. Sandra Saenz was twenty-nine and had received her undergraduate degree in sociology at the University of California, Los Angeles. She was a doctoral student in the program of higher education at the University of California, Los Angeles. Her mother had been both Catholic and Jehovah's Witnesses and her father did not belong to any religion.

14. Although I am using the ethnic identifier "Latino" to be inclusive, most respondents were raised in communities that were predominantly of Mexican descent.

15. Gloria considered herself Catholic and was about to be married in the Catholic Church. Her parents were also Catholic. For more biographical information, see chapter 2.

Notes to Chapter 5

1. Reports of the results of this study appeared in the following newspapers: the *McAllen* (Texas) *Monitor*, *USA Today*, the *Houston Chronicle*, the *Santa Cruz Sentinel*, the *Los Angeles Times*, and the *New York Times*.

2. Claudia Rodriguez was an undergraduate at the University of Illinois, Chicago, working part-time as a clerical worker on campus.

3. For biographical information on Patricia Alvarez, see chapter 3.

4. For biographical information on Carolina, see chapter 3.

5. Alicia Granillo had a long work history in Las Vegas, where she had spent most of her life. At age fourteen, she started working twenty-five hours a week in her aunt's restaurant and stayed there until she graduated from high school. During college she worked two jobs while she took a full academic load. After college she was an analyst with the city of Las Vegas in the Department of Human Resources, mostly doing training and development for city employees. For more biographical information, see chapter 3.

6. Rita's mother worked in a day care center and her father worked as a laborer at Martinelli's, a company that produced apple juice. For more biographical information, see chapter 2.

7. Tomasa described her class background as working-class. Her mother was a janitor in a bank and her father was a clerk for an electric company. For more biographical information, see chapters 3 and 4.

8. For biographical information on Irma Martínez, see chapter 4.

9. Carina García Guzmán described her class background as "poor." For more biographical information, see chapter 2.

10. Carina and her family were farmworkers, so they traveled for much of the year following the crops in South Texas as well as in Florida.

11. Rosa Lazo was twenty-eight and a part-time undergraduate student majoring in occupational therapy at the University of Texas, Pan American. She was working full-time as a secretary at the same university she was attending.

12. Guadalupe described her class background as poor. Both of her parents were farmworkers. For more biographical information, see chapter 3.

13. Maritza C. Resendez was twenty-two and a senior majoring in Latin American/Latino studies at the University of California, Santa Cruz. Maritza described her class background as working-class. Her mother worked in a factory as a sewing machine operator and her father was a painter.

14. Colorado College is a private liberal arts institution with a student population of 1,910 and tuition of about $22,800 a year.

15. In the 1940s, when labor was scarce, the United States established the Emergency Labor Program, popularly known as the Bracero Program. Braceros, whose name derived from the Spanish word *brazo* (arm), were Mexican manual laborers allowed to enter the United States to replace U.S. workers who joined the armed forces (http://encarta.msn.com).

16. Agustina described her class background as working-class. For more biographical information, see chapter 3.

17. Zulma Rodriguez was twenty and an undergraduate majoring in psychology at the University of Illinois, Chicago. Zulma identified as working-class.

18. Gloria described her class background as lower-middle-class. Her father had been a farmworker but had finally saved enough to own his small upholstery shop. For more biographical information, see chapters 2 and 4.

19. María del Rosario Santos was twenty-two and a senior majoring in sociology at Colorado College. By the time I wrote this chapter, she had received her master's degree in public administration from the University of Houston. María del Rosario described her economic background as poor.

20. Aixa was twenty-three and had received her bachelor's degree in English and American literature and women's studies from Brown University. At the time I was writing this chapter Aixa was in her first year of the doctoral program in modern thought and literature at Stanford University.

21. Mieka Valdez described her class background as middle-class. For more biographical information, see chapters 2 and 3.

22. Lemon Grove is a predominantly Mexican American community in Southern California.

23. Nicole Rodriguez identified as lower-middle-class. Both of her parents had attended college and had advanced degrees. For more biographical information, see chapters 1 and 2.

24. Misty was twenty-four and had received her bachelor's degree in Spanish and English at the University of Nebraska. She was in the master's program in higher education at Arizona State University and had applied to the doctoral program in educational leadership in policy studies at the same institution. Misty identified as middle-class because both of her parents had attended college and were high school teachers.

25. Tonantzin was twenty-five and a senior at the University of Texas, Pan American, majoring in history. Tonantzin described her class background as "rich."

26. To give someone "props" is a slang phrase that means to give someone recognition.

Notes to Chapter 6

1. Dolores del Río was a famous Mexican actor who was very successful in Hollywood beginning with silent films in the late 1920s and into the 1940s. *Mariachis* are musical groups that play folkloric Mexican music and are known for singing passionate love songs. *Alarma* magazine is a tabloid published in Mexico that specializes in gruesome "crimes of passion." Mostly working-class people in Mexico and the United States read it.

2. There is a folk legend in Mexico that is repeated in many U.S. Chicano communities about a young woman sneaking out to a dance without her parents' per-

mission. She encounters a very handsome, elegantly dressed man and dances with him. As she is dancing, she notices he has "rooster's feet," and concludes it is the devil who has come to tempt her because of disobedience to her parents. It is a tale told to keep young women in line. There are many variations to the story, but the punch line is always that the young disobedient woman is "dancing with the devil" (Limón 1991).

3. Coatlicue is an Aztec earth goddess known as the "mother of gods." She is an "insatiable goddess" who feasts on the corpses of men. Coatlicue is the giver of life and death, the instigator of war, and the eater of filth (http://www.zihrena .com/ixhelm/coaticlue.htm).

4. Jessica Delgado had a long-term relationship with her partner and had no children. For more biographical information, see chapters 2 and 3.

5. Maria Villa was a junior majoring in psychology at the University of New Mexico. She was in the honors program in the psychology department and hoped to have a career in research. Her husband was of Mexican descent and was also attending the university.

6. For biographical information on Cristina, see chapter 2.

7. Cristina was English-dominant, and her parents only spoke Spanish.

8. A total of thirteen of the respondents were already married to Latinos.

9. Alicia Granillo had divorced and was engaged to marry a Mexican-descent Latino. She had no children. For more biographical information, see chapters 3 and 5.

10. *Posadas* are a re-creation of the Bible story of Mary (on a donkey) and Joseph searching for a room at the inn. They are usually accompanied by a choir of small children who walk through neighborhoods knocking on doors asking for lodging for the couple. As in the Bible, there are no takers. The procession takes place every day for twelve days before Christmas. As the procession moves along, more people join in until they reach the church where mass is held. After the service, there is usually a celebration. *Posada* literally means inn in Spanish (http//www.mexonline.com/xmas.htm).

11. Agustina was single and had no children. For more biographical information, see chapters 3 and 5.

12. Tomasa was single and had no children. For more biographical information, see chapters 3–5.

13. Sonya K. Smith was single and had no children. For more biographical information, see chapter 2.

14. Gloria was engaged to be married with a person of German descent. She had no children. For more biographical information, see chapters 2, 4, and 5.

15. Valerie was married to a Mexican-descent Latino and did not have children, although she and her husband planned to eventually have two or three children. For more biographical information, see chapter 4.

16. Lucinda was thirty-two and had received her bachelor's degree in communications from the University of Texas, Austin. She was part owner of an advertising

agency that specialized in political advertising for the Hispanic population. Lucinda was engaged to a Mexican-descent Latino.

17. Frida was single and had no children. For more biographical information, see chapter 2.

18. Sobeida was twenty-four and had received her bachelor's degree in psychology from the University of California, Santa Cruz, and her master's degree in education from Stanford University. At the time I was writing this chapter, she was about to start her doctoral dissertation in education at the University of Colorado, Boulder. She was single and had no children. For more information, see chapter 3.

19. Rosario had received her bachelor's degree in elementary education from Heritage College and her master's degree in education from Washington State University.

20. Jocelyn Solis was single and had no children. For more biographical information, see chapter 2.

21. Rita was single and had no children. For more biographical information, see chapters 2 and 5.

22. Nicolasa Sandoval was single and had no children. For more biographical information, see chapter 3.

23. For biographical information on Bianca see chapters 1, 2, and 4.

24. Jennifer Trujillo was twenty-one and a junior majoring in biology at Colorado College. She planned to attend medical school. Jennifer was single and had no children.

25. Christine Granados was twenty-nine and had received her bachelor's degree in journalism from the University of Texas, El Paso. She was a freelance writer and a contributing editor to *Hispanic* and *Moderna* magazines. At the time I was writing this chapter she had been accepted to the master's program in creative writing at Southwest Texas State University, San Marcos, Texas. Christine was married, and by the time I was writing this chapter, she had had her first child.

26. Carina García Guzmán was single and had no children. For more biographical information, see chapters 2 and 5.

27. Dorian López was single and had no children. For more biographical information, see chapter 2.

28. María del Rosario Santos was single and had no children. For more biographical information, see chapter 5.

Note to Part III

1. *Día de los Muertos* encompasses All Saints' (November 1) and Souls' Day (November 2), and is celebrated in most Catholic countries. The celebration begins on the evening of October 31. The purpose is to remember dead family members, who are believed to return to their gravesites, so gifts and flowers are placed there. Families also construct altars with the favorite foods of the deceased. (http://www.usc.edu/isd/locations/ssh/boechmann/Dead/index.html).

Notes to Chapter 7

1. I use the plural for womanhoods because there is no singular definition of womanhood; rather, the intersection of race, ethnicity, and class produces different definitions for different groups of women. Also, a woman's womanhood may be defined differently within her own class, racial, and ethnic group than from the perspectives of individuals outside her group.

2. *Con el nopal en la frente* (with the cactus on your forehead) is a metaphor for an individual who looks racially Mexican Indian but wants to deny their indigenous heritage. The *nopal* is often associated with Mexican indigenous people.

3. Anna Reyes was twenty-six and had received her bachelor's degree in psychology and pre-medicine from the University of Texas, Austin. She was in her fourth year of medical school at the University of Texas, San Antonio.

4. Patricia Alvarez was very fair-skinned and was often confused for Italian or some other European ancestry. For more biographical information, see chapter 3.

5. *Mestiza* refers to the racial mixture present in Mexican descent people as a result of miscegenation with various ethnic and racial groups that came to Mexico during the European colonization of the Americas and during subsequent waves of immigration.

6. For biographical information on Claudia Rodriguez, see chapter 5.

7. Belinda Martínez did not see herself as beautiful, because she felt she was very dependent on what others thought of her. She was very fair-skinned. For more biographical information, see chapter 2.

8. For biographical information on María del Rosario Santos, see chapters 5 and 6.

9. Norma I. Garza believed she was beautiful, although it took her a while to arrive at that conclusion. Her family and friends called her *morena* (dark-skinned), which they told her was "prettier" than being fair-skinned. Norma's boyfriends also mentioned an admiration for her dark skin color. For more biographical information, see chapter 3.

10. For biographical information on Carina García Guzmán, see chapters 2, 5, and 6.

11. For biographical information on Gloria, see chapters 2, 4, 5, and 6.

12. For biographical information on Jennifer Trujillo, see chapter 6.

13. Cynthia Duarte was twenty-four and had received her bachelor's degree in Spanish and political science from the University of California, Los Angeles. She was a third-year graduate student in the doctoral program in sociology at Columbia University. Cynthia considered herself physically beautiful.

14. Camila Fuentes was twenty-six and had received her bachelor's degree in international affairs and Spanish from the University of Nevada in Reno. She received her master's degree from Harvard in education. At the time I was writing this chapter, she was in her first year of the doctoral program in education at the University of Michigan. Camila considered herself physically beautiful.

15. Alicia Granillo considered herself physically beautiful, largely due to her mother's reinforcement. For more biographical information, see chapters 3, 5, and 6.

16. Misty did not consider herself beautiful because "beautiful" "was too strong a word." Instead she thought she was "cute." For more biographical information, see chapter 5.

17. Tomasa did not consider herself physically attractive. For more biographical information, see chapters 3–6.

18. For biographical information on Jessica Delgado, see chapters 2, 3, and 6.

19. Lucinda's parents and her boyfriends always told her she was "pretty." However, she felt that her "selling point" was not her looks but the fact that she was nice to everybody. Lucinda's entire family was fair-skinned and nobody in her family "looked Mexican." For more biographical information, see chapter 6.

20. Ignacio García defines Chicanismo as a political movement that "emerged as a challenge to the dominant institutions, assumptions, politics, principles, political leaders, and organizations within and without the community" (1997, 6). The emphasis was on "dignity, self-worth, pride, uniqueness, feeling of cultural rebirth, and equal economic opportunity" (ibid.).

21. Emiliano Zapata (1879–1919) was a Mexican revolutionary leader and agrarian reformer. He was an illiterate tenant farmer whose indigenous background inspired the recruitment of others like him to form an army from the villages and haciendas in Morelos, Mexico. Under the rallying cry *Tierra y Libertad* (Land and Liberty), they joined the uprising led by Francisco Madero in the 1910 revolution against Porfirio Díaz. Although regarded by his enemies as a "pillaging bandit," Zapata was idolized by indigenous people in Mexico (http://encarta.msn.com). Chicano activists in the United States embraced Zapata as one of the historical figures used to symbolize the Chicano movement.

22. Mary Anne and Ginger were two characters in the popular television series *Gilligan's Island*.

23. Buffy and Joey were two child characters in the popular television series *A Family Affair*.

24. Patty stated that "beauty has a lot to do with how you're feeling" and that beauty was "a package deal. You can't just have my face and my body. It's my brain and my heart." For more biographical information, see chapter 2.

25. For biographical information on Desireé, see chapter 2.

26. "Pocha" is a derogatory term used in the United States and Mexico to describe a U.S. Mexican who cannot speak "proper" Spanish and who is "Americanized."

27. For biographical information on Leticia Sedano, see chapter 2.

Notes to Chapter 8

1. Alicia Granillo's educational experiences at Harvard exposed her to different ways of thinking about many social issues, including gender. She had read and en-

joyed Latina feminist writers and was still trying to sort out whether she was a feminist or not. For more biographical information, see chapters 3, 5, 6, and 7.

2. Marissa was twenty-four and had received her bachelor's degree in political science from the University of Michigan. She was finishing a master's degree in international education policy at George Washington University. She felt she might be "a feminist with restrictions," because she had very liberal views in general. She was reluctant to join what she considered "radical feminists." She had taken women's studies courses and identified with those who had "moderate feminist views."

3. Alicia Z. Maciel was twenty-six and had obtained her bachelor's degree in business at the University of California, Berkeley. She was in her final year of the master's program in business administration at Harvard. Alicia considered herself a feminist "with reservations," because although she believed in complete independence, she also enjoyed the nurturing and support offered by her husband.

4. Valerie identified herself as a feminist but still liked "to be treated as a lady." She believed that gender equality and chivalry were separate from one another. She believed that everyone should be paid the same rate for the same job and expected people to respect her opinion. See also chapters 4 and 6 for biographical information.

5. For biographical information on Rosario, see chapter 6.

6. Conchita was twenty-eight and had graduated from the University of New Mexico with a double major in sign language and Spanish. Conchita was working on her master's degree in bicultural studies at the University of Texas, San Antonio.

7. Sofia was twenty-six and had received her bachelor's degree in psychology from Williams College. She was obtaining her master's degree in education from Harvard. She considered herself a feminist, although she associated feminism with white women because they started the movement. She had a critique of white feminism because of its exclusion of nonwhite women.

8. Magdalena identified as a feminist, because she did not live at home and she did not consider her boyfriend the center of her life. She also clarified that she did not consider herself "an extreme feminist." See chapters 3, 4, and 6 for more biographical information.

9. Irma Martínez believed she was a feminist. She thought that women should have command over their lives. See chapter 4 for more biographical information.

10. Christine Granados felt that she was a feminist when she was growing up, but after attending a reading of the Susan B. Anthony–Elizabeth Cady Stanton conversations, she grew reluctant to identify herself as one. She was in a panel with "several Anglo women" and decided she felt disconnected from the feminist movement, because it did not reflect her life experiences. For more biographical information, see chapter 6.

11. Sonya K. Smith identified as feminist but used the term in "a racialized way" by calling herself a Chicana feminist. For more biographical information, see chapters 2 and 6.

12. Misty considered herself a feminist although she was aware of the negative connotations the label had for many people. For biographical information, see chapters 1, 5, and 7.

13. Victoria considered herself a feminist because she believed in equality between women and men, which is the way she and her husband related to each other. They divided all housework equally and made all decisions jointly. See chapters 2 and 3 for more biographical information.

14. Camila Fuentes considered herself a feminist.

15. Carolina considered herself a feminist. For more biographical information, see chapter 3.

16. For biographical information on Cristina, see chapters 2 and 6. Cristina considered herself a feminist.

17. Although Maritza C. Resendez thought that everybody had a different definition of the word "feminist," she nonetheless identified with the label. She did not openly assert her identification; rather, it was "what she did" and how she "lived her life that fit the definition." For more biographical information, see chapter 5.

18. Sandra Saenz did not know whether to call herself a feminist, because she associates the word "feminist" with "radical political views." In spite of her ambivalence about the label, she considered herself an "independent woman" who lived her life according to her own desires. For more biographical information, see chapter 4.

19. Kim Rivera-Figueroa was twenty-six and had received her bachelor's degree in elementary education at Arizona State University. She was a graduate student in the master's program in education leadership and policy studies at Arizona State University. Kim believed that she was a feminist, but only to a certain degree. She acknowledged that boys are not better than girls, having learned this lesson as a child directly from her mother. She felt that women can do anything men can do and has never had to fight for equality.

20. Maria Villa identified as a feminist and believed in equality between the sexes, but when at home with her husband, she "fell back a little bit on her feminist beliefs." For more biographical information, see chapter 6.

21. Lucinda identified as a feminist, especially because she wanted equality in the workplace. At the same time, she wanted men to treat her "like a lady" and do such things as open doors. For more biographical information, see chapters 6 and 7.

22. For biographical information on Bianca, see chapters 2, 4, and 6.

23. Jennifer Trujillo identified as a feminist. She believed that women have the right to work outside the home and not be required to only raise children. She also felt that it was a woman's right to stay home, but it should be a choice, not a requirement. For more biographical information, see chapter 6.

Notes to Chapter 9

1. Canela was twenty-seven and had received her bachelor's degree in education from Incarnate Word College, and was working on her master's degree in bicultural/bilingual studies at the University of Texas, San Antonio. Canela was not involved in any ethnic or political organizations during high school. After college she worked in grassroots issues, because she missed the political activism she experienced in college. At the time of the interview she was not a member of any organization, although she taught English to recent immigrants. She was also beginning to write children's books to counteract the Latino stereotypes in most children's literature.

2. Liza Flores Owens was twenty-seven and had received her bachelor's degree in speech and hearing sciences from the University of New Mexico. At the time of the interview, she considering entering a master's program in the same field. In high school, Liza was a member of the Hispanic Honor Society, an organization that raised money for scholarships for Hispanic students. During college she was not politically active because she was a reentry student and was raising a daughter. In the future Liza wanted to work with and be an advocate for minority children, especially Hispanic children.

3. Josefa was twenty-five and had received her bachelor's degree in Spanish from the University of New Mexico. Josefa had not been involved in any organizations in high school or as an undergraduate but she had taken many classes on Chicanos and had been deeply inspired by them. She hoped to be involved with Latino issues in the future through her profession.

4. As an undergraduate student, Anna Reyes was an officer in the National Chicano Health Organization. Currently she was an officer for the American Medical Student Women's Association, an organization with mostly members who were women of Color. She was also very involved with a battered women's shelter and was the co-president of the Association for Latin American Students in medical school. She planned to continue her involvement in ethnic and women's organizations after she finished medical school. For more biographical information, see chapters 7 and 8.

5. Aixa, as an undergraduate, was part of the MEChA governing board at Brown University. Since her graduation she had been working at the Esperanza Center, a progressive, politically active cultural arts organization. Aixa had a very active role in planning the meetings of the National Association for Chicana/Chicano Studies (NACCS). She planned to gear all her personal and professional decisions toward maintaining her activism on behalf of Chicanas, women of Color, and queer issues. For more biographical information, see chapter 5.

6. Maria Villa had never been politically involved because she married before she finished high school and had a child shortly after. She considered her involvement with Latinos as limited to the research she was helping a professor conduct

on the effects of bilingualism on cognitive processing. For biographical information, see chapters 6, 7, and 8.

7. Mariquita had received her bachelor's degree in communications from the University of Arizona. She was the administrative assistant for the Department of Institutional Advancement at Arizona State University. During high school, Mariquita worked with Student International, because there were no ethnic or women's organizations. As an undergraduate, she joined MEChA. She plans to be politically involved in the future helping people of all ethnicities and races.

8. Irasema was twenty-six, had received her bachelor's degree in broadcast management from Arizona State University, and was working in the Department of Institutional Advancement in special programs and graphic design. As an undergraduate, Irasema was involved in MEChA. At the time of the interview, she was involved in a group called SVR 015, which was fighting an anti–affirmative action bill in Arizona. Irasema saw her political involvement in Latino issues as a lifetime commitment.

9. Anita L. Verdugo was twenty-six, had received her bachelor's degree in business management and Spanish from the University of Notre Dame, and was working on her master's degree in public administration at Arizona State University. When Anita was an undergraduate at Notre Dame, she was involved in a group called the Hispanic American Organization (HAO) and also belonged to LULAC (League of United Latin American Citizens). She felt she would always be committed to working on Latino issues.

10. Jennifer Dominguez was twenty-one and a senior majoring in speech and hearing sciences at the University of New Mexico. She was planning to apply to the master's degree program in the same area of study. Jennifer was involved in MESA, a group that concentrated on math and the sciences geared toward minorities in high school. Jennifer did not have a concrete connection to Latino issues. She planned to work with "underserved populations," which in New Mexico by default included "Hispanic people." For more information see chapter 1.

11. Isela Moncada was nineteen and a freshperson at Colorado College. She had not yet decided on a major. Isela was a member of MEChA. She was also involved in a program tutoring minority students at a local high school. She hoped to continue to work on minority issues in the future.

12. Christina M. Cota was twenty-seven and had received her bachelor's degree in biology at George Washington University. Christina was working as a medical assistant at a radiology group. Christina was active in "pro-life organizations" and attended marches against abortion rights. In the future she would like to become involved in Latino issues.

13. Alicia Granillo was pro-choice but would not consider having an abortion herself in the case of an unplanned pregnancy. Alicia had always been politically involved since her years as an undergraduate. At Harvard, she was involved in Latinos Unidos. She saw her political commitment on behalf of Latinos as central to her profession. For more biographical information, see chapters 3, 5, 6, 7, and 8.

14. Carolina was pro-choice and had no qualms about using her right if she had an unplanned pregnancy. In college, she joined MEChA and interned at the Santa Cruz Women's Collective, a women's health center. Carolina planned to be involved in Latino and women's issues at the university level when she became a professor. For more biographical information, see chapters 3 and 8.

15. Misty was pro-choice but would not consider having an abortion herself in the case of an unplanned pregnancy. In college, Misty was very much involved in a group called the Mexican American Student Association (MASA). She was not involved in women's organizations, but she took many classes that dealt with women's issues. She plans to continue to be involved in ethnic organizations when she becomes a professional. For more biographical information, see chapters 1, 5, 7, and 8.

16. Sofia believed that abortion should be legal although she would never consider one for herself. As an undergraduate, Sofia helped coordinate a group called Vista, a student organization dedicated to increasing the number of Latina students at Williams College. She had also worked against the passage of Proposition 187, which was designed to deny publicly funded health care and public education to California residents who were suspected of being "illegal immigrants." In the future, she will work on behalf of the Latino community, which she considered very important. For more biographical information, see chapter 8.

17. Camila Fuentes was pro-choice but unsure of opting for an abortion in the case of an unplanned pregnancy. In college Camila had a feminist professor who encouraged her to get involved with feminist issues by joining a women's political group. She planned to be involved in political issues in the future. For more biographical information, see chapters 7 and 8.

18. Mariela was "pro-life" and did not think "abortion should be legal under any circumstances." In high school she was in the Spanish Club but did not participate in any ethnic organizations in college because of lack of time. She believed she would be politically involved in the future on "behalf of Hispanic issues." For more biographical information, see chapter 3.

19. Minerva was twenty-four and had received her bachelor's degree in liberal arts and sciences at DePaul University. Minerva was pro-choice, although she was adamant that women should not use abortion as a form of birth control. In case of an unplanned pregnancy, she would not consider having an abortion. Minerva never joined ethnic or women's organizations because she felt that most did "not live up to their expressed goals." She planned to be involved in Latino issues in the future.

20. Sachel was twenty-two and had attended Smith College her Freshman year but returned to Alberquerque and received her bachelor's degree in American studies at the University of New Mexico. At the time of the interview, she was about to start the master's program in American studies at the University of New Mexico, Albuquerque. Sachel was pro-choice but was uncertain of whether she would have an abortion in the case of an unplanned pregnancy. At Smith she was a member of

a group called Nosotras, a Latina organization that held protests and strikes. She definitely planned to be involved with ethnic issues when she became a teacher.

21. Lidia Tovar was twenty-four, married, and raising a little girl. She was a part-time student while she worked full-time as a secretary in the History Department of Pan American University, Edinburg, Texas. Lidia was pro-choice. She had not been involved politically but was interested in becoming involved in the future.

22. Noelia was twenty-six and worked as a secretary for the Economics and Finances Department at the University of Texas, Pan American, Edinburg, Texas, where she had earned enough hours to be a sophomore. Noelia was against abortion except in cases of rape. She had no interest in becoming politically involved.

23. Ruth N. Lopez Turley wanted to work with Latinos socially but not necessarily politically. She wanted to provide guidance and resources to insure Latino students' success in college. For more biographical information, see chapter 2.

24. Noemi Vazquez was twenty-seven and had received her bachelor's degree in biology at the University of Houston. She was doing her medical residency at the University of Texas, San Antonio. Noemi was pro-choice. During medical school she was part of a women's support group. In high school she was involved in several "Mexican-Hispanic clubs." She would like to be involved in Latino political issues once she graduates from medical school.

25. Gloria was pro-choice and believed women had the right to choose what to do with their bodies. Although she might have considered an abortion in high school, now that she was older and had a degree, abortion was no longer an option. Gloria also considered herself Catholic, and this influenced her views on having an abortion herself in case of an unplanned pregnancy. For more biographical information, see also chapters 2, 4, 5, 6, and 7.

26. Nina D. Sánchez was twenty and a junior at Colorado College majoring in anthropology and international affairs. Nina was pro-choice and believed that the government should ensure a woman's right to make her own decisions. She also would not hesitate to use her abortion rights in case of an unplanned pregnancy.

27. MEChA is an acronym for Movimiento Estudiantil Chicano de Aztlán, an organization founded in the late 1960s as a direct result of the Chicano movement. MEChA chapters exist in many institutions of higher education. On the University of California, Los Angeles's Web site, the organization's name is explained:

> M — Movimiento — signifies that the organization is dedicated to the movement for self-determination and identity.
>
> E — Estudiantil — identifies the organization as a student group.
>
> Ch — Chicano — here lies the fire of the name. It is a symbol of pride, a new identity for those of us taking an active role in our destiny and the struggle against oppression.
>
> A — Aztlán — the name of the original birthplace of the Aztecs. Today is known as the American Southwest. (http://students.asucla.ucla.edu /MEChA/newmskdocuments.html)

28. Gabriella Gonzalez was twenty-six and had received her bachelor's degree in sociology from Harvard University. She was in her third year of the doctoral program in sociology at Harvard. Gabriella was pro-choice and in 1999 founded the Harvard Graduate School of Arts and Sciences Women in the Social Sciences. She was also involved in the W. E. B. Du Bois Society and Concilio Latino.

29. "Pocho" has been used as a slang to describe the mixing of Spanish and English languages used by many Mexican descendants in the United States. It is usually used as a derogatory term but the use of "pocho" language is also used by Mexican descendants to create ingroup solidarity (Gurin, Hurtado, and Peng 1994, 529).

30. Frida was pro-choice "under all circumstances" and would not hesitate to consider an abortion in the case of an unplanned pregnancy. See also chapters 2, 6, and 9.

31. According to its Web site, "Mujeres Activas en Letras y Cambio Social (MALCS) is an organization of Chicanas/Latinas and Native American women working in academia and in community settings with a common goal: to work toward the support, education, and dissemination of Chicana/Latina and Native American women's issues" (http://spot.colorado.edu/~facio/malcs.htm).

32. Tonantzin was pro-choice. She had an abortion at her parents' insistence, when she became pregnant at a very young age. For more biographical information, see chapter 5.

33. Xochiquetzal was twenty and had attended Dartmouth College for a few semesters before deciding to return to San Antonio, where her parents lived. She was taking classes part-time at the University of Texas, San Antonio. Xochiquetzal was pro-choice and aware of the fragility of women's right to choose.

34. Rebeca was pro-choice and supported abortion but not as a means of birth control. At the same time, she believed that people who were not ready to have a child should have abortion as a legal option. Rebeca was twenty-three at the time of the interview and was working as an outreach counselor for California State University, Monterey Bay, in charge of the Northern California region. She had received her bachelor's degree from the University of California, Santa Cruz in Latin America/Latino studies. By the time I wrote this chapter she had finished her master's degree in education from Harvard University and had applied and been accepted to the doctoral program in education at the University of California, Los Angeles.

35. Mieka Valdez was pro-choice. In the case of an unplanned pregnancy, Mieka would consider having an abortion. There were many things she wanted to do and thought it unfair if she did not give her full attention to a child. For more biographical information, see chapters 2, 3, and 5.

36. The Pilsen neighborhood in Chicago transitioned from "an essentially Eastern European enclave in the early 1950's to an explicitly Chicano settlement" (Kerr 1976, 194). By 1969, Latinos in the Pilsen area formed successful organizations that focused on health care, improved school facilities, bilingual programs,

and job training (196). Currently, the Pilsen neighborhood remains one of the largest Mexican-descent Latino communities in the United States (http://chicagohistory.org/DGBPhotoEssay/plvintro.html).

37. Ana Castillo is a renowned writer. Among her books are *The Mixquiahuala Letters*, *So Far from God*, and *Massacre of the Dreamers*.

38. Proposition 209 specifically prohibits "the state, local governments, districts, public universities, colleges and schools, and other government instrumentalities from discriminating against or giving preferential treatment to any individual or group in public employment, public education, or public contracting on the basis of race, sex, color, ethnicity, or national origin" (http://Vote96.ss.ca.gov /Vote96/html/BP/209.htm).

Notes to Review of Part III

1. Susana L. Gallardo describes herself as "a third/fifth generation chicana from East L.A. / Yorba Linda / Palo Alto," who is a doctoral candidate at Stanford University and is writing her dissertation on "chicana/o catholic religious history." She identifies herself as "a proud chicana and a proud feminist, and a proud chicana feminist" (http://chicanas.com/justme.html).

2. Christine Granados, one of my respondents, wrote an article for *Latina* magazine that featured another one of my respondents, Anna Reyes.

Notes to Chapter 10

1. Many scholars have used a Chicana feminist framework to write about Mexican-descent women, but they have not asked them directly their views on feminism.

2. See introduction to part 2.

3. *Las mañanitas* are the Mexican equivalent to the "Happy Birthday" song in the United States.

4. The image can be seen on the Internet at http://www.almalopez.net.

5. For a recent example, see the article "Who's Failing Our Girls" by Mireya Navarro in *Latina* magazine (2001).

6. San Martín de Porras was the first Black saint in Latin America. He was a very hardworking and kind man. He helped those in need of food and was believed to look after orphaned children. His handshakes could cure a soul in pain (Mora 1997, 14–15).

7. See chapter 2.

8. See chapter 9 for a discussion of MEChA and MALCS.

Bibliography

Alarcón, Norma. 1989. "*Traddutora, Traditora*: A Paradigmatic Figure of Chicana Feminism." *Cultural Critique* 13: 57–87.

———. 1990. "The Theoretical Subject(s) of *This Bridge Called My Back* and Anglo-American Feminism." In *Making Face, Making Soul/Haciendo Caras*, ed. Gloria Anzaldúa, 356–69. San Francisco: Aunt Lute Press.

———. 1994. "Conjugating Subjects: The Heteroglossia of Essence and Resistance." In *An Other Tongue*, ed. Alfred Arteaga, 125–38. Durham: Duke University Press.

Allen, Myria Watkins, Patricia Amason, and Susan Holmes. 1998. "Social Support, Hispanic Emotional Acculturative Stress and Gender." *Communication Studies* 49: 139–57.

Almaguer, Tomás. 1991. "Chicano Men: A Cartography of Homosexual Identity and Behavior." *Differences: A Journal of Feminist Cultural Studies* 3 (2): 75–100.

Anzaldúa, Gloria. 1981. "La Prieta." In *This Bridge Called My Back: Writings by Radical Women of Color,* ed. Cherríe Moraga and Gloria Anzaldúa, 198–209. Watertown, MA: Persephone Press.

———. 1987. *Borderlands—La Frontera: The New Mestiza.* San Francisco: Spinsters/Aunt Lute.

———, ed. 1990. *Making Face, Making Soul/Haciendo Caras: Creative and Critical Perspectives by Feminists of Color.* San Francisco: Aunt Lute Press.

Arce, Carlos H., Edward Murguía, and W. Parker Frisbie. 1987. "Phenotype and Life Chances among Chicanos." *Hispanic Journal of Behavioral Sciences* 9: 19–32.

Arguelles, Lourdes, and Anne M. Rivero. 1993. "Gender/Sexual Orientation, Violence, and Transnational Migration: Conversations with Some Latinas We Think We Know." *Urban Anthropology* 22 (3–4): 259–76.

Arredondo, Gabriela, Aída Hurtado, Norma Klahn, Olga Nájera-Ramírez, and Patricia Zavella, eds. Forthcoming. *Chicana Feminisms: Disruptions in Dialogue*. Durham: Duke University Press.

Baca Zinn, Maxine. 1975. "Political Familism: Toward Sex Role Equality in Chicano Families." *Aztlán* 6 (1): 13–26.

———. 1995. "Social Science Theorizing for Latino Families in the Age of Diversity." In *Understanding Latino Families: Scholarship, Policy, and Practice*, ed. Ruth E. Zambrana, 177–89. Thousand Oaks, CA: Sage.

Behar, Ruth. 1993. *Translated Woman: Crossing the Border with Esperanza's Story*. Boston: Beacon.

Bellafante, Ginia. 1998. "Feminism. It's All about Me!" *Time* 151 (25): 54–62.

Bem, Sandra L., and Daryl J. Bem. 1997. "Training the Woman to Know Her Place: The Power of a Nonconscious Ideology." In *The Lanahan Readings in the Psychology of Women*, ed. Tomi-Ann Roberts, 419–28. Baltimore: Lanahan Publishers.

Benke, Richard. 2001a. "'Bikini Virgin' Prompts Debate." *Santa Cruz Sentinel*, 17 April, A12.

———. 2001b. "Speakers Demand Museum Remove Bare-Midriff." *San Jose Mercury*, 17 April, 13A.

Bernal, Dolores Delgado. 1998a. "Grassroots Leadership Reconceptualized: Chicana Oral Histories and the 1968 East Los Angeles School Blowouts." *Frontiers* 19 (2): 113–42.

———. 1998b. "Using a Chicana Feminist Epistemology in Educational Research." *Harvard Educational Review* 68 (4): 555–82.

Blackwell, Maylei. Forthcoming. "Contested Histories: *Las Hijas de Cuauhtémoc*, Chicana Feminisms and Print Culture in the Chicano Movement, 1968–1973." In *Chicana Feminisms: Disruptions in Dialogue*, ed. Gabriela Arredondo, Aída Hurtado, Norma Klahn, Olga Nájera-Ramírez, and Patricia Zavella. Durham: Duke University Press.

Broyles-González, Yolanda J. 1994. *El Teatro Campesino: Theater in the Chicano Movement*. Austin: University of Texas Press.

———. 2001. *Lydia Mendoza's Life in Music, La Historia de Lydia Mendoza*. New York: Oxford University Press.

Burciaga, Rebeca, and Ana Tavares, eds. 1999. *Meet Us at the River*. Cambridge: Harvard University.

Cantú, Lionel. 1999. "Border Crossings: Mexican Men and the Sexuality of Migration." Ph.D. diss., University of California, Irvine.

———. 2001. "A Place Called Home: A Queer Political Economy of Mexican Immigrant Man's Family Experiences." In *Queer Families, Queer Politics: Challenging Culture and the State*, ed. Mary Bernstein and Renate Reimann 112–36. New York: Columbia University Press.

Cantú, Norma E. 1995. *Canícula: Snapshots of a Girlhood en La Frontera*. Albuquerque: University of New Mexico Press.

———. 1999. "*La Quinceañera*: Towards an Ethnographic Analysis of a Life-Cycle Ritual." *Southern Folklore* 56 (1): 73–101.

———. 2002. "Chicana Life-Cycle Rituals." In *Chicana Traditions: Continuity and Change*, ed. Norma Cantú and Olga Nájera-Ramírez 15–34. Chicago and Urbana: University of Illinois Press.

Castañeda, Antonia I. 1990. "The Political Economy of Nineteenth-Century Stereotypes of Californians." In *Between Borders: Essays on Mexicana/Chicana History*, ed. Adelaida R. Del Castillo, 213–36. Encino, CA: Floricanto Press.

Castillo, Ana. 1982. "In My Country." Printed on a lithograph.

———. 1986. *The Mixquiahuala Letters*. Binghamton, NY: Bilingual Press.

———. 1994a. *Massacre of the Dreamers: Essays on Xicanisma*. Albuquerque: University of New Mexico Press.

———. 1994b. *So Far from God*. New York: Plume.

———. 1995. *Massacre of the Dreamers*. New York: Plume.

———. 1999. *Peel My Love Like an Onion*. New York: Doubleday.

———, ed. 1996. *Goddess of the Americas/La Diosa de las Américas: Writings on the Virgin of Guadalupe*. New York: Riverhead Books.

Cervantes, Lorna Dee. 1981. *Emplumada*. Pittsburgh: University of Pittsburgh Press.

Chabram, Angie. 1990. "Chicana/o Studies as Oppositional Ethnography." *Cultural Studies* 4 (3): 228–47.

Childers, Joseph, and Gary Hentzi, eds. 1995. *The Columbia Dictionary of Modern Literary and Cultural Criticism*. New York: Columbia University Press.

Cisneros, Sandra. 1991. *Woman Hollering Creek and Other Stories*. New York: Random House.

———. 1994. *Loose Woman*. New York: Knopf.

———. 1996. "Guadalupe the Sex Goddess." In *Goddess of the Americas/La Diosa de las Américas: Writings on the Virgin of Guadalupe*, ed. Ana Castillo, 46–51. New York: Riverhead Books.

Collins, Patricia Hill. 1991. *Black Feminist Thought*. New York: Routledge.

Cooper, Catherine R., and Jill Denner. 1998. "Theories Linking Culture and Psychology: Universal and Community-Specific Processes." *Annual Review of Psychology* 49: 559–84.

Córdova, Teresa. 1994. "The Emergent Writings of Twenty Years of Chicana Feminist Struggles: Roots and Resistance." In *The Handbook of Hispanic Cultures in the United States*, ed. Félix Padilla, 175–202. Houston: University of Houston, Arte Público Press.

Cuádraz, Gloria Holguin. 1989. "I Want to Be Known as a Hurdle-Jumper, Not as a High-Achiever." *Revista Mujeres* 6 (2): 69.

Dávalos, Mary Karen. 1996. "*La Quinceañera*: Making Gender and Ethnic Identities." *Frontiers* 16 (2–3): 101–27.

Davis, Angela Y. 1971. "Reflections on the Black Woman's Role in the Community of Slaves." *Black Scholar* 3 (4): 3–15.

Davis, Angela, and Elizabeth Martínez. 1994. "Coalition Building among People of Color." *Inscriptions* 7: 42–53.

Deaux, Kay, and Kathleen A. Ethier. 1998. "Negotiating Social Identity." In *Prejudice: The Target's Perspective*, ed. Janet K. Swim and Charles Stangor, 301–23. San Diego: Academic Press.

Díaz Guerrero, Rogelio. 1975. *Psychology of the Mexican: Culture and Personality.* Austin: University of Texas Press.

Dominguez, Virginia. 1992. "Invoking Culture: The Messy Side of 'Cultural Politics.'" *South Atlantic Quarterly* 91 (1): 19–42.

Dworkin, Andrea. 1987. *Intercourse.* New York: Free Press.

Feldman, Edmund Burke. 1967. *Varieties of Visual Experience.* Englewood Cliffs, NJ: Prentice-Hall.

Fine, Michelle, and Lois Weis. 1998. *The Unknown City: Lives of Poor and Working Class Young Adults.* Boston: Beacon.

Fine, Michelle, Lois Weis, Linda C. Powell, and L. Mun Wong, eds. 1997. *Off White: Readings on Society, Race, and Culture.* New York: Routledge.

Forbes, Jack. 1968. "Race and Color in Mexican-American Problems." *Journal of Human Relations* 16 (1): 55–68.

Frankenberg, Ruth. 1993. *White Women, Race Matters: The Social Construction of Whiteness.* Minneapolis: University of Minnesota Press.

Fregoso, Rosa Linda. 1990. "The Discourse of Difference: Footnoting Inequality." *Critica: A Journal of Critical Essays* 2 (2): 182–87.

———. 1993. *The Bronze Screen: Chicana and Chicano Film Culture.* Minneapolis: University of Minnesota Press.

———. Forthcoming. "Reproduction and Miscegenation on the Borderlands: Mapping the Maternal Body of Tejanas." In *Chicana Feminisms: Disruptions in Dialogue*, ed. Gabriela Arredondo, Aída Hurtado, Norma Klahn, Olga Nájera-Ramírez, and Patricia Zavella. Durham: Duke University Press.

Friedan, Betty. 1963. *The Feminine Mystique.* New York: W. W. Norton.

Frith, Hannah. 2001. "Young Women, Feminism and the Future: Dialogues and Discoveries." *Feminism and Psychology* 11 (2): 147–51.

Gallardo, Susana L. 2000. "Making Face, Making Soul." Web site. http://chicanas.com/defs.html.

Gamboa, Suzanne. 2001. "Diploma Deficit: Fewer Caps, Gowns for Hispanic Girls." *Monitor,* 25 January, 1A, 8A.

García, Alma. 1989. "The Development of Chicana Feminist Discourse, 1970–1980." *Gender and Society* 3 (2): 217–38.

———, ed. 1997. *Chicana Feminist Thought: The Basic Historical Writings.* New York: Routledge.

García, Chris. 1973. *Political Socialization of Chicano Children: A Comparative Study with Anglos in California Schools.* New York: Praeger.

García, Ignacio M. 1997. *Chicanismo: The Forging of a Militant Ethos among Mexican Americans.* Tucson: University of Arizona Press.

Gaspar de Alba, Alicia. 1992. "Juana Ines." In *New Chicana/Chicano Writing*, ed. Charles M. Tatum, 1–15. Tucson: University of Arizona Press.

Gonzales, Patrisia. 2001a. "Grieving and Transforming Rape." http://www.uexpress.com/columnoftheamericas/.

———. 2001b. "Lupe and the Buddha." http://www.uexpress.com/columnoftheamericas/.

Gonzales, Patrisia, and Roberto Rodriguez. 2001. "The Body of the Sacred Feminine." http://www.uexpress.com/columnoftheamericas/.

Gonzalez, Jennifer A., and Michelle Habell-Pallán. 1994. "Heterotopias and Shared Methods of Resistance: Navigating Social Spaces and Spaces of Identity." *Inscriptions* 7: 80–104.

Granados, Christine. 2001. "La Nueva Latina." *Latina,* February 100–104.

Griffin, Christine. 1989. "'I'm Not a Women's Libber, but . . .': Feminism, Consciousness, and Identity." In *The Social Identity of Women,* ed. Suzanne Skevington and Deborah Baker, 173–93. London: Sage.

Guinier, Lani. 1998. *Lift Every Voice: Turning a Civil Rights Setback into a New Vision of Social Justice.* New York: Simon and Schuster.

Gurin, Patricia, Aída Hurtado, and Timothy Peng. 1994. "Group Contacts and Ethnicity in the Social Identities of Mexicanos and Chicanos." *Personality and Social Psychology Bulletin* 20 (5): 521–32.

Gurin, Patricia, Arthur H. Miller, and Gerald Gurin. 1980. "Stratum Identification and Consciousness." *Social Psychology Quarterly* 43 (1): 30–47.

Gutiérrez, Elena. 1999. "The Racial Politics of Reproduction: The Social Construction of Mexican-Origin Women's Fertility." Ph.D. diss., University of Michigan, Ann Arbor.

Gutiérrez, Ramón A. 1993. "Community, Patriarchy and Individualism: The Politics of Chicano History and the Dream of Equality." *American Quarterly* 45 (1): 44–72.

Harris, Cheryl I. 1993. "Whiteness as Property." *Harvard Law Review* 106 (8): 1709–91.

Hayasaki, Erika. 2001. "Latinas Face Obstacles in Education, Study Says." *Los Angeles Times,* 25 January, B1, B4.

Heller, Celia Stopnicka. 1966. *Mexican American Youth: Forgotten Youth at the Crossroads.* New York: Random House.

Henley, Nancy. 1977. *Body Politics: Power, Sex, and Nonverbal Communication.* Englewood Cliffs, NJ: Prentice-Hall.

Henry, Tamara. 2001. "Study: Latinas Shortchanged by U.S. Schools." *USA Today,* 25 January, 8D.

Herrera, Hayden. 1983. *Frida: A Biography of Frida Kahlo.* New York: Harper and Row.

Herrnstein, Richard J., and Charles Murray. 1994. *The Bell Curve: Intelligence and Class Structure in American Life.* New York: Simon and Schuster.

Hochschild, Arlie Russell. 1999. *The Second Shift.* New York: Bard.

Holvino, Evangelina. 2001. *Complicating Gender: The Simultaneity of Race, Gender, and Class in Organization Change(ing)*. Working Paper Series, ed. Bridgette Sheridan. Boston: Center for Gender in Organizations, Simmons Graduate School of Management.

Horowitz, Ruth. 1993. "The Power of Ritual in a Chicano Community: A Young Woman's Status and Expanding Family Ties." *Marriage and Family Review* 19 (3–4): 257–80.

Hurtado, Aída. 1986. "Mi Padre el Filósofo." *Revista Mujeres* 3 (1): 22.

———. 1989. "Relating to Privilege: Seduction and Rejection in the Subordination of White Women and Women of Color." *Signs* 14 (4): 833–55.

———. 1990. "'Woman' of Color." *Revista Mujeres* 7 (1–2): 83.

———. 1996a. *The Color of Privilege: Three Blasphemies on Feminism and Race*. Ann Arbor: University of Michigan Press.

———. 1996b. "Strategic Suspensions: Feminists of Color Theorize the Production of Knowledge." In *Knowledge, Difference and Power: Essays Inspired by Women's Ways of Knowing*, ed. Nancy Goldberger, Jill Tarule, Blythe Clinchy, and Mary Belenky, 372–92. New York: Basic Books.

———. 1997. "Understanding Multiple Group Identities: Inserting Women into Cultural Transformations." *Journal of Social Issues* 53 (2): 299–328.

———. 1998. "*Sitios y Lenguas*: Chicanas Theorize Feminisms." *Hypatia* 13 (2): 134–59.

———. 1999. "A Crossborder Existence." In *Women's Untold Stories: Breaking Silence, Talking Back, Voicing Complexity*, ed. Abigail Stewart and Mary Romero, 83–101. New York: Routledge.

———. 2000. "'La Cultura Cura': Cultural Spaces for the Generation of Chicana Feminist Consciousness." In *Construction Sites: Excavating Class, Race, Gender, and Sexuality among Urban Youth*, ed. Michelle Fine and Lois Weis, 274–89. New York: Teacher's College Press.

———. n.d. *El Colorete*. Unpublished manuscript.

———. Forthcoming. "Underground Feminisms: Inocencia's Story." In *Chicana Feminisms: Disruptions in Dialogue*, ed. Gabriela Arredondo, Aída Hurtado, Norma Klahn, Olga Nájera-Ramírez, and Patricia Zavella. Durham: Duke University Press.

Hurtado, Aída, and Patricia Gurin. 1994. "Ethnic Identity and Bilingualism Attitudes." In *Hispanic Psychology: Critical Issues in Theory and Research*, ed. Amado Padilla, 89–103. Thousand Oaks, CA: Sage. Reprinted from *Hispanic Journal of Behavioral Sciences*, 1987, 9 (1): 1–18.

Hurtado, Aída, Patricia Gurin, and Timothy Peng. 1997. "Social Identities—A Framework for Studying the Adaptations of Immigrants and Ethnics: Mexicans in the United States." In *New American Destinies: A Reader in Contemporary Asian and Latino Immigration*, ed. Darrell Y. Hamamoto and Rodolfo D. Torres, 243–67. New York: Routledge. Reprinted from *Social Problems* 41 (1): 129–51.

Hurtado, Aída, and Raúl Rodríguez. 1989. "Language as a Social Problem: The Repression of Spanish in South Texas." *Journal of Multilingual Multicultural Development* 10: 401–19.

Hurtado, Aída, and Abigail J. Stewart. 1997. "Through the Looking Glass: Implications of Studying Whiteness for Feminist Methods." In *Off White: Readings on Society, Race, and Culture*, ed. Michelle Fine, Linda Powell, Lois Weis, and L. Mun Wong, 297–311. New York: Routledge.

Janofsky, Michael. 2001. "Santa Monica Artist's Image of Mary Rouses Ire at New Mexico Museum." *San Jose Mercury News*, 6 April, 27A.

Keating, AnaLouise, ed. 2000. *Interviews, Entrevistas/Gloria E. Anzaldúa*. New York: Routledge.

Kerr, Louise Año Nuevo. 1976. "The Chicano Experience in Chicago, 1920–1970." Ph.D. diss., University of Chicago.

Klahn, Norma. 1994. "Writing the Border: The Languages and Limits of Representation." *Journal of Latin American Cultural Studies* 3 (1–2): 29–55.

Lamphere, Louise, Helena Ragoné, and Patricia Zavella, eds. 1997. *Situated Lives: Gender and Culture in Everyday Life*. New York: Routledge.

Lamphere, Louise, Patricia Zavella, and Felipe Gonzales with Peter B. Evan. 1993. *Sunbelt Working Mothers: Reconciling Family and Factory*. Ithaca: Cornell University Press.

Lankford, Mary D. 1994. *Quinceañera: A Latina's Journey to Womanhood*. Brookfield: Millbrook Press.

Latina Feminist Group. 2001. *Telling to Live: Latina Feminist* Testimonios. Durham: Duke University Press.

Lewin, Kurt. 1948. *Resolving Social Conflicts, Selected Papers on Group Dynamics, 1935–1946*. Ed. Gertrud Weiss. New York: Harper and Brothers.

Leyveld, Nita. 2000. "Latinas Lead the Way in L.A.: Two Women Hold Key Positions in Demographic Convention Planning." *San Jose Mercury News*, 3 July, 1D.

Limón, José. 1991. *Dancing with the Devil: Society, Gender, and the Political Unconscious in Mexican-American South Texas*. Durham: Duke University Press.

Lopez, Alma. 2001. "Chicana Artist Needs Our Support!" http://calacapress .com.

Lorde, Audre. 1984. *Sister Outsider*. Trumansburg, NY: Crossing Press.

Lugones, María C. 1992. *Structure/Antistructure and Agency under Oppression*. Unpublished manuscript, Carleton College.

MacKinnon, Catharine A. 1982. "Feminism, Marxism, Method, and the State: Toward Feminist Jurisprudence." *Signs: Journal of Women in Culture and Society* 7 (31): 514–44.

Madsen, William. 1964. *Mexican-Americans of South Texas*. New York: Holt, Rinehart and Winston.

Martínez, Elizabeth. 1989. "That Old (White) Male Magic." *Z Magazine* 27 (8): 48–52.

Martínez-Chávez, Diane. 1989. "Quinceañeras." *Hispanic*, October, 11–12.

May, Patrick. 1999. "Where Did the Hatred Come From?" *San Jose Mercury News*, 15 August, 1A, 26A.

Mirandé, Alfredo. 1997. *Hombres y Machos: Masculinity and Latino Culture*. Boulder: Westview.

Mora, Magdalena, and Adelaida R. Del Castillo. 1980. *Mexican Women in the United States: Struggles Past and Present*. Los Angeles: Chicano Studies Research Center Publications.

Mora, Pat. 1993. *Nepantla: Essays from the Land in the Middle*. Albuquerque: University of New Mexico Press.

———. 1996. "Coatlique's Rules: Advice from an Aztec Goddess." In *Goddess of the Americas/La Diosa de las Américas: Writings on the Virgin of Guadalupe*, ed. Ana Castillo, 88–91. New York: Riverhead Books.

———. 1997. *Aunt Carmen's Book of Practical Saints*. Boston: Beacon.

Moraga, Cherríe. 1981. "La Güera." In *This Bridge Called My Back: Writings by Radical Women of Color*, ed. Cherríe Moraga and Gloria Anzaldúa, 29–34. Watertown, MA: Persephone Press.

———. 1983. *Loving in the War Years/Lo Que Nunca Pasó por Sus Labios*. Boston: South End Press.

Moraga, Cherríe, and Gloria Anzaldúa, eds. 1981. *This Bridge Called My Back: Writings by Radical Women of Color*. Watertown, MA: Persephone Press.

Morrison, Toni. 1992. *Playing in the Dark: Whiteness and the Literary Imagination*. Cambridge: Harvard University Press.

Nájera-Ramírez, Olga. Forthcoming. "Unruly Passions: Poetics, Performance and Gender in the Ranchera Song." In *Chicana Feminisms: Disruptions in Dialogue*, ed. Gabriela Arredondo, Aída Hurtado, Norma Klahn, Olga Nájera-Ramírez, and Patricia Zavella. Durham: Duke University Press.

Navarro, Mireya. 2001. "Who's Failing Our Girls." *Latina* 5 (12): 88–93, 132–33.

NietoGomez, Anna. 1974. "La Feminista." *Encuentro Femenil* 1 (2): 34–47.

———. Forthcoming. "Chicana Print Culture and Chicana Studies: A Testimony to the Development of Chicana Feminist Culture." In *Chicana Feminisms: Disruptions in Dialogue*, ed. Gabriela Arredondo, Aída Hurtado, Norma Klahn, Olga Nájera-Ramírez, and Patricia Zavella. Durham: Duke University Press.

Ochoa, María, and Teresia Teaiwa. 1994. "Enunciating Our Terms: Women of Color in Collaboration and Conflict." *Inscriptions* 7: viii–x.

Ogbu, John. 1987. *Minority Education and Caste: The American System in Cross-Cultural Perspective*. New York: Academic Press.

Orbach, Susie. 1997. *Fat Is a Feminist Issue: The Anti-Diet Guide for Women*. New York: Galahad Books.

Orlean, Susan. 1990. "Old-Fashion Girls." *New Yorker* 65 (52): 82–88.

Oyserman, Daphna, and Hazel Markus. 1990. "Possible Selves in Balance: Implications for Delinquency." *Journal of Social Issues* 46 (2): 141–57.

Pacheco, Sandra, and Aída Hurtado. 2001. "Media Stereotypes." *Encyclopedia of Women and Gender* 1–2: 703–8.

Pardo, Mary S. 1998. *Mexican American Women Activists: Identity and Resistance in Two Los Angeles Communities.* Philadelphia: Temple University Press.

Paz, Octavio. 1961. *The Labyrinth of Solitude: Life and Thought in Mexico.* Trans. Lysander Kemp. New York: Grove Press.

Pérez, Emma. 1991. "Sexuality and Discourse: Notes from a Chicana Survivor." In *Chicana Lesbians: The Girls Our Mothers Warned Us About,* ed. Carla Trujillo, 159–84. Berkeley: Third Woman Press.

———. 1993. "Speaking from the Margin: Uninvited Discourse on Sexuality and Power." In *Building with Our Hands: New Directions in Chicana Studies,* ed. Adela de la Torre and Beatríz M. Pesquera, 57–71. Berkeley: University of California Press.

———. 1999. *The Decolonial Imaginary: Writing Chicanas into History.* Bloomington: Indiana University Press.

Pesquera, Beatríz M. 1991. "'Work Gave Me a Lot of Confianza': Chicanas' Work Commitment and Work Identity." *Aztlán* 20 (1–2): 97–118.

Pesquera, Beatríz, and Denise A. Segura. 1993. "There Is No Going Back: Chicanas and Feminism." In *Chicana Critical Issues,* ed. Norma Alarcón, Rafaela Castro, Emma Pérez, Beatriz Pesquera, Adaljiza Sosa Riddell, and Patricia Zavella, 95–115. Berkeley: Third Woman Press.

———. 1996. "With Quill and Torch: A Chicana Perspective on the American Women's Movement and Feminist Theories." In *Social, Economic, and Political Change,* ed. David R. Maciel and Isidrio D. Ortiz, 231–47. Tucson: University of Arizona Press.

Phinney, J. S. 1996. "When We Talk about American Ethnic Groups, What Do We Mean?" *American Psychologist* 51 (9): 918–27.

Portillo, Lourdes. 1990. *La Ofrenda: The Day of the Dead.* Film, Xochitl Productions, San Francisco.

Quintana, Alvina E. 1996. *Home Girls: Chicana Literary Voices.* Philadelphia: Temple University Press.

Roa, Jessica. 2001. "Reclamation." *La Revista* 3 (spring): 55–56.

Rodriguez, Roberto. 2001. "When Sanctuary Becomes Hell." http://www.uexpress.com/columnofthe americas/.

Romero, Mary. 1992. *Maid in the U.S.A.* New York: Routledge.

Ruiz, Vicki. 1998. *From Out of the Shadows: Mexican Women in Twentieth-Century America.* New York: Oxford University Press.

Rushin, Donna K. 1981. "The Bridge Poem." In *This Bridge Called My Back: Writings by Radical Women of Color,* ed. Cherríe Moraga and Gloria Anzaldúa, xxi–xxii. Watertown, MA: Persephone Press.

Saldívar-Hull, Sonia. 1991. "Feminism on the Border: From Gender Politics to Geopolitics." In *Criticism in the Borderlands: Studies in Chicano Literature, Culture, and Ideology*, ed. Héctor Calderón and José David Saldívar, 203–20. Durham: Duke University Press.

———. 2000. *Feminism on the Border.* Berkeley: University of California Press.

Sánchez, Elba Rosario. 1992. *Tallos de Luna/Moon Shoots.* Santa Cruz: Moving Arts Press.

———. Forthcoming. "Cartohistografía: Continente de Una Voz/Cartohistography: One Voice's Continent." In *Chicana Feminisms: Disruptions in Dialogue*, ed. Gabriela Arredondo, Aída Hurtado, Norma Klahn, Olga Nájera-Ramírez, and Patricia Zavella. Durham: Duke University Press.

Sandoval, Chela. 1991. "U.S. Third World Feminism: The Theory and Method of Oppositional Consciousness in the Postmodern World." *Genders* 10 (spring): 1–24.

———. 2000. *Methodology of the Oppressed.* Minneapolis: University of Minnesota Press.

Segura, Denise A. 1994. "Beyond Machismo: Chicanas, Work, and Family." Paper presented at the Sixth European Conference on Latino Cultures in the United States, Bordeaux, 7–10 July.

———. 2001. "Challenging the Chicano Text: Toward a More Inclusive Contemporary Causa." *Signs* 26 (2): 541–50.

Segura, Denise A., and Beatriz M. Pesquera. 1992. "Beyond Indifference and Antipathy: The Chicana Movement and Chicana Feminist Discourse." *Aztlán* 19 (2): 69–91.

Sennett, Richard, and Jonathan Cobb. 1993. *The Hidden Injuries of Class.* New York: W. W. Norton.

Serros, Michele M. 1993. *Chicana Falsa: And Other Stories of Death, Identity, and Oxnard.* Valencia, CA: Lalo Press.

———. 2000. *How to Be a Chicana Role Model.* New York: Riverhead Books.

Spender, Dale. 1980. *Man Made Language.* London: Routledge, Chapman and Hall.

Steele, Claude M. 1997. "A Threat in the Air: How Stereotypes Shape Intellectual Identity and Performance." *American Psychologist* 52 (6): 613–29.

Steinem, Gloria. 1983. *Outrageous Acts and Everyday Rebellions.* New York: Holt, Rinehart, and Winston.

Sterngold, James. 1999. "3 Small Boys Are Shot at a California Day Camp." *New York Times*, 11 August, A1.

Summers, Laurie Kay. 1995. *Fiesta, Fé y Cultura: Celebrations of Faith and Culture in Detroit's Colonia Mexicana.* East Lansing: Michigan State University Museum; Detroit: Casa de la Unidad Cultural Arts and Media Center.

Tajfel, Henri. 1981. *Human Groups and Social Categories: Studies in Social Psychology.* London: Cambridge University Press.

Tajfel, Henri, and John C. Turner. 1979. "An Integrative Theory of Intergroup Conflict." In *The Social Psychology of Intergroup Relations*, ed. W. G. Austin and S. Worchel, 33–47. Pacific Grove, CA: Brooks/Cole.

Telles, Edward, and Edward Murguía. 1990. "Phenotypic Discrimination and Income: Differences among Mexican Americans." *Social Science Quarterly* 71 (4): 682–93.

———. 1992. "The Continuing Significance of Phenotype." *Social Science Quarterly* 73 (1): 120–22.

Triandis, Harry C. 1995. *Individualism and Collectivism*. Boulder: Westview.

Trujillo, Carla, ed. 1991. *Chicana Lesbians: The Girls Our Mothers Warned Us About*. Berkeley: Third Woman Press.

———. 1998. "La Virgen de Guadalupe and Her Reconstruction in Chicana Lesbian Desire." In *Living Chicana Theory*, ed. Carla Trujillo, 214–31. Berkeley: Third Woman Press.

Van Derbeken, Van Jaxon, Bill Wallace, and Stacy Finz. 1999. "History of Erratic Behavior, Ties to Neo-Nazi Group Seen." *San Francisco Chronicle,* 12 August, 1A, 16A.

Vidal, Mirta. 1971. "Chicanas Speak Out. Women: New Voice of La Raza." In *Chicana Feminist Thought: The Basic Historical Writings,* ed. Alma García, 21–24. New York: Routledge, 1997.

Villanueva, Alma. 1978. *Mother May I*. Pittsburgh: Motheroot Publications.

Viramontes, Helena María. 1993. "The Moths." In *Growing Up Chicana/o*, ed. Tiffany Ann Lopez, 117–24. New York: Morrow.

West, Candace. 1992. "Rethinking 'Sex Differences' in Conversational Topics: It's Not What They Say but How They Say It." *Advances in Group Processes* 9: 131–62.

———. 1995. "Women's Competence in Conversation." *Discourse and Society* 6 (1): 107–31.

Witt, Barry, Tracey Kaplan, and Brandon Bailey. 1999. "Rampage Was 'Wake-Up' Call to Kill Jews." *San Jose Mercury News,* 12 August, 1A, 18A.

Yarbro-Bejarano, Yvonne. 1986. "The Female Subject in Chicano Theater: Sexuality, 'Race,' and Class." *Theater Journal* 38 (1): 389–407.

Zavella, Patricia. 1987. *Women's Work and Chicano Families: Cannery Workers of the Santa Clara Valley*. Ithaca: Cornell University Press.

———. 1991. "Reflections on Diversity among Chicanas." *Frontiers* 12 (2): 763–85.

———. 1997. "Playing with Fire: The Gendered Construction of Chicano/Mexican Sexuality." In *The Gender/Sexuality Reader: Culture, History, Political Economy,* ed. Roger N. Lancaster and Maraela di Leonardo. New York: Routledge.

———. Forthcoming. "Talk'n Sex: Chicanas and Mexicanas Theorize about Silences and Sexual Pleasures." In *Chicana Feminisms: Disruptions in Dialogue,* ed. Gabriela Arredondo, Aída Hurtado, Norma Klahn, Olga Nájera-Ramírez, and Patricia Zavella. Durham: Duke University Press.

Zimmerman, Donald H., and Candace West. 1975. "Sex Roles, Interruptions and Silences in Conversation." In *Language and Sex: Difference and Dominance,* ed. Barrie Thorne and Nancy Henley. Rowley, MA: Newbury House.

Index

Index

About the Author

AÍDA HURTADO is Professor of Psychology at the University of California, Santa Cruz. Her research focuses of the effects of subordination on social identity, educational achievement, and language. She is especially interested in group memberships like ethnicity, race, class, gender, and sexuality, that are used to legitimize unequal distribution of power between groups. Hurtado's expertise is in survey methods with biligual/bicultural populations, qualitative methods, and feminist theory. Hurtado received her B.A. in psychology and sociology from the University of Texas, Pan American University in Edinburg, Texas, and her M.A. and Ph.D. in social psychology from the University of Michigan. She is the author of *The Color of Privilege: Three Blasphemies on Race and Feminism* (1996).